CONCORDIA UNIVERSITY

F390.H6
THE TEXAS REPUBLIC NORMAN

C0-AQX-808

3 4211 000032579

WITHDRAWN

THE TEXAS REPUBLIC

THE TEXAS REPUBLIC

A SOCIAL AND ECONOMIC HISTORY

BY

WILLIAM RANSOM HOGAN

KLINCK MEMORIAL LIBRARY
Concordia Teachers College
River Forest, Illinois

UNIVERSITY OF OKLAHOMA PRESS

NORMAN

COPYRIGHT 1946 BY THE
UNIVERSITY OF OKLAHOMA PRESS
PUBLISHING DIVISION OF THE UNIVERSITY
ALL RIGHTS RESERVED
COMPOSED AND PRINTED BY THE UNIVERSITY OF OKLAHOMA PRESS
AT NORMAN, OKLAHOMA, U.S.A.
FIRST EDITION

F 390 .H6

12296

1946-EW-180

*This book is for a valiant
and sweet-spirited Texas lady—my grandmother*
MRS. FRANCES NERREN LOGAN
of Fort Worth

Preface

THE REPUBLIC OF TEXAS, born in 1836 in the bloodletting ordeal of revolution, maintained a virile independence for almost ten years before it joined the American Union. In the minds of Texans, this phase of their historical heritage has marked their state as a region apart. For more than a century, moreover, both Texans and non-Texans have agreed that Texas and its citizens have had a special quality of their own, although outsiders have not always given unalloyed admiration to certain brash characteristics commonly attributed to inhabitants of the Lone Star State. To the question whether the Texas reputation has a historical basis, this study of the life of the people during their decade of independence may provide a partial answer.

This volume is focused upon the everyday existence of a frontier democracy. Devout circuit riders, pioneer physicians and school teachers, unruly young lawyers, gun-bearing rowdies and duelists, town builders and land pirates, planters and farmers—here is a part of the record they made at work and at play. What kind of houses sheltered them and their families? What clothes did they wear? What did they eat and drink? What bodily afflictions beset them? How did formal religion affect their lives? What were their ideals and aspirations? The answers to questions such as these, considered in the light of their social setting, are fundamental to the understanding of any people.

Government is here viewed as a part of, and not directing, the social mechanism. The maneuverings of politicians receive little attention, but there is much about the social ground swells that moved them to action.

This volume contains no extended treatment of the Mexicans, Germans, and Indians. The explanations are simple: There was more culture conflict than assimilation between the Anglo-American immigrants and the resident Mexicans, whose influence and numerical strength were comparatively insignificant. Spanish and German influences began to make themselves felt while Texas was independent, but they produced no sharp modifications of Anglo-American culture. As for the Indians, their resistance to steady encroachments upon their domain resulted in episodes of dramatic escapes and somber tragedies in the lives of individual white settlers. Yet the tribes which occupied areas within the partially settled frontier did not present an effectual barrier to expansion, and contemporary evidence is plain that they caused ordinary settlers less anxiety than malaria and crop failures.

The writer confesses to a belief that the so-called objectivity of the modern historical method defeats its own purpose if the color and warmth of past life is ironed out by a hypersensitive critical spirit. Mythology, for example, has a genuine place in American history. On the one hand, Western tall tales often were offsprings of crude but creative imaginations. On the other, the courses of historical currents have been altered by widespread belief in myths, however implausible they may seem to modern products of a technological age (who, of course, have no folklore of their own).

Critics of social history have often pointed out that it languishes for lack of a method. In this volume, the division of past Texas life into the segments indicated by the chapter headings undoubtedly is arbitrary over-simplification, but an effort has been made to indicate relationships between the segments. Regardless of the total effect, the writer has enjoyed attempting to give coherent pattern to a mammoth puzzle in which the various parts, under the impulse of the surge of life on the Texas frontier, kept moving about.

The preparation of this study was necessarily a co-operative undertaking. Scores of persons gave friendly help in locating widely scattered source materials, and the following acknowledgments of especially heavy indebtedness are gratefully made: The editors of the *Southwestern Historical Quarterly,* the *Southwest Review,* and the *Journal of Southern History* granted permission to include portions of articles by the writer. Winnie Allen and Marcelle Hamer rendered aid that far exceeded the normal requirements of their library duties; my mother, Irene Hogan, collaborated in research; and Professor Charles Edward Smith and Evelyn Hayes assisted in final revision. The manuscript in an early stage had the benefit of a critical examination by Professors Eugene C. Barker and Walter P. Webb; and Charlie Jeffries, Rev. J. Hoytt Boles, and Dr. P. I. Nixon read chapters dealing with their fields of special interest. Finally, this book would not have been completed if certain friends, who modestly prefer to remain anonymous, had not periodically mailed the writer generous quantities of an especially potent brand of Louisiana coffee.

WILLIAM RANSOM HOGAN

Norman, Oklahoma
  September 15, 1946

The Chapters

The Illustrations

THE

TEXAS

REPUBLIC

I

Gone to Texas

NIGHTFALL and a drizzling rain drove an elderly horseman traveling a road to Vicksburg to seek shelter near a roadside fire. As he approached, he saw around it the encampment of a family "a-moving" to Texas—a very common sight in Mississippi in the year 1841. Two bodies wrapped in blankets lay close to the blaze. Near them a tow-headed boy, crying loudly, leaned against a front wheel of a wagon.

The old horseman rode up and addressed him in a mollifying voice, "What's the matter, son?"

"Matter!" roared the piney-woods lad. "Fire and damnation, stranger! Don't you see mammy there shaking with ager! Daddy's gone a-fishing! Jim's got every cent of money there is, playing poker at a bit ante! Bob Stokes is gone on ahead with Nance! Sal's so corned she don't know that stick of wood from seven dollars and a half! Every one of the horses is loose! There's no meal in the waggon! The skillet's broke! The baby's in a bad fix, and it's half a mile to the creek. I don't care a damn if I never see Texas!!!"[1]

This family was one of thousands surging westward to the Republic of Texas, created in 1836 by representatives of about 30,000 Anglo-American colonists during their uprising against Mexico which history calls the Texas Revolution. Since the early eighteen twenties, when Stephen F. Austin began the introduction of colonists under contracts with the government, increasing numbers of immigrants had been settling in Mexico's northeastern province. Like many other frontiersmen moving in the current of the Westward Movement across mid–North America, a large majority of the Texas settlers were homemakers in search of desirable land.

[1] New Orleans *Weekly Picayune*, July 5, 1841 (quoting Yazoo City [Mississippi] *Whig*).

These individualistic, forthright Anglo-Americans almost inevitably drifted into opposition to the sensitive, devious Latin Americans. Dissimilar political experience and folkways made mutual tolerance difficult. In the early eighteen thirties clashes occurred between Mexican officials and the colonists, whose grievances were further aggravated by the aberrations of a state government in which they were inadequately represented.

The Texas Revolution—a complex popular movement which can be understood only in the light of the intricacies of Mexican politics and the instability of the national government—was precipitated by President Santa Anna's dictatorial seizure of power. In the fall of 1835 the settlers in Texas openly revolted and cleared the region of Mexican forces, but a "consultation" of their representatives voted against a declaration of independence and declared that they were fighting for the maintenance of constitutional government. Early in the following year a large Mexican army under Santa Anna invaded Texas. Two groups of Texans defending the Alamo (at San Antonio) and Goliad were overwhelmed by the superior numbers of the invaders. Not one of the defenders of the Alamo survived their desperate stand, while most of the Texans who surrendered at Goliad were massacred by their Mexican conquerors. The Anglo-American colonists began a pell-mell rush toward the haven of the United States border, but on April 21 the main body of the retreating Texas Army under General Sam Houston finally turned against a part of the pursuing Mexican force on the battlefield of San Jacinto. In the carnage there the Texans avenged the Alamo and Goliad in Mexican blood. Santa Anna was captured the next day, and the remainder of his army retreated across the Rio Grande.

Meanwhile, in March, 1836, a Texan convention had declared independence, set up a provisional government, and drafted a constitution. For nearly ten years thereafter, Texas was a republic with independent membership in the society of nations. In successive national elections, the electorate chose Houston as the first president, Mirabeau B. Lamar as the second, then Houston again, and finally Dr. Anson Jones. The national government maintained a small navy and army, established a judicial system and local government, and sent and received diplomatic representatives. The independence of the new country was recognized in 1837 by the United States, in 1839 by France, and in 1840 by Great Britain and The Netherlands.

When Sam Houston's second presidential administration ended in 1844, the strong possibility of annexation by the United States (which previously had been successfully opposed by antislavery elements in the mother country) overshadowed all other political interests. "Old Sam" generally is credited with using the opposition of England and France to annexation in such a way as to hasten favorable action by the United States Congress on the proposal to admit Texas as a state. President Anson Jones, the fourth and last chief executive, was able to submit to Texans a choice between joining the American Union and recognition of independence by Mexico. In June, 1845, the Texas Congress accepted the proposal of the United States by an almost unanimous vote. A state convention also accepted the annexation terms and drew up a state constitution, subsequently approved by the electorate. In December, 1845, the constitution was approved by the United States Congress and President Polk. On February 16, 1846, the first state legislature was formally organized, and three days later, President Jones relinquished executive authority to Governor J. Pinckney Henderson. "The final act in this great drama is now performed," Jones said in his valedictory address. "The Republic of Texas is no more."

A century ago the expression "Gone to Texas" (or simply "G. T. T.") chalked on the doors of houses in the Southern states gave information that the former occupants had departed for the frontier Republic, sometimes with a suddenness explainable only by a desire of the dweller to avoid an appearance as a principal in a court action. Many of the immigrants traveled to Texas by Gulf steamer and schooner. Some journeyed overland by wagon or horseback, possibly with a portion of their trip by stagecoach or river boat. A few simply walked.

The principal land route to Texas was the road from Natchitoches in Louisiana to San Augustine and Nacogdoches in Texas, crossing the Sabine River border at Gaines Ferry. An overland trek which took immigrants to Texas by this or any other road was not prohibitive in cost. In the early eighteen forties, two families numbering about fifteen persons and their fifty Negro slaves removed from Alabama to Texas by wagon and horseback at a total expense of $120, a considerable part of which was spent for ferry fees and repairs to three wagons. The ordinary family or single man also traveled with a very small outlay of money; in 1833 Asa Hoxey wrote from San Felipe de Austin: "The expenses of removing to the country are much less than I expected. It did not cost more than ten dollars per head."[2] One of the largest caravans was that of Jared E. Groce, who migrated from Alabama to Texas in 1821–22. Quite an impressive sight was his train of more than fifty covered wagons, some carrying the women and children and others the furniture, spinning wheels, looms, and provisions; white and Negro men on horseback, herding horses, mules, oxen, cows, sheep, and hogs; and finally Groce and his son, mounted on thoroughbred horses and accompanied by their personal body servants.

Many immigrant families were practically self-sufficient en route, for their carefully hoarded stocks of food were supplemented by game. By the time they arrived, however, their reserves of provisions usually were low, and the supply of corn meal in Texas often was depleted by the demands of newcomers. Typical and sound advice to farming immigrants was given by the anonymous author of *Texas in 1840; or, the Emigrant's Guide to the New Republic,* when he strongly recommended that prospective settlers should visit Texas and select a location before moving their families. He advised immigrants making the final trip to bring with them "small establishments" of furniture, cooking utensils, wagons, farming implements, and tools, as well as supplies of provisions and plain clothing, in order that they could begin life on the frontier without undue handicaps. This excellent advice was not always heeded, and numbers of farmers arrived with inadequate household and farming equipment and only a vague idea of where they were to settle.

Meanwhile, some travelers made part of the journey to Texas by river steamboat. As early as the eighteen twenties, when the Red River was high enough and obstructions did not make navi-

---

[2] Hoxey to Edward Hanrick, November 27, 1833, Hanrick Papers. See bibliography for locations of manuscripts cited in this study.

gation too difficult, steamboats began to come up the river to Alexandria and Natchitoches, and in 1836–37 to Coates Bluff and Shreveport. In the late eighteen thirties a few steamboats managed to circumnavigate the small log jams above Shreveport, and in the succeeding decade more light-draught steam vessels plied the river between Shreveport and landings to the northwest in Red River County, Texas; while in 1843–44 small steamers—including the *Llama,* the *Elizabeth,* the *Robert T. Lytle,* the *New Brazil,* and the *Douglas*—also ran westward from Shreveport to Port Caddo, Texas, on Cypress Bayou. Soon steamers pushed on beyond Port Caddo to Jefferson, one boat arriving in April, 1845, with more than 130 passengers. It is therefore not surprising that Jefferson shortly became an East Texas reception center for supplies and immigrants from the east as well as an outlet for Texas exports.

The Red River steamers made no pretense of providing comfortable accommodations. One traveler who went from Natchez to Natchitoches on the *Concord* complained that the boat "should be named Discord, for the firemen abused the mate, the cook fought the steward, the mosquitoes waged war on the passengers, and the passengers are not yet done cursing mate, firemen, steward, mosquitoes—in fine, the boat and all connected with her. A more miserable, dirty, slow moving, improvided, chicken thievish craft never walked the waters. . . . it excites my spleen to think of her."[3]

Immigrants also reached Texas by sea, usually by embarking at New Orleans, whence schooners, sloops, and steamboats ran more or less regularly to Galveston, beginning in 1837. The first well-equipped steamboat to enter this trade was the Charles Morgan steam packet *Columbia,* which could accommodate more than thirty cabin passengers and an equal number on deck. Either the service was better or the passengers more tolerant than on the Red River steamers, for one cabin passenger, a woman, reported that the vessel's accommodations were excellent: "The Captain a gentleman—always at the head of his table—set out in the best style—silver forks, or what looks like silver—large & small, with ivory knives. White waiters, neat & orderly—French Cook . . . & Bedding

[3] "Sketches of Texas. From the Journal of a Tourist. No. 1," San Luis *Advocate,* November 11, 1840 (quoting Vicksburg *Sentinel*). Unless otherwise indicated, all newspapers cited in this study were published in Texas or New Orleans.

the finest & whitest linen—water closets—& lady-like chamber maid, every thing nice."[4]

So impressed was the same observer with the *New York,* which began making the run from New Orleans to Galveston early in 1839, that she used romantic language in describing it. The boat was so beautiful, she wrote, that she could "think of nothing but Cleopatra" as she lay on the "luxurious couch" in her stateroom. She added that the upper-deck cabin of the *New York* was constructed entirely of mahogany "polished like the finest pianos," with drapery of "blue satin damask and dimity." In the dining room richly painted lamps were both suspended from the ceiling and on the table, while the ivory-handled knives and silver forks and spoons had the name of the vessel engraved on them.[5] The *Galveston,* which entered the trade in the middle eighteen forties, also was described as luxuriously furnished and—in contrast to the boxlike river boats of the period—built for seagoing voyages.

Planters en route to the Republic commonly occupied cabins, while their slaves huddled on a foredeck near their owners' horses and farming implements. But most immigrants who traveled by Gulf steamer could not afford the luxury of first-class cabins and went to Texas by steerage or deck passage. In 1840 James N. ("Uncle Jimmy") Smith and a friend named Matthews contracted with Captain Wright of the *New York* to transport them and their families from New Orleans to Galveston in steerage, and their freight and wagons elsewhere on the boat. The families of the two men were allowed to go on the upper deck to enjoy the Gulf breezes before retiring for the night in the curtained berths arranged along each side of the steerage cabin.

Among the passengers on the steamboats were returning citizens of the frontier commonwealth—the "old veteran who had braved the hardships of a new country and the sufferings of peace and war for fifteen years," the planter, and "the old Texian lady" and her fifteen-year-old son who had come to New Orleans to purchase flour, sugar, and potatoes for themselves and their neighbors. These old-timers rarely failed to cheer the immigrants with "flatter-

[4] Mrs. Mary Austin Holley to Mrs. William M. Brand, December 19, 1837, Holley Papers.

[5] Holley to Brand, November 12, 1840, *ibid.*

ing descriptions" of their destination. But the newcomers were "full of hope, then again desperately depressed" as optimism alternated with sober realization of the hardships and travail that lay ahead.

Chief rival of the *New York* in the first half of the eighteen forties was the *Neptune,* which carried thirty cabin passengers and about forty in the steerage. In 1841 it made an "unprecedented run" of forty hours in the voyage from Galveston to New Orleans, breaking the record of forty-five hours set by the *Cuba* three years before. Late in 1845, however, the *Galveston* reduced the time to thirty-four hours, "altogether the quickest passage ever made."

Wrecks and the withdrawal of steamships from the trade during the lax seasons resulted in interruptions to the New Orleans–Galveston traffic in the early eighteen forties. September, 1843, saw the wreck of the *Sarah Barnes* close "the communication for the present." Seventeen persons were drowned when the vessel went down in a gale, while fourteen escaped on a yawl and on rafts and were washed ashore approximately thirty miles from Galveston. But despite wrecks such as this, in 1844–45 the steamships *Republic, Galveston, McKim,* and *Alabama* began making the run to Galveston regularly.

At the same time, steamboat and schooner transportation occasionally was available between Galveston and New York. The steamer *Star Republic,* which made a number of voyages in the middle eighteen forties, usually required twenty to twenty-five days for the trip from New York to the Texas port. Also available to immigrants were schooners which plied between New York and Mobile in the United States and Matagorda and the mouth of the Brazos River in Texas. Moreover, numbers of European vessels began to arrive in Galveston Harbor. A significant entry dated March 10, 1844, in a contemporary journal reads: "There has never been so much shipping in the ports of Texas & principally foreign as this year. English, Bremen, French, Belgian, Hanover, bringing Emigrants & Manufactures & in return taking cotton, hides, &c."[6]

Between 1836 and 1846, tide after tide of immigration, coupled with natural increase, was to more than quadruple the population of the Republic. The immigrant population at the end of 1835, ac-

[6] William Bollaert, "Notes on Texas, 1843–1844," 233, Bollaert MSS.

cording to the most authoritative estimate, was between 25,000 and 30,000, including perhaps 3,000 to 4,000 Negroes, but not accounting for an undeterminable number of Mexicans. In 1847 the incomplete returns of the first state census showed a population total of about 142,000, including 39,000 Negroes, approximately 300 of whom were free.

Three years later the first United States census in Texas was taken; it affords significant data concerning the origins of the inhabitants—though it does not indicate the places from which settlers had migrated. According to this census of 1850, Texas had a population of about 212,000, including 58,000 slaves. Nearly a third of the 154,000 white persons and free Negroes were natives of the state itself; another third were born in the central Southern states, with Tennessee's 18,000 far in the lead; and of the 22,000 who had been born in the South Atlantic states, a substantial proportion had been provided by North and South Carolina. As Frederick Jackson Turner pointed out, "It is worth noting that the natives of Kentucky, Tennessee, and Missouri, where slavery was less extensive in proportion to population, surpassed those of distinctly slaveholding states."[7] There was also a foreign-born population (excluding persons born in Mexico) of more than 12,000, two-thirds of whom were natives of Germany.

Most immigrants were attracted to the Republic by governmental offers of large quantities of land to citizens. Under a provision of the constitution of 1836, all who were in Texas at the time of the declaration of independence from Mexico were entitled to extensive headrights; the head of a family was allowed a league (a Spanish land measurement of 4,428 acres) and a labor (177 acres), while an unmarried man who had reached the age of seventeen received one-third of a league. This gave settlers who had not located their holdings the same amount of land that ordinarily had been allowed under the Mexican regime, with the exception of the increase from one-fourth to one-third league for bachelors. Later, however, new arrivals received smaller grants, divided into blocks similar to those in the public lands of the United States. The head of a family migrating to Texas between

[7] Turner, *The United States, 1830–1850; the Nation and its Sections,* 357–58.

Gone to Texas

March 2, 1836, and October 1, 1837, was allowed 1,280 acres, while a single man received 640 acres; thereafter until the end of 1841, these grants were reduced by one-half. The land law of 1841 and supplementary acts also authorized the restoration of the Mexican practice of making grants of premium lands to specified individuals, called *"empresarios,"* if they induced a required number of immigrants to settle in certain frontier areas. This policy was discontinued in 1844, however, and early the following year a law was passed granting settlement rights in tracts of 320 acres in the vacant public domain to settlers fulfilling specified conditions.

Although a number of contracts with *empresarios* were made, only two resulted in substantial settlements in the "wild lands" of the frontier. Beginning in 1842, the Peters Colony hastened the occupation of the region in the vicinity of modern Dallas. And by 1846 Henri Castro had brought in several hundred Alsatians and some Swiss and Germans to his grant on the Medina River, west of San Antonio. In spite of the extreme hardships and sickness suffered by many of his settlers before reaching their destinations, they managed to establish Castroville, a town with a distinctly European flavor.

Another settlement with European characteristics was New Braunfels, the chief village established under the auspices of the Society for the Protection of German Immigrants in Texas, which in 1844 began to accelerate a German immigration already well under way. Continued predominance of the Germans in this and other communities in which they originally settled resulted partly from their strong attachment to the soil, a quality not possessed by numbers of Americans who, in migrating westward, changed locations as many as three or four times.

The establishment of sound titles naturally was a matter of gravest importance to newcomers. After 1830 many came to Texas with worthless land scrip purchased in the United States or Europe. Others, when they found on arrival that the choice lands had been taken up, often purchased fraudulent land certificates, which in 1837–39 were issued in enormous numbers with the connivance of corrupt local boards of land commissioners. Overlapping and dubious titles dating from the Mexican era created further uncertainty. Although this alarming situation was relieved somewhat by

11

Congress, which in 1840 selected two boards of traveling land commissioners to examine all land titles, progress in surveying the public domain was slow.

In the next five years the settlement of frontier lands was complicated further by conflicting claims arising under the *empresario* contracts. Speculators, the holders of land scrip and unlocated headrights, prominent politicians, and squatters demanded the nullification of these contracts, chiefly on the grounds of illegality and nonfulfillment. Yet it was not until 1850 that all colonists in Mercer's Colony (in North Texas), who had settled within the grant prior to October 25, 1848, were granted legislative assurance of relief. Many of them had been squatters for several years. Although Mercer and his associates eventually were denied compensation by a decision of the Supreme Court of the United States, the ruling did not adjust conflicting claims, and as late as 1936 many of the boundary lines were still in the process of adjudication.[8]

Even when sound titles could be secured, the puzzling question of the most advantageous location of settlement still confronted new arrivals. "All are land-hunting, seeking sugar, cotton and stock farm lands, but are as much at a loss in their selection as children in a toy-shop," reported one Texan in 1845. "Information and advice from old settlers is cheap and abundant, and the relative merits of particular portions of the country, are descanted upon with all the fanciful additions that the most imaginative could desire."[9] Pending a solution to the problem, some squatted on land they did not own or rented land on shares. Rather than attempt to settle on an unfavorably located headright, numbers of immigrants purchased land at bargain prices; in the early eighteen forties a down payment of a six-hundred-dollar slave or two and a long-term note could buy a farm of several hundred acres. Sometimes large landholders even donated land to desirable farmers.

In making a final decision, newcomers manifested a tendency to seek land similar to that of their home regions in other Southern states or in neighborhoods settled by people from their home states. Clarksville and Red River County thus attracted Tennesseans,

8 Nancy E. Eagleton, "The Mercer Colony in Texas, 1844–1883," *Southwestern Historical Quarterly*, Vol. XL, No. 2 (October, 1936), 114–44.

9 New Orleans *Daily Delta*, November 28, 1845.

while others chose the section around Huntsville for homemaking "because the red clay of the hills, and the sandy land between, and the trees—post oak and red oak and water oak, moss-bearded; and the pines, and the cedar groves—were like the home places back in Mississippi and north Alabama and Georgia."[10]

In selecting land, immigrants were forced to consider the constant possibility of invasion by Mexican forces. Throughout 1836 and 1837 rumors of invasion swept over the country. On Christmas Eve of 1837 "an Express" came into Houston, the capital, warning that invasion was imminent.

From that time commenced warlike preparations—all was business & bustle [wrote an eye-witness]. . . . Meetings were called, money $2000 to 3000 subscribed,—men enrolled (600 in one day) all was excitement. From Mrs. Allens gallery we could over look the whole town in motion like bees swarming—clusters of men in confab—a rushing to the Presidents house next door—every body in movement. Nobody was afraid, but everybody was busy. We were at the house of Mr Labranche (the U. S. minister) . . . *a good cabin*—he promised us the protection of the flag if necessary. We did not let all this interrupt our plans. Every body knew the Mexicans could not get into the country.[11]

Despite such alarms, renewals of the struggle with the enemy were prevented for several years by internal turbulence across the Rio Grande and the threat of French aggression against Mexico. Nevertheless, in 1841 President Lamar sent an ill-fated expedition to Santa Fé; in the following year Mexican forces took San Antonio for two brief periods; and late in 1842 a Texan expedition against northern Mexico proved abortive. As late as October, 1844, the border settlements were still in "a State of excitement and apprehension truly painful" as a result of "many excitements & rumors of Mexican invasions."[12] Though actual bloodshed was really quite negligible, the potential menace of the enemy army and

[10] John W. Thomason, Jr., "Huntsville," *Southwest Review,* Vol. XIX, No. 3 (April, 1934), 234. See also Archer B. Hulbert, *Soil; its Influence on the History of the United States, with Special Reference to Migration and the Scientific Study of Local History,* 77.

[11] Mrs. Mary Austin Holley to Mrs. William M. Brand, December 30, 1837, Holley Papers.

[12] Ira R. Lewis to James H. Starr, October 27, 1844, Starr Papers.

the activities of marauding bands of Mexi...
tonio and the Rio Grande were factors in res...
of the western counties. The Mexican scare...
decline in immigration, curtailed the acti...
private business, and practically depopulate...
Brazoria and Austin) of their able-bodie...
military forces. Through it all, however,...
temptuous of Mexicans, "a feble, dastard...
riden race of mongrels, composed of spa...
blood" and were "always willing to fight t...
to one."[13]

Indians also conditioned the direction a...
Occupancy of portions of East Texas nor...
Road was considered precarious until...
crushed and expelled the partially civiliz...
and other tribes at the Battle of Neches in m...
the lands claimed by the Indians were tem...
Mexicans were attempting to incite the...
"Cherokee War" was not wholly popular...
Indian scares also occurred along Red Ri...
Fannin County.

The Texas settler distinguished betwe...
Indians. After the expulsion of the Cheroke...
in the partially settled areas small groups...
Bidais, and Alabamas, while various tribes...
Wichita, lived along the middle Brazos an...
in a region overlapping the most advanced s...
of the Comanche country. The remnant of t...
kawas ranged an interior region between...
Brazos rivers, and the Lipan Apaches occu...
and northwest of San Antonio; both were...
white settlers' principal Indian enemies, the...
exception of the Comanches and the few hu...
Wacos along the Brazos above the San Ant...

[13] Joseph Eve to Richard Southgate, May 10, 184...
Letter Book of Joseph Eve, United States Chargé d'Affa...
Historical Quarterly, Vol. XLIII, No. 4 (April, 1940),...

March 2, 1836, and October 1, 1837, was allowed 1,280 acres, while a single man received 640 acres; thereafter until the end of 1841, these grants were reduced by one-half. The land law of 1841 and supplementary acts also authorized the restoration of the Mexican practice of making grants of premium lands to specified individuals, called *"empresarios,"* if they induced a required number of immigrants to settle in certain frontier areas. This policy was discontinued in 1844, however, and early the following year a law was passed granting settlement rights in tracts of 320 acres in the vacant public domain to settlers fulfilling specified conditions.

Although a number of contracts with *empresarios* were made, only two resulted in substantial settlements in the "wild lands" of the frontier. Beginning in 1842, the Peters Colony hastened the occupation of the region in the vicinity of modern Dallas. And by 1846 Henri Castro had brought in several hundred Alsatians and some Swiss and Germans to his grant on the Medina River, west of San Antonio. In spite of the extreme hardships and sickness suffered by many of his settlers before reaching their destinations, they managed to establish Castroville, a town with a distinctly European flavor.

Another settlement with European characteristics was New Braunfels, the chief village established under the auspices of the Society for the Protection of German Immigrants in Texas, which in 1844 began to accelerate a German immigration already well under way. Continued predominance of the Germans in this and other communities in which they originally settled resulted partly from their strong attachment to the soil, a quality not possessed by numbers of Americans who, in migrating westward, changed locations as many as three or four times.

The establishment of sound titles naturally was a matter of gravest importance to newcomers. After 1830 many came to Texas with worthless land scrip purchased in the United States or Europe. Others, when they found on arrival that the choice lands had been taken up, often purchased fraudulent land certificates, which in 1837–39 were issued in enormous numbers with the connivance of corrupt local boards of land commissioners. Overlapping and dubious titles dating from the Mexican era created further uncertainty. Although this alarming situation was relieved somewhat by

Congress, which in 1840 selected two boards of traveling land commissioners to examine all land titles, progress in surveying the public domain was slow.

In the next five years the settlement of frontier lands was complicated further by conflicting claims arising under the *empresario* contracts. Speculators, the holders of land scrip and unlocated headrights, prominent politicians, and squatters demanded the nullification of these contracts, chiefly on the grounds of illegality and nonfulfillment. Yet it was not until 1850 that all colonists in Mercer's Colony (in North Texas), who had settled within the grant prior to October 25, 1848, were granted legislative assurance of relief. Many of them had been squatters for several years. Although Mercer and his associates eventually were denied compensation by a decision of the Supreme Court of the United States, the ruling did not adjust conflicting claims, and as late as 1936 many of the boundary lines were still in the process of adjudication.[8]

Even when sound titles could be secured, the puzzling question of the most advantageous location of settlement still confronted new arrivals. "All are land-hunting, seeking sugar, cotton and stock farm lands, but are as much at a loss in their selection as children in a toy-shop," reported one Texan in 1845. "Information and advice from old settlers is cheap and abundant, and the relative merits of particular portions of the country, are descanted upon with all the fanciful additions that the most imaginative could desire."[9] Pending a solution to the problem, some squatted on land they did not own or rented land on shares. Rather than attempt to settle on an unfavorably located headright, numbers of immigrants purchased land at bargain prices; in the early eighteen forties a down payment of a six-hundred-dollar slave or two and a long-term note could buy a farm of several hundred acres. Sometimes large landholders even donated land to desirable farmers.

In making a final decision, newcomers manifested a tendency to seek land similar to that of their home regions in other Southern states or in neighborhoods settled by people from their home states. Clarksville and Red River County thus attracted Tennesseans,

8 Nancy E. Eagleton, "The Mercer Colony in Texas, 1844–1883," *Southwestern Historical Quarterly*, Vol. XL, No. 2 (October, 1936), 114–44.

9 New Orleans *Daily Delta*, November 28, 1845.

while others chose the section around Huntsville for homemaking "because the red clay of the hills, and the sandy land between, and the trees—post oak and red oak and water oak, moss-bearded; and the pines, and the cedar groves—were like the home places back in Mississippi and north Alabama and Georgia."[10]

In selecting land, immigrants were forced to consider the constant possibility of invasion by Mexican forces. Throughout 1836 and 1837 rumors of invasion swept over the country. On Christmas Eve of 1837 "an Express" came into Houston, the capital, warning that invasion was imminent.

From that time commenced warlike preparations—all was business & bustle [wrote an eye-witness]. . . . Meetings were called, money $2000 to 3000 subscribed,—men enrolled (600 in one day) all was excitement. From Mrs. Allens gallery we could over look the whole town in motion like bees swarming—clusters of men in confab—a rushing to the Presidents house next door—every body in movement. Nobody was afraid, but everybody was busy. We were at the house of Mr Labranche (the U. S. minister) . . . *a good cabin*—he promised us the protection of the flag if necessary. We did not let all this interrupt our plans. Every body knew the Mexicans could not get into the country.[11]

Despite such alarms, renewals of the struggle with the enemy were prevented for several years by internal turbulence across the Rio Grande and the threat of French aggression against Mexico. Nevertheless, in 1841 President Lamar sent an ill-fated expedition to Santa Fé; in the following year Mexican forces took San Antonio for two brief periods; and late in 1842 a Texan expedition against northern Mexico proved abortive. As late as October, 1844, the border settlements were still in "a State of excitement and apprehension truly painful" as a result of "many excitements & rumors of Mexican invasions."[12] Though actual bloodshed was really quite negligible, the potential menace of the enemy army and

[10] John W. Thomason, Jr., "Huntsville," *Southwest Review*, Vol. XIX, No. 3 (April, 1934), 234. See also Archer B. Hulbert, *Soil; its Influence on the History of the United States, with Special Reference to Migration and the Scientific Study of Local History*, 77.

[11] Mrs. Mary Austin Holley to Mrs. William M. Brand, December 30, 1837, Holley Papers.

[12] Ira R. Lewis to James H. Starr, October 27, 1844, Starr Papers.

the activities of marauding bands of Mexicans between San Antonio and the Rio Grande were factors in restricting the populating
of the western counties. The Mexican scares of 1842 caused a sharp
decline in immigration, curtailed the activities of the courts and
private business, and practically depopulated many towns (such as
Brazoria and Austin) of their able-bodied men, who joined the
military forces. Through it all, however, most Texans were contemptuous of Mexicans, "a feble, dastardly, supersticious priest
riden race of mongrels, composed of spanish Indian and negro
blood" and were "always willing to fight them or the Indians five
to one."[13]

Indians also conditioned the direction and extent of settlement.
Occupancy of portions of East Texas north of the San Antonio
Road was considered precarious until Texas volunteer forces
crushed and expelled the partially civilized Cherokees, Caddos,
and other tribes at the Battle of Neches in mid-July, 1839. Although
the lands claimed by the Indians were temptingly fertile, and the
Mexicans were attempting to incite them to depredations, the
"Cherokee War" was not wholly popular with all settlers. Serious
Indian scares also occurred along Red River, notably in 1841 in
Fannin County.

The Texas settler distinguished between "tame" and "wild"
Indians. After the expulsion of the Cherokees, there remained within the partially settled areas small groups of peaceful Coushattas,
Bidais, and Alabamas, while various tribes, mostly Caddoan and
Wichita, lived along the middle Brazos and upper Trinity rivers
in a region overlapping the most advanced settlements and the edge
of the Comanche country. The remnant of the once-powerful Ton-
kawas ranged an interior region between the San Antonio and
Brazos rivers, and the Lipan Apaches occupied an area to the west
and northwest of San Antonio; both were implacable foes of the
white settlers' principal Indian enemies, the Comanches. With the
exception of the Comanches and the few hundred Tahuacanos and
Wacos along the Brazos above the San Antonio Road, these tribes

13 Joseph Eve to Richard Southgate, May 10, 1842, in J. M. Nance (ed.), "A
Letter Book of Joseph Eve, United States Chargé d'Affaires to Texas," *Southwestern
Historical Quarterly*, Vol. XLIII, No. 4 (April, 1940), 494.

gave the colonists little trouble. The Wacos frequently were blamed for small-scale theft and murder.

The nomadic Comanches were the most menacing tribe, especially between 1836 and 1840, but fortunately the territory they frequented was located mainly to the west and northwest of the partially settled areas. The most horrible massacre of the period occurred on May 19, 1836, when a band of Comanches and Kiowas captured the stockade at Fort Parker (near modern Groesbeck) by a treacherous ruse. This was one of a series of Comanche depredations committed while the Republic was in a state of confusion following the Mexican invasion, which already had caused a recession of the settled frontier. During the next three years, small parties of whites were "balled off . . . as they facetiously term being shot by Indians in this country." While the danger from the Indians was comparatively slight in the more thickly settled areas, the chronicles of individual tragedy are numerous—particularly in the western counties. In 1837 "the frequent incursions of hostile Indians" in the Bastrop region caused families to defer returning to their homes there, and, as late as 1839, Bastrop was referred to in contemporary court records as "a depopulated County."

President Sam Houston's policy in dealing with the Indians was one of pacification, while President Mirabeau B. Lamar was much more aggressive. In 1839–40, during Lamar's term in office, both the Cherokees and the Comanches suffered decisive defeats at the hands of the Texan volunteers. In 1840 a melee at a council at San Antonio resulted in the death of about thirty-five Comanches, including one chief. The Indians retaliated with a raid in which they attacked Victoria and burned Linnville, a small port, but they in turn were defeated in two other fights. Concerning one of them —the Battle of Plum Creek (near modern Lockhart)—young Hamilton P. Bee wrote in typical Texas fashion: "You can imagine my mortification upon *arriving at the battle ground a few hours after the fight."* His mortification was well grounded, for Plum Creek was the last engagement of importance with the Comanches during this period, with the exception of a Texas raid that destroyed the chief Comanche village on the upper Colorado.

Despite the possibilities of meeting hostile Indians and Mexicans, the unceasing, restless search for virgin land continued. Led

15

by a few indomitable pioneers who moved when neighbors began to encroach on their "lone-wolf" solitude, the frontier advanced northwestward up the valleys of the rivers emptying into the Gulf of Mexico, and westward south of Red River. In 1846 the partially settled area included roughly the region east of the ninety-seventh meridian, with a large bulge in the south extending over the ninety-ninth to include Austin, San Antonio, Fredericksburg, and Castroville. Thus the resistless flow of population into the Republic had carried it to the western edge of the well-watered, partially wooded area which was to become a great cotton empire.

From the beginning of Anglo-American settlement it was agreed generally that the immediate economic advancement of Texas was primarily contingent upon cotton production. Before 1836 the San Antonio region produced relatively little cotton, while the yield in East Texas was believed to be less than one-half of that in the Brazos River sector. It was estimated that in 1828 the Brazos region, in which Austin's Colony was located, produced about five hundred bales for exportation; double that amount in the following year; five thousand bales (an exaggeration) in 1832; less than half that yield in the very wet year of 1833; followed by substantial increases in the next two years.

Early in 1835 Ira Ingram, an unusually well-informed planter of the lower Colorado River region, observed that the cotton crop in the previous year had been better than ever before and was bringing a high price. Many of the planters had sold their cotton at fourteen and one-half cents per pound. One of his friends, who owned ten slave "field hands," had sold his crop for $4,500. With prices so high, he estimated the value of a hand at $250 to $400 per year, and incidentally remarked that overseers were paid an annual wage of $500 to $1,000—a higher scale than that prevailing during the succeeding ten years. The price of prime cotton lands had risen 300 to 400 per cent in the last two years, but he was convinced, he said, that "there is land enough in Texas, within the fine staple region, to supply the demand, at present, of the whole civilized world."[14]

14 Ira Ingram to Roswell Ingram, January 9, 1835, Ingram Papers (University

After Texas began to seek economic recovery from the shattering effects of the Revolution, the correspondence of the period is replete with emphatic proclamations of the superiority of Texas cotton lands. The general belief was that despite unfavorable marketing conditions and the vicissitudes of the weather, agriculture yielded the most certain economic returns. In 1837 a Quintana citizen stated that a planter owning ten or twelve Negroes thought that he fared badly if he did not clear $3,000 to $4,000 per year.

As the early eighteen forties brought a disheartening depression, young men constantly were urged to turn to farming. President Lamar received a letter in 1841 from an East Texas supporter who thus analyzed the woes of many of his fellow countrymen: "Hard times press on every side but they are the consequence, where there are so few *cultivators* of the soil, and so *many poor gentlemen* as are in Texas, who have emigrated here to find money growing on trees, and it would be too much condescension on their part to labour, after having had such fine anticipations."[15]

The prospects for cotton and corn crops, always of paramount interest because they were the country's basic sources of revenue and sustenance, often were reported in the public prints and in personal letters. Eastern Texas crops were good in 1836, but the settlers in the western and southern regions had difficulty in securing even sustenance. Substantial increases in cotton exportation were reported in 1839, and there were also appreciable increases in the amount of cotton grown and exported in the two subsequent years. In 1842 long droughts in the early part of the season reduced the volume of corn yields in the counties along the United States border, and incessant rains and army worms hurt the cotton on the coast. Although the annual influx of immigrant farmers resulted in augmentation of the total yield, many planters failed to produce normal crops in 1842 and 1843, especially in the coastal counties. In the latter year, "the most unprecedented rains" caused the Brazos River to overflow again. Nevertheless, crops of both corn and cotton were more than satisfactory in the two following

of Texas Library); Ira Ingram to Mrs. M. B. West, February 10, 1835, Ingram Papers (Library of Congress).

15 James Armstrong to M. B. Lamar, June 12, 1841, in Charles A. Gulick, Jr., *et al.* (eds.), *The Papers of Mirabeau Buonaparte Lamar*, III, 537.

seasons, and as annexation approached, large crops of corn were planted to take care of the needs of immigrants. In October, 1845, Colonel James Morgan, looking back on an experience that had spanned the existence of the frontier Republic, wrote: "I have never known it so healthy in Texas any previous Summer—no sickness. ... This added to the fine prospects of Crops—peace—annexation and an expectation of an immense immigration serves to cheer up the drooping Spirits of many a poor Texan."[16]

Complete statistics concerning cotton production in the years following 1836 cannot be compiled, because much of the staple grown in East and Northeast Texas was smuggled into the United States to avoid payment of duties. Nevertheless, even the available incomplete statistics indicate that cotton was the Republic's only important export. The amount of cotton reported as clearing through the customhouses in the coastal towns for the year ending October 31, 1845, was approximately 29,000 bales, a figure that does not include either legal or illegal exports of East Texas cotton across the United States boundary. In the year ending July 31, 1844, the value of cotton exports from the coastal customhouses was more than $580,000, whereas hides, the second most important export commodity, were valued at only about $17,500.[17]

Agricultural techniques in the Republic are described in the voluminous unpublished papers of William Bollaert, accomplished British naturalist, ethnologist, and geographer, who lived in Texas and traveled over a considerable part of its settled area in the early eighteen forties. After plowing—according to Bollaert—the cotton was sown by hand late in February or early in March. When the plants were two or three inches high, they were thinned until what remained appeared to have been planted in rows. Corn was planted in rows three or four feet apart, with two seeds in each hole. On the Trinity River in one year, the annual corn yield was forty to fifty bushels per acre and the cotton yield about two thousand pounds of seed cotton per acre—admittedly a high average. (But cotton production often was computed in the number of bales raised per Negro hand; on the lower Brazos River plantation of

16 Morgan to Samuel Swartwout, October 3, 1845, Morgan Papers.
17 R. E. L. Crane, Jr., "The Administration of the Customs Service of the Republic of Texas" (M.A. thesis, University of Texas), 228–31.

The Capitol of the Republic of Texas at Houston

Reproduced from Homer S. Thrall, *Pictorial History of Texas,* 1879

Executive Mansion in Houston

Courtesy University of Texas Library

Diorama of houses of Peach Point Plantation, a few miles above the mouth of the Brazos River, which was owned by James F. Perry, second husband of Stephen F. Austin's sister.

Diorama of the capitol of the Republic of Texas at Austin

From photographs by Elwood M. Payne of a diorama, by Edward Wilkinson and staff, on display in the San Jacinto Museum of History.

James F. Perry, the annual average per hand was four and one-sixth bales for the period from 1838 through 1849.) Bollaert added that much more cotton would have been planted if a greater labor force had been available. Even so, many planters and farmers planted more than they could pick before inclement weather began in the fall.

Preparing the raw cotton for market engendered serious problems. If a farmer had no gin, he often had to pay a tenth or an eighth of his yield as ginning fee, and bagging and rope cost him an additional $2.50 per bale. To be sure, a number of planters owned gins, and cotton compresses were established in a few towns, but it was admitted that Texas cotton, though often fine staple, "has frequently been placed in the lowest class solely on account of the slovenly manner in which it has been put up."[18]

Many of the early settlers considered the possibilities of raising sugar in the river bottom lands near the coast, and even before 1830 produced a few hundred hogsheads. By 1840 most of the plantation owners on the Colorado and Brazos rivers and the intervening streams had a few "patches" of cane. The leaders in this experimental cultivation were E. Mercer on the Colorado, John Sweeny on the San Bernard, Major James P. Caldwell on the Brazos, a Judge Menifee, Colonel James Morgan on Galveston Bay, and Captain John Duncan on Caney Creek. Sweeny harvested one hundred hogsheads of sugar of an excellent quality in 1844, in addition to good crops of cotton and corn. Duncan, who used his mechanical bent in improving agricultural implements and machinery, put two steam engines into operation on his Caney Creek plantation; one of them furnished power for one of the first sugar mills erected in Texas. Although only fifty of his thirteen thousand acres were in sugar cane in 1844, he raised more than any other of the plantation owners. While the efforts of the sugar raisers were still on an experimental scale, they were able to meet the demands of their immediate communities and the families west of the Brazos; and the first exportation, from the crop of 1846, was approximately fifty hogsheads.

During the period of the Republic a lack of adequate capital

[18] *Civilian and Galveston Gazette,* September 21, 1844.

inhibited the growth of the sugar industry. In 1846 the estimated price of a sugar plantation on the Brazos, including buildings and a minimum of fifty slaves (at an average cost of $600 each), was about $50,000. The possession of a large force of Negroes commonly was considered requisite for any planter to raise sugar on a commercial scale, and except in Brazoria County—where at this time about two-thirds of the population was slave—such requirements were prohibitive. The industry developed moderately in Brazoria County during the eighteen fifties, but the frequent prediction that Texas would rival Louisiana in sugar production never approached realization.

Other crops were grown on a small scale by a few individuals. Wheat, rye, and oats were raised in the early eighteen forties with some success near Clarksville and Bastrop, as well as in other parts of "the upper country." One element of the intensive, diversified, free-labor farming system of the German-Americans was the cultivation of tobacco; Friedrich Ernst of Mill Creek (where he laid out the town of Industry in 1838) led his neighbors in producing small crops. A few abortive attempts at silk, rice, and indigo production also were made. Many settlers on the Guadalupe River profited considerably from selling pecans in 1842–43, but the following season found the trees almost bare. Although vegetables and fruits grew well in Texas, a large majority of settlers neglected their cultivation.

Texas generally was recognized as a fine stock-raising country. Prairies and river bottom lands in a temperate climate offered excellent pasturage without the attendant necessity of providing shelter for the animals. "Stock dose extremely well. all the trouble is to herd them and brand them. tha increase much faster than where you live," a young farmer wrote from Brazoria to his parents in the United States during the summer of 1834.[19]

Unnumbered thousands of wild cattle—called Spanish, black, or mustang cattle—were found in small groups from Red River to the Rio Grande in the eighteen twenties. Settlers and professional hunters who worked for plantation owners hunted these wild cattle for food or sport. Furthermore, importation of cattle from Mexico

[19] Pleasant M. Bull to "Dear parents," July 15, 1834, Bull Papers.

continued. In 1839 Dr. James H. Starr, on arriving at "Woods," about twelve miles from La Grange, saw "a Company of the Texas Cowboys" who had stolen hundreds of cattle as well as mules and horses from "the inoffensive inhabitants of Chihuahua."[20]

Cattle raising was the chief source of livelihood for many settlers near Houston and the region of the lower Trinity, eastward to the Sabine River. Improved breeds of livestock were introduced, and tax returns indicate that stock raising was especially important in Liberty, Jefferson, Fort Bend, Montgomery, and Harris counties. Cattle and horses were driven in indeterminable numbers to New Orleans, a long trip made hazardous by many water crossings. Taylor White, one of the Trinity River settlers, drove cattle to Louisiana long before the eighteen forties, and has been designated authoritatively as "the first cattle king of Texas."

Taylor White moved here nineteen years ago [an American diplomatic representative in Texas wrote in 1842] his whole fortune was three cows and calves two small poneys a wife and three children, he now owns about 40,000 acres of land upwards of 90 negroes about thirty thousand head of cattle, has sixty thousand dollars in specie deposited in new orleans, marked and branded thirty seven hundred calves last spring, and sold last fall in new orleans 11 hundred steers weighing about 1000 lbs each which he says cost him not more than 75 cents a head to drive them to market [at New] orleans and what is extraordinary he cannot read or write and has made his fortune raising stock alone.[21]

Negro labor became increasingly important in Texas agricultural economy during the period of the Republic, although as late as 1850 less than one-third of the 25,000 persons who listed their occupation as farming were slaveowners. Nevertheless, the proportion of slaves increased from an estimated 12 per cent of the immigrant population at the end of 1835 to about 27 per cent of the

[20] Starr, "Private Journal, 1839–1840," entry for September 21, 1839, Starr Papers.

[21] Joseph Eve to J. F. Ballinger, April 26, 1842, in Nance (ed.), "A Letter Book of Joseph Eve," *Southwestern Historical Quarterly*, Vol. XLIII, No. 4 (April, 1940), 488.

THE TEXAS REPUBLIC

total population in 1847, the year of the first state census. Of the 7,747 slaveholders listed in the census of 1850, only about 6 per cent owned twenty or more slaves, and more than half owned less than five. A large proportion of Texas farmers thus were either non-slaveholders or owned very few Negroes. These small farmers had to develop a high degree of self-sufficiency (they might be called upon to make a cart, a coffin, a cradle, a bucket, or shoes), but often they had to pay a substantial portion of their crops of cotton and corn for assistance in harvesting.

The largest concentrations of slaves were on the plantations of the lower Colorado and Brazos rivers—particularly in Brazoria County—and in scattered locations in East Texas. An account of the life of plantation Negroes is found in the manuscripts of William Bollaert, a sharp and usually accurate observer, whose four years in the Republic enabled him to write with authority. He testified that Negroes were well treated on the whole, and added that he could "bear witness that they are not over-worked, or ill-used"; most of them were "family Negroes," who were permitted to stay on the plantations in their old age and not sold to masters indifferent to their welfare. On well-regulated plantations, each slave family had its own log cabin, with a half or full acre of land behind it for a garden, as well as pigs and poultry which the family consumed or sold.

Bollaert estimated that in favorable weather "a good working hand" picked one thousand pounds of cotton per week. The slaves usually were allowed Saturday afternoon and Sunday as leisure time, but during cotton-picking season they could choose to work for pay on Saturday afternoons. On some plantations they were permitted to keep the cotton picked this half-day, by which means they could make as much as thirty dollars in a season.

During the busy season when the negro men & women go to their labours in the field [Bollaert continued], they intrust their young children to the care of old "Aunty Suky," or on very large plantations there are several of these old Auntys who look after them until their parents return to their meals. The "Nursery" is a large log-house & the collection of juvenile blacks of all sorts, sizes & colours, their cryings & screamings, the bawlings of "Aunty" & the what she wont do to them

22

if they dont "Quit" crying, her admonitions at their favourite pastime of eating dirt, which is only prevented by giving them a lump of fat bacon, is very amusing. It is said in Texas & in the U. S. by many as a *fact* that if a negro child be kept clean & well clothed it will pine & often die; but if allowed to roll & play about in the dirt there is no fear of its not thriving.[22]

The opinion generally prevailed that Negro labor was necessary for the agricultural development of the rich coastal lands. It was believed that white men, even those from Southern states, could not stand continued exposure to the sun and the malarial fevers there, whereas the slaves seldom were attacked. Negroes accordingly were in steady demand and as valuable property had to be controlled and protected. The fear of insurrection, possibly to be instigated by free Negroes, was constantly present, and patrol companies to force slaves to conform to regulations consequently were authorized by several county and city governments. Most reports of Negro uprisings, however, were nothing more than rumors. The court records contain very few entries in which individual Negroes —free or slave—were charged with crimes. These few indictments ranged from petit larceny to murder by poisoning, and convictions were not always returned. But slaveholders often settled cases involving Negroes without resort to the courts.

A small minority of the white population believed that slavery was morally unjustifiable or economically harmful. These included some Englishmen and Germans and an occasional American. Stephen Pearl Andrews, a lawyer from Massachusetts, became so unpopular in Houston because of his abolitionist sentiments that, in 1843, he was almost mobbed and barely was able to escape from the country. Colonel James Morgan, who used his fifteen or more slaves on his Galveston Bay plantation in raising corn, growing cattle, and experimenting with sugar production, came to consider his Negroes as a handicap. He expressed his attitude in the following words:

I am no abolitionist but like all mankind am governed by intellect therefore *facts* go before arguments with me. I feel assured that it is

[22] Bollaert, "Notes on Texas, 1843–1844," 148–50.

to my interest that Texas stand as a non slave holding country. Look at Ohio on one side and Kentucky on the other side of the river—Look at that part of Texas settled by a white population and that part settled with a slave population & see the difference—in happiness and Contentment. . . . I am a slave holder, was bred in a slave holding Country —am tired of slaves and slavery. I am the slave for my negroes—while they are happy and content I am unhappy and the loser by them—I wish to be free and hope to see Texas free'd of slavery—because it will be to *my interest* as a land holder.[23]

Most Texans approved the institution of slavery. In the few instances when it was thought necessary to defend the institution, the familiar arguments were advanced: By what right did the Northern and English abolitionists propose freedom for Negroes when many white paupers of the industrial areas enjoyed less freedom and ate worse food than the slaves of Texas? Did not the Scriptures contain almost countless verses approving and defining the relationship of master and slave? Perhaps the most striking index of public opinion was shown in the almost unanimous support given by Texas Methodists to the Southern point of view when the Methodist Episcopal Church split over the slavery question in 1844–46. It was deemed essential that the black quarter of the population remain in bondage for both its spiritual and economic welfare. Although a majority of the farmers owned no Negroes, most of them were ambitious to acquire at least a few, for they believed that profitable cotton and sugar-cane cultivation could be carried on only with slave labor. As long as this opinion prevailed, a civilization that was necessarily materialistic could be expected to greet abolitionist proposals with outraged contempt.

[23] Morgan to Mrs. J. M. Storms, January 26, 1844, Morgan Papers.

II

The Necessaries of Life

THE LOG CABIN HOMES of ordinary Texas settlers—marked by lack of pretense and often, in spite of their small size, an air of boldness and expansiveness—were expressions of the characters of the men who built and lived in them. "Fundamentally, early Texas architecture was plain, rough, strong, angular, and open," wrote Charlie Jeffries in a remarkable essay on early rural architecture. "It was more for utility than ornament. About it there was often grandeur, and sometimes beauty. About it, too, there was often originality of detail, and, not seldom, quaintness and grotesqueness."[1]

The Texans' houses also were expressions of their environment. Their cabins were located with more attention to elevated ground and proximity to water than to land lines and roads. Distance from towns fostered simplicity, and materials close at hand were used in a logical manner.

Most of the houses were one- or two-room log cabins, with lean-tos adding shed space. In 1836 a Virginia lawyer observed that "a rude house of two rooms and an open passage" was "the common style"; the two-room or double log cabin had a long porch or porches and an open central hall, designed to catch the breezes that tempered the scorching Texas sun. The walls were constructed of roughly hewn logs laid horizontally over each other, fitting together in grooves near or at the ends; the spaces between the walls were filled with clay mixed with grass, moss, or sticks. Hand-riven oak "shakes" or boards (placed like modern shingles) of the roof were held in place by stones and weight poles laid perpendicularly across the shakes and above wooden pegs; for protection against

---

[1] Jeffries, "Early Texas Architecture," *Bunker's Monthly*, Vol. I, No. 6 (June, 1928), 905.

rain, eaves extended twelve to eighteen inches beyond the walls. The floors were of dirt or clay, or were constructed of puncheons —split logs with roughly dressed flat sides up. Wooden doors and shutters were fastened with wooden or rawhide hinges; sometimes the windows were covered with a "kind of clarified raw-hide that admitted the light into the rooms much better than any one would imagine." Wide, deep chimneys of sticks and clay, with broad hearths of smooth rocks, were common, although occasionally more substantial chimneys were erected.

Differences in houses resulted from regional variations in availability of materials as well as from the diversity of settlers' backgrounds. In Southeast Texas extensive pine forests prescribed the kind of logs that went into the cabins, while in other sections oak, gum, and cedar prevailed. In 1843 a traveler noted that most of the buildings in the Rutersville vicinity had chimneys of "sandstone— with lime," and in East Texas today it is necessary to travel as far north as Angelina County before occasional examples of limestone chimneys on ante-bellum houses can be encountered.

A few second-generation settlers—with less need for haste— weatherboarded the log cabins and added wings or second stories. Some built houses of stone with great square chimneys—structures which have been described as "articulate and full of meaning, beautiful in their grace of line and softness of color." To these small early residences, as native to the Southwest as cowboy ballads, modern designers are turning as a source of inspiration for a truly indigenous architecture.

Wall pegs and shelves were the primitive equivalent of closets in the early cabins. Usually a low shelf near the door supported a water pail, while a long-handled gourd hung near by; clothing, rifles, and perhaps strings of beef and venison, furs, or a looking glass hung on pegs elsewhere. Homemade tables, stools, benches and chairs with rawhide bottoms, spinning wheel, and loom could be found in most cabins; and the utilitarian aspect of the furnishings often was enhanced by "one leg beds." Placed in corners, these beds were constructed of rails running from the one leg to the walls, with hemp ropes or rawhide stretching from rail to rail to support a prairie-grass mattress.

In contrast to the prevailing stark simplicity, a number of people of modest means, who apparently cared more for comfort than compactness, possessed bedsteads and even feather beds. Indeed, probate records show that an occasional poor man owned double bedsteads, or a cherry bedstead, or even a claw-foot mahogany table and a few Windsor chairs, his few pieces of fine furniture standing incongruously in crude surroundings.

This contrast between the primitive and the luxurious—noted in the simple cabins—was even more striking within the houses of the comparatively well-to-do, particularly those who lived in coastal towns and on plantations. In 1837 the home of one of the Allen brothers, Houston proprietors, contained such nineteenth-century conceptions of fine furniture as mahogany hair sofas and red-velvet rocking chairs—"all nice and new, and in modern style"; and the 1839 household inventory of James H. Davis, also of Houston, revealed that his furnishings included a mahogany sofa as well as such additional appurtenances of affluence as a "Grecian Breakfast Table," a marble-top center table and other marble-top furniture, a tin bathtub, a Franklin stove, champagne glasses, two china dinner sets, waffle irons, ivory-handled knives, sugar tongs, and two "Door Scrapers." In Henry Austin's home on the Brazos, "New York furniture adorned the puncheon-floored rooms; New York china was spread on the white board tables."

Some of the richest men in Texas lived in plantation homes along the Brazos. The home of Jared E. Groce, who settled near modern Hempstead in the early eighteen twenties, has been described as follows:

"Bernardo" was a large, rambling log house. There were many expert carpenters and brick masons among the slaves, and the house when finished was comfortable and had not the appearance of having been built with logs. The logs were cottonwood hewed and counter hewed, smooth as glass, about a foot thick; the edges were perfectly square. There was a broad hall fifteen feet wide, with two large rooms on each side twenty by twenty feet, which made the front of the house fifty-five feet across. A broad porch ran the full length supported by huge posts of solid walnut, beautifully polished. There was a broad staircase in the hall, which led to two bedrooms above, situated in the two gable ends. There was an old-fashioned fireplace in each room, built of sandstone, taken from the Brazos River. Shingles were of post oak, made with a drawing knife. The floors were of ash, sawed by hand, and planed. As was the custom in those days, the kitchen was built a few feet away from the house; a fireplace occupied one whole end of this kitchen, on which was done the cooking. Next to this was the dairy, ten by twelve feet, built of cedar. Two other rooms were in the back yard, one for the doctor, who cared for the negroes when sick, and the other a room thirty by thirty feet, with a rock fireplace in each end, called "Bachelor's Hall."[2]

Groce's son-in-law, William H. Wharton, built one of the first large frame houses in Texas. Situated about six miles from Velasco, the Wharton estate was called "Eagle Island," a name giving a picture of its locale inasmuch as the Texan definition of an "island" was a "clump of forest wood in the midst of a prairie."

Eagle Island captured the imagination of all who traveled in that part of the country. The house itself was situated in an "island" of live oaks near a horseshoe-shaped, clear-water lake of about fifteen acres. A New Orleans newspaper correspondent described the "mansion" as "one of the most picturesque kind" and the grounds as "ornamented with a great variety of shrubs and trees," while the garden—tended by a Scottish gardener—contained more than five hundred types of imported "exotic plants." This garden was described as "charming" by Mrs. Mary Austin Holley, who further commented that within the house the Whartons had "a great many beautiful books and other curiosities—centre table, woolen damask curtains—sofa, silver pitcher, white china &c &c. I hated to leave so agreeable a place."[3]

Most Texas villages were merely sprawling groups of cabins and shacks. Houston required several years to achieve an atmosphere of architectural respectability; in the interim, many of its early houses were crudely constructed by covering and weatherboarding with split-pine boards a framework of poles set in the ground. Few were painted, few had glass windows, and, in gen-

[2] Rosa G. Bertleth, "Jared Ellison Groce," *Southwestern Historical Quarterly,* Vol. XX, No. 4 (April, 1917), 360.

[3] Holley to Mrs. William M. Brand, March 6, 1838, Holley Papers; New Orleans *Weekly Picayune,* April 16, 1838; Abner J. Strobel, *The Old Plantations and Their Owners of Brazoria County, Texas,* 23.

eral, they impressed a traveler in 1839 as being "merely patched up shantees of rough boards." In the next six years, a number of two-story and a few brick structures were erected in Houston, but no dwellings comparable to the best in Galveston and San Augustine, where the Greek Revival influence, already discernible in the architecture of some of the plantation homes of the river lowlands, had begun to manifest itself.

After the devastating storm of 1837, Galveston sprang up as a village of shanties, sod huts, and houses improvised from wrecked vessels. But it soon became one of the two largest towns in the Republic, and the early makeshifts were superseded by more presentable structures. By 1840 it was reported that there were "some very pretty houses here of Grecian architecture, one story, with columns & windows to the floor like glass doors, all painted white & having a neat white paling around them."

While the larger houses derived their columned porticoes from classical prototypes, the typical Galveston residence was a small frame structure with a porch. Many homes were similar to the one described in the following 1840 contract "for doing the carpentering work of a House":

> The House is to be built twenty two feet front and twenty eight feet deep with a Portico in front 6 feet one Story high, two windows & one door in front, two windows in each side, and two doors in rear, the windows to have Glass. . . . The weather boarding is to be planed, plain cornice on the sides, with a pediment in front, supported by four square Collums. The floors to be laid out with narrow flooring, planed, tongued & grooved and secret nailed. The House to stand on blocks two and half feet high with steps to the ground, and also the said house to be petitioned [*sic*] off in three rooms . . . with three doors . . . the whole work to be done in a plain workmanlike manner for the sum of three hundred & forty dollars New Orleans money.[4]

In San Augustine, enough of the most beautiful houses remain to show that originally they were marked by simplicity in general outline combined with neoclassic details of dignity and charm. J. Pinckney Henderson's two-and-one-half story residence, modeled

---

4 Galveston County Deed Records, A, 383. See also *ibid.*, 83, 124, 265, 281, 438.

after a well-known Virginia mansion, has upper and lower galleries supported by large columns and is appropriately located in an oak grove, while the porch of Colonel S. W. Blount's one-story dwelling has small, finely proportioned Doric columns. These and other Greek Revival houses gave this East Texas town an architectural kinship with the plantation South. Many of them, as well as the handsome Berry Hotel and the buildings of two colleges, were designed and constructed by Sidney A. Sweet and Augustus Phelps, both skilled craftsmen and accomplished architects. In 1841 a well-known Methodist bishop noted that most of the town's houses were frame structures, painted white. On the whole, to the traveler of the eighteen forties, San Augustine presented surprisingly few marks of frontier crudity.

The Mexican population left an architectural imprint on several Texas towns. Colonel J. N. Almonte, visiting Texas in 1834, found that most of the houses at San Antonio and Goliad were of stone and mortar. Later many another visitor to San Antonio marked the resemblance to fortifications of the one-story, flat-roofed houses, constructed with typically Mexican thick stone walls. Here and at other towns there were also adobe buildings and Mexican picket huts, the latter constructed by placing stakes in the ground "as close to each other as their crookedness" would permit, with intervening spaces filled with a mixture of mud and moss and their roofs consisting of "palm leaves . . . confined with a strip of palmetto stalk, or of raw hide." As far east as modern Lavaca County, American settlers also lived in "picket houses" before they erected log cabins.

Fire control naturally was a serious problem in most wood-built Texas towns. A "fire guard" to inspect buildings, stoves, and chimneys was appointed by the mayor of Austin, and the city council of Houston prohibited the building of wooden chimneys in certain sections of the town. An organized fire company existed in Houston for a few months, but fire fighting usually was done by the first unorganized volunteers to reach a conflagration. Some towns bought ladders and leather buckets, and Houston even purchased an engine and hose. In 1845 a fire beginning in a San Augustine store destroyed several buildings before it was checked by tearing down a building. On the same occasion, a hotel was saved by the "indefatigable exertions of the citizens," who covered the roof with carpets and blankets and kept the front deluged with water thrown from windows.

Efforts of city councils to make Texas towns livable were criticized constantly for their futility. The corporation of Matagorda employed men to keep the streets in good condition, but the town newspaper pointed out in 1841 that some of the ditches had worn away to a depth of ten or fifteen feet. In rainy seasons mud frequently made Houston streets almost impassable; in 1839 the city council addressed itself to the related problem of preventing the passage of horses and carriages on the sidewalks; and six years later the town was compared to "a pig stye." The presence of stumps in many Texas towns rendered night walking hazardous; in Columbia, the seat of government in the fall of 1836, a man died after falling on a stump during a walk in the dark. The condition of Clarksville streets provoked this outburst by the newspaper editor:

Agreeable, very—To range about the streets, of the ancient, incorporated, and highly improved city of Clarksville on a dark, rainy night with no object distinguishable, but a light in some distant window. You grope your way towards that light with the happy expectation of trying the hardness of your limbs against some post oak stump, an expectation never disappointed, for you bark your knees successively against half a dozen before you reach your destination; after which you offer up sincere thanks to the giver of good that you did not break your neck, or fall in the mud, both very possible occurrences. With a most providential regard for their successors, the first settlers of the city, left the stumps of all the trees they felled just high enough to strike a man's knees, for which considerate kindness we return thanks with tears in our eyes.[5]

"Raising corn was a matter of life and death, since upon it depended the existence of the colony," wrote an observer of the initial development of a German settlement. This might well have

[5] Clarksville *Northern Standard,* December 31, 1842.

31

been a realistic statement of the experiences of thousands of settlers of all nationalities. Newly arrived pioneers always hastened to plant patches of corn, a grain distinctively adapted to its role as a fundamental factor in the conquest of the wilderness. Not only was it comparatively easy to grow, harvest, and prepare for eating, but it provided the basic food resource for the maintenance of the frontier.

Once matured, corn could be prepared for consumption in many ways. "Corn-stalk molasses" was produced from the pith of the stalk. When the ear had formed and was still on the stalk in a milky state, it could be toasted, boiled, or fried. After the grain hardened and before it was ready for grinding into meal, it could be grated and made into a sweet bread, or it could be boiled, roasted in ashes, or popped in an oven. But usually the grain was converted into meal by grinding. Corn meal boiled in water furnished the dish called mush, to which milk, honey, molasses, butter, or gravy might be added. Mixed with cold water and given a dash of salt, corn meal was ready for any one of several cooking processes. Batter covered with hot ashes became an old-fashioned ash cake. When the batter was placed upon a clapboard and set near the coals, the result was a "johnnycake"; placed in the same way upon a helveless hoe, the mixture became a hoecake. If the batter was put into an oven and covered with a heated lid, it was transformed into a pone or loaf, or if used in smaller portions, into "dodgers." Neither sugar, yeast, eggs, spices, soda, nor other ingredients were essential, although they could be used to advantage. Not only was bread prepared from corn meal cheap and nutritious, but most people found it palatable. One exception was an English diplomat who referred to Texas corn bread as "a modification of Sawdust."

Corn was prepared for cooking by mashing the grains in a wooden or stone mortar with a pestle, or by converting them into meal in a steel mill (also called an Armstrong mill). Eventually almost every family owned a steel mill, a hand-turned device which had a handle on each end of a spindle. Contemporary records unanimously describe it as irksome to operate, and corn meal was produced in it amid much noise, profanity, and sweat.

Parched corn pounded or ground into a coarse powder (called "cold flour" or *pinole*) and the meat of wild game were the chief dependence of expeditions into the wilderness in search of lands or Indians. Sometimes small quantities of dried beef, coffee, and salt also were carried. Nestor Clay, who in 1832 went on a trip of nearly seven hundred miles up the Colorado River and down the Brazos, wrote to a friend that his party had lived for two months on different kinds of wild flesh: "Buffalo Mustang horse wild Cow deer antelope, Panther Bear wildcat mountain cat Polecat Leopard Cat together with a variety of fish fowl turtle &c., making 19 in all." Clay and his companions stayed in the wilds much longer than they had intended when they set out, so they were "60 days without Bread salt Coffee sugar Tobacco or in fact anything but horse Beef at times." He assured his friend, however, that horse meat was "better than Buffalo, wild cow, or venison; so that if you have an old fat horse that is worth no more than an ox of the same size, you can try it, & I can also state that polecat is the worst meat I have ever tasted."[6]

Even at home the meat of wild animals was depended upon to add variety to meals or to provide food when all other expedients for obtaining sustenance failed. Before the corn crop was harvested, or if the supply was exhausted, venison and the dried breasts of wild turkey were used as staple foods. In any event, deer, wild turkey, or bear meat often was found on Texas tables, and occasionally the flesh of wild ducks, geese, and "prairie hens," as well as the highly prized buffalo steaks and tongue. In 1843 wild pigeons, fat and tender, were knocked down in Red River County; the oldest settlers had never seen them before, and cold weather was supposed to have driven them as far south as northeastern Texas. In the daytime deer were hunted with dogs, and at night they were lured by the flame of burning pine knots carried in large pans. Venison sometimes was eaten daily by backwoodsmen, who also fashioned deerskins into clothing and bags in which honey and bear fat (called bear oil) were kept. A young man recorded in his diary in 1838 that bear meat, prized above any other in the woods, was the finest he had ever tasted; it was fat and made an admirable supplement to venison. Although the members of his land-hunting

[6] Clay to James W. Johnson, April 28, 1832, Clay Papers (University of Texas Library).

33

party exhausted their supply of meal and rice and had nothing to eat but bear and deer, they ate the meat and drank the bear oil with as much satisfaction as if they were bread and milk. Clear, liquid bear oil also was used in cooking and in lamps.

Travelers often noted that milk and butter were scarce—and this in a land where the inhabitants numbered their cattle by the hundreds. In 1845 Washington on the Brazos, then the capital, was without milk and butter except at one boardinghouse. In 1840 no milk was available at Velasco because the cows had been driven into the woods "to recruit their energies, with the young grass." Two years before, the explanation given by a New Yorker at Bastrop was that the populace would not take "the trouble in the spring to keep their cows up when with calf but let them run at their leisure in the prairie."

The basic fare of most Texans was made up of corn-meal "dodgers," fried beef or venison, and black coffee. Sweet potatoes also were eaten frequently, and bacon gradually became a part of every Texan's food, perhaps because hogs could be raised in the woods "in great abundance," with no corn "excepting a little to keep them gentle." This lack of balance in rations was not confined to Texas, for in this period consumption of fresh vegetables was meager in the United States, and the three daily meals were practically identical.

The staple fare was partially responsible for a picturesque outburst by a young man who arrived in Tyler County in 1845. "I don't see how a man can live," he wrote, "as you folks do and be a Christian, for the Ticks, the black Mud, the sand flies, and musketoes— dry beef, black coffee, sweet potatoes, and other hard features of your country would ruin me. . . . It is the most perfect purgatory of any place on the Earth."[7]

The Texan diet gradually was expanded to include a few fruits, melons, and vegetables, and various wild nuts. Pumpkins, sweet potatoes, cabbages, turnips, and peas were among the first vegetables grown, while pecan trees flourished in many areas, particularly the river bottoms. A few bananas were grown on Galveston Island, but the orange groves planted around Galveston Bay were

7 William W. Arnett, "Reminiscences," 16, Arnett Papers.

Views of Fort Parker, as restored in 1936

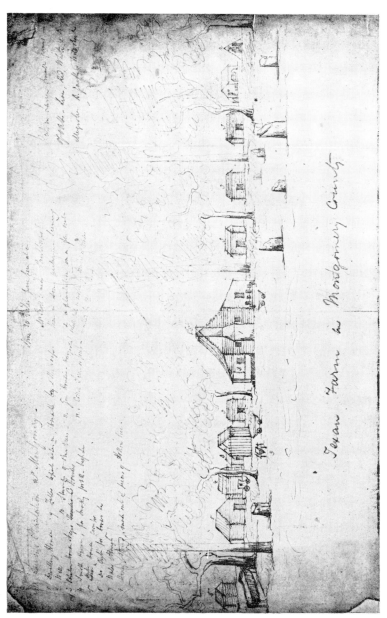

Sketch of the buildings of a cotton plantation in the interior, drawn by William Bollaert between 1841 and 1844

From the original in the Ayer Collection; reproduced by special permission of the Newberry Library.

unsuccessful. Unimproved peach orchards and wild grapes throve, but most travelers considered that farmers generally failed to give their gardens and fruit trees proper care. As late as 1846 it was reported that "no attention is paid to the cultivating of fruits. . . . Yams, melons, pumpions of finest size and flavour are produced almost without any care."[8]

The plantations in the river bottom lands of coastal Texas had a better quality and a much wider variety of food. They were operated by men who used their credit in the stores at Brazoria, Velasco, Quintana, Columbia, Houston, and Galveston or their access to ship wharves along the rivers to purchase a few of the foods, including flour, which were classifiable as luxuries. Yet the records of the James F. Perry plantation at Peach Point, one of the most efficiently managed on the lower Brazos, show very few purchases of flour. And in the spring of 1837 Colonel James Morgan wrote from his Galveston Bay plantation that he had "not a pint of corn— nor ten pounds of breadstuff in the world—nor ten pds of meat! except Beef which, thank God, we have here great abundance in the prairies."

Even in the plantation homes, the customary food and drink were wild game, beef, fish, corn bread, and coffee, but poultry, figs, grapes, peaches, and melons were seen more often on planters' tables than on other settlers'. In the spring of 1838 optimistic Mrs. Mary Austin Holley reported concerning Bolivar, her brother's plantation on the Brazos: "They brought in a fine buck this morning. We get rabbits like chickens, & fish great buffalo & perch whenever we choose to catch them. There is a lake back, too, fed by springs, full of fish." A party of New Yorkers who visited a plantation on the San Bernard River reported that they were served a dinner that would satisfy the appetite of an epicure, but noted that bowie and pocket knives, forks made from cane, and gourds for drinking purposes were used at the table. In 1844 the ranch of Colonel H. L. Kinney (approximately the site of modern Corpus Christi) was making "a good show in Indian corn, pumpkins, melons, sweet potatoes, beans, tomatoes . . . and Sea island cotton."

[8] William A. McClintock, "Journal of a Trip Through Texas and Northern Mexico in 1846–1847," *Southwestern Historical Quarterly*, Vol. XXXIV, No. 2 (October, 1930), 150–51.

But this generation of Americans was only in the process of learning to eat tomatoes and salads.

Those who enjoyed good meals had ample grounds for complaint, even in the towns. Before 1835 Harrisburg, Brazoria, San Felipe, and other towns often were reported to be without flour, sugar, and coffee. Indeed, citizens occasionally were unable to purchase these staples in interior towns in later years. On March 9, 1842, Adolphus Sterne, one of the prominent citizens of Nacogdoches, made this entry in his diary: "how the People of this Country can get the necessaries of life till next fall god only knows, a perfect Barrier is placed now between the introduction of even the Staff of Life (Bacon & flour) because those who have the fortune to raise enough money to purchase a little at Natchitochez [Louisiana], have not the means to pay the duties on them." A short time later, Sterne had no money to buy sugar, flour, and coffee. He had not been without them since he had been in Texas—for him they had become "rather necessaries, than Luxuries of life." In the following fall, however, he was housing his corn and pumpkin crops, and since he previously had recorded that he had found his hives productive of fine honey (often used for sweetening purposes), he was not actually facing starvation.

Flour was regarded as a luxury by many Texans. It sold in Houston at prices ranging between $10 and $30 and even as high as $75 per barrel; sometimes it was unavailable at any price. But after 1843 the price gradually went down, so that within two years it was no longer a luxury except for the poor. When the capital was moved to Austin on the extreme frontier, Houston editors were fond of pointing out that the cost of transportation to the new seat of government made flour twice as dear there as in the former capital. Some families living in the interior rarely saw a biscuit, and occasionally children reached adolescence without tasting wheat bread. On the whole, foodstuffs on the Texas frontier did not present the same startling contrast between luxury and simple necessity that was exhibited in furniture and wearing apparel.

In the coastal towns, apples, rice, molasses, raisins, beans, onions, sugar, coffee, tea, salt, mackerel, and codfish frequently were listed as importations. Cheese and butter usually were noted as "scarce," while eggs and poultry sold at prohibitive prices. In 1838 Samuel

M. Williams of Galveston made a gesture of marital affection when he directed his wife to sell a town lot and buy several boxes of cherries. Occasionally cakes and pies were available for sale in restaurants and bakeshops, which sometimes sent bread carts through the streets. In the eighteen forties ice cream and candies also were proffered to the public by Houston and Galveston confectioners.

Fish and oysters were a customary part of the diet in the coastal towns. A visitor to Quintana reported that she and her friends had eaten there "the finest oysters you ever saw—as long as your hand —some of them" and that ducks and fish were abundant. She was impressed particularly by the high quality of the red fish. At Aransas, south of Goliad, the fish, oysters, and turtle delighted those who loved good sea food. The German geologist, Ferdinand Roemer, observed that there were several shops in Galveston which served oysters raw or prepared in any way desired—fried, roasted, or stewed. Although the size of the oysters impressed him, he considered them inferior in quality and piquancy to the smaller European varieties.

The proximity of groups of Europeans and Mexicans helped to add variety to the Anglo-Americans' eating habits. The German and French settlers applied their native industry to the production of the best vegetable gardens in Texas, and some Anglo-Americans imitated them and profited by their example. Figs, pomegranates, other fruits, and sugar cane in small quantities flourished in the vicinity of San Antonio, and their growth presaged San Antonio's modern truck-farming industry. The Mexicans there made thin, flat, unleavened tortillas from corn meal, and Anglo-Americans learned to like them. Eggs prepared in various unusual ways and "a sort of stew made of beef, chicken or any sort of meat with pumpkin and a large quantity of red pepper" were among favorite Mexican dishes. In 1845, at Corpus Christi, an American army officer was introduced to "a Mexican preparation called themales [tamales], made of corn-meal, chopped meat, and Cayenne pepper, nicely wrapped in a piece of corn-husks, and boiled." He added, "I know of nothing more palatable."[9]

[9] W. S. Henry, *Campaign Sketches of the War with Mexico*, 27.

The potency of early Texas coffee, usually drunk without sugar or cream, frequently was a matter of comment. Although all settlers could not afford to purchase coffee in their initial years in Texas, the pot or can in which it was brewed came to be a necessity in every home and was standard traveling equipment. In the river town of Brazoria, the custom of drinking coffee immediately before or after rising in the morning was followed by some families; this early-morning potion occasionally was strengthened with brandy. Dr. Alexander Ewing, surgeon general of the Texas Army in 1836–37, prescribed the early morning use of coffee as a malaria preventive. One prominent Texan testified in later life that he had followed the practice for more than fifty years and never had chills and fever in his family, though residence in the coastal country had been maintained during most of that period.

Among the men tobacco was almost as indispensable as coffee. In the year ending July 31, 1844, the value of tobacco officially imported into the Republic was more than three-fifths of that of spirits importations. Texans chewed an inordinate amount of tobacco, two of the most highly regarded types bearing the names "honeydew" and "Brown and Niger's best Cavendish." Except among the Germans, cigars were much more commonly smoked than pipes, and an English observer noted that Mexicans of both sexes in San Antonio "indulge largely in the delicate form of cigarrits of finely divided tobacco rolled up in the shuck or leaf which envelopes the head of the Indian corn." The same observer denied that all the Anglo-American women were pipe smokers; on the contrary, most women addicted to the habit were of an advanced age. According to the usually accurate Dr. John Washington Lockhart, when the women took their children outside the building during lengthy religious services, "the elderly ones would draw their pipes from the long calico bag and have a good smoke, while the younger ones would draw from their dress pocket the box and brush and have a social dip"—of snuff.[10]

Tobacco chewing prevailed among all classes of men. The veranda of Galveston's Tremont Hotel, the finest in Texas, saw much

[10] J. L. Wallis and L. L. Hill (eds.), *Sixty Years on the Brazos; the Life and Letters of Dr. John Washington Lockhart, 1824–1900*, 151.

consumption of "the 'weed' per humo and per mastico," while the observation of a visitor at a session of Congress was typical: "the way the members were chewing the tobacco & squirting was a sin to see." The English diplomat, Francis C. Sheridan, was especially disgusted with this "universal" practice. "High & low," he wrote, "rich & poor, young & old, chew, chew, chew, & spit, spit, spit, all the blessed day & most of the night." He saw a man in Galveston teaching a child about two years of age to chew. Furthermore, as late as 1849, a church near Austin found it necessary to post this admonition in verse:

TOBACCO IN CHURCH
Ye chewers of that noxious weed
Which grows on earth's most cursed sod
Be pleased to clean your filthy mouths
Outside the sacred House of God.

Throw out your "plug and cavendish,"
Your "Pig Tail," "Twist," and "Honey-dew,"
And not presume to spit upon
The pulpit, aisles, or in the pew.

Although Stephen F. Austin attempted to limit his colonists to persons "absolutely free from the vice of intoxication," whisky was admitted free of tariff duties under the Mexican regime, and drunkards caused some confusion and disorder in San Felipe de Austin. Usually a realist, however, Austin went so far as to give reluctant approval to the beginning of the distilling industry:

Philanthropy cannot but weep [he wrote] at the incalculable mass of human misery and degradation which the use of ardent spirits heaps upon mankind, and were it possible to exclude it from our country for ever, the first who attempted to introduce it would be ranked by me on a level with the fiend who first introduced sin into the garden of Eden, but like sin, the use of spirits pervades the whole civilised world, (savages and barbarians are not sufficiently civilized to brutalise in this refined way) and Philanthropy has no consolation, other than that derivable from the hope that the sound judgement and moral rectitude of men will restrain the use of spirits to proper and safe limits.

I am therefore not displeased to see this branch of business com-

39

menced. Spirits will be imported and if not manufactured in the country, money will be sent out to import it, and it is better that the money which is thrown away by the drunken and worthless part of our citizens should go into the pockets of our own distillers, than into the pockets of foreigners.

For these reasons I accept of the present of the bottle of Rum which you have sent me, and in return wish Mr Varner and yourself success and prosperity in your distillery.[11]

The rugged generation that maintained Texas as a republic drank heavily and frequently. Enormous amounts of intoxicants were imbibed in the boom towns, chief among which was Houston.

While there were a few who did not exceed the limits of moderation [at Houston in 1837], a large majority knew no restraint to their appetites. The extent to which this vice was carried, exceeded all belief. It appeared to be the business of the great mass of the people, to collect around these centers of vice, and hold their drunken orgies, without seeming to know that the sabbath was made for more serious purposes, and night for rest. Drinking was reduced to a system, and had its own laws and regulations. Nothing was regarded as a greater violation of established etiquette, than for one who was going to drink, not to invite all within a reasonable distance to partake; so that the Texians being entirely a military people, not only fought, but drank, in platoons.[12]

The inhabitants of Galveston and Houston in the late eighteen thirties were largely bachelors who found in the barrooms both companionship and opportunities for business chances. Houston merchants left their businesses several times daily to enjoy pick-me-ups; the crowded, smoky barrooms—redolent with the smell of whisky, tobacco, and the unwashed male—served both as clubs and as commercial meeting-places. Here the merchants could make business contacts with farmers, freighters, and newly arrived immigrants, as well as with local customers.

Grogshops were among the first business houses in Houston

11 Austin to Israel Waters, July 30, 1829, in Eugene C. Barker (ed.), *Austin Papers*, II, 243.

12 "Notes on Texas," *Hesperian; or, Western Monthly Magazine*, Vol. I, No. 6 (October, 1838), 431.

and Galveston, and their number multiplied with the rapid growth of the towns. A saloon built in 1837 in the shape of an octagon, boarded up about ten feet and covered with canvas, was one of Houston's principal early structures. In the following year, Houston was reported to have between twenty-five and fifty saloons, with gambling a side line in many of them. By 1846 Houston's most sumptuous business houses were barrooms, magnificently furnished in comparison with the surrounding buildings, and constantly filled with customers. The patron stepped through folding doors into a large room where long rows of crystal bottles lined a lavishly decorated bar, attended by an experienced barkeeper who served both plain and mixed drinks. Although two Galveston business establishments abandoned liquor sales in 1842 (Cornelius O'Connor advertised that his "Family Temperance Grocery Store" had abandoned the traffic in intoxicants "from a consideration of his immortality"), there were "grogshops innumerable" there, and the Tremont Hotel bar had become a noted dispensary.

The "Texas passion for erecting grogshops" prevailed in other towns in varying degrees. In December, 1845, it was reported that the number of barrooms in Corpus Christi had increased from two to more than two hundred in response to the demands of the United States troops there. In other towns, such as Nacogdoches, "the hard times" infrequently caused the "doggeries" (known also as "drunkeries," "grogshops," or "groceries") to close, yet even in the middle of the depressive conditions of the early eighteen forties, a diarist recorded: "every body in Town drunk, nothing doing, idleness Root of all evils." The records of the Fort Bend County Clerk's office show that, between 1838 and 1846, more licenses were issued to retail wines and spiritous liquors than for all other businesses combined. The Mexicans of San Antonio loved their alcoholic drinks, but were credited with being fairly temperate. Likewise, in smaller villages and at crossroads stores all over Texas, whisky flowed from barrels at the order of men in all walks of life, among them farmers who had brought their products to exchange for necessities of life. At home, some settlers also prepared various fermented home-brews, such as "persimmon beer" and "potato beer."

The most common drinks were whisky, brandy, and cognac,

while gin, champagne, claret, and port also arrived in Texas ports by the boatload. In 1838 it was reported that "London Porter and champagne were constant drinks" among the families of merchants at Quintana. The more expensive drinks usually were served at hotel bars in the coastal towns, while the common "groggeries" served inferior liquors at about one-half the price charged in the more pretentious establishments. After 1839 imported ice and lemons occasionally were available in Galveston and Houston, facilitating the concoction of fancy drinks.

By 1842 cocktail mixing had become an art in the best Texas hotels, although the term "cock tail" was applied to only one drink. The list of mixed drinks was headed by whisky punch, "the national drink" during the Christmas season. As served at the Tremont Hotel in Galveston, it was described as "nectar of the Gods." In addition to such familiar concoctions as gin sling, eggnog, variations of the mint julep, various types of cobblers, and "Tom and Jerry," the intriguing list of drinks prepared in Galveston hotel bars included the following, priced at twenty-five cents each: "Tip and Ty," "I.O.U.," "moral suasion," "vox populi," "silver top," "poor man's punch," "epicure's punch," "peach punch," "deacon," "stone wall," "Virginia fancy," "Knickerbocker," "heater," "smasher," and "cock tail."[13] Barrooms in inland towns, such as Bastrop, charged higher prices for less complicated drinks—a reflection of the high cost of transportation.

Carousing in saloons and at private drinking parties was a major sport. One of the most captivating spectacles that Houston citizens were privileged to see in 1838 was that of a local doctor ghoulishly drinking whisky "out of a scull that had yet brains in it." In June, 1846, a traveler spent two days at the town of Buffalo (or Goddards Bluff) in "drinking whiskey, listening at some new fangled Texas oaths in real Texas style occasionally lookin on at a verry interesting game of dollar pitching that lasted the entire two days that we staid between Loafers on one side and Loafers on the other—the Stake Liquor a game."[14] Many fights occurred in tippling bouts. A few began as the result of a forceful infusion of

13 William Bollaert, "Personal Narrative, 1840–1844," 75.

14 [A. W. Moore?], "A Reconnoissance in Texas in 1846," Southwestern Historical Quarterly, Vol. XXX, No. 4 (April, 1927), 266.

frontier democracy into barroom manners—since it was a violation of any man's hospitality to refuse to drink with him. In 1839 a sailor in the Republic's navy had been criticized severely, and the "only honest charge [wrote a friend] that can be preferred against him by his most bitter and unrelenting enemies is simply that he will not indulge with them in their bachanilian meetings and midnight revelrys."[15]

Holidays, election days, and campaign speakings were times for unrestrained license in drinking. As elections approached, politicians often took the lead in providing as well as in drinking liquors.

Nothing is now talked of [wrote Charles S. Taylor of Nacogdoches] but the approaching elections. I was present yesterday at a "stump speechification." There was much recrimination and but little discrimination between the Candidates. One of them carried his best speech in his saddle Bags in the shape of a bottle of whiskey which *ever* and anon we had recourse to, as it were to cheer us on our weary way. This speech though short made on *some* a very *visible impression.*[16]

Many drinking exploits of the greatest politician of them all bore the stamp of his flair for the spectacular. Among the countless stories concerning Sam Houston's drinking bouts, there was one to the effect that in 1839 he went on a spree, had his coat burned off, and was seen with a large cloak wrapped around him on a warm day. But such actions always were forgiven by the electorate. In 1840, before his second election to the presidency, Colonel James Morgan wrote to a mutual friend: "Genl. H. is now inclined to be more dissipated than ever—though being lately married he may reform. If he lives, there is no doubt about his elevation to the next Presidency." The following year he made one of his periodic resolutions to stop drinking and even addressed a large group of persons at a barbecue, which "strange to say ... was a cold water *doins.* The Old Chief [Houston] did not *touch,* taste or handle the smallest drop of the *ardent.*" In later life, Houston looked back upon the drinking feats of his past with mellow tolerance. In a

[15] John S. Evans to M. B. Lamar, May 22, 1839, in Gulick *et al.* (eds.), *Lamar Papers,* V, 287.
[16] Taylor to James H. Starr, August 30, 1839, Starr Papers.

speech on the floor of the United States Senate, in 1854, he said: "Now, it is very well known that I quit barrooms in 1845 [laughter], and I only patronized them in a small way before that [laughter]."[17]

The "Old Chief" had the physique and temperament to endure self-indulgence, whereas many other able men in public life did not. In 1838 Chief Justice James Collinsworth, a candidate for the presidency against Lamar, leaped from the deck of a steamer and was drowned in Galveston Bay. Concerning the circumstances of his death, Thomas F. McKinney wrote to his business partner: "Collingsworth went exactly as you and B. presumed. I was here and had been with him to Houston and we had returned and he was under the influence of Ardent Spirits for a week before hand."[18] Indeed, a list of Texas tipplers would have included many a prominent name. Attorney General F. A. Morris was said to have been intoxicated habitually for a period in 1841 but seems to have reformed. Judge Charles S. Taylor, one of Nacogdoches' most reputable citizens, was accused of being unreasonable while "under the influence"; in 1842 a quarrel with General Thomas J. Rusk caused a temporary cessation of their friendship: "the Cause of the quarrel was—*whiskey* & Taylor was in the wrong." But other contemporaries stated that Rusk himself had difficulty in remaining sober during certain periods of his life, and eventually he committed suicide. On March 31, 1843, Colonel James R. Cook, a well-known Texan, was shot and killed by a friend in a drunken row. This is only a small part of the record which indicates the baleful effect whisky consumption may have had upon the actions and life spans of a number of the country's leaders.

The army of the Republic also was known for its ability to consume intoxicants in large quantities. Officers stationed at Galveston in 1838 were heavy drinkers, one of them having "the conviction that the water did not agree with his constitution." In 1841 one company at Camp Cook, near Austin, had a "great reputation"

---

[17] Sources of the three quotations in this paragraph are as follows: Morgan to Samuel Swartwout, July 6, 1840, Morgan Papers; E. H. Winfield to Ashbel Smith, September 22, 1841, Ashbel Smith Papers; and *Congressional Globe*, 33 Cong., 1 sess., Appendix, 1086.

[18] McKinney to Samuel M. Williams, October 13, 1838, Williams Papers.

because of its good music and because it "passed through town without a man's attempting to stop at a Grocery (which they say is the first time that such a thing ever happened)."

Recourse to the bottle helped travelers endure their journeys. William D. Wallach, editor of the *Colorado Gazette and Advertiser*, related a story of his trip by horseback from Matagorda to Austin in the company of a doctor "whose penchant for good living induced him to carry a bottle or so of the best 'Old Nash.'" Early in the morning they were overtaken by "a tar river cracker," who was invited to join a prebreakfast "antifogmatic." The newcomer accepted the offer, and toasted his benefactor with "Here's luck, *Captain.*" Another "dose of the same physic" was swallowed shortly before breakfast by the stranger with a "Here's your health, *Major.*" A noontime drink brought a "Thank you, *Colonel.*" At dinner his comment on his "whetter" was "Mighty fine liquor this, *General.*" Shortly thereafter, before the travelers took different roads, a last dram produced this earnest question: "*Governor,* whar did this liquor come from? It's the best I ever see. I wish I know'd any thing higher nor a governor, and I would call you so, for any man that totes such stuff ought to have the biggest sort of title."[19]

Modes in clothing both reflect the cultural pattern of a people and are an integral part of it. On the Texas frontier, life that was a mixture of the crude and the cultivated was manifest in dress that ranged from the reliable roughness of buckskin to the refined elegance of broadcloth.

Whole families of Texans occasionally were outfitted completely in buckskin, sometimes with both clothing and moccasins trimmed with self-fringe and beaded. However, such garb was more general in the early days of colonization when many had to depend on animal skins for wearing apparel. As other types of clothes became available with the passage of time, less buckskin was worn, one reason being that it left something to be desired in comfort. Francis R. Lubbock, twice comptroller of the Republic of Texas, attested to this fact when long after his one and only wearing of such a suit, he wrote, "Buckskin is more romantic and

19 Matagorda *Colorado Gazette and Advertiser*, March 27, 1841.

entertaining in romances and pictures than on one's own shanks." He had, it seems, set out from Houston on an Indian-hunting expedition which he expected to last only a few days and therefore had taken no change of clothes from the buckskin suit which he had deemed the practical attire for venturing into the wilderness. When rain drenched his suit, he dried it—and himself—near the campfire only to discover when he was thoroughly warm and dry that his breeches had shrunk to above his knees and were stuck so tightly to his skin that they had to be cut off. But the "old stagers" knew better than to dry buckskin near a fire, and Texas pioneers continued to wear it on hunting and fighting expeditions throughout the period of the Republic. Headgear often was fashioned from coonskin, and one individual who lived near Washington on the Brazos won local notoriety by donning a snakeskin vest, "a very odiferous affair."

As soon as sufficient cotton was produced, homespun became the standard dress material for the entire family. The clothes were made by Texas pioneer womenfolk who carded, spun, and wove cotton and wool, sometimes even concocting their own homemade dyes. Thus, women and girls usually wore "linsey" homespun made from home-raised cotton dyed with bark and berry juices. By virtue of these improvised dyes, they managed to achieve colorful blue, yellow, purple, and red effects in their raiment. Their head coverings usually were bonnets—sunbonnets for summer wear, in some cases fashioned from a "bonnet squash" plant, and poke bonnets for state occasions. For the man of the family, the women made coat and pants, dyed a rich walnut brown, and perhaps a hat out of palmetto and straw. Coarse blankets were formed into overcoats which became standard for those Texas farmers who did not wear a bearskin or buffalo-hide outer covering in winter. In fashioning the blanket coats, the women sometimes made decorative use of a striped border across the shoulders and on the lapels; and expert matching of stripes was considered—then, as now—the test of designing skill. Many wore blankets poncho-fashion with a slit in the middle, faced to prevent raveling, in the style of the expensive Mexican blankets which were worn only by the fortunate few who could afford them.

When the family status was such as to include slaves, the wife sometimes made their clothes from white and blue cottonades, although often a dexterous Negro made outfits for a group of slaves. In 1843 Mrs. James F. Perry wrote to her planter husband: "If the negros should want any over coats, there is plenty of linsey in the Box. Let Clarissa keep to Sewing, she & Milley could make old Mary & Sarah dresses." Even stockings were knit at home in a day when the whirr of the spinning wheel, the beating of the loom, and the click of the knitting needles were as familiar household sounds as in the first colonies on the Atlantic coast. Rough shoes also were made at home out of deer or cow skins, although some persons went barefooted. Occasionally the shoe and clothing scarcity was relieved by visits from an itinerant shoemaker or a strolling peddler whose stock included calico.

For "Sunday best" the frontierswoman saved a calico dress or perhaps a cherished old black silk gown, brought from "the States" in a battered hair trunk along with her worn black silk bonnets in an ancient hatbox.

As some families became more affluent, and the stores in the towns became more accessible, a few women were able to enjoy the luxury of ready-to-wear clothes—or at least fabrics purchased by the yard. Sometimes, with the returns from the first crops, the family obtained "store-boughten" shoes as well as calico and checked shirting materials for Sunday and holiday wear, but in all except the large settlements, the rare individual who wore "store clothes" habitually was distinguished by that fact in his community. Occasionally, a townswoman might make a selection from an assortment of fabrics that included silk crepes and ginghams as well as domestic cottons, or she might have a choice of walking shoes in black, white, or colored kid; even dancing pumps were sometimes to be found.

Frontierswomen were no different from their less adventuresome sisters in their desire for self-adornment, and the Texas women who were fashion conscious attempted to learn from every traveler and available publication what styles were in vogue. They tried to copy them, if possible, although there is reason to believe that in some instances they may have been misled by local storekeepers. For example, in 1839 one Charles Hoffman of Baltimore, in sending a consignment of bonnets to his partner, P. McLaughlin, a Galveston storekeeper, wrote that they "were old stock and out of fashion, but believe they will sell in Texas."[20]

The young lady of fashion in the larger towns, however, was not altogether dependent for style hints on the likes of Hoffman and McLaughlin. The following is a description of a fashionable young lady's "holiday suit" worn in Houston in 1837:

A black silk dress with very full skirt reached to the ankles, a low-necked waist had long leg-of-mutton sleeves, tight fitting below the elbow, but puffed out very full at the arm-holes, a double shoulder cape of white embroidered mull called a Vandyke was trimmed with lace, and concealed the neck and shoulders. This out-door costume was completed by a pink satin bonnet, with brim of eight or ten inches projecting over the face, and a crown three or four inches high towering above the head. Close to the face inside was a double ruching of tulle, with minute bows of pink satin and sprigs of flowers interspersed. Fastened by a ribbon around the crown and hanging over the face was a white blond veil a yard wide and about a yard and a quarter long; this was elaborately wrought in flowers, all in white, and furnished at the lower end with a rich border.[21]

White silk stockings and black slippers were worn with this suit— a costume that was more likely inspired by pictures in *Godey's Lady's Book* than by anything in McLaughlin's emporium. Nor were some of the men of the time much behind in sartorial distinction. Elegantly dressed gentlemen frequently were seen in Galveston and Houston, and in 1838 a visitor recounted that at Velasco "the gentlemen dress remarkably well—the clothes being all brought from New York, ready made & of the newest fashions."

Few men, however, were able to import their clothes from that fashion center. A traveler stepping into the rather bare front room of a Houston hotel early in 1846 would have found himself in the midst of a number of men, evidently farmers, standing around the stove talking animatedly about the news of the annexation of Texas by the American Union. His eye would have been caught by the

[20] Hoffman to McLaughlin, June 28, 1839, in Galveston County Probate Records, File No. 0195.

[21] Dudley G. Wooten (ed.), *A Comprehensive History of Texas, 1685 to 1897*, I, 665.

brightness of their coarse blanket coats in mixtures of bright red, white, and green. If the visitor was uncomfortable in such crude surroundings or annoyed by the farmers' continual expectoration of tobacco juice, the innkeeper probably would lead him to a parlor in which a few more refined guests were gathered. These men wore black frock coats, the invariable mark of the American gentleman of the period. When they had entered the parlor, they in all probability had doffed overcoats, cloaks, or roundabouts.

In addition to frock coats and lighter linen coats (for summer wear), the wardrobes of the countless "colonels," "majors," and "captains" usually included military coats, often blue in color. The tendency toward military dress resulted from the martial spirit of the times and the related existence of many militia organizations, which attempted to maintain a semblance of similarity in their uniforms. At one time (1838) the Milam Guards of Houston, parading in the mud, found it necessary to stick their white pantaloons into their boots, which "at a short distance gave each man the appearance of a pair of black boots drawn over his inexpressibles." Yet the boots may have been of good quality, for it was possible for men to purchase from a selection of "Wellington, military, Cossack, opera, and high" shoes and boots in Galveston stores.

The shining item of attire for any male was a dazzling "vest," without which not even the poorest "Texian" was seen at a public function. An elaborately adorned waistcoat allowed for the free play of sartorial individuality against the background of the long, close-fitting, black frock coat, and a particularly ornate vest would be borrowed by a succession of bridegrooms for appearance at their weddings. If a man was able to own a frock coat, his costume also included a false collar, ruffled shirt front, and black string cravat. For ordinary wear, the Texan preferred a hat with a wide, floppy brim, but he covered his head with whatever he could obtain, whether beaver, Mexican hat, "stovepipe," or coonskin.

Whiskers were worn to suit the fancy of the individual man, but many Texans were clean shaven at least part of the time and nearly everyone owned a razor. In the towns there were usually barbers, one of whom offered not only to shave his customers and to cut their hair—which was worn long by many men—but also to "make guard chains and finger rings of hair."

A considerable minority of the men owned watches and fewer carried canes. Some of the canes were strikingly ornamented with carved ivory heads and silver tips. In 1840 an Austin newspaper carried the following fashion advertisement of locally made canes, together with a facetious note, perhaps the prototype of some of today's semihumorous advertising copy: "Walking-canes are all the rage in Austin now, and the way our friend BROWNING does the thing *brown* is a caution to all foreign cane importers. Ye admirers of buffalo horn, Austin pearl, and hickory (when done up in the shape of a fashionable walking-stick), give Browning a call."[22]

Although the frontier obviously was not a region where one would expect to see a general display of the latest fashions, a number of beautiful gowns were worn at the balls which were given in the largest towns to commemorate military victories, to celebrate the opening or conclusion of the races at Houston or Velasco, or to pay homage to foreign envoys who arrived at Austin. For these occasions women saved their best costumes—dresses that had been imported from England or France, or purchased in American cities, and carried with them among their most valued possessions when they had come to the Republic.

From all accounts, one of the most sparkling fashion and social events of the times was the San Jacinto Ball in Houston in 1837, invitations to which were printed on white satin. To this great gala, ladies and gentlemen rode as far as fifty to sixty miles on horseback "accompanied by men servants and ladies' maids, who had charge of the elegant ball costumes for the important occasion." A fashion reporter covering the event might have noted that Mrs. Mosely Baker, who led the first cotillion with the President, was gowned in white satin with black-lace overdress and that Mrs. Sidney Sherman, wife of the Colonel, was lovely in a bouffant white velvet. Our hypothetical fashionist, groping for a trend to report, probably would have added that several of the ladies who attended the San Jacinto Ball wore soft white mull gowns gleaming with touches of rich satin—the gowns bare-necked and billow-skirted. With these gowns they affected coiffures that were parted in the middle, with curls caught at the nape of the neck.

22 Austin *City Gazette*, October 21, 1840.

This part of the S. W. Blount residence was erected in 1838

Courtesy Historic American Buildings Survey

The Cartwright home, built in 1839 by Isaac Campbell, has been occupied by descendants of Matthew Cartwright for more than one hundred years.

Both of these houses, and several other structures in San Augustine, show a Greek Revival influence.

Courtesy Historic American Buildings Survey

Chambers residence, Anahuac, reputedly built in the 1840's.
Note winding outside staircase and Texas star in the gable.

Courtesy Historic American Buildings Survey

French Legation at Austin, occupied by Chargé d'Affaires Count de
Saligny in the early 1840's

Courtesy Historic American Buildings Survey

But the fashion scribe probably would not have given substance to the provocative thought that style varied at this social affair, as at later ones in the Republic, according to the dates most of the wearers migrated there. For years Mrs. Francis Yoast, Jr., of Bastrop appeared at dances dressed in a full-skirted, off-shoulders gown with lace bertha, together with a matching necklace, earrings, and bracelets of amethysts and pearls. This was the costume in which she had made her debut in Virginia.

Of the men who attended the San Jacinto Ball of 1837, it has been reported that all wore white dancing slippers except President Sam Houston, who because of a wounded ankle wore boots, red-topped and silver-spurred. Most of the men probably dressed in black frock coats—with the exception of those in blue broadcloth uniforms and of the President, who must have been a dashing figure in a gold-corded black velvet suit with ruffled shirt and crimson waistcoat. During his first administration, he often wore this apparel, sometimes complementing it with a large hat ornamented by waving plumes.

On the other hand, in his early years in Texas, Sam Houston frequently appeared in buckskin and a Mexican or Indian blanket. In 1841 this same gentleman, recently elected president for the second time, wore a hunting shirt and pantaloons when he delivered his inaugural address before an Austin audience of about one thousand persons.[23] At this time he was worried about the financial situation of the Republic, which, as he stated in his message to Congress about two weeks later, was "not only without money but without credit." Thus, in "dressing down" to the inaugural assemblage, it was as though the "Old Chief," good actor that he was, may have been attempting personally to demonstrate the need for governmental economy. And, when the capital was moved to Washington on the Brazos, it was observed that Houston was still wearing a similar type of rude costume, though not exclusively, for the spectacular Sam occasionally appeared in "a garment of fine broadcloth, in the style of a Mexican blanket, lined with yel-

---

[23] Maurice G. Fulton (ed.), *Diary and Letters of Josiah Gregg*, 109; James Morgan to Samuel Swartwout, January 12, 1842, Morgan Papers; Harriet Smither (ed.), "Diary of Adolphus Sterne," *Southwestern Historical Quarterly*, Vol. XXXIII, No. 1 (July, 1929), 76; Mrs. Julia Lee Sinks, "Texas Reminiscences," VII, 10.

low satin, with gold lace all around it."[24] In 1845 he visited various courts in New Orleans clad in a "blue cloth military frock and pantaloons and buff vest, and the fingers of his left hand were ornamented with massive rings."[25] Sam Houston's choice of clothes marked the extremes of dress in the Republic just as his life epitomized the contrasting strengths and weaknesses inherent in an individualistic frontier society.

[24] H. F. Gillett to Ashbel Smith, December 8, 1843, Ashbel Smith Papers.
[25] New Orleans *Daily Picayune,* May 27, 1845.

III

Roads of Mud and Slush

TRANSPORTATION DIFFICULTIES which largely shaped the whole economic and social pattern were the chief obstacles to prosperity. The slow, uncertain trips to local markets for supplies were vexatious and often hazardous, and it was imperative to develop facilities for transporting cotton to American markets. Economic advancement beyond the level of family self-sufficiency almost was precluded until cotton, hides, and other products could be sent safely to the outside world. It was natural, therefore, that within the limitations of the means and knowledge of a new, raw country, the Republic's settlers made strenuous efforts to travel dirt roads and to navigate the long, snag-ridden rivers with light-draught steamboats or other suitable craft.

Texas roads which bore a major portion of travel and internal commerce were mere dusty trails in dry weather and quagmires in wet seasons, as many wayfarers ruefully narrated. Early in 1838 Sam Houston wrote that he had been unable to start on an intended trip from Houston to Nacogdoches because "at this time the roads are most terrible and impassable in this section of the country." Near the end of the same year a San Antonian wrote concerning his trip to Houston:

I did not get here until last night, about 10 o'clock; the roads and the weather were very bad indeed. . . . I must tell you a little more about the roads, as I wish to get rid of the subject forever; So much rain has fallen that about one half of the road from the Navidad and a good portion of that back to Victoria is under water. Between the Colorado & Brazos I was obliged in the worst places to relieve the mule by getting off and leading for a mile at a time, with water to my knees and sometimes to my britches pockets. The weather was very wet &

53

cold most of the time and I suffered for want of thick boots and a heavy blanket. My cloak being of very little use at all.[1]

When dry spells occurred in summer, Texans were able to find consolation in their effect on the roads. A Methodist preacher wrote from Fort Bend County to his brother: A "great benefit of the drought is dry roads; this is more favorable on me than the farmers. As you have never travelled in this country, you have no idea of the state of the roads in wet weather; and if you remain in ignorance on this point, you will lose nothing."[2] Although in dry seasons the roads in the Nacogdoches–San Augustine region of East Texas made a favorable impression on some tourists, the creeks and rivers in this area were very difficult to cross in wet weather and even the hardiest horseman dared not venture abroad in the face of the winter "northers." Indeed, the abrupt drop in temperature produced by the bone-chilling "northers" could mean death to a lone traveler. Shortly before the Republic's existence terminated, a company of Rangers found a horse and rider frozen to death within a few miles of the Ash Creek settlement, high on the Brazos River—and others died in similar fashion.

Travelers usually made their way across the country on horseback or—if baggage had to be carried—in wagons drawn by oxen. Horsemen often traveled in small parties, each rider equipped with a blanket or two, a rope, pistols or a short rifle, saddlebags or wallet for provisions and perhaps a few changes of clothing, a gourd, and the inevitable coffeepot. If a saddle were not available, one could be fashioned out of wood, possibly held together with wooden pins and rawhide strings. The horseman had to be prepared to swim rivers, face sudden changes of weather, or walk if his animal strayed during the night—one accident "which happens quite frequently and belongs to the 'petites miseres' of traveling in Texas."[3] Yet a horse was a necessity for many persons, among them a

---

[1] Samuel A. Maverick to Mrs. Mary A. Maverick, December 29, 1838, Maverick Papers. On January 14, 1844, he wrote to Mrs. Maverick that it would be impossible to go from Washington to Houston: "We can't go till the roads are passable, even to Houston, say April or thereabouts."—*Ibid.*

[2] O. M. Addison to M. H. Addison, June 18, 1848, Addison Papers.

[3] Ferdinand Roemer, *Texas* (1935 translation by Oswald Mueller), 176, 183.

man who wrote to President Lamar that penury compelled him to forego sufficient food while he was paying $1.25 per meal for his horse. "Him I must feed," he stated, "or I have to walk, which at times would be impossible."⁴

But relaxation around the evening campfire was ample compensation to resilient spirits for the rigors of the day's journey. William Bollaert, camped on the San Bernard River en route from Houston to Columbus, wrote in August, 1843:

The night was beautiful, the heat of the day was passed & the cool & refreshing breezes from the South were invigorating indeed. A fire was soon kindled, the coffee pot was called into requisition, each cut a twig and broiled his strip of dried beef & with corn bread & cheese, et voila! notre souper. Each took his pipe, the evening chat was soon over, our horses watered & then hobbled, buffalo robes & blankets spread and now, good night.⁵

Transportation by wagon was exceedingly difficult and snail-paced. In the summer of 1839 one of President Lamar's advisers predicted that existence would be arduous for the citizens of Austin in the ensuing winter; for, until the roads greatly improved, no provision wagons could reach the frontier capital. In the spring of 1845 an editor of the New Orleans *Daily Picayune* made a journey from Houston to Washington on the Brazos River, but was not impressed with the advantages of travel by wagon:

Here [Washington] have we been, ever since Wednesday last [he wrote], swimming, digging and floundering from Houston to this place, two days of the time completely weather and water bound. With our horses we could get along well enough—they could swim the swollen creeks and bayous—but the Count's lameness, although he is now nearly over it, induced us to purchase a wagon at Houston, and it is not altogether so simple a matter to swim a vehicle of that particular de-

[Fiske?], *A Visit to Texas,* 55, states that horses were tethered by tying both forelegs with short cord, and not one hind leg and one foreleg as in the Northern states.

⁴ Richard R. Wilkins to M. B. Lamar, February 12, 1839, in Gulick *et al.* (eds.), *Lamar Papers,* II, 450.

⁵ Bollaert, "Notes on Texas, 1843–1844," 7. For a similar expression, see Mrs. S. J. Allen to Mrs. Isabella H. Gordon, January 20, 1845, Gordon Papers.

scription, neither is it so easy to drag it through the deep, heavy, black mud of the prairies.[6]

Indeed, a long trip by cumbersome, wooden-axle ox-wagon was likely to be interrupted by days spent in mending broken parts. A letter from Bastrop County in 1838 characteristically complained that "we have traveled a long and crooked road to get here. We traveled from 9 of Oct til 12 of December. We lost 3 days; one to wash, two to make axle trees which broke both times by the box in the hub breaking."[7] Even short trips by individuals who lived near towns were accomplished principally on horseback, and the owner of a vehicle was a marked man; Rev. J. W. Kenney of the Washington community owned one called "the Old Ship of Zion," which was prevented from falling to pieces by repairs made with rawhide and bars of iron. In the larger towns or on the plantations a few buggies or barouches were available, and the inhabitants of Galveston found driving along the beach in a light cabriolet a pleasurable experience.

If a traveler visited many parts of Texas, he often would employ several different types of transportation. In 1833 Thomas Drummond, a Scottish naturalist, went by boat up from Velasco to Bell's Landing and walked to San Felipe, and on another trip paddled a canoe from Galveston Bay to Harrisburg, at which place he hired a cart and oxen to return to San Felipe, and finally rode a wagon to Gonzales. In 1845 John C. McCoy and Charles Hensley traveled from Galveston to the present site of Dallas by raft, oxcart, horseback, canoe, and horseback again.

The experiences of that greatly traveled lady, Mrs. Mary Austin Holley, offer an instructive commentary on the variegated travel facilities of the period. "We were fortunate in finding a barouche returning empty to Matagorda [she wrote to her daughter in De-

[6] New Orleans *Daily Picayune*, April 26, 1845. George Wilkins Kendall, the writer of this account, was accompanied by Count Zondogi, a Hungarian; Mr. Wade, an "English pleasure traveller"; and Stephen Whitney, Jr. Kendall came to Texas in the spring of 1845 to hunt and to report the activities of English and French diplomats who were attempting to block the annexation of Texas to the United States.—Fayette Copeland, *Kendall of the Picayune*, 133.

[7] John Hobbs to "Brother and Sister," February 1, 1838, in Canton *Van Zandt Enterprise*, June 28, 1906.

cember, 1837], having brought on the family of Mr. Horton of the Senate to get passage in the steamboat. This we chartered for the ladies, together with an ox wagon going to Brazoria for corn, for our baggage." The following February she and Mrs. James F. Perry descended the Brazos River below Brazoria to Quintana "going down one side of the river, & up the other, visiting all along shore—on horseback." While at Quintana and Velasco, she became acquainted with Mrs. William H. Wharton, who invited her to visit her home, Eagle Island, a few miles away. Mrs. Holley drove there "in a barrouche & four—I will not say how elegant—the leaders being plough horses, in plough harness." And in May she came sixty miles down the Brazos in "a dug out, or Indian Canoe, the water within 2 or 3 inches of the top—considerable swell in the river most of the way. We had to sit very still. . . . The Columbia [a steamboat] was waiting outside [the bar at Quintana] & we had to cross the breakers in a whale boat on the top of the surf."[8]

A few sanguine individuals operated stagecoach lines over some of the fearful Texas roads. In the summer of 1837 passengers could travel from Houston to near-by Harrisburg for "$1 *in dry weather*"; in the following spring passengers were taken as far as Richmond once a week for seven dollars per head; and in the summer of 1839 a stage line ran weekly from Houston to Egypt. Afterward there was usually transportation from Houston to the capital, whether it was Austin or Washington on the Brazos. When the capital was moved to Austin in the fall of 1839, P. B. Starke and a Mr. Burgess of Mississippi brought thirty-six horses and "two first rate stage drivers" to Texas and established service from Houston to Austin via Washington. The schedule called for the negotiation of the distance in three days, with two trips per week each way. One man remembered in later life that the coaches were old and rickety and "the passenger who travelled in these had to work his way by carrying a fence rail on his shoulder for long distances and helping to pry the vehicle out of mudholes in order to reach his destination at all." Starke and Burgess also inaugurated four-horse stage con-

---

[8] Mrs. Mary Austin Holley to Mrs. William M. Brand, December 30, 1837, February 8, March 6, May 13, 1838, Holley Papers.

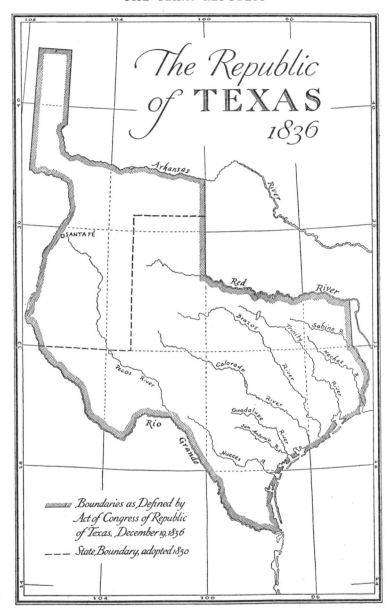

The Republic
of TEXAS
1836

Boundaries as Defined by
Act of Congress of Republic
of Texas, December 19, 1836

State Boundary, adopted 1850

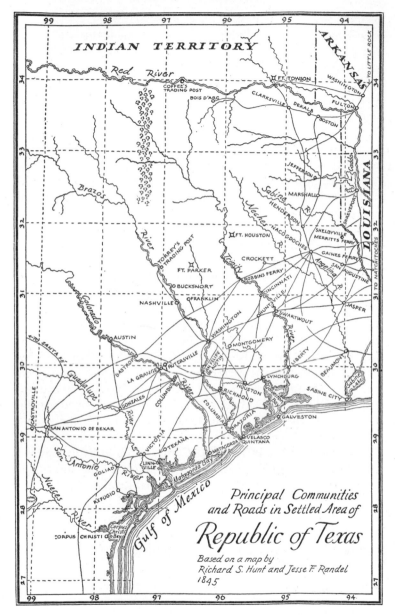

Principal Communities
and Roads in Settled Area of

Republic of Texas

Based on a map by
Richard S. Hunt and Jesse F. Randel
1845

nections between Houston and Velasco, operating on a prospective twenty-four-hour schedule. A minister who made the trip records that he paid nearly twenty cents a mile, "the highest fare I ever paid." But the Starke-Burgess venture apparently failed, for the following spring found "Smith and Jones," mail contractors for the Austin-to-Houston route, making arrangements for carriage communications.

After the spring of 1843, Houston had fairly regular weekly stage connections with Washington on the Brazos.[9] The trip was estimated to require thirty hours. In the fall of 1844 J. F. Brown became the proprietor of this line, and the next year, associated with a Mr. Tarbox, made Austin a terminus. Travelers paid fifteen dollars for the Houston-to-Austin journey, and six cents per pound for baggage in excess of thirty pounds. Houston also had weekly connections with Huntsville for a time.

The county courts and later the commissioners of roads and revenue (presided over by the chief justice of the county) were authorized by law to construct and maintain roads, arrange for the establishment of ferries, and contract for erection of toll bridges. All free males between the ages of eighteen and forty-five and all male slaves between sixteen and fifty were alike subject to calls to work on the roads of the precinct in which they lived, but these legal sanctions often were ignored. The national government in a few cases attempted to supplement the efforts of the counties in their road-building activities. In 1839 Congress directed that the counties concerned should construct a road from Washington on the Brazos to Jasper and thence to the Sabine River, later granted the Houston and Austin Turnpike Company authority to construct a toll road via San Felipe, and in 1844 authorized the survey and initial development of the "Central National Road of the Republic of Texas" from a point in what is now central Dallas County to northwest Red River County. But the Republic was too poor to give substantial assistance in the development of highways, and most of the roads were no more than trails from which the brush had been cleared away.

[9] Stage connections to Washington were advertised as early as May 15, 1839. —Houston *Morning Star,* July 26, 1839. See also Houston *Telegraph and Texas Register,* March 6, 1841.

One of the irksome transportation problems was that of crossing the rivers. As the country developed, ferries were installed at strategic points, usually on authority of the county governments. The customary procedure was for an individual to apply to the commissioners of roads and revenue, who issued the requisite license and set the rates. The usual charges were light and heavy wagons, one to two dollars; man and horse, twenty-five cents; single footman, six and one-quarter or twelve and one-half cents; cattle, four to six cents per head; and sheep and hogs, lesser amounts. Special provisions often were allowed for increasing the rates if service was performed between nine or ten P.M. and daylight, or in high water. Less frequently, the erection of a toll bridge by a private party was authorized. In 1846 the town of Nashville on the Brazos River had neither ferry nor bridge, and travelers paid for the privilege of swimming their horses across by the side of a canoe.

The uncertainty of travel in the Republic was one of the chief causes of the breakdown of the postal system. Although modern Western fiction and the movies always depict mail riders as galloping safely to their appointed stations, the mail often failed to go through in that segment of the frontier called the Republic of Texas.

From the beginning of Anglo-American settlement to the end of the administration of Dr. Anson Jones as the last president of the Republic, Texas had no postal system that functioned with even moderate efficiency. Though this provoked frequent and bitter complaint, neither the Mexican state government nor its successor could remedy the situation. A few post offices and mail routes connecting the principal towns were established before the Revolution, but service was hampered by inadequate roads, high water, official mismanagement, and robberies. Furthermore, communication by mail with the United States was very precarious. Although the establishment of official connection between the Mexican and United States postal systems was urged by Stephen F. Austin on behalf of the colonists as early as 1824, more than ten years elapsed before the establishment of a weekly mail to the United States border was sanctioned by official action. The inefficiency and inadequacy of mail service seem to have been minor irritants among the grievances of the Texas colonists against the Mexican governmental administration, and the poverty-stricken government of the Republic of Texas could do little to improve the service.

The business of carrying the mail in the Republic often was neither lucrative nor tranquil. The person who contracted with the government to transport mail frequently had difficulty in collecting his compensation, or currency depreciation might make his contract practically worthless. In 1840 the mule carrying the Houston-to-Austin mail escaped from the carrier, and it was announced that "those who sent letters in this mail must write again." On other occasions Indians attacked mail carriers, but chief among the carriers' woes were the bad roads and the vagaries of Texas weather. Naturally, mail contractors and their riders were not overly popular, and the opprobrium heaped upon many of them apparently was partly deserved. Mail was found in ditches, and carriers were accused of failing to stop unless it was convenient. Riders occasionally encountered open antagonism. In 1843 Dr. James H. Starr received a letter which stated in part: "Still I assure you such has been the bad faith of contractors on this line of road that but for your letter stating that Mr Clevinger was a punctual man, that rare phenomenon in Texas, which letter I shewed to several, his rider would not have found food or shelter in this country."[10] But at least one mail carrier, Peter Carr (on the Austin-to-La Grange route in 1839), delivered mail to many of his numerous acquaintances gratis and accordingly was in good standing with the community.

Emoluments of the office of postmaster were not compatible with such honor as the position may have entailed. On December 29, 1841, G. Stubblefield, postmaster at Houston, petitioned Congress for relief because he had been compelled to hire clerks to work all night to care for the "large packages of letters which are distributed at Houston." In 1843 the Galveston postmaster wrote that his compensation was totally inadequate; he found it necessary to advance sums from his own pocket in order to continue the work of his office, and he was not in a position to work for nothing. Noah

10 J. H. Kirchhoffer to James H. Starr, February 11, 1843, Starr Papers.

Smithwick, Bastrop postmaster (as well as justice of peace, blacksmith, and militia officer), testified that he never received any compensation for his services or office rent beyond a few worthless "shinplasters." The following illustrative excerpts from the diary of Adolphus Sterne of Nacogdoches reveal many of the tribulations which beset a Texas postmaster:

[March 2, 1841] news was received that the mail rider between this place and Cincinnatti was arrested at Crockett on an accusation of having stolen Judge Hart's monay, and that, a large mail is now at Douglass, brought there in a waggon, all this is rumor—however something must be wrong, or else the mail would have been here before this time. . . .

Saturday the 27th [of March, 1841] . . . a Mr. Caldwell from Fanning County came from Austin last night he has all the mail Contracts East of the Trinity, he let out to day the Cincinatti contra[c]t to Mr Davison, the Epperson ferry contract to [blank] and the Sabine or McLanahan's to Mrs. Hubert, all to commence running after the 1st April next. . . .

[October 30, 1841] received a letter from G. W. Sinks Chief Clerk of Post office Department, Drawing upon me for $470.00. I owe nothing to the Department, which is acknowledged in the Letter, but poor Devils it was their only chance. . . .

[February 6, 1842] the mail from the west arrived, Mr. Hall the Subcontractor informed me he would not carry said mail any longer. . . . Communicated the actual distracted situation of our mail routes . . . to the general Post office Department. . . .

[March 28, 1842] Judge Mason one of the Contractors of mail rout No 3 made an arrangement for George Clevenger to carry said mail from and after the 1st April next and to receive *all* the pay pr quarter for which said route was contracted. . . .

[August 1, 1842] have a serious Idea of resigning my Postmastership it is a loss to me, every day, and the government is so destitute of means that the Establishment can not be kept up as it ought to be—it is the *beginning of the End*—God grant it may not be—but!!!

[August 25, 1842] Started a Supscription to have the Eastern mail transported again, made arrangements to have it carried for $12.00 pr

Month by getting a horse furnished etc. have $32.00 subscribed, want 18 more to carry it from now, till first January next. . . .

17th [of November, 1842] *allmighty* Cold this morning, the wind is N. W. and nearly blowing t[h]rough a body . . . did not send off the western mail, was afraid the little mail rider would freeze—however the Eastern mail came in but did not bring any thing ex[c]ept Red landers [San Augustine newspapers]. . . .

[December 8, 1842] the western mail arrived last night, did not see it till this morning, nothing but a few Letters (apparently such) were put in but the Boy having rode two days in the rain so that the whole Contents were so mangled, and mixed up that it looked more like mush than anything else, so that nothing can be read to find out to whom the documents belong or where they came from.[11]

The irregularity of the arrival of the mails was particularly galling to the newspapers because they were dependent upon regular postal service to reach their subscribers and to obtain data from other newspapers with which to fill their columns. In October, 1837, the Matagorda *Bulletin* protested that "here is one of the principal ports of entry of the country—where in the space of ten days have landed 300 foreigners . . . the county seat of justice—the designated point for locating a land office,—without any communication except in one direction . . . and that as uncertain as the wind." The newspapers frequently carried similar complaints which reveal intermittent breakdowns in the postal system. Three years later, communication by mail between Matagorda and the neighboring county of Brazoria was "very contracted," and as late as the spring of 1844 the Matagorda mail was two months overdue in Houston, whereas mails from the eastern counties had not arrived there for nearly a month. In May, 1842, the East Texas town of Nacogdoches had received no mail from Galveston and Houston for six weeks, and in the fall of 1845 no mail from any direction reached neighboring San Augustine during a two-week period.

11Smither (ed.), "Diary of Adolphus Sterne," *Southwestern Historical Quarterly*, Vol. XXXI, No. 3 (January, 1928), 288; Vol. XXXI, No. 4 (April, 1928), 375; Vol. XXXII, No. 4 (April, 1929), 344; Vol. XXXIII, No. 2 (October, 1929), 161; Vol. XXXIII, No. 3 (January, 1930), 235; Vol. XXXIV, No. 1 (July, 1930), 72; Vol. XXXIV, No. 2 (October, 1930), 159; Vol. XXXIV, No. 4 (April, 1931), 343, 347.

Mail communication between the United States and the Republic of Texas was chronically slow and uncertain. In August, 1837, Surgeon General Ashbel Smith wrote to a friend in New York: "The other day I received nine letters, by a single mail—the first and only time I have heard from the United States since quitting New Orleans. Among them all there was not even one from you.—I have written to you several times."[12] In 1839 Mrs. Mary Austin Holley claimed that letters sent from one country to the other often failed to reach the addressees; "Brother H[enry Austin] does not get half mine." Although in 1843 and 1844 an arrangement was in force whereby letters from the United States were forwarded free of charge from New Orleans to Texas, this practice later was discontinued.[13] Meanwhile, mail was reaching Nacogdoches, San Augustine, and Clarksville from the United States, though never regularly. Adequate arrangements for postal communication between the Republic of Texas and its sister nation were never made, and as late as January, 1844, a Brazoria citizen wrote to Secretary of State Anson Jones: "Cannot something be done to facilitate intercourse between Texas and the United States by mail? As matters now stand, it is almost wholly impracticable to get a newspaper from the United States."[14]

The untrustworthiness of the governmental mails compelled resort to private carriers, and many letters which have been preserved are indorsed with the name of the carrier instead of a postal mark. When the postal system broke down almost completely in 1842, groups of citizens of Houston, Nacogdoches, and elsewhere contributed to private subscriptions with which to pay mail carriers; similar arrangements existed for long periods in many backwoods communities. Even in Austin, capital in late 1839, a prominent Texan wrote to his wife: "Mr. Welsh leaves here today for Galveston, and I take advantage of it to write you a line—since I have been

[12] Smith to Daniel Seymour, August 6, 1837 (letter-book MS), Ashbel Smith Papers.

[13] New Orleans *Daily Picayune,* June 29, 1843, August 4, 1844; Houston *Telegraph and Texas Register,* December 24, 1845. For President John Tyler's message to Congress on this subject, see "Trade and Mail Arrangements with Texas," No. 162, *House Exec. Documents,* 27 Cong., 2 sess.

[14] James Burke to Jones, January 4, 1844, in Jones, *Memoranda and Official Correspondence Relating to the Republic of Texas,* 297.

here the mails have been so irregular that I did not think it worth while to attempt forwarding a letter thro the Postoffice."[15] And if a writer at Galveston or Houston could get a friend to take his letter to New Orleans for mailing there, it was judged to be not only more economical but safer.

A large portion of the commerce of the Republic was carried by freight wagons, usually drawn by three to eight yoke of oxen or less often by horses or mules. The use of oxen had several advantages: their hoofs did not sink into the mud as readily as those of horses and mules; the purchase price of a yoke of oxen was about forty to fifty dollars (in 1846) compared with a figure at least three or four times as high for a pair of draft horses; and the oxen could subsist almost entirely on the prairie grass. Therefore, oxen-drawn wagons carried produce from the interior to markets and seaports and returned with goods and provisions, a trip that required many weeks or even months. A load for several yoke was three thousand to five thousand pounds, which could be transported at a rate of ten to fifteen miles per day in dry weather. If the streams were swollen by rains, progress was halted for days. Under such conditions, several "freighters" generally traveled together for mutual protection and assistance; by co-operating, teams could be doubled or goods lightened in crossing miry places and watercourses—all of which was accompanied by lurid swearing to which the oxen seemed to respond better than to whipping. German immigrants very often found that their lack of experience in handling oxen compelled them to seek help in stimulating the stubborn beasts to movement or finding them if they had escaped during the night. On the other hand, Negroes appeared to possess a particular knack for driving oxen. "It almost seemed to me [wrote Ferdinand Roemer] as if they understood it better than the whites, on account of a certain intellectual relationship" which enabled them "to see the viewpoint of this horned beast of burden."

"Teamstering" or "freighting" was carried on by men who owned their own outfits or by others who worked for half the

15 Samuel M. Williams to Mrs. Samuel M. Williams, December 29, 1839, Williams Papers.

profits. One of the few examples of an attempt to conduct this business on a schedule was revealed in the 1840 newspaper advertisement which stated that three wagons would leave Matagorda and Austin on the first and fifteenth of each month. Many farmers became freighters in their spare time, since the traffic provided a ready supplement to their incomes. Farmers also employed oxen to draw sleds loaded with cotton or hides to market. Dr. Pleasant Rose of Stafford's Point, who used a sled in 1834, humorously divided the settlers into three classes: the aristocrats who owned wagons, the middle class who owned carts, and the lower class who owned sleds.

Houston became the most important center of the freighting business because of the location of the capital there and the town's accessibility to water communication with Galveston Harbor. Trade with the Brazos River cotton-growing areas quickly sprang up, and the city became a "commercial mart" with a population variously estimated at two to three thousand souls. By 1840–41 the streets of Houston frequently were crowded with wagons being loaded to carry merchandise inland. In November, 1841, Josiah Gregg found that the town "has a brisk trade supporting from a dozen to 20 dry goods stores. It has indeed several tolerably extensive foreign importing houses." During the two following years the volume of trade lessened because of partial crop failures, river-boat competition, and bad roads. But early in April, 1844, the local press noticed "that the commerce of this city, which has been languishing to an unprecedented extent for the last two years is slowly and steadily reviving," and on May 22 that approximately a thousand bales of cotton had been brought into Houston in the preceding three weeks.[16] A part of the explanation of the revival of trade, according to the editor, was that many wrecks and accidents had occurred in transporting cotton by river boat; two Brazos River steamboats had sunk in the preceding winter.

Ox-wagons also carried freight from Natchitoches, Louisiana, to San Augustine, in East Texas. Wagons drawn by three yoke of oxen could transport about three thousand pounds; they carried freight at one dollar per hundred pounds and returned with six

---

[16] Houston *Telegraph and Texas Register,* April 3 and May 22, 1844.

bales of cotton. The round trip required three to four weeks in good weather.

While the rivers of Texas seemed to offer a tempting possibility for solving the transportation problem, the story of river navigation is largely one of frustration and disappointment. The long, meandering rivers were difficult for even shallow-draught steamers to negotiate. Many overflowed during spring rains, while all needed clearing and some were choked by long masses of tangled driftwood called "rafts." Most of the principal waterways flowing into the Gulf had shallow bars at their mouths, and these bars, as well as the passes and channels in the Texas coast, often shifted. Bolivar Pass, at the east end of Galveston Island, had a depth of twelve feet over hard sand, while the bar at the mouth of the Brazos usually had not more than three to five feet of water running over it. The earliest river-shipping efforts were directed chiefly toward navigation of the Brazos, which ran through the most productive cotton region in Texas, but the difficulties proved too great, and the Brazos trade gradually was diverted by the access to Galveston Harbor offered by Houston and Galveston.

The first steamboat to navigate the waters of Texas probably was the *Ariel,* commanded and owned by Henry Austin, cousin of Stephen F. Austin. In the summer of 1829 Henry Austin began to run the vessel on the lower Rio Grande, but from the beginning the prospect was enough to discourage even such a persevering optimist as he. Sickness disabled his crew during the fall months, the season when the boat might have been most profitably employed; he himself was ill in the following spring, and he was further handicapped by "the crudeness of the people, who, taking his boat for a living thing, were afraid of it." Trade with the suspicious Mexican merchants on the sluggish, shallow Rio Grande soon disgusted this strenuous New Englander; and, although conditions had sufficiently improved to enable him to make expenses for three months, he wrote that "nothing but my pride and the censure to which I should expose myself by abandoning a project of my own choosing has induced me to continue here so long." This was not quite the whole truth, for he estimated the value of his Rio Grande interests at six to eight thousand dollars and hesitated to leave them in the hands of an agent. He therefore persisted in carrying on the business until July, 1830, when he perfected arrangements to visit his cousin's colony in Texas, despite the fear, expressed only half-facetiously, that the "river may dry up and prevent my departure."

In August, 1830, Austin reached the mouth of the Brazos in the *Ariel* and ascended the river to Brazoria. The country that he saw en route impressed him favorably, especially when contrasted with the arid territory from which he had come. Nevertheless, cursory investigation convinced him that the prospects for a profitable steamboat business on the Brazos were poor, unless the river could be made more navigable and connected by canal with Galveston Bay. Throughout the fall months he explored the river and considered possible locations for a ten-league grant, for which he had made formal application on the ground of his services to the commercial and agricultural development of northern Mexico. Not only had he introduced steam navigation on the rivers of the country, he declared, but if the grant were allowed, he would settle his large family in Texas.

Indeed, he set out for New Orleans to secure supplies and make arrangements for settlement in Texas, but the *Ariel* never reached its destination. Four of the crew deserted; a part of the provisions spoiled; and the vessel, being nearly wrecked on the Brazos bar, put to sea in a damaged condition. Two cannon had been left at Brazoria to lighten the boat's draught, but the additional weight of wood and supplies for the run to New Orleans nearly caused disaster on the shallow, treacherous bar at the mouth of the river. After three fruitless attempts to reach the United States, the ship put back into Galveston Bay and Buffalo Bayou, reaching Harrisburg on December 29. The boat, "leaking badly & her chimney blown away," was disabled beyond hope of repair.[17]

With the possible exception of a vessel which Ben Milam supposedly ran up Red River in 1831, the next steamboat introduced to Texas waters was the *Cayuga*. In November, 1833, a number of Texans signed a subscription list circulated in Austin's Colony to secure pledges to encourage "Robert Wilson and William P.

[17] For complete documentation of the career of Henry Austin, see the writer's study in *Southwestern Historical Quarterly*, Vol. XXXVII, No. 3 (January, 1934), 185–214.

Harris . . . [to] bring a Steamboat to Texas for the purpose of running in its Rivers, and to be and remain in Texas for the benefit of the Commerce of the Same." Henry Austin, William Barret Travis, Asa Brigham, and A. N. Breedlove pledged the largest donations of land with five hundred acres each. By the following April the subscription list contained promises amounting to five thousand acres of land and eight hundred dollars, and arrangements had been made to bring out the *Cayuga* from New Orleans. In the fall of 1834 it was operating on the Brazos, and occasionally reached San Felipe de Austin, where on January 8 a ball celebrating its arrival was held, but the vessel stuck on a sand bar on its return journey.[18]

In the eighteen thirties the Brazos River was navigated by schooners and sloops as far up as "Columbia Landing" and Brazoria. In 1831 the *Majesty* made the voyage to Brazoria by sending men ashore with ropes at every turn in the river, and other sailing craft slipped over the shallow bar at the mouth of the river. In 1836 schooners frequently were towed up to Columbia or Brazoria by the steamers *Ocean* and *Yellowstone*. In November the *Ocean* sank at the landing at Brazoria, and a schooner likewise was wrecked on the bar—no uncommon occurrence. While the *Yellowstone* advertised that it would make trips on the Brazos between Quintana, at the mouth, and Washington, "when the state of the water will permit," both this vessel and the small steamboat *Laura* soon quit the Brazos and entered the Galveston-Houston trade. In February, 1839, however, the *Laura* was back on the Brazos during a period of high water.

In 1843 two steamers—the *Mustang* and the *Lady Byron*—plied the waters of the Brazos above Brazoria. The *Mustang,* a small vessel, had a short piece of two-inch pipe extending from the boiler

18 "Proposal for Introducing a Steam Boat Into Texas," November 27, 1833, Franklin Papers; William P. Harris to Travis, April 16, 1834, *ibid.;* Robert Wilson to Samuel M. Williams, March 7, 1834, Williams Papers; Wilson and Harris to Williams, October 23, 1834, *ibid.;* James K. Greer (ed.), "Journal of Ammon Underwood, 1834–1838," *Southwestern Historical Quarterly,* Vol. XXXII, No. 2 (October, 1928), 132. On December 30, 1834, James Tylee paid $106.89 for transportation of forty-eight packages weighing 7,126 pounds on the *Cayuga* from "Columbia Landing" to San Felipe.—MS, Austin County Probate Records, Case No. 45.

instead of a whistle. A box placed over the pipe was blown high in the air when the engineer let off steam. "The crashing, rasping sound followed by the immense cloud of vapor, caused all to think that the whole thing had burst and was rapidly going up.... Such a scattering was never witnessed on the banks of 'the Arms of God' (Brazos de Dios) before." In the summer of 1843 the *Mustang* went as far as several miles above Nashville, but on November 19 she sank at Jones Landing.[19] Less than two months later, her successor, the *Lady Byron,* went down below Richmond, losing about half of the cargo of 370 bales of cotton.[20] Yet even in the face of such disasters, arrangements were being made to navigate the Brazos in the fall of 1845.

Steamboat transportation on the Brazos River was largely a failure because navigation was rendered precarious by the shallowness of the bar and obstructions in the tortuous channel. In February, 1840, the McKinney, Williams and Company steamer *Constitution* managed to negotiate the river outlet en route to Galveston with a cargo of three hundred bales—reputedly the largest cargo that had been transported across the bar—but larger vessels dared not attempt to enter the river. In 1838 the *Columbia,* which was running between New Orleans and Galveston, made side trips to the mouth of the Brazos, but she anchored outside the bar to take on passengers. Meanwhile, some of the farmers on the upper Brazos sent their cotton downriver in "flats," and merchants and newspapers along the river agitated loudly for river clearance but with practically no tangible results. Much of the cotton was transported by the safer if slower wagon-train method to Houston, which was making a determined and successful bid for the Brazos River trade.

The watercourse most traveled by steam navigation was Buffalo Bayou. Even before the removal of the capital to Houston in April,

---

[19] Wallis and Hill (eds.), *Sixty Years on the Brazos,* 84, 85; Washington *National Vindicator,* November 25, 1843; Houston *Telegraph and Texas Register,* November 29, 1843.

[20] Houston *Telegraph and Texas Register,* January 10, 1844; Washington *National Vindicator,* January 13, 1844; New Orleans *Daily Picayune,* January 23, 1844. The *Daily Picayune* announced in its issue of April 25, 1845, that the boat had been raised. But the vessel soon sank again. In 1842 both the *Mustang* and the *Lady Byron* had been in the Galveston-Houston trade.

1837, the possibilities of navigating this stream, which connected the site of that town with Galveston Bay, had been explored. In January the *Laura* had chugged up the bayou; "thus it is proved [said the Columbia *Telegraph and Texas Register*] that Houston will be a port of entry." The *Laura* found Buffalo Bayou deep and wide as far as the site of Harrisburg—which had been practically destroyed by the Mexicans in 1836—but it took three days to negotiate the narrow, log-obstructed channel from Harrisburg to the site of Houston. All the passengers had to lend a hand in clearing away the obstructions. The trip of the *Laura* was only the beginning of a substantial traffic on Buffalo Bayou. The Allen brothers were engaged in a skillful promotion of the town of Houston, which they had located on the Bayou in order to attract the cotton business of the fertile Brazos River region, less than twenty-five miles distant at its nearest point.

The initial issue of the town's first newspaper frankly stated the difficulty in navigating Buffalo Bayou: "The principal objection to this place is the difficulty of access by water; the bayou above Harrisburg being so narrow, so serpentine and blocked with snags and overhanging trees, that immense improvements will be required to render the navigation convenient for large steamboats." Though the "immense improvements" were not destined to be made until several decades had elapsed, small steamers and an occasional schooner began to ply between Galveston and Houston; they carried many loads of prospective settlers on the first lap of their journeys into the interior, and returned with cargoes of cotton, hides, and other products. The June 3 issue of the *Telegraph and Texas Register* (which had followed the seat of government from Columbia to Houston) pridefully announced the arrival of the steamboat *Constitution*. Early in August the *Leonidas* (later the *Sam Houston*) and the *Branch T. Archer* entered the trade, and by March, 1838, had been joined by the *Friend*. The *Sam Houston* and the *Friend* frequently made the trip in nine hours. When the boats reached Houston, a fork or inlet in the bayou was utilized in turning around. After 1838 there were usually four or five steamers in the Galveston-to-Houston trade, except for one period in 1844 when the *Dayton* was the only one. In 1841 the captains of the *Dayton* and the *Maryland* offered to carry passengers from Galveston to Houston free of charge. In 1845 several new steamboats, including the *Spartan,* the *Republic,* and the *Sam M. Williams* (a Texas-built boat capable of carrying eleven hundred bales of cotton) were making the run, and by March competition had reduced the rates for the Houston-to-Galveston run. Passengers were carried for one dollar, and cotton for thirty-seven and one-half to fifty cents per bale, whereas a few weeks before the rates had been four dollars per passenger and seventy-five cents per bale.

The early Galveston-to-Houston steamers were small, dirty boats. One was described as having the appearance of a wooden house on a large raft, and another, the *Sam Houston,* as "a small filthy, horribly managed concern." In late 1837 the captain told Mrs. Mary Austin Holley that "his accommodations, bad as they are, are better than Houston can furnish, crowded as it is." The fare of tough beef, Irish potatoes, and coffee was invariably poor, although often it was supplemented by venison and fish which the grumbling passengers obtained while the crew was attempting to dislodge the boat from bars or mud.

Traffic was conducted on Buffalo Bayou in spite of many handicaps. The boats frequently grounded on Red Fish Bar and Clopper's Bar in Galveston Bay, or scraped against the sides of the bayou, which in 1845 was still "so narrow [between Harrisburg and Houston], tortuous and overhung by the limbs of the adjacent forest," that it alarmed passengers "who had never navigated a *branch* in a steamboat till they *came to Texas.*"[21] The *Sam Houston* twice partially sank in Buffalo Bayou; on another occasion the grounded *Brighton* so obstructed navigation of the stream that more than a hundred Houston citizens had to work to get it loose. In the spring of 1840 donations were collected to clear the bayou of snags, and two years later the city of Houston was authorized by law to remove obstructions in Buffalo Bayou and to levy a tax on vessels to provide funds for that purpose. At times Buffalo Bayou overflowed its banks and the current became so strong that steamboats at Houston were prevented from leaving port. And on December 21, 1841, the *Albert Gallatin,* en route to Galveston,

[21] Unsigned letter written from Houston, dated November 21, 1845, in New Orleans *Daily Delta,* November 28, 1845.

burst a boiler and sank; five persons were killed and several wounded.

Such were the beginnings of a navigation which provided the principal basis for the growth of Houston and Galveston, the Republic's leading cotton and trading marts. Their victory in the duel with the Brazos merchants for the river's cotton trade was largely the result of the superiority of the Buffalo Bayou—Galveston Harbor outlet to the sea over the Brazos River's difficult course and shallow bar. Though Houston and Galveston had a healthy sense of civic rivalry, they complemented each other in transporting cotton to foreign markets; shallow-draught steamboats made the run from Houston to Galveston, where cargoes were transferred to ocean-going vessels.

Unsuccessful attempts also were made in the late eighteen thirties and early eighteen forties to connect the Brazos and Galveston Harbor by means of railroads and canals. Augustus C. Allen and associates organized the Houston and Brazos Rail Road Company, chartered in 1839, to run to some point on the river, later designated at the "City of Brazos," near the present town of Hempstead. On July 25, 1840, an elaborate "railroad meeting" to celebrate the beginning of construction was held at Houston in conjunction with the Odd Fellows meeting on their fourth anniversary in the Republic. After the Odd Fellows ceremony in the Presbyterian Church, a procession formed by Masons, Odd Fellows, the Milam Guards, city and county officials, army and navy officers, lawyers, doctors, company officials, and other dignitaries marched to the place selected as the terminus of the prospective railroad, where "a neat slab with fitting inscriptions was planted." After the militia organization fired a salute, the parade proceeded to Henri Corri's theater, where James Reily delivered a bombastic speech. A local newspaper reported that it had been many years "since we have heard so eloquent and powerful an effort." Sam Houston also spoke, the president of the railroad made a few remarks, and the Reverend William Y. Allen dismissed the assembly with prayer. This "auspicious and glorious commencement of the great system of Internal Improvements," as a local editor described the meeting, proved abortive, for, although contracts were signed for construction of two sections of the road, it was never built.

The Harrisburg Rail Road and Trading Company was formed early in 1840 as a phase of the attempt of the stockholders in the Harrisburg Town Company to promote their rivalry with Houston. Although a few ties were purchased and some work was actually performed on a section of the roadbed, sales of town lots and later of stock in the railroad company failed to provide sufficient capital for a thirty-mile railroad to the Brazos. An earlier company, the Brazos and Galveston Rail-road Company (chartered in 1838), was equally unsuccessful in its attempts to promote the development of Austinia and later of San Luis by connecting them with the Brazos by railroad. In the early eighteen forties this company considered building a canal instead of a railroad, and in 1842 some of the stockholders obtained a charter for the Brazos Canal Company, which apparently contemplated a waterway connection between San Luis Harbor, at the western end of Galveston Bay, and the Brazos River. The connection of the river with Galveston Bay had been the subject of much thought on the part of a number of Texans for fifteen years, but the anonymous author of *Texas in 1840* correctly held that schemes of this sort were still premature. Aside from the difficulties of constructing internal improvements in a new country, railroad and canal projects in the eighteen forties failed because they were launched in a period of acute financial stringency which blasted the prospects of town-promotion schemes with which the transportation ventures were largely associated.

On the other hand, the importance of Galveston as a commercial center was advanced by steamboat and flatboat navigation of the Trinity River. During the period of the Republic, the volume of cotton grown along the Trinity was much less than that produced in the Brazos watershed, but it was large enough to induce the owners of shallow-draught steamers to risk sending their vessels considerable distances from Galveston Harbor. One of the earliest trips up the Trinity was made by the *Branch T. Archer,* which took advantage of a series of rains in May, 1838, to ascend the river. In consideration of the enterprise shown by the captain and owners of the vessel, as well as their commitment that it would make the trip from Galveston to Cincinnati as regularly as possible, several settlers along the Trinity agreed to pay amounts ranging from five to fifty dollars to the owners. James C. Dewitt, the proprietor of Cincinnati, donated fifteen town lots.[22] In the following year the *Pioneer* also reached Cincinnati, and other small steamboats, such as the *Correo,* the *Friend,* the *Trinity,* and possibly the *Wyoming* and the *Victoria,* subsequently were in the Trinity trade for brief periods.

In the early eighteen forties the steamers *Ellen Frankland* and *Vesta,* operating out of Galveston Harbor, chugged up and down the Trinity more or less continuously. One writer hailed the *Ellen Frankland's* initial voyage, in 1840, as almost beginning "an era in the commercial history of the country."[23] Although in the winter of 1842–43 the *Vesta* steamed up the river as far as Magnolia (landing place for Fort Houston) and found that recent high water had washed away cattle, cotton, and other produce, both boats had about as much business as they could handle the following winter. However, the wreck of the *Ellen Frankland* with a considerable loss in April, 1844, was a blow to this trade; it was estimated that cotton then ready for shipment on the banks of the Trinity exceeded two thousand bales.[24] The *Vesta* continued to run on the Trinity, the *Scioto Belle* arrived in Galveston on May 7 to ply between that city and the various river landings, and it was reported that new steamers were being built for the Trinity trade.

Late in January, 1843, the Englishman William Bollaert descended the Trinity River by steamboat. His daily observations must have been somewhat similar to those of other travelers. On the morning of the twenty-fourth he boarded the *Ellen Frankland* at Cincinnati. The air was bracing, and a thick mist on the water cleared off as the sun rose. Six miles down, the boat passed a ferry

[22] Houston *Telegraph and Texas Register,* June 9, 1838; contract between Trinity River citizens and owners of steamboat *Branch T. Archer,* May 28, 1838 (copy); pledge of property by Trinity River citizens to Captain John E. Ross, undated (copy); George Weedon to John E. Ross, August 14, 1838–all in Ross Papers; James Morgan to James Treat, September 20, 1838 (marked *"Verbatim Copy"*), Swartwout Papers.

[23] Mrs. [Matilda C. F.] Houstoun, *Texas and the Gulf of Mexico,* II, 90. See also New Orleans *Daily Picayune,* December 6, 1840, and May 21, 1841.

[24] Galveston *Texas Times,* February 21, 1843; H. F. Gillett to Ashbel Smith, February 21, 1844, Ashbel Smith Papers; Houston *Telegraph and Texas Register,* April 24, 1844 (quoting Galveston *News*).

at Nelson's Creek; ten miles farther he saw Wright's Bluff, the site of the projected town of Trinidad. One fine cotton plantation was passed before the *Ellen Frankland* arrived at the town of Carolina (formerly Bath), a village of about twenty houses including the deserted "Carolina Hotel. Drygoods & groceries." Here the steamer docked for the night.

On the twenty-fifth, the traveler spent the morning exploring Bidais Creek, half a mile above Carolina. Here he saw deer, wild turkey, geese, and ducks in abundance. At two P.M., the *Ellen Frankland* left Carolina, passed Duncan's Ferry, and having traveled thirty-five miles stopped for the night at Patrick's Ferry, a small place boasting about a dozen houses, where the steamer refueled with wood, at two dollars per cord.

On January 26, the boat departed at seven A.M. and at noon passed Swartwout, "rather a considerable village, placed on rather high land but has no bluffs." Ten miles farther, Bollaert saw the two Coushatta Indian villages, and commented on their houses, which were nearly square and constructed of branches of trees. Before stopping for the night, the *Ellen Frankland* passed Smithfield, with its "few habitations" and "forests of Magnolias."

On the following day, the river bed widened, settlements were scarce, the banks lower, and many alligators basked on the sand. At four P.M. the town of Liberty was reached. Here was a ferry, one store, and "a beef preserving & salting machine" which had been practically ruined by a rise in the river.

On the twenty-eighth, the *Ellen Frankland* left Liberty, passed "the plantation of Mr. Van Pradilles (on the last bluffs on the river)," and at four P.M. arrived at the mouth of the "Old river," where there was a ferry on the road to Houston. The land was low and swampy. About a mile below was the real mouth of the Trinity River, which emptied into a big basin. Around this basin were large collections of driftwood, which with sand and "other earthy matters" formed several islands, between which the waters of the Trinity issued by seven or more passes. River boats generally used "Brown's Pass," which was less than three feet deep and obstructed with snags and logs. At highest tide and under the most favorable conditions, "such as freshets and S. E. winds," there were seldom more than four feet of water over the bar, which constituted one of the most difficult problems in navigating the river. In fact, both the *Ellen Frankland* and the *Vesta* had to lighten their cargoes to move through Brown's Pass.

Bollaert observed that what was called "the great nation of geese" had their residence in and about the passes of the mouth of the Trinity River. There he saw enormous numbers of wild geese, swan, duck, brant, cranes, and pelicans, as well as turtle, fish, and alligators.

On January 31 the *Ellen Frankland* grounded in the pass, but Bollaert transferred to the *Vesta,* which had negotiated the pass. The *Vesta* then proceeded cautiously to Galveston. A strong southeast wind forced the captain to order the anchor dropped, and a party had to go ashore to cut wood for fuel. At length Red Fish Bar was crossed at daylight on February 2, and the *Vesta* anchored in Galveston Harbor at noon.[25]

The most serious impediment to navigation of the Colorado River was "The Raft," which was a series of timber masses—some floating and others sunken and difficult to remove. The obstruction was variously reported as three to eight miles in length, with its northern end thirteen to fifteen miles above Matagorda landing, near the mouth of the river. The removal of "The Raft" was for many years a matter of concern to the citizens of Matagorda and settlers along the river course. It was estimated that it could be cleared away with an expenditure of approximately thirty thousand dollars. Congress incorporated two companies to clean out the river above Matagorda in return for certain concessions, but, in spite of much enthusiasm displayed at local "river navigation" meetings, neither enterprise was carried to conclusion.

In the summer of 1845 a steamboat especially built for the Colorado River trade, the *Kate Ward,* was launched at Matagorda. With its 110-foot keel and 24-foot beam, it reputedly could carry six hundred bales of cotton in three feet of water. The following spring a Texas newspaper reported that in March the *Kate Ward* had reached Austin, overcoming, once at least, difficulties presented by "The Raft."[26]

25 The above is a summary of Bollaert, "Notes on Texas, 1843–1844," 205–11.
26 New Orleans *Daily Picayune,* July 16, 1845; La Grange *Intelligencer,* July 7,

Meanwhile, keelboats and flatboats were bringing cotton, hides, pecans, and lumber down the Colorado to "The Raft," where they were unloaded and hauled overland to Matagorda. Sails and poles were used to propel the keelboats, which sometimes carried between two and three hundred bales of cotton. On April 11, 1838, the Matagorda *Bulletin* announced that the keelboat *David Crockett* had arrived at the head of "The Raft," having averaged more than sixty miles per day for five days of daytime navigation. "This is the first boat, of any dimensions," the *Bulletin* stated, "that has ever attempted the navigation of the Colorado river." It further was announced that the *David Crockett* soon would begin the ascent of the river with a full cargo.

Occasionally there was shipping on other Texas rivers. In 1840 the City Council of Victoria was granted congressional authority to clear out the Guadalupe River, including a raft a few miles below, and collect tolls. In the following spring the steamer *Swan* (which previously had been in Matagorda Bay) navigated the Guadalupe as far as the foot of the raft, and in June it was reported that a canal around the Guadalupe raft had been completed.[27] On the San Jacinto River, keelboat transportation of cotton from Montgomery County to Lynchburg likewise proved feasible, and similar navigation occurred on the Angelina and Neches rivers. A few steamboats ventured up the Sabine River as far as Sabine Town and even farther, and by 1845 lumber, hides, and more than four thousand bales of cotton from the Southeast Texas area were exported officially in one fiscal year through the Sabine customs district.

Finally, Northeast Texas cotton and hides were shipped by Red River keelboat and, beginning in the early eighteen forties, by steamboat to Shreveport. Among the steamboats in the intermittent upper Red River trade were the *Swan,* the *Yazoo,* the *Frontier,* the *Concord,* the *Cotton Plant,* and the *Hempstead.* In November, 1843, the *Swan* arrived in Shreveport with nearly five hundred bales

1845; San Augustine *Red-Lander,* April 2, 1846. See Austin *Texas Centinel,* July 25, 1841, for reference to previous attempts to operate a steamboat on the Colorado.

[27] New Orleans *Daily Picayune,* May 2, 1841; Houston *Telegraph and Texas Register,* June 2, 1841 (quoting Austin *Texas Centinel*); New Orleans *Weekly Picayune,* July 5, 1841 (quoting Houston *Houstonian*).

of upper Red River cotton. Most of these steamboats were operated by Shreveport commission merchants, particularly James H. Cane and Company and Lewis and Howell, who also maintained river-packet service to New Orleans. The *Red River Planter,* a steamboat built in Texas at Berlin Landing, was called "that dug out" and other uncomplimentary names by a Shreveport newspaper. Meanwhile, in the middle eighteen forties, steamboats began to edge over the East Texas border to Jefferson by way of the Lake Caddo–Cypress Bayou connection with Red River. This navigation had the immediate effect of expanding the Shreveport-Natchitoches trade area, which already included much of East Texas as well as part of the Red River country to the north, but it also presaged the rise of the rival border town of Jefferson as an important commercial depot throughout the next thirty years.

The hazards of navigation on the rivers of the Republic seriously retarded economic and social development. Though many of the farms and settlements of the Republic were on or near rivers, water was largely a failure as a transportation medium. Only canal-like Buffalo Bayou provided an effective outlet to the sea, and overland transportation was necessary before the head of navigation on that short stream was reached. Meanwhile, the difficulties of travel by unimproved roads were so great that the San Augustine–Nacogdoches district of East Texas, the Clarksville region of the Red River country, and the Brazos Valley–Houston area extending northward from the coast were isolated from each other for all practical purposes. The economic potentialities of Texas were great as she entered the American Union, but they were not to approach realization until the coming of the railroads.

IV

Times Are Terribly Severe

THE REPUBLIC OF TEXAS had the misfortune to be born shortly before the five or more years of financial stringency heralded by the world-wide Panic of 1837. "There were some *premonitory fits* before, but *then* the *great convulsion* came on."[1] In the United States the chief cause was speculation in lands, canals, and industry, although the situation was aggravated by crop failures in 1835, 1837, and 1838. As is well known, the crisis was hastened by the government's anti-inflation Specie Circular. In 1836 the Second Bank of the United States had ceased to exist, and some of the "pet" banks, in which federal funds had been deposited, contributed by credit inflation to the boom that preceded the break. The banks of New York City and other financial centers suspended payments in specie, and even the national government could not obtain gold and silver for its paper. Wildcat and state banks in Mississippi, Tennessee, Alabama, Arkansas, and Florida—as well as elsewhere in the United States—were compelled to close, ruined by the evils of mismanagement, dishonesty, and speculation they had encouraged.

The economic and political background of the panic and subsequent depression need not be detailed here. But it is worthy of note that speculators, bankers, borrowers, businessmen, and farmers in the United States were enmeshed by their inability to meet obligations and engulfed by a wave of paper money that became almost worthless. Even to a modern age that has experienced a frightening "bank holiday," the deadly stagnation of credit and lack of stable currency in the years following 1837 seem almost incredible. It is not surprising that the Texas government's currency became almost valueless, that banking was almost nonexist-

---

[1] Joseph G. Baldwin, *The Flush Times of Alabama and Mississippi*, 239.

81

ent in the frontier Republic, and that eventually the barter system was used to conduct a large proportion of business transactions.

Though the Panic of 1837 had immediate repercussions in Texas, the psychological depression came later and lasted longer there than in the eastern United States. A feeling of optimism actually prevailed in many quarters as late as the end of 1839. The lesson of the era of land-gambling in the United States meant little in Texas, where a dazzle of speculation imparted a spurious brightness to the economic picture. The anticipated relief from monetary constriction, chiefly through expectations of a rapid appreciation of choice properties resulting from the demands of a constant stream of newcomers, tempted many to buy agricultural land and town lots beyond their means. Scores of incipient towns were laid out, and the country became "town mad" in the face of "such scearcity and distress for money" as had never before been "seen in any part of the world."[2]

Speculation in Texas lands was nothing new. Since 1829 several companies had sought to capitalize on popular interest in Texas by selling land scrip that usually was fraudulent. The most notorious of these ventures was the Galveston Bay and Texas Land Company, organized in New York in 1830 by a New York banker and several individuals close to the Jackson administration. This company ostensibly attempted to exploit the colonization grants of three empresarios—Zavala, Vehlein, and Burnet, who had secured such rights for eastern Texas areas from the Mexican government. Not only did this firm's promotions fail to win the government's approval because they were illegal, but the company's land scrip was unloaded on a gullible American public in a fraudulent manner, and before 1834 its settlers had difficulties in securing titles. In addition, some of the members of the company plunged into other very large personal speculations. Though they were represented in Texas by such influential lawyers as Sam Houston, Thomas J. Rusk, J. Pinckney Henderson, and John C. Watrous, they failed to validate practically all of their mammoth land claims after Texas became independent.

[2] Henry Austin to Mrs. Mary Austin Holley, April 24, 1838, Henry Austin Papers.

In 1834–35 General John T. Mason, the chief agent of the Galveston Bay and Texas Land Company, obtained a personal grant of at least 300 leagues of land (more than 1,300,000 acres) under an act passed by the legislature of Coahuila and Texas. General Houston introduced a resolution at the Consultation of 1835 voiding this and other grants, "purchased . . . under the most suspicious circumstances of fraud." The resolution was adopted in an altered form, and Mason's grant was among those specifically voided by the constitution of 1836,[3] while Houston continued to attack "the unholy dictation of speculators and marauders upon human rights." His public record against speculation was continued in 1841 in an attack on David G. Burnet as a land speculator; he was particularly vehement in condemning Burnet's connection with "a company [the Galveston Bay and Texas Land Company] who have swindled by the millions."[4]

However, Houston's private dealings with this company and its members were radically different. This was the same company that he himself had offered to represent in 1834, demanding an initial fee of two thousand dollars before he should "feel bound to be subservient, or to promote the interest of any Company by which I am not employed."[5] During the early eighteen thirties Houston himself may have been interested in securing large grants. Soon after he had led the Texans to victory at San Jacinto, the soldier-barrister was retained by Mason. On June 4, 1836, the speculator wrote to an associate, Samuel Swartwout of New York, that Houston had been advanced "$2,000 as the advocate and agent for our land business in Texas." But the type of assistance that Mason expected from "the advocate and agent" was too great for even a victorious general to render in a country already aflame with resentment against large-scale speculations. "I think Houston will be able

[3] "Resolution to Annul Land Grants," October 18, 1835, in Amelia W. Williams and Eugene C. Barker (eds.), *Writings of Sam Houston*, I, 306; H. P. N. Gammel, *Laws of Texas*, I, 1080–81; Eugene C. Barker, "Land Speculation as a Cause of the Texas Revolution," *Quarterly of the Texas State Historical Association*, Vol. X, No. 1 (July, 1906), 93.

[4] Houston *Houstonian*, August 18, 1841; Williams and Barker (eds.), *Writings of Sam Houston*, II, 383, 386.

[5] Houston to James Prentiss, March 28, 1834, in Williams and Barker (eds.), *Writings of Sam Houston*, I, 284.

to get us a commissioner from the next Congress without waiting for a general land law & a regular land office," Mason added. "His power in Texas will be very great, & he has now a double motive in interest and friendship to serve us." Moreover, a few months after Houston became president, he wrote Swartwout a letter in which he stated that, while the New Yorker's claims would be subject to settlement by the courts, the rights of aliens had not been impaired by the constitution of the new Republic. He expressed the opinion that the Texan constitutional convention of 1836 had no power to invalidate any act previously passed by the Mexican legislature—a reassuring opinion but not a very realistic appraisal of the actual situation.[6]

The two-thousand-dollar payment to General Houston undoubtedly met with Swartwout's complete approval, for they long had been friends. In 1835 the New Yorker had written to the Texan: "If I mistake not Texas will be U States in 5 years, or an independent Empire, when you'l be King."[7] Furthermore, in accordance with the attitude held by many of his contemporaries toward such matters, he doubtless considered Houston's acceptance of the fee both legally correct and ethically defensible. But Swartwout's record as a high government official was none too savory. After he fled to Europe in the fall of 1838, his accounts as collector of the port of New York revealed that he "was entitled to the distinction of being the first American to steal a million dollars."[8] Some of this money probably was used to finance his support of the Texas Revolution as well as his various speculations, while the shortage of his accounts gave rise to a contemporary slang term, "a Swartwouter," to designate an embezzler.

In the months preceding the Revolution, Texas lands became

[6] Mason to Swartwout, June 4, 1836, Swartwout Papers; Houston to Swartwout, March 22, 1837, in Williams and Barker (eds.), *Writings of Sam Houston,* VI, 3; and see also Marquis James, *Andrew Jackson: Portrait of a President,* 411.

[7] Swartwout to Houston, May 10, 1835, Houston Papers (in possession of Sam Houston, III, Oklahoma City, Oklahoma), quoted in Marquis James, *The Raven; a Biography of Sam Houston,* 211–12.

[8] James, *Andrew Jackson: Portrait of a President,* 444; *Congressional Globe,* 25 Cong., 3 sess., 19, 21, 89–103, and Appendix, 16, 378. A report of the Secretary of Treasury indicated that Swartwout's defalcations had begun in 1830, the year after he took office.

increasingly attractive to other speculative Americans. "They did much [states Marquis James] to keep alive the patriotic cry for a rectification of the international boundary which would bring their holdings under the stars and stripes." Not the least of these patriots was Colonel Anthony Butler, United States diplomatic representative in Mexico, whose interest in acquiring Texas or a portion of it by purchase, bribery, or otherwise, was enhanced by his own landholdings there. In Florida, the Texas Land Company—headed by Thomas Jefferson Green and Achille Murat—invested in lands on the Sulphur Fork of Red River and elsewhere in Texas.[9] Major Green proceeded to Texas with "capital destined to be invested to a large amount in similar speculations," but his business transactions were interrupted by his appointment as a brigadier general in the Texas Army. After the Revolution had begun, the Mississippi Texas Land Company was formed at Pontotoc "for the purpose of trading and Speculating in land in the provinces of Texas and Cohela [Coahuila] and the contiguous borders of the United States."[10]

Meanwhile, Mason, Samuel M. Williams and his associates, and other persons had secured a number of large grants of land in Texas from the Mexican legislature under very questionable circumstances. Many colonists keenly resented these speculations of 1834 and 1835, as well as ten-league grants to individuals in Austin's Colony in return for special services—some of dubious value—in the development of Texas. They also were embittered by sales by the Mexican government of eleven leagues each to Mexicans who resold them to speculators. Yet some of the best citizens encouraged Mexicans to buy land for resale, Jim Bowie alone obtaining control of fifteen or sixteen of these eleven-league grants. In addition to his grants from the legislature, Mason bought several eleven-league grants at six and one-quarter cents per acre on behalf of himself, Swartwout, James Treat, and others. Moreover, some

[9] Juan N. Seguin to "Mi querido amigo," February 4, 1834; [F. M.?] to T. J. Green, October 14, 1835; Achille Murat to Anthony Butler, November 2, 1835 (copy); Monroe Edwards's bond for future delivery of an eleven-league grant of land made to Mexican citizen, [*c.* November] 1835–all in Green Papers; Leon County (Florida) Deed Records, E, 224.

[10] Articles of association, January 8, 1836, Franklin Papers.

of the Texans allowed eleven-league grants to be held in their names when the real owners were citizens of the United States— thus evading the intent of the law requiring owners to be Mexican citizens.[11]

The framers of the constitution of 1836 took drastic steps to outlaw land speculations, past and future, by non-Texans. Two of the laws of 1834 and 1835, and all grants (including Mason's grant) founded thereon, specifically were annulled. It further was decreed that no alien should hold land in Texas except by titles obtained directly from the government of the Republic. Finally, all eleven-league claims located within twenty leagues of the former boundary between the United States and Mexico were voided. In spite of President Houston's reassurances, both Swartwout and Mason, the non-Texans with the highest stakes in Texas speculations, were unable to establish their claims and died in comparative penury.

Furthermore, any attempt to secure large grants of land from the government of the Republic was regarded with instant suspicion. One of the chief reasons for the violent opposition to the Texas Rail-Road, Navigation and Banking Company (chartered in 1836) was the possibility of its pre-empting the country's choicest lands. In April, 1838, David G. Burnet, candidate for the vice presidency, made an utterance typical of the political doctrine (if not the practice) of the period when he declared that "an excessive accumulation of lands in the hands of one or a few individuals, is eminently injurious to the public weal."[12]

This condemnation of large landholders, who, in anticipation of unearned increment, were withholding lands—particularly the most fertile and favorably located—from the "real cultivators" was a point of view that had a real basis in fact. Yet few individuals who were able to offer credit or cash abstained from the practice. In a sense, even the small farmers were speculators who hoped to recoup crop losses and ameliorate discomforts with the profits of land sales, but public opinion held that the real enemies of eco-

---

11 Barker, "Land Speculation as a Cause of the Texas Revolution," *Quarterly of the Texas State Historical Association,* Vol. X, No. 1 (July, 1906), 77–78; Mason's statement of account with Swartwout, February 4, 1836, Swartwout Papers.

12 Brazoria *The People,* April 18, 1838.

nomic advancement were the large-scale speculators. The correspondence of the late eighteen thirties is filled with condemnation of "the artful and unprincipled speculators of the country," particularly those who were buying up soldiers' bounty land. Even in the eighteen forties participation in an "eleven league speculation" was a damning charge, yet ventures of this kind supplied a major portion of the holdings of a number of citizens of substance, including two prominent East Texans, Frost Thorn and Phil Sublett. A recent study of the career of Frost Thorn concludes that "he accomplished in land acquisitions by legitimate means what many of the land sharks failed to accomplish under questionable circumstances."[13]

Speculators without reserve capital were caught in the web of their own design. The anticipated period of prosperity failed to materialize; instead, land values tumbled. Henry Austin, a large landholder who had stretched his credit to the limit in order to add to his original eleven leagues, along with many others was forced to sell land very cheaply. As early as April, 1839, he wrote that although his estate was assessed at $81,000, he was unable to pay his taxes, for he was "a beggar so far as money is concerned.... Matters must soon be much better or much worse."[14] His fears of intensification of the economic blight were only too well grounded.

The paradoxical existence of inflation in a time of economic depression and the sudden collapse of the boom spirit is revealed strikingly in the correspondence of Dr. Ashbel Smith, surgeon general of the Texas Army, who lived at Houston and Galveston. On December 22, 1837, he wrote that "times here are very easy—money plenty—and the people much better satisfied, I will venture to assert, than our brethren in the United States," and "the accounts published in the News-papers, of the unsettled and distracted state of Texas and its government, are utterly false.—Our new promisory notes pass curently here for everything—and will in my opinion, constitute a safe and permanent currency." Throughout 1838 his confidence was not shaken, and he continued

[13] Lucy May, "Life and Activities of Frost Thorn" (M.A. thesis, University of Texas), 99.

[14] Henry Austin to Mrs. Mary Austin Holley, April 8, 1839, Henry Austin Papers.

to invest his money and that of his friends in lands. In April and June he noted that Texas money and credit were improving, although in August he wrote: "Every thing goes on smoothly and prosperously here. Money is quite scarce, in great demand: and yet times are easy." In November land values were increasing and he was buying more property: "There is a general scarcity of money in Texas as elsewhere. Still I have aplenty, always keeping a respectable sum by me for chance occasions. I have within three weeks bought upwards of nine thousand acres of land, and a likely negro fellow—for all of which I paid the cash—and I have now in hand several hundred dollars." In the following month he admitted that the discount of Texas currency at 40 per cent in New Orleans bank notes was an indication of "the deranged state of our currency," yet "sales are commonly made for cash—if on credit—debts are as easily collected as elsewhere."

Throughout 1839 Dr. Smith continued to report that the country was in a flourishing condition, crops excellent, "times easy," business brisk in Houston and Galveston, and lands rising in value, though the currency was even more depreciated. In November he wrote from Galveston: "Times are very brisk here, and the country is flourishing admirably notwithstanding the depreciation of our currency.—Good lands are augmenting in value far beyond my former expectations.—Wild lands on Galveston Bay are worth from $15. to $30. *in specie* per acre in tracts of a thousand acres.— And everything is high and of course whatever we do is well paid. I am as well pleased with this country as ever." At the end of the year he was convinced that he soon would be able to command at least eight thousand dollars in sound funds, and perhaps twice that sum by the following October, though money was exceedingly rare. Accordingly, as late as the first three months in 1840, the doctor continued to buy lands.

But the Smith correspondence takes on a sharply different tone in the spring and summer of 1840. In April he admitted that he had very little cash on hand. In May he wrote that times were extremely hard, Texas currency was worth only sixteen cents on the dollar, and business was "much depressed, unless an exception be made to Law." In July he thought that "times are terribly hard I think every body almost must break and go to work." In August he stated that debts could not be collected by law until the expiration of twelve or eighteen months, and as for selling land, "property in these times of scarcity will not command cash." By September he was writing that he gladly would sacrifice a part of his valuable holdings in order to obtain money. But there were no purchasers, because there was no money in circulation.[15] Values had proved to be chimerical, and Texas had to begin following the United States on the long, tortuous climb back to prosperity.

A notable feature of the persistent mania for speculation in Texas, even during a depression period, occurred in 1837–39 in the craze for establishing towns. Scores of landholders laid out townsites and gave them fanciful names. Rival claims energetically were advanced that Columbia, Montezuma, Richmond, and Nashville, as well as two different sites called Bolivar, were each the head of navigation on the Brazos River. The deed records of every county contain evidence of the dreams of town-makers that resulted in no more than a survey or the erection of a few cabins at such places as Oregon, Manhattan, Dollar Point, Powhatan, and Monadelphia.

Many prominent men were interested in the promotion of one or more embryo towns. Sam Houston and Phil Sublett were the chief promoters of Hamilton (in East Texas) and Sabine City, neither of which made much money for their backers. Mirabeau B. Lamar's share in a Copano Bay townsite—named after himself—was equally unprofitable, although one of his associates had hoped that the five principal backers might make "a cool half million" in six months. Anson Jones had an interest in Manhattan; Henry Smith was one of the proprietors of Aransas; William H. Wharton, John A. Wharton, General Thomas Jefferson Green, and Branch T. Archer were the guiding lights of Velasco; others like James Collinsworth bought lots in a number of towns while they were living on credit.[16]

15 All of these quotations are from letters written by Dr. Ashbel Smith between December 22, 1837, and September 6, 1840, to friends and business firms in the United States. See letter-book MSS in Ashbel Smith Papers.

16 Before Collinsworth committed suicide in 1838, he had been secretary of state, and at the time of his death he was chief justice of the Supreme Court and a

Not all of the town promoters were Texans. Sam Swartwout's most ambitious Texas speculation was the New Washington Association. He was leading spirit in this organization (formed in 1834), which was owned by a group of New Yorkers, Mexicans, and Colonel James Morgan, resident agent. In 1838 the company had located about 100,000 acres on the Trinity, San Jacinto, Neches, and Sabine rivers, and on Galveston Bay. Wrote Colonel Morgan: "I feel fully justified in asserting, that the lands owned by the New Washington Association, from the quality of soil, peculiarity of location, well known situation for townsites & other advantages, are among the best body of lands ever Selected in any Count[r]y & must in time be of immense Value."[17] The association's chief enterprise was the development of the town of New Washington, on the upper arm of Galveston Bay. Though the town never was rebuilt after the devastation wrought by the Mexicans in 1836, the New Washington Association continued to send funds to Morgan until 1840 and participated in developing another townsite, a Trinity River village appropriately named Swartwout. Colonel Morgan often was downhearted about the failure of New Washington, but the optimistic Swartwout continued to send cheering letters to his Texas agent, even after hopes for the town practically were abandoned. On one occasion the New York politician-speculator wrote:

Have you not made judicious purchases for us, fine selections of land, procured titles that are good, watched over our interests as though they were exclusively your own—why then fret about the "Flash" [a boat belonging to the company, which had sunk]? . . . Why man, our merchants who were worth 500,000$ in cash 90 days ago, cant buy a loaf of bread to feed their starving families with. They have lost all & more, but we have lost only 12,000 out of an hundred—so huzza and the Devil take the crockery![18]

candidate for the presidency. His estate was probated in 1843. He owed more than $15,000 and his creditors received less than $1,100.—MSS, Brazoria County Probate Records, Case No. 79.

17 Morgan to James Treat, September 20, 1838 (marked "Verbatim Copy"), Swartwout Papers. The articles of association of the New Washington Association were drawn up on October 25, 1834, revised October 23, 1835, and filed in 1850 in Harris County Deed Records, N, 587–89.

18 Swartwout to Morgan, May 27, 1837, Morgan Papers.

The town promoters were inspired by the earlier successes of the backers of Galveston and Houston. But certain factors in the development of these towns were not present in the beginnings of other towns. Both Galveston and Houston had favorable locations; both were developed by energetic capitalists fortunate enough to obtain special consideration for their sites from the government.

Among the earliest laws passed by the First Congress of the Republic was a grant to Michel Branamour Menard of one league and one labor of land on the eastern end of Galveston Island. This law confirmed Menard's claim, which dated from the year 1834, although his right to the harbor-city location was violently contested. His agreement to pay fifty thousand dollars to the poverty-stricken Republic doubtless was the deciding factor in the congressional decision. The action of Congress in awarding the promising Galveston site to Menard was condemned bitterly in many quarters. As late as October 25, 1839, a Fayette County grand jury returned a "true bill" in a case entitled "Public Weal vs. Inconsistent Legislative Acts." The jury argued that the land belonged either to Menard or the national government, and should have been awarded to one or the other without the payment of a sum representing but a paltry fraction of the townsite's value; actually, the grand jury stated, "the bargain and sale to Mr. Menard was indeed a *bargain* by which the Government *chiselled* itself out of $2,-000,000, Minus $50,000."[19] Menard apparently obtained at least a portion of the money from David White of Mobile, and sold shares in the Galveston City Company to other moneyed Texans, including Thomas F. McKinney, Samuel M. Williams, Levi Jones, and James Love. Regardless of the validity of Menard's claim, or the justice of the congressional act confirming it, Texas was fortunate in that its best harbor town was developed by a company headed by McKinney, Williams, and Menard. They continued an energetic and liberal promotion of the town and its port facilities in the face of several discouraging storms and the depreciation of shares in the Galveston City Company to ten cents on the dollar.

In December, 1837, a visitor to Galveston reported that the devastating gale of the preceding October had destroyed all of the

[19] Fayette County District Court Minutes, A–C, 19.

buildings except "a frame house or two, here or there," but some of the vessels cast "high and dry on the shore" were "already transformed into dwelling houses. One is the custom house. So quick is anything put to use here."[20] Fifteen months later a Texan wrote that whereas two years before he had seen only a single house on the island, "the city is now twice as large as Salisbury [North Carolina] with 25 or 30 sail boats at all times in her harbor and upwards of a dozen Steamboats plying in her waters. These changes, the bustle in the streets and the French fleet riding at anchor in the offing seemed to me like the magic of the Arabian Nights Stories."[21]

Meanwhile, after much bickering the First Congress located the seat of government at Houston, a prospective townsite laid out in the fall of 1836 on Buffalo Bayou by John K. and Augustus C. Allen. The wealthy Allens spent much money on the location, and Houston sprang into being in the first half of 1837. Lots sold for high prices. Early in May Colonel Morgan wrote from near-by New Washington: "*Houston* it is said now *nos.* 1200 inhabitants and has grown like magic. Lotts now sell as high in some instances as $10,000—$1,000 the lowest price at which rate a block of ten was lately sold. Say 10 lotts in one block for $10,000! So much for Town making."[22] Morgan's hearsay population estimate doubtless was too high, but by the spring of 1839 a local census recorded the resident population as 2,073 (including 453 "females"), and the town was established as a center of commerce and trade.

Many of the town-makers attempted to emulate the methods of the Allens. While only one town could be the capital, inducements still could be offered to county governments. Lots were donated to churches and schools, and it was considered an amiable gesture as well as sound business to give lots to ladies and influential politicians. And as one traveler observed in his diary after he had reached Cincinnati, on the Trinity River: "Every set of proprietors boast of the pecular advantage of their new formed towns, and invariably try to depreciate all others—the way these spoke of Oceola *was a sin.*"[23]

[20] Mrs. Mary Austin Holley to Mrs. William M. Brand, December 19, 1837, Holley Papers.

[21] Ashbel Smith to Charles Fisher, May 24, 1839 (letter-book MS), Ashbel Smith Papers.

The experience of Henry Austin was typical. His sister revealed his expectations in a letter written in March, 1838:

I am growing rich in Town Lots—all the town-makers, & they are not few, are ambitious to have me in their town & present me with a lot. Mr Wharton has given me one in Velasco—Dr Jones in Manhattan . . . & Dr Stone at Orregon (Galveston Bay). [She had already been given a lot at Quintana.] . . . Brother will have a sale of town lots in Bolivar 14 April (¼th cash) which can not fail to bring money. It is a favorite situation & many are pledged to buy. He expects at least $100,000. Others go on at that rate, & I do not see why he should not. He has a ware house already built, & contemplates a rail road towards Houston, which will take with people there. They say I should not know Houston it has *grown so much* since I was there. The proprietors have made an immense sum.

But the fate of Bolivar, which Henry Austin claimed was at the head of navigation on the Brazos River, became apparent when he was in Houston a year later "to collect town lot notes payable in good money" from the purchasers of Bolivar locations. He reported that "not a man of them can pay me a dollar."[24]

In 1843, after the town boom had subsided, William Bollaert came down the Trinity River in a steamboat. He noted that, between the villages of Cincinnati and Swartwout, "on nearly all the Bluffs speculators have marked out town sites, with high sounding names"—Trinidad, Carolina (formerly Bath), Rome, Pompei, and Geneva. The principal building at Carolina was unoccupied; a proprietor of a cotton gin was the only inhabitant of Rome; and most of the other towns either had never achieved physical existence or had been abandoned.[25] Texas was dotted with dozens of similar reminders of the town-maker's futile hopes.

In 1840 the illusion of hastily acquired riches was dissipated by

[22] James Morgan to Samuel Swartwout, May 3, 1837, Morgan Papers.

[23] Smither (ed.), "Diary of Adolphus Sterne," *Southwestern Historical Quarterly,* Vol. XXX, No. 4 (April, 1927), 318.

[24] Mrs. Mary Austin Holley to Mrs. William M. Brand, March 6, 1838, Holley Papers; Henry Austin to Mrs. Holley, April 8, 1839, Henry Austin Papers.

[25] Bollaert, "Notes on Texas, 1843–1844," 205.

the fall of fictitious real-estate values. The Galveston *Daily Courier,* in a discussion of "our present dubious prospects," warned against extravagance lest there should follow "still greater embarrassments in our monetary affairs." The advice was appropriate but unnecessary. One Houston citizen wrote that money was so scarce that "I doubt much whether our citizens will be able generally, to get hold of enough to pay their taxes with.—I never have witnessed anything like it before.—Nevertheless it is still passing at 6 for one."[26] In December the Houston *Telegraph and Texas Register* announced that eight counties had paid no taxes to the Republic during the past year. In the early eighteen forties newspapers were filled with accounts of foreclosures and sheriffs' sales, in some of which property formerly owned by prominent persons was announced for auction. As late as the spring of 1845 many town lots in Houston—boom town of the late eighteen thirties—were being seized for nonpayment of taxes and auctioned at prices ranging from ten cents to two dollars per lot, plus costs.

Everywhere the picture of stagnation in business was etched in grim black lines. "San Luis is experiencing the terrible pecuniary depression [wrote Dr. Ashbel Smith in 1840] which is every where felt ... no sales can be made of any property for want of Currency. Times are terribly Severe." A citizen of Crockett reported on conditions there: "Times here are perfectly ruinous. Our most solvent men are unable to meet their lightest obligations and property of every description is unsaleable."[27] Early in 1842 one of the two most stable business firms in the Republic wrote from Galveston that "the wretched condition of everything of a monetary nature in the U. S. renders all business doubtful and unpleasant."[28] Adolphus Sterne of Nacogdoches made two significant diary entries on February 5 and March 17, 1842: "Grog Shops all Shutt up *no Cash";* and "times have never been so hard in Texas, like they are now, I have never known the *want* of two bits untill now,—!!!!!"

The national government likewise suffered bankruptcy. At

[26] J. D. Andrews to M. B. Lamar, August 18, 1840, in Gulick *et al.* (eds.), *Lamar Papers,* III, 433.

[27] J. H. Kirchhoffer to James H. Starr, January 5, 1841, Starr Papers.

[28] McKinney, Williams & Co. to James H. Starr, February 21, 1842, *ibid.* See also Henry Smith to George W. Fulton, December 3, 1841, Fulton Papers.

the end of 1841, as Sam Houston assumed the presidency for his second term, he pointed out to Congress that there was not a dollar in the Treasury, and the nation, without credit, owed several million dollars. "Patriotism, industry, and enterprise," he said, "are now our only resources, apart from our public domain and the precarious revenues of the country." The President was able to speak from personal experience, because in the preceding summer he himself had been completely without cash. But even the application of the virtues he recommended could not control insects and the weather. The partial failure of the Texas cotton crops in 1842 and 1843 and a continuation of low cotton prices had the effect of retarding the revival of economic stability until annexation to the United States was imminent.

As conditions became worse, the amount of business conducted by barter or "trade" increased. In the early eighteen thirties peltries as well as cows and calves had been used extensively as media of exchange. It was a commonplace that a cow and a calf were worth ten dollars. In the early eighteen forties there was widespread reversion to barter for both business and personal service transactions. Doctors and newspaper editors advertised that produce of all sorts would be accepted in exchange for medical services and newspaper subscriptions. A carpenter's labor might be exchanged for a gun, and a boarder might pay for his meals with a cow. The land market had collapsed, and as one citizen wrote in 1842, "Texas lands will not sell for any thing. . . . There seems to be no kind of property here now that would answer in the place of money except good work Mules or Negroes at a fair price."[29] In fact, wealth came to be gauged in terms of slaveholdings; a person's financial condition was shown in the phrase "ten or twelve Negroes' worth."

Even business on a large scale was transacted without the use of money. In April, 1839, William R. Smith of Texas obtained more than "$8,000 worth of goods" from a Mobile merchant in exchange for half of a Velasco town property; Smith planned to retail the merchandise through a Velasco merchant, who probably would exchange it for cotton.[30] As late as the summer and fall of

[29] [Henry Smith] to James Power, January, 1842 (copy), Henry Smith Papers.
[30] William R. Smith to Thomas Jefferson Green, April 18, 30, 1839, Green Papers.

1843, William Bollaert found the barter system still extensively used. At Columbus on August 12–15 he was so impressed with the trading in progress that he recorded in his notes that a Columbus trader's account book would be an interesting manuscript for the British Museum: "Cotton for sugar and Coffee—Bacon for boots —Corn for Calomel and quinine & Whiskey—Beef for Brandy." The system whereby commission merchants in Galveston, Houston, San Augustine, Shreveport (Louisiana), and other towns advanced supplies to planters before selling their cotton amounted to a combination of barter and credit.

In February, 1844, Bollaert returned to Galveston after an absence of six months and noted that "considerable improvements here have & are still going on. No longer does the 'picayune' system of bartering continue, but a good *cash trade*."[31] Money circulated somewhat more freely thereafter, but trading habits were not to be discarded easily. In 1846 Ferdinand Roemer, the German geologist, stopped at a farm between Gonzales and New Braunfels, where he had an experience which prompted him to make the following observation:

During our extended stay, the young people in the home of Mr. King made us all manner of offers for bartering. One wanted to trade or sell a horse; the other who was soon to be married, wanted to trade a good cow and calf for a black frock coat; a third wanted my saddle with which he had fallen in love, and offered me a much better one in trade, according to his opinion. Boys from eight to ten years participated in the bartering with articles of small value and showed a shrewdness seldom found in boys of the same age in Germany. Trading and bartering are more common in Texas than in any other part of the United States. A Texan is ready at any moment, even while traveling, to trade or sell anything he wears, whether it be his coat or shirt, if he can make an advantageous trade. He expects this from anyone else. He has no conception of becoming attached to an article . . .[32]

The reliance upon barter is understandable in view of the con-

31 Bollaert, "Notes on Texas, 1843–1844," 9 (quotation about barter at Columbus), 217 (quotation about Galveston), 2, 108, 159.
32 Roemer, *Texas,* 89.

fusing variety of currency in circulation. Between 1820 and 1860 the state banknote circulation in the United States multiplied five times, and there were alternately violent expansion and contraction of loans and issues in periods of prosperity and depression. Currency issued by Alabama, Mississippi, Louisiana, South Carolina, Georgia, New York, and Indiana banks was accepted in the Republic of Texas at continually varying rates of discount. "New Orleans City Money" and "Alabama Money" usually were scarce but generally circulated at a rate nearer their face value than did the currency issued by the Texas government. In October, 1838, "Brandon [Mississippi] money" was accepted in Texas as equivalent to notes issued by the government of the Republic, but many state-bank issues were distrusted because of constant fluctuation. In 1838 a Houston newspaper stated that "many of our citizens have been cheated by the holders of West Florida, Holly Springs, Pontitock, Chickasaw bills and similar trash." Furthermore, counterfeit notes often were unloaded on the gullible; at one time spurious notes were said to be flooding the Houston market. In 1837 a Brazoria merchant wrote to a business associate: "There is such a medley of Paper money on ma[r]ket that one does not know what is good and the only safety is to pass it on as you get it."[33]

The prospective establishment of a bank or banks was a bitterly fought political issue throughout most of the Republic's existence. The question whether banking privileges should be granted to corporate groups was presented in 1836 to the first session of Congress, which incorporated two banks contingent upon their fulfilling certain obligations. One of them was the Texas Rail-Road, Navigation and Banking Company. This corporation was the creation of a group of prominent men (headed by James Collinsworth and Branch T. Archer) who proposed to build a network of canals and railroads and to establish a banking system somewhat like the Second Bank of the United States—the whole to be "a sort of Credit Mobilier that should have control of the banking and transportation facilities of the country."[34]

[33] Edmund Andrews to Zacheus Hamblin, August 3, 1837, in "Estate of Z. Hamblin," MSS, Bastrop County Probate Records.
[34] Charles S. Potts, *Railroad Transportation in Texas*, 23, 24; Gammel, *Laws of Texas*, I, 1188.

The capital stock of the corporation was to be $5,000,000, and the banking privileges (including the power to issue notes as money) were to begin after one-fifth of this amount had been collected in specie and $25,000 had been paid into the government treasury. The government also was to receive 2½ per cent of net profits of all tolls and fees collected on the prospective canals and railroads, 1 per cent of bank dividends, and the right to transport ships of war, transports, soldiers, provisions, and munitions free of charge. The charter authorized the company to build railroads and canals anywhere in Texas. If General Thomas Jefferson Green (one of the stockholders) was correctly quoted, he thought the corporate privileges were "beyond arithmetical calculation," and he proposed that the company take full advantage of its possibilities. He suggested that the corporation (operating as a bank) should use one million dollars to purchase lands at fifty cents an acre, thus acquiring an investment that would increase in value not less than 1,000 per cent within two years.[35]

The fight against the Second United States Bank in the United States and a current distrust of all banking operations were reflected in a similar Texas campaign in 1837–38 against the Texas Rail-Road, Navigation and Banking Company. Its proposed bank was condemned as "the Vampire, which was to lick up the life's blood of the country." The opposition cried that this potentially all-powerful organization would become "a hydra" with a strangle hold on the country's finances and that the corporation threatened to gobble up the best lands. In the public mind these considerations outweighed the possibilities of bolstering the national credit and constructing internal improvements that would strengthen the country's defenses and better transportation facilities. Although many of the prominent politicians of the country were connected directly or indirectly with the passage of the law granting the company's charter, the fervor of their support waned in the face of vehement public opposition. President Houston approved the act of Congress creating the company, but later refused to allow stockholders to make the required payment of $25,000 to the govern-

---

[35] Matagorda *Bulletin,* August 30, 1837. See also Houston *Telegraph and Texas Register,* September 16, 1837.

ment in depreciated treasury notes rather than in gold and silver.[36] The company never fulfilled the condition requiring that this payment be made before banking operations could be undertaken.

Although President Lamar in his first message to Congress strongly recommended the establishment of a government bank, which should be backed by a portion of the public domain, specie, and the public credit, he unfortunately neglected to suggest a definite source for obtaining the specie. As late as July, 1841, one of his partisans wrote from Austin: "Politics is the great theme now, and Bank or no Bank the leading question." Public sentiment gradually solidified against all banks. Both Lamar and President Anson Jones opposed private banking of any type, and in 1844 an act "to suppress Private Banking" was passed by Congress. Finally, an antibanking clause was incorporated into the constitution of 1845: "No corporate body shall hereafter be created, renewed or extended, with banking or discounting privileges."

Meanwhile, the government had begun to issue paper money, and in the course of its career introduced three principal types. The first consisted of interest-bearing promissory notes that appeared late in 1837 and throughout 1838. This paper was backed by public lands as well as by the faith and credit of the government, and it was made receivable in all payments to the government. By March, 1838, the Texas promissory notes had depreciated to fifty cents on the dollar in New Orleans "in consequence of the scarcity of money," although they circulated at a higher rate through most of Texas. However, in May a discount of 50 per cent likewise was demanded and secured at San Antonio. According to one J. W. Garraty, "this depreciation in our Currency is Created by a few Pedlars (and Would be Brokers) who has brought a few goods to the place —and linked themselves with a few Mexicans that has the principal supplies, with the understanding to sell, for Nothing but Silver, or to take the Currency of our Country at the enormous discount of 50 per Cent."[37]

But depreciation of these interest-bearing notes was mild compared with that which assailed the non-interest-bearing "red back"

[36] Houston *Telegraph and Texas Register,* June 16, 1838; Treasury Department letter-book, 1836–1841 (MS), 67.

[37] Garraty to Henry Smith, May 6, 1838, Henry Smith Papers.

currency issued, in 1839–41, during the administration of President Mirabeau B. Lamar. When he took office, the outstanding circulation of the Republic's money was about $800,000, but by the end of 1841 the total probably had mounted to more than $2,500,000.[38] Depreciation began with the initial issue of the red backs; in 1840 they fell to less than sixteen cents on the dollar, and in early April, 1841, to twelve and one-half cents, although a few weeks later a rumor that a governmental loan had been negotiated in Paris brought them up to between thirty cents and forty cents. But between midsummer and the end of the year the Texas money gradually went down to as low as eight to ten cents. In January, 1842, both the interest-bearing notes and the red backs were practically repudiated: The Texas Congress made them no longer acceptable for duties and taxes, and the value of a single note dropped to as little as two cents. They had never been legal tender for the payment of private debts.

Lamar's administration often has been condemned for its reckless issuance of paper money, prodigal expenditures, and the abortive expedition to take Santa Fé—which the President earnestly believed would open up a trade that would relieve the widespread economic distress. Doubtless these were contributing factors to the failure of the circulating medium. But the chief causes were the subsiding of the boom in Texas land prices in both the United States and Texas and the failure of the United States to regain prosperity. Lamar and Van Buren had the same misfortune—each became president at a time when economic collapse was inevitable.

The "exchequer" currency that succeeded the red backs was made the only paper that could be used for payment of taxes and duties, but the Houstonian policies of limiting the issue and of rigid governmental economy were necessary to raise exchequer bills from a depreciation that ranged as low as thirty cents on the dollar in July, 1842, to forty to ninety-five cents at various times in the following two years. To be sure, the approach of annexation to the United States brought them close to par, but at no time had the official currency of the Republic provided an effective and adequate medium of exchange.

[38] E. T. Miller, *A Financial History of Texas,* 70.

Although there were Mexican coins circulating in Texas both before and after the Revolution, there was little specie exchanged during the ten years following the issuance of the Specie Circular of 1836 and the suspension of specie payments by most American banks. In 1838 David G. Burnet (claiming to have secured his information from the Secretary of the Treasury) wrote: "You are in error as to specie being very abundant with our government. I doubt if the desk of the Treasurer has heard the jingle of it for the past year."[39] The problem of making change was partially solved by the issuance of "change notes" by a few towns, as well as "change notes" issued by individuals in violation of the law.

Notes legally issued by one business firm and circulated as money were considered a sound medium of exchange. In 1841 Congress authorized the firm of McKinney, Williams and Company, Galveston mercantile and commission merchants who had aided the Texas government during the Revolution and thereafter, to issue thirty thousand dollars in notes to circulate as money. These notes were secured by mortgages, real estate, Negroes, and a sawmill valued at sixty thousand dollars, with the added requirement that the firm not be permitted to issue "more than two dollars of their own notes for every dollar of their actual monied capital on hand."[40] McKinney and Williams were conservative and careful in their operations, and their notes were considered to be among the most reliable in Texas. On March 16, 1844, the Houston *Texian Democrat* listed the following wholesale money prices: ninety to ninety-five cents in specie for a dollar of McKinney and Williams notes, and only fifty to sixty cents for Texas government "exchequers." But in 1844, as confidence in the government and its currency was increasing, Congress repealed all authorizations granted to any corporation or persons to issue notes.

Meanwhile, both government land scrip issued to soldiers and officeholders and promissory notes signed by private individuals in the course of business transactions were virtual substitutes for

[39] Burnet to Alex Grant, April 24, 1838, Burnet Papers.

[40] Gammel, *Laws of Texas,* II, 598. McKinney, Williams & Company also had a charter to operate a bank, which apparently was not opened until near the end of 1847, although a note in the New Orleans *Daily Picayune,* December 17, 1840, stated that a Galveston "Real Estate Bank has commenced issuing its notes."

money. Commission merchants accepted many promissory notes at a discount, and a single negotiable instrument of this type sometimes became the property of a succession of individuals.

McKinney, Williams and Company, "the Barings of Texas," was one of the two great commission-merchant firms in the Republic of Texas. Thomas F. McKinney had been a merchant at Nacogdoches in the eighteen twenties, while, beginning in 1824, Samuel M. Williams had served as secretary of Austin's Colony, as Stephen F. Austin's confidential assistant, and later as his co-*empresario* in a contract with the Mexican government to settle Mexican and foreign families. In 1834 McKinney and Williams formed a mercantile partnership. Three years later the firm moved its chief base of operations from Quintana (at the mouth of the Brazos River) to Galveston, gradually acquired banking functions, and became a decisive factor in the early economic advancement of the island city. Although McKinney and Williams sustained severe losses in two Galveston storms, and in the sinking of several of their schooners and steamboats, their business interests gradually expanded. On October 13, 1838, McKinney wrote to his partner: "I feel that with our present prospects we can control to a great extent all the valuable business of the country."[41] McKinney was not given to rash statements about his business affairs, and his prediction partially was realized. He and Williams combined in an unusual degree talents for land speculation, industrial and town promotion, and careful business operations.

During the next decade the Galveston firm's only real rival was the succession of enterprises formed by Robert Mills, "the Duke of Brazoria." McKinney, Williams and Company and the Mills concerns practically controlled the cotton trade of the Brazos River watershed, and much of the cotton sold at Galveston and Houston passed through their hands. Several years before the Revolution, Robert Mills had joined his brother, Andrew G. Mills, in a merchandizing business in Texas. After the death of the elder partner in 1835, Robert and his younger brother, David G. Mills, had continued to conduct the business. The mercantile firm at Brazoria

41 Williams Papers.

was known as R. Mills and Company in 1836–37; and Mills and (Theodore) Bennett in 1838 and for several years thereafter. The Mills brothers retained their mercantile and commission business at Brazoria through the eighteen forties, but—like McKinney and Williams—they gradually transferred the center of their operations to Galveston. Eventually Robert Mills became the senior partner in R. and D. G. Mills and Company, as well as a member of New York and New Orleans firms. The Mills brothers' operations had widespread ramifications: the advancing of credit in the form of all sorts of supplies—food, clothes, and furniture—to planters and farmers in exchange for cotton; shipment of the cotton in their own boats; marine insurance; and the operation of their Brazos River plantations. In 1844 it was estimated that Robert Mills would make nearly six hundred bales of cotton, probably the largest crop raised in the Republic, and during the eighteen fifties R. and D. G. Mills and Company reissued the money of a Mississippi bank and became the largest slaveholders and sugar raisers in Texas.

The Mills brothers were among those who engaged in the sporadic trade with Mexican towns, particularly Laredo. But the trade with the Mexican frontier was held in check by governmental restrictions prior to early 1839 as well as by the activities of bands of marauders and the Mexican invasions of 1842. Trade with Indians likewise was dependent upon whether they were on the warpath; the most important trading stations were those of the Torrey brothers and associates, near modern Waco, and Holland Coffee's two posts, on Red River.

Although in 1850 Texas had only five towns with a population exceeding one thousand, and none with more than five thousand, yet even in the preceding decade its economy was complex enough to enable many persons to work at least part of their time at jobs not directly connected with the professions, farming, or stock raising. There were far more grogshops, or saloons, than any other type of business. Clerks found employment in stores, many of which were stocked with an amazing variety of goods. Surveyors, blacksmiths, gunsmiths, wheelwrights, an occasional silversmith and watch repairer, tanners and saddlers, tailors, carpenters, and cabinetmakers worked at their trades. At least one cabinetmaker announced that he would "also act as an undertaker for funerals, and will prepare coffins at the shortest notice."[42]

But all did not find clear sailing in these pursuits. In 1845 a carpenter wrote that business was dull in Galveston, lumber was scarce, and the place was "overstocked with Dutch carpenters, no less than three brigs now lying in port from Bremen." Peddlers, particularly clock peddlers, often encountered antagonism and prohibitive license taxes.

Twenty-eight Nacogdoches blacksmiths presented Congress with a masterly statement of their grievances in the midst of the economic disarrangements of 1841. They pointed out that the blacksmith was particularly important to farmers, and indeed "to Earn their Bread . . . all classes of mankind are directly or indirectly dependent on the Black Smith, and of all of them he has the poorest chance in Texas." He has to pay high prices, including tariff duties, for the materials of his trade, and then perform work of "the most filthy, disagreeable, unhealthy and laborious kind." Immigrants arrive from the east (said the petitioners), get work done on credit by a blacksmith, make crops on rented land, and neglect to pay their creditor before moving westward. The petition further stated that when a blacksmith shod a traveler's horse, "it would be irksome to our feelings to demand pay before we did the work." He gives us a ten-, fifty-, or a hundred-dollar bill, and we are unable to change it (the petition stated), "even if we were assured it was neither . . . spurious, raised or counterfeit." The blacksmiths concluded that if no relief were forthcoming, they would be forced to take up farming—an eventuality that would be distasteful because they wanted to help "rear up our infant republic." They petitioned for relief in the form of authorization to take liens on crops or other property.[43] Doubtless most of the artisans who did other types of work had similar grievances.

A few precursors of modern labor unions were organized. The journeymen printers of Houston formed the Texas Typographical Association in 1838, and struck for higher wages in the following

---

42 Clarksville *Northern Standard,* November 6, 1844. Probate records reveal that coffins usually cost between twenty and fifty dollars, including expenditures for planks, nails, a lining of black cloth, and labor in construction.

43 Memorials and Petitions, Congress of Republic of Texas, File 69, No. 14.

year. In 1845 the "mechanics" and workingmen of Houston and Harris County established an organization. On the other hand, groups of merchants at Houston, Matagorda, and Galveston associated themselves in "chambers of commerce," chiefly for the purpose of establishing uniform and equitable rates of settling litigation between members without resort to courts.

Two common trades were barbering and auctioneering. The diary of an Englishman who visited Galveston early in 1840 contains two passages which reveal something of the atmosphere in which barbers and auctioneers labored. Having entered a barbershop, wrote Francis C. Sheridan,

I examined the ornaments of the Shop w^h consisted of a wretched print of Napoleon . . . and a likeness of General Jackson. If it is a likeness the Generals no beauty, or it must have been taken when in a state of alarm—a complaint w^h I never heard he laboured under. . . . Beneath the picture of the old Hero, was the following notice attached with four red wafers to the wall.

"Gentlemen that washes in this shop & does not get barbered at the time must pay 12½ cents to the Shop."

Sheridan also described an auction:

Fancy a tall man with a red nose dressed in the deepest mourning mounted on a flour cask in the middle of the principal street of the Town, & surrounded by a heterogeneous collection [of] Coats, Coffee Pots, Hams, Hammers, Sugar, Saws, Spurs, Trowsers, Butter, Cart wheels Pocket handkerchiefs—Bowie Knives—Plough Shares, Eggs, Gin &c &c &c & God knows what besides. The Value of each & all appeared to be as accurately known to the Auctioneer as if the price had been labeled on every article. . . . The rapidity of his elocution unfettered as it was by the gew-gaws of trope & metaphor was only equalled by the dramatic powers he ever and anon exhibited. For instance, having soothed the feelings of a German pastry-cook who had out-bid (evidently from motives of pique or ambition) the Barber for a doubtful Ham the Auctioneers assistant,—a bandy-legged, brandy stunted youth with a putty face & vacant eye—presented to the gaze of an admiring crowd a pair of bright bottle green Trowsers, w^h no sooner caught the eye of the Auctioneer [than] his whole countenance, over which a slight cloud had passed during the ham episode, instantly beamed with admiration and he executed as effective a Melodramatic start as the flour cask would permit of. Then taking the trowsers very carefully and slowly from the hands of his assistant, he shook them proudly aloft, & with a triumphant smile w^h plainly said "no—I am *not* deceived," he shouted "a pair of Breeches, *Brand* new &—Bosting built." To this succeeded a solemn silence w^h occupied some moments, during w^h the auctioneer gazed on the crowd with a kind smile as if he delighted in doing good. On resuming he slowly lowered the trowsers & gazing fondly on them, he said emphatically "What *can* I say for them"—At this point an expression of serious embarrassment turned out the kind smile, & his eye as it ranged round the wrapt crowd seemed to say—"Gentlemen I throw myself upon you—assist me with your counsel I conjure you in this emergency." After w^h he again raised the trowsers, again lowered them & again put the question with a earnestness w^h went to the marrow of the Assembly—"What *can* I say for them"—"Two Bits" roared out an irreverent wretch at w^h of course the crowd laughed because it was so witty—"A pair of *breeches brand* new & Bosting built," thundered the auctioneer & sending a severe glance of stern reproof round the throng to shew them that a pair of Bottle-green Boston breeches were not subjects for thoughtless levity. "One dollar" said a cautious gentleman after reflectively picking his teeth with a Bowie Knife—On w^h the Auctioneer commenced in the following way increasing in volubility as he proceeded until it was marvellous how he contrived to speak at all. "One dollar is bid for the pair of breeches brand new & Bosting Built, one dollar is bid—one dollar is bid for the Boston breeches a dollar is bid, is bid, is bid—a dollar is bid"—&c[44]

The operation of hotels and boardinghouses in the towns was an important occupation in a country with a predominantly male population. In addition to providing sleeping quarters, food, and drink, they were also the scene of cotillions, concerts, and organizational meetings. Among the best known were the Tremont Hotel and the Caravansary (later Shaw's Hotel) at Galveston, Floyd's Hotel, the Old Capitol Hotel, and the Houston House at Houston,

[44] Francis C. Sheridan, Diary, 1839–40, entry for February, 1840. In a letter written from Galveston, dated March 18, 1840, and published in the Cincinnati (Ohio) *Chronicle,* April 25, 1840, the statement was made that business was "very dull, except with auctioneers."

the Archer House at Velasco, Berry's Hotel at San Augustine, and the Eberly House and Bullock's Hotel at Austin. The superior accommodations at the Tremont—which was owned by McKinney, Williams and Company in 1840—were widely acclaimed, but they were by no means typical.

The problems of hotel proprietorship were formidable. The procurement of a variety of fresh food was virtually impossible, and though sensitive palates were rare in that day of five- to fifteen-minute meals, complaints about the "bad fare" were common. Limited accommodations often made necessary the sharing of a room by several men, a circumstance which resulted in a number of unfortunate occurrences. Indeed, an unruly guest was a nuisance to both his roommates and the proprietor. When Mr. H. Baldwin of the Houston House civilly requested payment by one guest whose account was several weeks overdue, the delinquent replied: "If you come to insult me again, sir, by God, I'll shoot you, sir."

Nevertheless, a number of women earned livelihoods by operating hotels and boardinghouses. Mrs. Jane Long, wife of the filibusterer, General James Long, and Mrs. Angelina Eberly, who is given credit for repelling the attempt to remove the Archives from Austin in 1842, were well-known innkeepers, and Mrs. Pamelia Mann of the Mansion House in Houston achieved widespread notoriety. Some of the female boardinghouse proprietors were hardened individualists while others were women of refinement.

In the larger towns industries were beginning to flourish. Several brickyards were established in the eighteen forties, although it was announced that the brickmaker in Clarksville had turned to farming for a livelihood. But in 1842 this town claimed nine gins, four gristmills, and three tanneries within a radius of four miles. Other towns could make similar and additional claims indicating that specialization in industry was underway. A few had cooperages and "beef preserving and salting machines"; Houston boasted a "lard oil manufactory"; and in 1845 Galveston had a small foundry, supposedly the first successfully operated in Texas. Salt being a luxury in many homes and often listed among imports, small "salt manufactories" were established near Victoria, at Matagorda, at the mouth of the Brazos, at "the Neches Saline" in eastern Texas, and elsewhere.

A few sawmills were placed in operation, occasionally in conjunction with a gristmill and cotton gin. A steam sawmill, probably the first in Texas, was erected at Harrisburg in 1830 by members of the Harris family and Robert Wilson; it continued to run until destroyed in 1836 by the Mexican Army. Afterward small steam mills were operated at or near Houston, Matagorda, Velasco, Richmond, Bastrop, and San Augustine and at other places in East Texas. The San Augustine mill used an "old fashioned sash saw, moving up and down through the timber, which was fed to the saw on an ordinary carriage." Yet the hand whipsaw was commonly used, construction materials were so scarce that buildings often were temporary structures, and schooners continued to import building materials and even a few complete buildings.

In the summer of 1844 a Galveston newspaper summed up industrial progress in the following booster report:

The process of developing its resources was never carried on more rapidly in any country than it has been in Texas for the last year. The establishment of several new ship-yards—the machinery of hauling out vessels—new cotton presses—the erection of machinery of manufacturing lard oil, and extracting tallow by the new process—the curing of beef on the new plan—tanneries, soap factories, the manufacture of lucifer matches, and the great extension of operations in a variety of the more common branches of mechanical industry have kept pace with the rapid extension of agricultural production and the introduction of capital, and afford the most gratifying evidences of the improvement and prosperity of the country.[45]

Some observers, however, particularly Germans and New Englanders, stigmatized Texans as slothful. In 1834 a young German, George Willich, Jr., wrote: "So great is the indolence of the present inhabitants, that they hate everything that causes the least work like death, and they know no greater happiness than eating, drinking brandy, and sleeping. What a future stands open for the only average industrious and busy European. . . . [These Texans] are so lazy that they hardly want to open their mouths to push in the food, and . . . largely do not know how to write their mother lan-

[45] New Orleans *Daily Picayune*, July 12, 1844 (quoting *Civilian and Galveston Gazette*).

guage." Frances L. Trask, school teacher from Massachusetts, commented in a letter to her father written in the following summer: "The white people if ever so poor, consider it degrading to work, and would rather stay at home in their dirt, and rags, than do the first days work for another—this is one of the evils of slavery." Five years later, the English diplomat, Francis C. Sheridan, was more discriminating: he found only certain classes unwilling to work— notably the "loafers" and "rowdies." A loafer he defined as "one of those unfortunate young men who feel it beneath them to dig and are ashamed to Beg,—altho' not to borrow." Rowdies were "a class if possible lower than the Loafers . . . combining the qualities of a Loafer of the lowest caste with pugnacious propensities."[46]

On the other hand, Southerners, and even persons from the Northeastern states who had good prospects, frequently commented on the enterprising, "go-ahead" spirit of the populace in the late eighteen thirties, although it must be admitted that enterprise often may have been confused with speculation. In the midst of the economic stringency of 1841, an American diplomat from Kentucky wrote from Austin: "we know that it is the bould fearless and enterprising that emigrate to new countries, while [the] slouthful, the indolent and timid, like the drones remain in the old hive."[47] Yet even such qualities had not availed to dissipate the effects of the depression. Gloom had settled over both small and large landholders, most of whom had seen their chances for hasty riches go up in the smoke of futile hopes. But the depression caused some of them to increase their agricultural labors as a final resort, while other Texans began to occupy themselves with building businesses of a solid nature instead of putting their faith in speculative ventures. The approach of annexation to the United States brought rapid increases in population and commerce, the currency situation was improving, and crops were good. In 1845 most Texans felt with justification that "better times" were an immediate prospect.

[46] The three quotations in this paragraph are from the following sources: George Willich, Jr., to Mrs. George Willich, Jr., September 8, 1834, Willich Papers; Judith Trask [known in Texas as Frances L. Trask] to Israel Trask, July 5, 1835, Trask Papers; Sheridan, Diary, 1839–40, entry for February, 1840.

[47] Joseph Eve to John White, December 29, 1841, in Nance (ed.), "A Letter Book of Joseph Eve," *Southwestern Historical Quarterly,* Vol. XLIII, No. 2 (October, 1939), 217. Similar statements are in many contemporary letters.

──❦ V ❦──

Fun and Frolic Were the Ruling Passions

HE UNCEASING QUEST for diversion in past American life has been almost ignored by social scientists. A few lines or paragraphs describing man's behavior in his leisure hours occasionally have been included in historical monographs or textbooks, but interpolations such as these apparently have had the dubious purpose of adding inconsequential piquancy to weighty and seriously considered facts, or perhaps of indicating the writers' broadminded tolerance of social history. Sociologists, cultural anthropologists, and even so-called social historians have never given thoroughgoing attention to amusements. Horse racing, social dancing, amateur theatricals, and the circus—to mention only a few—have yet to find their historians.

This reluctance to unearth the facts about various amusements should be abandoned in favor of the logical point of view that the record of *all* human experience is significant. Indeed, the recreation and fun-seeking devices of a people should be considered one of the decisive factors in their history. Will the historian of the future, as he attempts to take an objective view of our own generation, be able to quiet his professional conscience if he ignores the amusements, recreations, sports, and other diversions which have had such important "escape values" (vicariously or directly) and furnished employment for millions of Americans in the first half of a highly geared, mechanistic twentieth century?

Similarly, an examination of the amusements of the Texans of a century ago will illuminate other phases of their existence, as well as reveal much of the lusty spirit of their frontier.

The well-known forms of neighborly frolicking connected with labor were common. Newcomers to a community often were greeted by house-raisings and housewarmings. Later, they in turn helped give similar welcomes to other new settlers, and took part in rail-splittings, chopping frolics, and quilting bees. The struggle for survival in Texas was not so rigorous that the settlers were prevented from having a great deal of wholesome fun, much of which was with their neighbors. The "lone-wolf" pioneer, who moved on when neighbors began to settle about him, was not an ordinary type; on the contrary, even the expanding edges of settlement were marked by small clusters of the houses of homemakers, often grouped around protective stockade forts. Beginning almost contemporaneously with house-raisings and logrollings, barbecues and dances were held (especially on holidays and election days) with increasing frequency.

Noah Smithwick was an old-timer who vividly described the bitter experiences which were the lot of the settlers in Stephen F. Austin's first colony of three hundred persons. Smithwick quoted the old commonplace that "Texas was a heaven for men and dogs, but a hell for women and oxen." But the same author also wrote: "They were a social people, these old Three Hundred, though no one seems to have noted the evidence of it. There were a number of weddings and other social gatherings during my sojourn in that section."[1] A few years afterward Texas was characterized accurately, if not fully, in a settler's letter to a friend in "the States" as "a free fighting, stock raising, money hunting country."[2] Accordingly, a major portion of its amusements were vigorous and masculine.

Various diversions were in the border zone between sport and the actual labor of searching for food. Fishing and hunting, including co-operative bear and buffalo hunts and wolf chases, naturally had more of an aspect of sport to visitors than to many permanent settlers, except on a few coastal plantations. Yet a German scientist reported that, in the middle eighteen forties, buffaloes were killed more often by settlers for sport and meat than for skins. In their descriptions of hunting methods outsiders were more explicit than were inhabitants of Texas. An Englishman writing from Fort Bend in 1843 described the typical method of attracting deer at night with fire, or crude lamps, adding, "I suppose few

[1] Smithwick, *Evolution of a State,* 15, 39.
[2] Nestor Clay to James W. Johnson, from "Austin's Colony," April 28, 1832, Clay Papers (University of Texas Library).

Englishmen would credit the fact that in this land of Leather-stockings, Hawkeyes, and Crocketts, deer are killed with greater ease at night than previous to sundown."[3] And after several trips to Texas, George Wilkins Kendall, an editor of the New Orleans *Daily Picayune,* wrote articles containing enthusiastic descriptions of the hunting and fishing between the San Gabriel and the Little rivers.

Another type of hunting was mentioned in an 1841 newspaper report, which stated that 180 volunteers and 10 or 12 Indian spies had left Houston "in pursuit of Comanches and for sport general-ly; and a determination was expressed by them to remain out dur-ing the whole summer unless a respectable body of Indians could be found sooner."[4] Similar testimony came in 1838 from young James Nicholson as he wrote from Bastrop to his wife in New York: "my landlady tells me she kept at bay 50 Indians by pointing a gun at them. . . . The children here have no fear of them—the women care nothing about them and the men think no more of hunting and fighting them than they do deer—nay they think it sport." Since the writer of the letter probably was reassuring his wife that life in the new country was not so hazardous as she had feared, his testimony deserves a reasonable discount, but a sense of sport in the unequal though precarious warfare against both In-dians and wild animals did occasionally exist among experienced Indian fighters.[5]

The same hardihood or daredeviltry or desire to escape laws and customs which brought immigrants to the new country, and enabled them to stay there, led them to seek diversions with ve-hemence. Dancing and horse racing were among the most com-mon amusements. This was true even on the borders of settlement in the interior, though the *Spirit of the Times*—widely read Amer-ican journal dealing with sport, humor, literature, and the stage—

[3] "A Correspondent of the London 'Sunday Times,' Fort Bend, Texas, August 20, 1843," who signed the initials "P.B.," in *Spirit of the Times,* Vol. XIII, No. 37 (November, 1843), 433. See also A. A. Parker, *Trip to the West and Texas,* 140–41.

[4] Houston *Morning Star,* June 2, 1841 (quoting Houston *Telegraph and Texas Register*).

[5] Nicholson to his wife, June 27, 1838, Nicholson Papers. J. Frank Dobie, *The Flavor of Texas,* 139, supports the general idea of this paragraph.

expressed a measure of astonishment in noticing the racing meet held in 1838 at Velasco, on the coast, with a column headed: "Jockey Club in Texas!—We shall hear of one in Astoria directly." If opportunities for dances were sometimes few, they were extended to last all night and even for days as compensation. If the social standards of the period prohibited the appearance of women in amateur theatrical productions, the men in the small Texas villages organized dramatic clubs and played the female parts themselves. The more robust among them, with a healthy and humorous outlook on life, found one emotional floodgate in enormous numbers of practical jokes. This form of amusement probably reached its all-time height in American frontier communities such as those in Texas.

Humorous, sentimental, and camp-meeting songs were sung in Texas, as elsewhere. Typical songs were: "Am I Not Fondly Thine Own," "The Carrier Dove," "The Banks of the Blue Moselle," "Haste to the Wedding," "Yankee Doodle," "Will You Come to the Bower," and "The Minute Gun at Sea." In 1840 the tune "Rosin the Bow" was being whistled and sung in many places in Texas and Louisiana. In group singings of these and other songs, the young people from the "forks of the creek" often found an adequate substitute for dancing when a musician was not available.

The exuberance of the frontier had one characteristic musical expression in the sentimental and ribald tunes chorused by roisterers in the saloons. Carousing was not always confined to the otiose "rowdies" who spent a major portion of their time in the grogshops. J. H. Herndon, who was in Houston on March 16, 1838, made the following entry in his candidly written diary: "Had a serenade and much carousing—The Vice-Pres^t. Atty. Genl . . . & others arraigned for riotous conduct."[6] Rev. Littleton Fowler, a Methodist preacher stationed in Houston early in 1838, with unwitting indiscretion made a holiday trip to Galveston with a congressional party. His account of his experience in a letter to a friend reveals a condition not infrequent aboard Galveston-to-Houston excursion steamboats:

So soon as I recovered from my serious illness I took a trip to Gal-

[6] Herndon, Diary, 1837–38, 44.

veston Island with the President [Sam Houston] and the members of Congress, and saw *great* men in *high* life. If what I saw and heard were a fair representation, may God keep me from such scenes in the future. . . . On our return on Sunday afternoon, about one-half on board got mildly drunk and stripped themselves to their linens and pantaloons. Their Bacchanalian revels and blood-curdling profanity made the pleasure boat a floating hell. . . . I relapsed from the trip and was brought near to the valley of death.[7]

Carousing was especially common on the numerous holidays. The anniversaries of the battle of San Jacinto (April 21), the Texas Declaration of Independence (March 2), the Fourth of July, and Christmas were the most generally celebrated.

Before the dances on patriotic holidays, there were always restrained exercises such as parades by militia organizations, public reading of patriotic documents, and singing by children, as well as barbecues and "collations." Prayers and the inevitable orations were delivered in the grandiloquent manner of the period by ministers and lawyers such as "one of the most distinguished orators of the country, who had to arouse him besides his own genius, the thought that he was himself one of the heroes of the day."[8] Then came dinners, usually beginning in the middle of the afternoon and featured by toasts. Typical toasts were: "Texas on the 2nd March '36, and Texas now. By her annual return from her hitherto unprescribed orbit, she has proved to the world that she is no transient meteor," and "The ladies, God bless them, they expect us at a ball tonight, and require every man to keep himself in condition for duty."

Other parts of holiday festivities have a more familiar ring to modern ears. In 1844 two local doctors arranged a "Montgolfier balloon" and fireworks display for the Fourth of July celebration at Clarksville. Unfortunately, on March 2 of the following year, one of the persons engaged in firing a salute at Galveston had an arm blown off.

The decoration of trees and the exchange of presents at Christ-

---

[7] "Jottings from the Old Journal of Littleton Fowler," *Quarterly of the Texas State Historical Association,* Vol. II, No. 1 (July, 1898), 82.

[8] "Notes on Texas," *Hesperian,* Vol. I, No. 6 (October, 1838), 435.

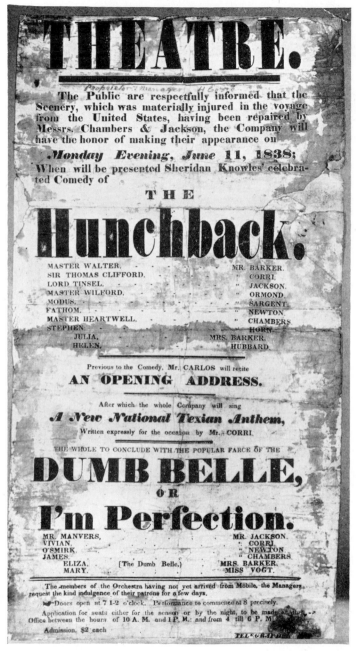

Playbill distributed to advertise the first professional theatrical performance in Houston

Courtesy The Grand Lodge of Texas, A. F. & A. M., Waco

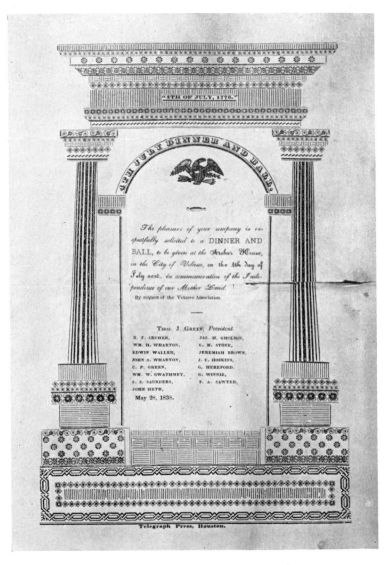

Invitation to a Fourth of July dinner and ball; printed on one of two green-tinted pages.

From Ashbel Smith Papers, courtesy University of Texas Library

mas time were probably not customary in Texas before it was annexed by the United States except among the German settlers. On Christmas Eve and the following day friends assembled to make merry in small groups. The festivities often were enlivened by the drinking of whisky punch, "the national drink with which Christmas is celebrated here." Afterward Negroes and whites had separate dances. The sounds of dance music tormented a Nacogdoches lawyer who sat writing a letter on Christmas Eve of 1839. He had "been on the water wagon" for nearly four months, and deserved commiseration as he wrote the following postscript:

It is now 9 o'clock, P.M., and tomorrow's Christmas. The way the votaries of that jolly God Bacchus are now "humpin" it is curious. Fiddles groan under a heavy weight of oppression, and heel-taps suffer, to the tune of "We Won't Go Home 'Till Morning," and now and then the discharge of firearms at a distance, remind me that merriment now despotic rules to the utter discomfiture of dull care, while I, O Jeminy! have nothing stronger wherewith to lash my cold sluggish blood than cold Water.[9]

No pastime in American history has been indulged in with more gusto than frontier dancing. A Texas woman explained how it met the psychological requirements for a Western diversion:

Times were too pregnant with excitement for grave pleasures to take strong hold of the minds of the people. . . . How could people sit often to listen to grave discourses when at every random shot of a gun their ears were on the alert for the cry of Indians. To be so situated as to have these quick vibrations operate nervously upon the brain predisposes the mind to seek relief in softer emotions of pleasure, but still one of excitement, consequently the dancing master found favor with the majority instead of the philosopher.[10]

Dances were held on every possible occasion, and the scarcity of women only accentuated the frontier passion for dancing. In 1839 a young man wrote: "We had three balls in Bastrop lately.

[9] Charles S. Taylor to James H. Starr, December 24, 1839, Starr Papers.
[10] Sinks, "Texas Reminiscences," V, 2.

. . . I paid little attention to the ladies, contenting myself with a little girl about 11 years old for my partner. The men were so crazey after the grown up ladies that I never interfered with them."[11] To these dances, as was customary, mothers brought their babies, wrapped them in shawls and blankets, and left them beneath the temporary benches along the walls while they participated in the merriment.

A single violinist customarily provided the music, and many Negroes fiddled their way into the white folks' favor. But the lack of a musician was often a serious problem. A partially facetious contemporary newspaper story reported that an army captain, according to his own account, had found dancers in an East Texas tavern attempting to revive the only available fiddler, victim of an overdose of inspiration from his whisky bottle. "The dancers," so went the story, "rolled the drunken man upon the floor, they stirred him up, they rubbed his head with vinegar, and they crammed an entire jar of Underwoods' pickles down his throat—but all would not do." Although the captain had never played any sort of musical instrument, he offered to substitute for the drunken musician. When the dancers accepted enthusiastically, the captain took his place in the violinist's chair, picked up the fiddle, and made a few musician-like flourishes and preliminary motions.

At length, thinking he had infused a sufficiency of the effervescence of dancing into the eager set, he drew the cork by giving every string on the violin a general rake with the bow. Away they went like mad, Captain H. still sawing away, stamping his right foot as if keeping time, and calling the figure. . . .

It may readily be supposed that the dancers had but a limited knowledge of music; but still they could tell, in their cooler moments, a tune from a tornado. The first two couple[s] had by this time finished, and the second had commenced, when one of the former addressed his partner with:

"Eliza, did you ever hear that tune he's aplaying afore?"

"Can't say that I ever has," was the response, and this within hearing of Captain H. who was still punishing the violin as severely as ever.

"Does it sound to you like much of a tune . . . any how?"

11 James Nicholson to Mrs. James Nicholson, April 19, 1839, Nicholson Papers.

"Well, it doesn't."

"Nor to me either," said the first speaker, who all the while had his head turned to one side after the manner of a hog listening. "My opinion is that that feller there is naterally jest promiscuously and miscellaneously sawin away without exactly knowing what he's a doin."[12]

Other accounts of dances are more descriptive. From them it is clear that it was no drawback that a log-cabin floor was made of puncheons or consisted of bare earth. Even as the prevailing type of women's skirts has influenced dance styles in modern times, so the roughness of cabin floors made smooth dances impossible. As one settler said, "When young folks danced in those days, they danced; they didn't glide around; they 'shuffled' and 'double shuffled', 'wired' and 'cut the pigeon's wing' making the splinters fly." After the men with boots had danced awhile, they exchanged their footgear for the moccasins worn by their less fortunate companions, who were thus enabled to take the floor and make the proper amount of noise. If "the din of clattering feet" drowned out the music of the fiddler as he played "Molly Cotton-Tail," "Money Musk," or "Leather Breeches," his efforts often were supplemented by those of other musicians using crude instruments such as a clevis, hoe and case knife, or a tin pan. Other dances included "Roaring River," "Piney Woods," "Killiecrankie," "Harper's Creek," and "My Wife's Dead and I'm a Widower." "Fandangos" were also common among the Mexican population in Texas, and some startling variations of Spanish dances were learned by a few Anglo-Americans.

Weddings and christenings were the occasion of especially large dances in "the woods"; as many as two hundred persons traveled the "horrible roads of mud and slush" to attend the ceremony, supper, and dance. In 1843 a visitor to a rural wedding near Huntsville found that by late afternoon perhaps 175 persons—men, women, boys, girls, and babies—had assembled, all dressed in "their best with a sprinkling of fashionables." A shout of "here he comes" heralded the arrival of the bridegroom and his friends in front of the log cabin which was to be the scene of the wedding. After the groom had dismounted from his horse, he had to shake hands

[12] New Orleans *Daily Picayune,* March 11, 1843.

with perhaps a hundred persons, a number of whom volunteered the single word "courage" accompanied by a smirking smile as they pressed his hand. Meanwhile, the females of the party were "closeted with the bride, comforting and consoling her" and arranging her white bridal dress. The minister then conducted the ceremony, the newlyweds were congratulated, and supper was announced in the "No. 2 Room." The repast continued for several hours "owing to the great number of visitants and the small quantity of crockery." Singing and afterward dancing to the music of a fiddler followed the supper, the dances including "Rosin the Bow," "Jin along Josey," "Zip Coon," and variations of "Roaring River." About midnight the elderly persons and mothers with babies departed, the road being lighted by Negroes who went ahead with fire pans of the type used in deer hunting. But the younger guests continued dancing and playing such games as "forfeits" until dawn and breakfast concluded the festivities.

In the larger towns and on a few plantations, many dances were conducted with a considerable amount of style. Some of them were memorable events. In the spring of 1845 a visitor described a Galveston ball honoring the officers of a squadron of the United States Navy then in port as a magnificent affair: "There was an elegance and refinement about it belonging to older and more favored cities, a grace shown by the many beautiful women present, not only as regards dress but all the accomplishments which must adorn the sex."[13] Similar terms were used to describe the San Jacinto balls at Houston in 1837 and 1838, the "levee" in the same town given by President Sam Houston as he left office in 1838, and the ball at Austin in 1841 in honor of the minister from Yucatán. These dances, as well as other social affairs, were characterized by the elegancies of the Southern cavalier and lady; as early as 1839 Galveston and Houston had a professional dancing master, one "Mon. Amadee Grignon," who charged one dollar per lesson for instruction in the performance of the cotillions and reels of the day.

A chivalrous approach to ladies was quite customary on the part of a limited number of gallants, even among those who indulged in robust carousals on occasion. In 1838 President Houston

13 *Ibid.,* June 1, 1845.

paid his addresses to Miss Frances L. Trask by proffering her a seat in a carriage for transportation to a party. "Should Miss Trask conclude to ride," he added, "Gen¹ H—— assures her Ladyship that the steed, as well as the carriage, shall be of the first order in appearance and in qualities." Or, preliminary to a May Party, a gentleman might send his lady a bouquet together with an appropriate note.

There is little evidence that dancing met with the strong religious objections which were a part of the prevailing moral code in many Texas communities after the country became more settled. A Methodist circuit rider wrote from the village of Montgomery in 1843 that he had gone three-fourths of the way around his circuit and found "nothing cheering, or encouraging, many of the members having backslidden and are spiritually dead—some have been going to dancing school, and some have joined the Baptists!"[14] But few preachers of any denomination crusaded against dancing, and even if they had been inclined to preach against square dancing, their condemnation may not have been effective because, as late as 1845, not more than one-eighth of the white population were church members. Furthermore, the frequency of dances points to a strong public sentiment supporting the amusement.

Both professional and amateur theatricals also met with popular favor.[15] A major portion of the professional theatrical performances were staged in Houston. The first dramatic season there was launched on June 11, 1838, with a program presented by a professional stock company of eight men and three women under the management of Henri Corri. An opening address was given by John Carlos, local merchant who had prepared a room in a building for dramatic performances. The "New National Texian An-

14 Oscar M. Addison to Mr. and Mrs. Isaac Addison, February 12, 1843, Addison Papers.

15 The following discussion of theatrical and vaudeville entertainment is a part of the writer's "The Theater in the Republic of Texas," *Southwest Review*, Vol. XIX, No. 4 (July, 1934), 374–401. An earlier theater than any discussed here may have had a brief existence at Columbia in the fall of 1836 when that town was the temporary seat of government, but the evidence examined is by no means conclusive. See New Orleans *Le Courrier de la Louisiane*, October 28, 1836, for reference to a "well supported" theater at Columbia.

them," sung by the company and written expressly for the occasion by Corri, preceded the presentation of Sheridan Knowles's comedy, *The Hunchback*. The performance came to an end with a popular farce, *The Dumb Belle, or I'm Perfection*. The company fared remarkably well in its succeeding presentations, which included *The Stranger, Therese, The Rent Day,* and the *Maid of Munster*. Indeed, one lady remarked some years later that this "first theatrical company to come to Texas . . . not only ran the young people wild, but the old people were not much better." The season of 1838 was marked by an increasing lack of harmony between Corri and Carlos, and both proceeded with plans to erect new buildings for the following year.

The Houston season of 1839 was the high peak of professional dramatics in the Republic of Texas. For several months two new theaters vied for public favor by importing, for limited engagements, nearly a dozen actors who had received top billing in playhouses in the United States and usually had last appeared in New Orleans. The lure of the young Republic must have been very insistent to have drawn so many, even from a profession which was notably venturesome. Their appearance marked the formation of a slender cultural tie between the expanding frontier and the United States.

The beginning of this eventful season occurred on January 21, when Carlos opened his Houston Theatre with an entirely new stock company from "the States" playing in the fashionable comedy, *Charles the Second,* and the popular farce, *The Secret, or Hole-in-the-Wall,* together with the usual assortment of dances, comic songs, and orchestral selections—customary *divertissements* in American playhouses and precursors of modern vaudeville. The cast was headed by the tragedian H. L. Waldron, who was commended by a writer in the local press for his "vigor, energy, and pathos"; but the same critic was not so charitable in his suggestion that certain lesser lights in the company would improve with a "greater dislike to the prompter." The Houston Theatre gave continuous performances for several months. During the last two weeks in March, Henry James Finn, hailed by a local critic as "the most original actor now living in either country," drew good crowds, his engagement terminating with a series of lectures on astronomy "and other subjects of a novel and interesting character; which are calculated to improve, refine, and please the juvenile members of the community." Finn had enjoyed continuous popularity in the leading theaters of the United States for about two decades; in 1822 he had turned to eccentric comedy, in which he became one of "the distinguished actors of the day." But in the latter part of April Carlos could present only a steadily decreasing number of attractions, for he was beginning to feel the stress of competition with Corri's new theater, which had been in operation for two months, and in July he advertised "theatrical property" for sale.

On February 25 Corri had opened his New Theatre on Market Square. The cast, which included the tragedian Forbes, the comedian Barnes, Mrs. Barnes, and their daughter, Charlotte, was judged by the press to be the finest "array of Histrionic talent" ever assembled on Texas boards. This judgment was not without foundation in view of "Old Jack" Barnes's sustained popularity in low comedy in New York, and the indubitable talent of the other three; for many years Mrs. Barnes was the leading actress in both tragedy and comedy at the Park Theatre, New York. One feature of their initial program was an address, written by Judge Henry Thompson and delivered by Forbes. A short excerpt will indicate sufficiently the grandiloquent nature of this poetic effusion, which the first-nighters greeted with prolonged applause:

> *Yes—now where late the forest stood,*
> *In Nature's mildest solitude,*
> *Where all was but a Prairie sod*
> *Which human foot but seldom trod—*
> *We hail the Drama's spotless page,*
> *And breathe its pathos from the stage.*

The play which followed, Sheridan's *School for Scandal,* received "unanimous approbation." Its plot, revealing the hopeless depravity of the European nobility, made a natural appeal to the equalitarian spirit of the frontier audience.

Throughout the spring the New Theatre carried on with a series of spirited programs which were generally considered superior to those of the opposition house. After the financially successful performances of the Barnes family, John R. Scott and Charles H. Eaton were the next United States headliners engaged, Scott's engagement terminating on March 27 with a presentation of *Othello*. Scott and Eaton were regarded by New York critics of the period as having approached without quite attaining greatness. Joseph Burke, the young "Irish Roscius," followed for a short period in the middle of April. His renditions of Irish comic parts in the *Irish Ambassador* and the *Irish Tutor* and his playing of the violin delighted Houstonians just as they had thousands of Irish, English, and American listeners—and he made a New York appearance in the same year. On April 22 the resident stock company, which had been engaged in supporting the visiting stars in their specialties, gave *Macbeth,* "acted for the first time in Texas."

The last important player of note to appear at the Corri establishment during 1839 was Mrs. Henry Lewis, an English actress —who with her husband and small daughter, billed under the name of "La Petite Bertha"—played an engagement in the latter part of May and early June. One Texas critic conceded that Mrs. Lewis was an actress whose reputation "has been well and justly acknowledged by the *Literati* of England and the United States." Although he found no suggestion of incongruity in her playing of male Shakespearian roles, he considered her appearance in "that tasteless exhibition denominated 'Dancing in Cachuca'" disgusting in the extreme.

The theatrical season at Corri's theater in Houston dragged on apathetically during the summer of 1839. A part of his theatrical corps played several nights in Galveston, a town often visited for short periods by the same actors who came to Houston. Throughout the subsequent fall and spring, Corri managed to remain open, but aside from a reappearance of Mrs. Henry Lewis and her daughter—who had been gathering "golden opinions" in New Orleans— no stars were imported. Corri did not suspend operations until the spring of 1841, but the performances during his final year were marked by the frequent appearance of amateurs and the presentation of parts of plays. In the end he was reduced to the expedient of holding masquerades and fancy-dress balls in his theater.

From 1840 to 1844 Texas was laboring to recover from the effects of a violent economic depression and offered but indifferent prospects of success to professional actors. Nevertheless, in various Texas towns a few of them appeared, usually supported by amateur talent. At Matagorda in 1840, and at Clarksville in 1842, professionals made brief but, to the amusement-hungry citizens, delightful appearances. And in June, 1843, a Mr. Harris from New Orleans played the leading role in the tragedy *Douglas,* a presentation of the San Augustine Thespian Society. Soon Harris was joined by his wife and two other professionals, and they continued in San Augustine until early in 1844. Among the plays presented were *Golden Farmer,* which ran for several nights, and *The Lady and the Devil.*

In 1845–46 the professional drama was revived in Houston and Galveston. One group of professionals headed by Mrs. Hart and the tragedian Charles Webb played in both towns. Mrs. Hart and her actor-husband followed the United States Army to Corpus Christi, where two theaters thrived while the soldiers were encamped near there, and ultimately even went into Mexico in the wake of the armed forces. Another dramatic company traveled the same theatrical trail, first to Galveston and Houston and then to the Rio Grande. Included in this group was young Joseph Jefferson, then seventeen years of age, who was acting under the tutelage of his mother.

Jefferson's autobiographical account of one of the performances in Houston is diverting. The actors induced "Pud" Stanley, a former actor who then was operating a saloon and gambling hall in Texas, to take the leading role in *Richard III*, a part in which he believed himself unsurpassed. The citizens of Houston, who had given very indifferent patronage to the stock company, packed the house to hear the barkeeper play Shakespeare. A few ladies came, but their escorts took them home when they saw that the audience was going to be turbulent, "so that the friends and admirers of the star were unchecked in their cat-calls and noisy demonstrations." The retired actor had not forgotten some of the "old-fashioned tricks of the art," and would take tremendous strides from the center to the extreme right or left, "thereby signifying to the audience that if they desired to applaud *that* was their time." The audience interrupted the performance from time to time with "expressions of approval in complimentary but rather familiar terms." *Richard's* love scene with *Lady Anne* was interrupted by a heckler who warned her that the tyrant already had two Mexican wives in San Antonio, and as the curtain went down at the end of the final scene, "Pud" was bandying insults with an onlooker.

The programs of the day offered an incongruous mixture of established classics, low comedy, and an occasional equestrian drama. Melodrama and Shakespeare, delivered with vociferation and overemphasis on the action, were reliable vehicles to gain the favor of a generation of Texans who admired any public exhibition of excessive rhetorical skill. Comic relief followed in the form of songs and dances, some of which were offensive to the refined tastes of self-appointed critics. The final performance was usually a farce. In the words of one of the newspaper editors, these were too often "common, low, vulgar comedies, replete with the most vulgar *'entendres'* that are . . . served up to the mortification of the boxes and the uproarious applause of the galleries."

A few plays were written by Texas authors, and some of them were produced. In March, 1839, it was announced that *The Milesian,* an original drama by a citizen of Houston, would be presented shortly thereafter at one of the local houses, but whether it was played is not known. A published synopsis revealed that the play had a setting in eighteenth-century Ireland and a plot with numerous complications eventually concluding in a duel and the demise of the poisoned heroine in her lover's arms. In 1841 two take-offs on the current elections were played. And *The Fall of the Alamo, or, The Death of Col. Crockett,* a "national piece" written by a former Texan army officer, proved popular enough to warrant more than one showing.

In spite of complaints concerning the behavior of ruffians and gamblers in the audiences and the vulgar character of many performances, the introduction of the professional theater into Texas met with the general approval of the classes recognized as reputable among the townspeople. In Houston the President and his cabinet, many other influential men, and (less often) the women and children of the community attended. The efforts of the theatrical managers received the backing of the newspapers, most of which served as self-constituted forces for the maintenance of moral standards. One note of protest may have been sounded in 1839 when the

Young Men's Society of Houston debated the subject, "Have the-
atres an immoral tendency?" But there was no organized opposition. Both Matagorda and Houston had substantial theater buildings before churches were erected, and the preachers laboring there,
as elsewhere in the Republic, found evils more noxious to combat
in excessive fighting, gambling, swearing, drinking, and misuse of
the Lord's Day. Texas, eager for relief from the hardships of frontier life, readily welcomed a diversion as stimulating as the drama.

Texans were not altogether dependent on outsiders for their
theatrical entertainment, for they had amateur dramatic organizations, which not only supported but were also in some instances the
outgrowth of the professional theater. These lively amateur organizations were usually called "Thespian" societies. The Matagorda
Thespians, who reached their highest point of activity in 1840 and
1841, received constant encouragement from both reader corre-
spondents and editorial writers in the local newspaper. One com-
mentator urged the support of the amateurs on the grounds that
"the Thespian institution is not only harmless, but in fact may be
considered a beneficial establishment 'for useful mirth and salutary
woe' "; and the local editor encouraged "the two blackest beards in
town" with the comment that "they costumed with great effect."
The Houston Thespians, organized as early as 1840 and still func-
tioning in 1845, became especially energetic in the spring of 1843,
when they presented *The Heir at Law, The Bee Hive, All the
World's a Stage,* and the historical drama, *Charles the XII.* The
donation of their net proceeds for that year to charity provided one
basis for their claim that "they have the satisfaction to know that
their efforts have not been in vain, seconded as they were by the
beauty and fashion of our city."

San Augustine also developed an invigorating communal spirit
in support of its enthusiastic Thespian Society. Colonel John S.
Ford—doctor, editor, lawyer, politician, and Indian fighter—records that the "Thespian corps," organized in 1838, was composed of a number of prominent young men, including the newspaper editor, a district judge, and a future Confederate general,
who played heroes and "ladies in sorrowful moods and in scenes
where death cast a mantle of gloom." The San Augustine Thespians presented two comedies written by Ford, *The Stranger in*

Texas and *The Loafer's Courtship,* both based on the author's observations of life in the Republic. The first of these plays related the saga of a swindler who received spurious land certificates in return for worthless "wildcat" paper money, while the second drew a large house and "increased the writer's vanity to an alarming extent." The San Augustine amateur organization continued in intermittent operation for at least six years.

Dramatic productions also were staged in rural communities, but to what extent is difficult to determine. In an autobiographical manuscript, James N. ("Uncle Jimmy") Smith has left an account of one attempt in 1840 in the Cuero Creek community, a scattered settlement on the Gonzales–Austin road, and one by no means free from Indian raids. On Saturday nights the young people were accustomed to assemble to sing, and occasionally some of the young men performed plays written by a local doctor. The female parts were taken by men. In one play a duel was fought between two of the actors who were aspirants for the hand of a "young lady"; when a pistol was fired, one of the duelists fell dead "to the great consternation of many in the house who thought it was a real fight. . . . This indeed was a brilliant affair for Cuero Creek, and the older citizens were much amused and the younger part never saw the like before."

No amateur group was in any sense in competition with the professional troupes which visited Texas during the same period; on the contrary, the Thespians constantly encouraged the influx of professional companies and often took parts when extra players were needed. Even if their acting had been on a par with that of the professionals, the amateurs would have been at another serious disadvantage in that prevailing social standards prohibited the appearance of women in their plays. An actress was a person of uncertain caste, while the appearance of a lady in an amateur play was strictly taboo. On the other hand, the select young men of these communities—the lawyers, doctors, and editors—could don wigs and costumes for a night, and even play female parts, with no loss of social standing; and their participation gave the Thespian offerings an air of high, though often hilarious, respectability.

The flow of immigration made Texas increasingly attractive to a variety of traveling entertainers. Gerard, "The Texian Magician," appeared at the Houston Theatre in the spring of 1839 and received the compliments of the press for his "skill in legerdemain." In 1843 a visitor to San Antonio saw a small company of Mexican performers present rope dances and "very, very *low* comedy." In the autumn of the previous year ventriloquist E. L. Hervey had visited several East Texas towns, and in the following spring turned up at Houston. Concerning one of his Nacogdoches performances, the postmaster recorded in his diary that Hervey "amused the people this Evening with his rare powers notwithstanding the mud"; and at Clarksville the ventriloquist "astonished the good citizens . . . by a masterly and skillful exhibition of his extraordinary powers." "Wyman's Exhibition" followed a similar route in the spring and summer of 1844, showing at San Augustine, Shelbyville, Nacogdoches, Houston, and Galveston. In addition to an Italian puppet show, the chief drawing cards were a ventriloquist, Mr. Wyman, advertised as "the most popular *putrilognist* of the present day," and Miss Wyman, a magician. A Houston editor was moved to eloquence after attending one of their exhibitions: "The 'fascinating' powers of the latter make us incredulous of the evidence of our own eyes; while the ventriloquism of the former makes us doubtful of the sense of hearing." Wyman was a showman of many years' experience who had traveled thousands of miles over the United States and, although he rarely appeared in the larger cities, was considered "one of the best entertainers of the day."

Negro ministrel shows and "strong men" had their innings in the eighteen forties. Early in 1845 T. W. Tanner, bearing the self-awarded title of "The American Hercules," appeared in Houston, supported by a banjoist and a dancer, and by "Master J. R. Tanner, the unequalled India Rubber Child," whose contortions were advertised as "incredible and must be seen to be believed." Their efforts gave ample satisfaction. The elder Tanner performed one feat in particular that excited admiration. He allowed a large rock to be placed on his chest, and "although this rock was repeatedly beaten with a sledge hammer by a strong man, Mr. Tanner continued to support it as if it were merely a toy." In August of the same year the "Ethiopian Minstrels," fresh from a successful stay in New Orleans, played a short engagement in Houston. These five men—singers and Negro imitators—frequently closed "amid rapturous shouts of applause." Their three concerts at Washington on the Brazos in early September likewise were given to full and appreciative houses.

The traveling circus, more far reaching than the theater in American life of this period, also came to Texas. In the spring of 1843 the "Olympic Circus" gave performances of "varied representations of Horsemanship, and a variety of Gymnastics and Olympic games" in Galveston, Houston, and San Augustine. "These merry fellows," said the Houston *Morning Star,* "have indeed arrived at a most opportune season, and we hope that their lively jokes, fun and feats of horsemanship will tend to dissipate a portion of the gloom and melancholy, that have originated from the hard times." But the times were not so hard that the lower stratum of society was welcome; the advertisements promised the exclusion of forward females with this proscription: "No ladies admitted unless accompanied by a gentleman." This circus was followed by other equestrian organizations. At Galveston, in the spring of 1844, "a group of Franconi's horses, or at least their owners called them such," entertained the citizens in a large temporary pavillion. And on January 16, 1846, the "Olympic Arena and New York Circus" opened a four-night stand in Houston. The proprietors gave promise to young Houston and its indulgent parents that at least eleven "distinguished Equestrians" and a large brass band would appear, and that "strict attention will be had to the maintenance of good order and decorum."

A fever for gambling ran in the blood of the age. It was a chronic social ailment in the South and reached even higher virulence in Texas. In this Western republic the very presence of an individual was an indication of willingness to take a chance, and speculation in land and town futures was a common form of legal gambling. Nacogdoches in the pre-Republic days had been known as a "gamblers' heaven" where every immigrant was considered fair sport for trimming by an organized ring. At San Felipe de Austin and Brazoria, leading villages in Austin's Colony, much of the gambling centered around the game of billiards, which eventually became widely played in Texas towns. Wagering also was carried on at cockfights and probably at a few bowling alleys which had brief existences.

Gambling was prevalent at Houston, especially in its early years. After it became the capital in 1837, it was one of the boom towns that have marked the early development of the agricultural, as well as the cattle-raising and mining, trans-Mississippi West. The records of the district court there show scores of indictments, although few convictions, for "dealing faro," for "permitting gaming," and for "playing at cards." On January 24, 1838, a traveler in Houston made the following notation in his journal: "Took lodging at Floyds Hotel. . . . Visit Billiard room play games of B[illiards]—successful—in the same house are 4 Faro Banks in addition to which are a large number of others in the place—the greatest sink of disipation & vice that modern times have known —Place but nine months old & has a population of 2000."[16] Anti-gambling laws passed in 1837 and 1840 did little to discourage chance-taking at the card table. A few months after passage of the second law, a Houston newspaper (whose editors were not among the town's righteous elements) gleefully commented on the ineffectuality of the new law:

Since the law for the suppression of gambling has passed, we have seen more card playing than ever.—New games have been instituted and old ones revived. The Texians play at *rounders;* the Frenchmen at *vingt-et-un;* the Mexican at *monte;* the Kentuckian, Mississippian and Tennesseean at *poker;* the Dutch at *euchre;* the sons of Erin at *forty-fives;* and the negroes at *old sledge.* They all *cut* and *shuffle* to get rid of paying the liquor bill, for now that we have to pay 50cts per glass it takes but a few to spoil a V or an X. We hope congress will take this matter into consideration and repeal a part or the whole of it.[17]

In the following year District Judge R. E. B. Baylor called gambling "this fashionable but too prevalent vice of the day." The judge was correct on both counts. Any man could take risks at roulette or poker, promote a lottery, or place high wagers on a horse without loss of community standing.

16 Herndon, Diary, 1837–38, 17.
17 Houston *Weekly Times,* April 30, 1840.

Gambling prevailed in connection with horse racing. Even in "a little place like Columbus," wrote the German geologist, Ferdinand Roemer, "the wagers are sometimes quite large, single bets ... amounting to as much as five hundred dollars."[18] Probably as a result of the rousing of tempers following losses at wagering, the race tracks were occasionally the scenes of quarrels and fights which had fatal results. But much of the highest betting was between owners in match races. The following advertisement, inserted in a Clarksville newspaper by C. E. Hilburn, is typical of published challenges, and incidentally contrasts the two best tracks in the Red River region, at the small villages of Clarksville and Boston:

A CHALLENGE

Hart and Co. are hereby informed that my horse *Woodpecker* can take their horse, *Albert Gallatin,* two mile heats, over the Boston track, on the 1st Monday in May next, for a negro boy worth six hundred and fifty dollars, and three hundred and fifty dollars in cash. The objection I have to the Clarksville track is, that it is too muddy in wet weather and too hard in dry.[19]

Horse racing, a universal American sport in this period, was widespread in the Republic of Texas. Some of the very earliest American settlers in Texas, Oklahoma, and Arkansas built race tracks. As early as 1834 there were several in sparsely settled portions of East Texas. In 1834 and 1835 the Texas village of Columbia had a track on which match races were run for purses as high as five hundred and one thousand dollars. Even though Columbia was captured and partially devastated by the invading Mexican Army shortly before the Battle of San Jacinto, the Texas Revolution did not end the sport in that town. The Columbia Jockey Club held racing meets in both of the seasons immediately preceding and following the invasion, as well as in later years. And in November, 1836, P. R. Splane of Columbia publicly offered to wager ten thousand dollars or less on one of his horses against any competition.[20]

18 Roemer, *Texas,* 81.
19 Clarksville *Northern Standard,* November 6, 1844.
20 Brazoria *Texas Republican,* October 25, 1834, May 2, June 6, September 19,

In the period of the Republic, most of the small Texas towns, including the few predominantly Spanish, had race courses. Some were owned by individuals, some by clubs. They were located at Galveston, Houston, Velasco, Washington, Columbus, Columbia, Richmond, Crockett, Texana, Bastrop, San Augustine, Nacogdoches, Clarksville, Boston, Brazoria, San Antonio, and Goliad. In 1838 a traveler from Natchez, Mississippi, wrote to the *American Turf Register and Sporting Magazine* that he had been struck with "the spirit of the people for racing." He had seen side bets of twenty-five hundred dollars made by owners on one race late in 1837, and he believed that "Texas is going to be one of the greatest racing countries in the world, to be racing and betting the way they do now, and the Mexicans now on their Western frontier."

In 1839 a Louisiana visitor gave similar testimony: "The spirit of racing is already current there. Indeed this ... amounts to almost a positive mania."[21]

The chief racing centers were on the coast, at Velasco, Houston, and Galveston. The meetings of their jockey clubs received extended notices in 1838 in the *Spirit of the Times,* partly because their purses were high enough to publicize. Before the expiration of intensive speculation in Texas towns, and before the removal of the seat of government from Houston, these clubs offered purses which compared favorably with those of many clubs in the United States.

General Thomas Jefferson Green was a moving spirit among several prominent men who were officers of the New Market course at Velasco, a town at the mouth of the Brazos River. General Green, soldier of fortune and one of the leaders of the luckless Texan expedition which attempted to take the Mexican town of Mier in 1842, had been the most successful operator on the Texas tracks. He was president of the Velasco club in 1839 and the owner of a string of horses which ran successfully in both Texas and the United States.[22] Other leading turfmen in Texas were Shelby

1835; Columbia *Telegraph and Texas Register,* October 25, November 2, 9, 12, 16, 19, 1836.

[21] *American Turf Register and Sporting Magazine,* Vol. IX, No. 2 (February, 1838), 51–52; *Spirit of the Times,* Vol. IX, No. 24 (August, 1839), 282.

[22] For Green's racing activities in Texas, Mississippi, and Alabama, see *Spirit*

Smith and David Random, of Galveston and Houston; John W. Hall of Washington; and Dr. W. F. T. Hart of Clarksville.

Races held in the coastal towns had a concurrent social side in the balls arranged by the managers of the races. Though bachelor Dr. Ashbel Smith may have tinted the following account of the Houston fall races of 1838 with optimistic colors (since he confessed that his chief interest was in the beauty and chivalry attending the races), his version merits consideration:

As an evidence of the progress of civilization or as some regard it of its vices in this remote land, I may mention that we have a race course near the seat of Government: there and in different sections of the country. Our fall races came off last month. There was some very pretty running especially on the four mile day. I have sent you a newspaper containing an account of the races. There is a larger proportion of well bred geldings about Houston than I have seen in any other part of the world. The days of the races were concluded by a ball given by the Club. It was a large assembly of elegant ladies and high bred gentlemen; the festivities of the night were unmarred by any adverse incident.[23]

Enthusiasm for racing persisted throughout the period of the Republic, one result being the continued importation of blooded stock. C. C. S. Farrar of St. Francisville, Louisiana, took four racing horses to Texas in the summer of 1839 and sold them for eleven thousand dollars. A few months later Dr. R. W. Withers, who had raced extensively in Alabama, sent ten blooded horses to Texas under the care of Isaac Van Leer, "the well known trainer." In the spring of 1840, there were race horses "all the way from Long Island" training for the first meet of the newly organized San Augustine Jockey Club. And several well-bred English and American stallions, including "the celebrated Leviathan," were brought to Texas.[24] These importations did not mean that Texas racing

of the Times, Vol. VIII, No. 45 (December, 1838), 356; Vol. VIII, No. 46 (December, 1838), 364; Vol. IX, No. 2 (March, 1839), 18; Vol. X, No. 4 (March, 1840), 43; Vol. X, No. 5 (April, 1840), 55. Also Green to Ashbel Smith, February 17, 1839, and Smith to H. P. Brewster, April 22, 1839 (letter-book MS), Ashbel Smith Papers.

23Ashbel Smith to "My dear Will," December 20, 1838 (letter-book MS), Ashbel Smith Papers.

24 Among the sources on which this paragraph is based are *Spirit of the Times,*

stock was uniformly good, for the contrary was true; it merely presented further proof of interest in the sport.

Private race tracks were laid off on the plantations along the coast and even on farms in the interior. Conclusive evidence exists that, both on some of these tracks and on prairie straightaways, horse racing often occurred in the last outposts of settlement. Consider the experience of Rev. Z. N. Morrell, when, in 1846, he reached the village of Springfield, which only recently had sprung up near the site of the Fort Parker massacre. He had been forced to swim several rivers to reach the place; he was undoubtedly on the edge of settlement in that region. Yet he found, to his sorrow, a fine race track "on which much labor had been expended."[25] A few months before, Ferdinand Roemer had seen one at Bucksnort, "the farthest settlement," he said, "on the Brazos River." At Bucksnort he lodged with a farmer who told him of the troubles he had had to suffer on account of Indians, and offered him corn-meal mush and milk, "the simplest supper" he had eaten in Texas. Afterward, Roemer's companion informed him that the settler had once been well-to-do but that he had been ruined by making unfortunate bets on his expensive horses. "To hear people speak of racing on the extreme outposts of civilization, sounded peculiar to me, but on the following day I actually saw a race track which had been recently used. Later I had other occasions to observe, that the love for this national sport asserted itself in these places, far removed from civilization."[26] Such is the testimony of a trained and accurate observer.

A less reliable reporter was Mrs. Matilda C. F. Houstoun, an English lady whose yacht touched at Galveston, starting point for her brief visit into the interior in 1844. She wrote, perhaps with unconscious humor, that the national amusement of the frontier

Vol. VIII, No. 5 (March, 1838), 36; Vol. IX, No. 2 (March, 1839), 18; Vol. IX, No. 24 (August, 1839), 282; Vol. IX, No. 38 (November, 1839), 450; Vol. X, No. 2 (March, 1840), 18; Vol. X, No. 12 (May, 1840), 138; Vol. XII, No. 9 (April, 1842), 103; Vol. XII, No. 16 (June, 1842), 183. Also Matagorda *Colorado Gazette and Advertiser,* January 9, 1841; Galveston *Texas Times,* February 25, 1843; San Augustine *Red-Lander,* March 12, 1846; and Sheridan, Diary, 1839–40, entry for February, 1840.

25 Morrell, *Flowers and Fruits from the Wilderness,* 241–42.
26 Roemer, *Texas,* 190.

Republic was *whittling,* a sport which seemed to be carried to its point of highest dexterity in the halls of its Congress. Her estimation of the importance of whittling may not have been far from the truth because yarn-swapping and the playing of rough practical jokes on newly arrived "greenies"—in the concoction of which whittling and the chewing of tobacco were natural concomitants—were perhaps the greatest amusements of all.

"Fun and frolic were the ruling passions of the hour," wrote Dr. John Washington Lockhart, "and woe to the one who came in green from the states, particularly if he were in the least presumptious and loved good whisky. The old stager would have an especial series of lessons for him to learn and some were so severe that they were never forgotten." The lessons in the curricula of the schools of horseplay not only were severe but also occasionally served a social purpose. Dr. Peebles of the village of Washington aided "the boys" in getting rid of a loafer by dissolving nitrate of silver in the water for his bath (his first in many months), which they had persuaded him to take. After exposure to the sunlight, the loafer's skin began to turn dark, and when a plunge in the river failed to deterge his dark coating and his friends were threatening to have him enslaved as a Negro, he departed in great haste.

Another very practical joke consisted of trading spurious head-right certificates for worthless "wildcat" paper money brought in by visiting sharpers. It was customary to conclude the proceedings with the "Spanish Burying," which ended in the administration of a blistering "paddling to the gentlemen in search of landed estates."

Finally, an incident involving the second President of the Republic of Texas reflected, through a mild bit of buffoonery, the free-and-easy character of the country. The citizens of Austin "framed" President Mirabeau Buonaparte Lamar, a dreamer by nature, who was especially absent-minded early in the morning— a condition doubtless aggravated by engrossment in the pressing affairs of the infant Republic. As he walked from his log cabin "White House" to the crude capitol building in Austin one morning, groups of passersby bade him "good morning"; all the inhabitants of the capital seemed determined to greet Lamar before he reached his office. Near the end of his walk, a final group of young state employees surrounded the Chief Executive, and all yelled "good morning" in concert. The President thereupon came out of his self-absorption, removed his hat, and with a good-humored and profound bow to his tormentors, made this rejoinder: "Good morning, gentlemen; in the name of God, good morning to you all."[27]

[27] Sinks, "Texas Reminiscences," VII, 4.

VI

Education, Both Solid and Ornamental

RONTIER LIFE was in itself a phase of education for young Texans. Yet this was the age when the beginnings of formal education for everyone—later to become almost a religion with
Americans—were discernible, and many Texas parents were pa-
thetically eager to provide at least elementary facilities for educating their children. Teachers usually were given cordial receptions,
but it was difficult to find means for conducting schools by private
endeavor in a land where money and books were at a premium.
Meanwhile, the Congress of the Republic of Texas set aside large
grants of land which provided the basis of the public school system
of the future, and Protestant ministers took the lead in educating
the generation rising to manhood. Texas preachers—particularly
the Methodists, "Old School" Presbyterians, and Protestant Episcopalians—taught in various types of schools and actively promoted the establishment of elementary schools, academies, and
"colleges." And at the end of the period of the independent existence of Texas, a convention dominated by preachers took the first
steps toward standardization of teacher training and instructional
methods.

The Texas declaration of independence of 1836 listed the failure of the Mexican government to provide a public school system
as one of the grievances that moved the colonists to revolt. This
statement smacked of the lawyer's brief that included all conten-
tions, logical and fallacious alike, for in the period of colonization
the Mexican government ostensibly had been strongly in favor of
the establishment of public schools conducted in the Spanish language. Although both the Mexican authorities and the colonists
continually avowed their eagerness for government schools, the
numerous laws and official correspondence on the subject form a
record of beautifully phrased plans that never materialized.

136

One illustration will suffice. In 1830 the state legislature passed Decree No. 129 providing for the establishment of primary schools, but the Texas *ayuntamientos* of Nacogdoches and San Felipe de Austin reported that it was impossible to obtain capable teachers for the government schools. Instructors who spoke both Spanish and English probably were unobtainable, although the San Felipe jurisdiction then had four schools conducted in English by private teachers,[1] who probably were included in the list of thirty or more who taught a few brief terms among the colonists before the Texas Revolution. In addition to the insurmountable difficulty involved in securing bilingual school teachers, it is doubtful that the poverty-stricken colonists would have tolerated any serious attempt of the Mexican authorities to introduce a system of tax-supported schools in which instruction was carried on chiefly in Spanish. Meanwhile, the Spanish towns of San Antonio de Bexar, Nacogdoches, and La Bahía (or Goliad after 1829) had a few struggling schools, supported by a population even poorer than the Anglo-Americans.

The most influential newspaper in the Republic advanced the claim that Texas yielded to no other country in realizing "the importance of firmly establishing beyond the reach of all vicissitude or chance of change that rock on which the whole structure of freedom rests—the education of the whole people."[2] This sentiment had considerable backing in public opinion and law. The constitution of the Republic enjoined Congress "to provide by law, a general system of education," and in 1838 A. J. Yates, a lawyer, and sixty-one other persons memorialized Congress to implement this provision, with the result that various bills were introduced into Congress. But the immediate impetus for the passage of acts providing the basis of the modern Texas school system was afforded by a stirring and often quoted portion of the message which President Mirabeau Buonaparte Lamar sent to the Congress of the Republic in December, 1838:

[1]*Laws and Decrees of the State of Coahuila and Texas,* 148; and Ramón Músquiz to *ayuntamiento* of San Felipe de Austin, May 13, 1830; Thomas Barnett to the government of Bexar, August 10, 1830—both in Bexar Archives. The *ayuntamiento* was the governing body of a municipality, the most important unit of local government in the pre-1836 period.

[2] Houston *Telegraph and Texas Register,* January 20, 1841.

If we desire to establish a Republican Government upon a broad and permanent basis, it will be, our duty to adopt a comprehensive and well regulated system of mental and moral culture. . . . It is admitted by all, that [a] cultivated mind is the guardian genius of democracy, and, while guided and controlled by virtue, is the noblest attribute of man. It is the only dictator that freemen acknowledges [*sic*] and the only security that freemen desire. . . . Our young Republic has been formed by a Spartan Spirit. Let it progress and ripen into Roman firmness, and Athenian graccfulness and wisdom. . . . Let me therefore urge it upon you, gentlemen, not to postpone the matter too long. The present is a propitious moment to lay the foundation of a great moral and intellectual edifice, which will in after ages be hailed as the chief ornament and blessing of Texas.

A suitable appropriation of lands to the purpose of general education, can be made at this time without inconvenience to the Government or the people. . . .[3]

Congress granted four leagues (17,712 acres) to each county for the creation of common schools and academies, and designated the chief justice and two associate justices of each county as a school board to administer the lands and schools, but a system of public common schools never was established in the Republic. There was no general opposition, yet in vain did the newspapers call attention to "the want of a general system of education." The newspapers could not add value to school lands in the midst of a depression and could not force the officials of the more thickly settled counties to have their land surveyed (in accordance with the law), if it was located in distant counties.

A public school was established in only one town—Houston— where in 1839–40 the city council employed Rev. Richard Salmon to conduct a school, with low tuition rates and free instruction for the indigent. Salmon was a Protestant Episcopal minister from New York who had brought a small group of immigrants to Brazoria in an abortive effort to establish a church colony in Texas. They had "suffered indescribably from Poverty, Sickness, and Death," while Salmon himself and his family had been so ham-

---

[3] *Journal of the House of Representatives of the Republic of Texas: Third Congress*, 168–70.

pered by sickness that he had been unable to preach regularly until after his appointment as chaplain of the Senate of the First Congress. This teacher of the first public school in the Republic of Texas had not found it a beneficent land, and he accepted a teaching position to relieve his monetary distress. The school opened on February 11, 1839, but in the following January the city council accepted his resignation after investigating "some supposed evils" in his administration.[4]

Houston attracted more teachers than any other town; several schools were always open there. The public school was in operation at least occasionally in the eighteen forties. In addition to the schools for girls, young ladies, and small boys, taught by women, the outstanding private schools with male teachers were, in the order of their appearance, the Houston Select School (W. J. Thurber, instructor); the Select Classical School (taught by Rev. Henry Reid, a Presbyterian minister); and the Houston Academy (under Thomas J. Pilgrim, and afterward the Protestant Episcopal minister Charles Gillett, his nephew H. F. Gillett, and Mrs. M. H. Bigelow). Other teachers occasionally advertised in the newspapers; among them was B. Miller, apparently a linguist, for he offered to teach Latin, French, German, Greek, and Hebrew, as well as mythology, ancient and modern history, and geography. He claimed to be a graduate of the University of Göttingen, where he had studied theology, philology, and philosophy. By the spring of 1848 there was a sufficient number of school teachers in Houston to warrant the epistolary comment that "Houston is glutted with School Teachers—This is good news if they are of the right kind; but if they are a set of fawning pretenders, then woe be to Houston."[5]

A typical academy course was that of the two Gilletts, who offered in 1845 a beginning course of reading, writing, and orthog-

---

[4] Memorials and Petitions, File 80, No. 15½; Salmon to Henry Smith, February 16, 1839, in John H. Brown, *Life and Times of Henry Smith,* 358; Houston *Telegraph and Texas Register,* January 30, February 20, August 7, 1839; Houston *Morning Star,* April 12, 1839, January 23, 31, 1840; Salmon to M. B. Lamar, December 5, 1839, in Gulick *et al.* (eds.), *Lamar Papers,* V, 330; letter from Houston dated January 30, 1839, in Columbus (Mississippi) *Democrat,* March 9, 1839; Minutes of Houston City Council, A, 4–19.

[5] R. Crawford to O. M. Addison, April 17, 1848, Addison Papers.

raphy (tuition: $2.00 per month, par funds); a secondary course in arithmetic, grammar, and geography ($2.50 per month); and a final course in Latin, Greek, philosophy, "and higher matter" ($3.50 per month).[6] Boys and girls were instructed in separate rooms; and the advertisements of the academies frequently assured the public that vulgar or profane language would be prohibited.

There were also academies at Galveston, Matagorda, Velasco, Quintana, Brazoria, Richmond, Gonzales, Columbia, Washington, Independence, Austin, Caldwell, Clarksville, DeKalb, San Augustine, Nacogdoches, Huntsville, even in Corpus Christi, and probably elsewhere. Among the teachers whose services extended over periods of several years were James P. Nash and E. Walbridge at Galveston; Frederick Dean at Velasco and Galveston; H. F. Gillett at Houston, Washington, and Independence; Rev. James Sampson at Clarksville; and Rev. and Mrs. Caleb S. Ives at Matagorda.

Some of the academies were conducted under the auspices of a board of trustees or a proprietor, who, when possible, secured subscriptions in advance from prospective patrons. The Washington Academy, under the superintendence of Rev. L. P. Rucker, was "in an old shell of a house"; it was advertised that no corporal punishment would be inflicted on boys over twelve years of age, but Rucker's failure to control them was the cause of the closing of the school. The Reverend Mr. Ives' Matagorda Academy was conducted continuously after 1839, and was very successful. In 1845 it was chartered under the more ambitious name of Matagorda University, but it may well be doubted that it had the faculty or facilities to justify the new designation; less than a year before, the head of the school had inserted this suggestive item in the local newspaper: "Notice—Mr. Ives has loaned Turner's Chemistry to some friend in Town; he now needs it and will feel greatly obliged to have it returned."[7]

Other institutions which were not above the academy level appropriated grandiose names with even less justification. Often they were a part of town-promotion schemes. Pete Whetstone—credited by the Houston *Telegraph and Texas Register* with being a "noted

[6] Houston *Morning Star*, September 13, 1845; Houston *Telegraph and Texas Register*, September 17, 1845.
[7] Matagorda *Weekly Despatch*, March 23, 1844.

freebooter," a "violent and bloodthirsty renegade" who had mur-
dered at least twenty persons—donated ten acres of land to Marshall
University, the consideration being one dollar and Pete's "interest
in the progress of literature." Since he had to make his mark in
signing the deed, this interest was commendable, but still another
consideration unmentioned in the deed record was Mr. Whetstone's hope that the value of his considerable holdings in Marshall
townsite property would be increased. Manhattan University was
projected as a part of a campaign to boom the prospective town
of the same name, but the school never opened. In noticing the
opening of the "preparatory department" of DeKalb College in
1844, the Clarksville *Northern Standard* observed in its editorial
columns: "We do not admire the plan of terming these incipient
institutions by the lofty names of Universities and Colleges."

The ordinary rural or village school was in session from early
morning until nearly sundown. In the first month or two the pupil
read the beginning of Webster's spelling book in which the letters
of the alphabet were printed up and down the page. Then he was
promoted to words of one syllable, to "baker" and "crucifix," and
on to "Constantinople" and "immateriality." During this time he
perused the various readers by McGuffey, if they were available,
and afterward advanced to the arithmetic class, where he studied
arithmetic books by Pike, Smiley, or Emerson. These texts often
were too difficult for the immediate comprehension of the young-
sters, and it sometimes took one or two years to learn the most
elementary arithmetic. After the boy had mastered the multiplica-
tion table, he might become a "trusty" and retire to the shade of a
tree, where in solitary communion with himself he worked arithmetic problems on his slate.

Grammars by Murray, Smith, and Kirkham were those most
often used. The most advanced reading class studied the writings
of eminent authors, including a few poets. The most common
geography textbooks were those written by Smith, Parley, Olney,
and Adams, but the subject was not stressed. Textbooks in all subjects were always at a premium, even though the stores in Houston
and Galveston generally offered a few for sale. Advanced students
usually were inducted into the mysteries of chemistry (taught chief-

ly by the lecture method), history, rhetoric, and "natural, mental, and moral philosophy," and less often were given training in book-keeping and other business subjects. Practically all schools, from the elementary to those offering college work, closed their sessions with public examinations. At these exercises, diaries kept by advanced students were exhibited and their compositions read to the patrons, and the head of the school invariably gave an address on "Education" or a similar subject that manifested "a correct moral tone."

The problem of the education of the children in strictly rural districts was even more difficult than in the towns. In the half-isolated areas mothers attempted to give their children the benefit of what education they might possess, or families sometimes combined to employ teachers, who lived in the homes of patrons and took part of their pay in produce. The teachers, who often were ill trained, rarely taught in one neighborhood for more than a year or two and usually regarded their positions as providing only temporary means of subsistence. Log cabins, frequently lacking floors or windows, were utilized as school buildings. All of the books of any kind in a neighborhood were gathered together for use in the school; all too often the supply was inadequate. The time and length of the terms were regulated by the state of the weather, the condition of the crops, and the likelihood of Indian attacks. Thus many Texans of this generation reached manhood or womanhood with only a smattering of formal education.

The antecedents of modern educational problems began to appear in debates concerning curricula and teaching methods. In 1845 the "lyceum" of Wesleyan College debated the question "Should the dead languages be excluded from a college course?" While a few teachers of elementary schools claimed to use a modified and improved Pestalozzian system of teaching, and an occasional attack was made on "the rote method" of instruction, the doctrines of the educational reformers of the period received no widespread application in Texas. Spelling and reading still were taught as memory exercises, and a delinquent male student was rewarded with a vigorous application of the switch. "Did one ever think how tiresome it is to read without mastering the ideas intended to be conveyed by the words?" wrote one Texan critic. But there were also those who opposed deviation from the discipline of hard work by children both in and out of classroom. Dr. Francis Moore, Jr., stated his point of view in no uncertain terms in the editorial columns of the *Telegraph and Texas Register*:

There is a great, a terrible evil springing up in this country that unless seasonably checked will be productive of immense mischief. We allude to the method of educating children. In many instances the doctrine is encouraged that it is disreputable to work, and the children are brought up in perfect idleness. . . . The consequence will be, that the boys will give loose to the natural buoyancy of youth in dissipation and extravagance. . . . The *girls,* we will not say young ladies, will grow up like mere parrots, accomplished in nothing except the art of "killing time," and spending their days in alternately lolling on a rocking chair, or prosing over useless insipid novels, thus making themselves instead of objects of love and admiration, the mere toys, to be trifled with an hour and then cast aside with disgust and contempt. What a contrast will there be between these dull, shiftless, stupid females, and the intelligent, refined, active, and accomplished ladies who adorn the first society of the United States.[8]

The literate elements of the citizenry were firmly committed to a belief in the necessity for educating girls. Sentiments such as "on female education depends the future destinies of our Republic" frequently appeared in the speeches and newspapers of this period, and women teachers who could give their feminine charges what was called "a complete and thorough English education" were warmly welcomed and supported. The first boarding school for "young ladies and misses" was put into operation in Coles Settlement early in 1835 by Miss Frances L. Trask of Gloucester, Massachusetts—one of the countless New England women who carried the torch of education into what was considered the cultural darkness of the West. A letter written by Miss Trask to her father reads in part:

As to my prospects in this country, I can hardly say what they are, but I am in hopes that they are improving. My school is small, but profitable, as tuition is high, from $6.00 to $10.00 per quarter—I have

[8] Houston *Telegraph and Texas Register*, July 14, 1841.

but 7 boarders at $2.00 wk but my housekeeping expenses are trifling, *Corn bread* and *Bacon* being the chief [items] of our diet. As to furniture no hermit's cell was ever more simply furnished, *two* chairs, a table, a few trunks, benches, and boxes, sundry articles of crockery, and iron ware, compose all my household stuff, with the exception of my bedding, which consists of mattresses of my own making, and a decent supply of bed clothes—

My buildings (for I have two) rank second to none in Texas. One is a frame building 15 by 20 ft. with two *glazed* windows on a side, and folding doors at each end. This answers for schoolroom, parlor, bed chamber, and hall. The other is of more humble pretensions, being a rugged black log house, with a very forbidding exterior, but the interior very decent, that is my kitchen. My dining room is of magnificent dimensions, for it extends all over creation . . . that is, I dine under the oaks, and have a plenty of corn bread, and bacon. My domicile I presume you will think is of very mean pretensions, quite a caricature of a boarding school—but I assure you my Dear Father, that with the Texas public that it not only ranks *respectable,* but *quite genteel,* and indeed I know of no reason why it should not, for it is much better than some of our Texas planters occupy with their twenty, or thirty negroes.[9]

After the Texas Revolution, schools for girls and young ladies were numerous, though few had a continuous existence for more than two or three years. Among the first educational institutions chartered by the Congress of the Republic was the Independence Female Academy, which was the successor of Miss Trask's school for girls. Another early school was the Montville Boarding School for young ladies, run by Miss Lydia A. McHenry and Mrs. David Ayers. In his richly flavored recollections, M. M. Kenney states that Miss McHenry taught a boarding school for girls at the same time that his mother directed a class of boys. "There were in all twenty or more lodged and boarded as best we could in our unfinished cabins in the wilderness. . . . The studies were of every grade. The

[9] Judith Trask to Israel Trask, July 5, 1835, Trask Papers. Miss Trask used this signature in writing to her father, but she was widely known in Texas as Frances L. Trask. A possible explanation is that she changed her name when she came to Texas.

pupils were carefully instructed in the art of reading well, and as a help to that end were encouraged to memorize verses, some of which I can still repeat from hearing them recited so long ago."

As the population of the Republic increased, female "seminaries" or "academies" (for girls of all ages, and often with classes for small boys as well) appeared in twenty or more towns and villages. Newspapers consistently gave them strong editorial support. Their teachers doubtless possessed the qualities of perseverance and nerve, and a number of them pushed forward the educational frontier by carrying at least a modicum of culture from one place to another. Mrs. George Todd taught "every branch" of female education, "both solid and ornamental," in two Texas towns, Boston and Clarksville. Miss A. E. Madden moved from San Augustine to Houston and afterward to Galveston. The Sims sisters transferred their school from Nacogdoches to Washington on the Brazos. Mrs. Gibbs (of Boston, Massachusetts) and her daughters taught in Tuscumbia, Alabama, and later conducted a boarding school at Quintana, Texas.

The curricula of the "female seminaries" bore the stamp of the ideas of the eighteen forties concerning what a well-educated woman should know. A course comprising orthography, reading, and writing usually came first, followed by arithmetic, grammar, geography, and history (ancient and modern) in a second group. This "thorough English education" was completed by the study of "the higher branches of science and literature." It was announced that the education of the young ladies attending the Pine Creek Female Institute, about fifteen miles north of Clarksville, would conclude with courses in philosophy, astronomy, rhetoric, composition, logic, and chemistry, while Mrs. Gibbs's school in Quintana advertised that "Chemistry, Philosophy and Botany will be impressed by lectures." French and Italian were taught for small extra fees, and music lessons (piano, guitar, and voice), drawing and painting, "ornamental needle work and wax work" always were offered by the more pretentious establishments. But Mrs. Gibbs was the only instructress who advertised that calisthenics (three dollars for three months' training) would be included in the curriculum.

Parents who could raise the money and were particularly anxious that their children secure well-rounded educational training sent them to schools in the United States. Planter Jared E. Groce arranged to have his children remain in Southern institutions for several years, while José Antonio Navarro of San Antonio, a Mexican who had been a signer of the Texas declaration of independence, sent his son to a college in "the States." The younger members of the family of planter James F. Perry were educated at Kenyon College in Ohio, Trinity College in Connecticut, and other American schools. One of his wife's sons by a former marriage, Guy M. Bryan, drew more heavily on Perry's agents than he thought necessary. He therefore wrote to Guy that he would allow him five hundred dollars each year for his expenses at Kenyon College and enjoined him to try to live within his income. President Lamar's own daughter, Rebecca Ann, was educated in Georgia until her death in 1843, and Henry Austin made severe financial sacrifices to keep his children in Kentucky schools.

The alluring vision of an American education for their children constantly was held in mind and sometimes was realized by many other parents. Few letters from children in the United States to their families in Texas have been preserved; one letter—bearing a New Jersey postmark and written after the end of Texas' independent existence—from a girl to her father in San Augustine, bears the poignancy of extreme homesickness that must have marked many such communications, particularly from the very young:

It is now sunday evening [wrote Mary Garrett] and I have again to sit down to write you to come for me—but I know you are very tired of listening to me. [I] beg you to let me come home. I cant help it for it is very disagreeable to stay here we have no fire in our rooms and I tell you it is soo cold we do not know what to do. the ice is on windows where we breathe and the windows is wet. it is frozen in the mornings thick and the water that we have to wash in so cold that it makes our fingers ache so that we can scarcely make our bed up . . . this is a very lonesum place although there is so many girls but they will not go with us they think that they are too good. Pa, you must be sure and come after me. I cannot keep from crying to think of the many happy days I have spent at *home*. and then to think that I will

146

Miss Frances (Judith) Trask, 1835, wearing a green satin redingote over hand-embroidered white muslin underdress.

From a water-color sketch by Mary Reid

Port of Galveston

Reproduced from Mrs. Matilda C. F. Houstoun, *Texas and the Gulf of Mexico*, 1844

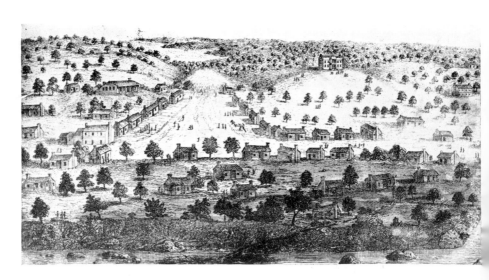

Austin, as it appeared in January, 1840

Reproduced from *Texas in 1840, or the Emigrant's Guide to the New Republic*, 1840

have to stay here. I could not think of such a thing I know I would die. Just to think of *home* that sweet place home pa you do not know how much we suffer here it is so hard for us to stay. I know that you can not say *no* when I have asked you so often to let me come home. . . . you must excuse all mistakes and the bad writing. and write immediately to your daughter.[10]

The practice of sending the children of the comparatively well-to-do to schools in the United States deprived Texas educators of one of the most likely sources of possible income. The government considered itself obligated to assist colleges, but it had difficulty in meeting its own expenses. Despite the interest of many individuals in the establishment of a state-supported college and the direct appropriation by Congress of fifty leagues of land "for the establishment of two colleges or universities hereafter to be created," the chief immediate assistance rendered by the government of Texas to the development of colleges was in grants of four leagues of land to each of seven private or religious institutions.

The Republic of Texas—in common with other American frontiers—witnessed the birth of a number of "colleges," though many were stillborn. Ministers of the Methodist and "Old School" Presbyterian churches were the founders of, or connected with, all that became active.[11]

The first "college" that had the barest claim to the designation was Rutersville College, which was officially opened on February 1, 1840, at Rutersville, a new town near La Grange. The establishment of a Methodist college was suggested by Rev. Martin Ruter, Methodist missionary and former president of Allegheny College in Pennsylvania, whose death in 1838 inspired his Methodist brethren to name a town and college in his memory. The president of Rutersville College was Rev. Chauncey Richardson, A.M., former president of Tuscumbia Female College in Alabama. Then, as now, a college president's qualifications for office included the

[10] Mary Garrett to William Garrett, December 31, 1854, Cartwright Papers.

[11] Baylor University was chartered and plans made for its establishment by the Baptists before the end of the Republic of Texas, but its actual opening occurred after Texas was annexed by the United States.

ability to secure endowments, and the Reverend Mr. Richardson was not deficient in that respect. He traveled in Texas and the United States to plead for support for his college, and in the midst of an economic depression not only obtained donations of land, money, and books, but also influenced the Texas Congress to include a grant of four leagues of land in the college charter. By 1842 the main building had been completed and presented "quite an imposing appearance." In 1844, during the fourth year of official operation, Rutersville College announced that "one hundred and ninety-four students have shared, in a greater or less degree, its valuable advantages." But the burden of paying the salaries of the faculty, three to five in number, was always onerous, and in the late eighteen forties the school was in dire financial straits.

The enrollment of Rutersville College occasionally reached one hundred students (more than half of whom were girls). The catalog contemplated the issuance of two degrees (Bachelor of Arts and Bachelor of Science and English Literature); and instruction in Latin, Greek, German, French, Italian, Spanish, calculus, logic, philosophy, surveying, geology, and botany could be obtained by the few advanced students. Nevertheless, most of the students were not advanced enough to attempt collegiate work, and the disdainful characterization of the college by Prince Solms of Germany as "an American elementary school" was partly justified.

It often became the duty of the boys at school to mount their ponies and accompany their elders in pursuit of bands of Indians. A notable instance occurred at Rutersville College soon after the opening of the school. Two young boys in the neighborhood while hunting horses were attacked by Indians, and one of them, Henry Earthman, was killed; his brother Fields escaped and brought the news to the school. The excited boys joined in the search for the body, which lay a mile away in a dreadfully mutilated state. The scalp had been taken, the hands cut off and thrown into the grass, and the heart, with ligaments unsevered, laid on one side of the body; it was found to have a bullet in the centre, and was, no doubt, exposed in a spirit of bravado to show how unerring was the aim of the red man. Nearly all the boys in the school, ranging from fourteen to sixteen, joined in the pursuit of the Indians, which lasted about three weeks. In fact, one of them still liv-

ing says they did little but hunt Indians while at school at Rutersville prior to 1842.[12]

In 1840 Galveston University opened its doors to five students.
The first president was the Reverend W. L. McCalla, a Philadelphia Presbyterian preacher and a powerful speaker and controver-
sialist, who soon was reported to have left for England where "it is
said he intends challenging Daniel O'Connell [the famous Irish
orator and political reformer] to wordy combat." Galveston University was still in operation in 1844, with an annual enrollment of
nearly one hundred students. It had acquired a library (according
to newspaper reports) of almost a thousand volumes and offered
the customary ambitious curriculum ranging from common-school
subjects to history, natural philosophy, "intellectual philosophy,"
moral philosophy, bookkeeping, chemistry, "phisiology," botany,
rhetoric, political economy, astronomy, and three modern languages.[13]

The University of San Augustine achieved the greatest ephem-
eral success of any of the colleges that were established in the Republic of Texas. As usual in such cases, the institution was built
around the personality of one man. Although the "University" was
incorporated on June 5, 1837, with a group of representative citizens of varying political and religious views as trustees, it was not
until the summer of 1842 that they were able to employ a man with
energy and intellectual attainments. Their choice was Rev. Marcus
A. Montrose, a Scotsman who let it be known that he was a graduate of the University of Edinburgh (though the institution has no
record of his graduation) and a minister of the Presbyterian
Church.

An amusing though unauthenticated tradition concerns the circumstances of his interview with a committee of the board of
trustees:

It was evident that no one in the town was adequate to the examina-

[12] Wooten (ed.), *Comprehensive History of Texas*, I, 656.

[13] New Orleans *Daily Picayune*, September 8, 1840, January 18, February 9,
1842; Houston *Telegraph and Texas Register*, October 20, 1841, January 4, July 12,
1843; W. L. McCalla, *Adventures in Texas, Chiefly in the Spring and Summer of
1840 . . . Accompanied by an Appendix, Containing an Humble Attempt to Aid
in Establishing and Conducting Literary and Ecclesiastical Institutions.*

tion of so learned a man. The committee, consisting of I. D. Thomas, Matthew Cartwright and Phillip A. Sublett, decided to make it a mere matter of form. Mr. Thomas asked, "Can you figure?" Mr. Montrose, who was a master of calculus, modestly admitted that he thought he could, and Mr. Thomas announced that he was satisfied. Mr. Cartwright then asked, "Can you calculate interest?" Mr. Montrose thought he would be equal to the task, and Mr. Cartwright declared himself satisfied. Mr. Sublett then asked, "Can you turn the grandmother's trick?" (a trick at cards well known among gamblers). This puzzled the worthy Scotchman and he was obliged to confess his ignorance. "Then I am satisfied," exclaimed Mr. Sublett, and Mr. Montrose was accordingly employed.[14]

The learning of the Reverend Mr. Montrose made a tremendous impression upon the inhabitants of East Texas. The trustees believed that they had found "a gentleman of no ordinary capacity and enterprise, possessing in eminent degree the learning and talents to command respect and inspire confidence; to impart instruction, and conduct with skill . . . all the various departments."[15] He began his tenure in San Augustine by delivering three lectures on different subjects, "evincing to his audience the highest order of talents." Adolphus Sterne of the neighboring town of Nacogdoches was introduced to President Montrose, "a Scotchman who is no doubt a very Clever fellow and has seen the world, but makes the *Natives* of San Augustine belive he is a perfect curiosity—!! go it my Montrose [Sterne wrote in his diary]—gull the Augustin Classic parents with your Greek, Latin, and Algebra, but you can not cram your learning down the —— of such Ignoramuses as we are in Nacogdochez."[16]

Montrose soon had a chance to display his talents in Nacogdoches. San Augustine University developed a working agreement with the Presbytery of Eastern Texas of the "Old School" Presbyterian Church (which was formed in 1843 chiefly to assist the school), and Montrose became involved in a debate with a Method-

14 George L. Crocket, *Two Centuries in East Texas,* 302.

15 San Augustine *Red-Lander,* February 16, 1843.

16 Smither (ed.), "Diary of Adolphus Sterne," *Southwestern Historical Quarterly,* Vol. XXXV, No. 2 (October, 1931), 157; R. Whittlesey to Thomas J. Rusk, August 28, 1842, Rusk Papers (University of Texas Library).

ist minister that aroused the brethren of that sect to establish the rival Wesleyan College. In the spring of 1845 the president resigned from San Augustine University to begin a very brief term as head of the newly organized Nacogdoches University. His letter of resignation modestly called attention to the remarkable progress that had been made during his administration, and claimed that "our Philosophic and Chemerical Apparatus are nearly complete." He lauded the trustees for being among those "who have aided to establish a system of general education, free from Ecclesiastic Monopoly and Church Laws, to the blessing and benefit of the rising generation." Finally, he pointed out the superiority of his "Electic System of Universal Education." One group of his critics had attempted to rob him of credit for developing this revolutionary set of methods, he said, while another group

declaim against the system, knowing that if it becomes general, they will be compelled to adopt it, or leave off teaching altogether—hence they exclaim, it is superficial!—it is mushroom education. . . . It is true that a teacher, although endowed with the talents of an angel, and making the use of the most efficient system of instruction, upon some children or youth, can make no lasting impression, for what nature hath denied, all art cannot supply.

But for instructing those who could learn, he claimed that his "Electic System" was far superior to the "Old Plodding System."[17]

Whatever innovations in imparting wisdom to the young may have been introduced, the general course of instruction in the San Augustine school was similar to that at Rutersville, though slightly more ambitious. At San Augustine University instruction ostensibly was available in chemistry, mineralogy, conchology, and the Hebrew, Syriac, Chaldean, and Arabic languages, as well as in the ordinary courses. Painting, music, and "stenography" also were a part of the curriculum. A few lectures on law, medicine, and patriotic subjects were given by local professional men.[18] A complete education from grammar school through the young men's college course and the young women's female academy was advertised,

[17] Washington *Texas National Register,* May 22, 1845.
[18] San Augustine *Red-Lander,* January 5, 1843, September 11, 1845; William S. Red, *History of the Presbyterian Church in Texas,* 222.

although one suspects that most of the work was much below collegiate level. At any rate, the school never granted a college degree. The largest enrollment reached was approximately two hundred, but the establishment of a rival institution in the same place in 1844 reduced this number by more than half.

The Reverend James Russell, holder of a genuine Master of Arts degree from Edinburgh University, was promoted, in 1845, from the faculty to the presidency of San Augustine University. He conducted himself much in the manner of his predecessor. He gave a series of lectures on magnetism in which he "performed upwards of forty amusing and highly interesting experiments," using apparatus which was announced as "the largest and best selected west of the Mississippi river." His lecture topics also included "The Phenomena of Volcanic Eruptions" and "Astronomy." He improved his faculty, and inserted a statement in the newspaper that "a highly accomplished female teacher is engaged—*there is no mistake on this occasion.*" He developed his own method of instruction, "the analytic," and engaged in controversies with the Wesleyan College adherents. But his frank expression of opinion concerning the character of a lady brought about an encounter with her brother in which the educator was killed in the summer of 1847. San Augustine University thereupon ceased to exist.[19]

Meanwhile, early in March, 1844, the Wesleyan Male and Female College opened its doors in San Augustine. The establishment of this Methodist institution was largely a result of the labors of Rev. Francis A. Wilson. This uneducated circuit rider raised most of the funds for the erection of a three-story building, and the cornerstone was laid on August 26, 1843, with appropriate addresses by two prominent lawyer-orators, Kenneth L. Anderson and David S. Kaufman. Theoretically, the curriculum was almost as comprehensive as that advertised by its local rival and was intended to be largely nonsectarian except for candidates for the Methodist ministry. The initial enrollment in Wesleyan College was 155 students, and in 1846 two students actually were granted degrees. But the institution was financially weak, and attempts to merge with San

19 San Augustine *Red-Lander*, November 3, 1845, January 15, February 5, 12, 1846; Crocket, *Two Centuries in East Texas*, 228, 306; Huntsville *Texas Presbyterian*, September 4, 1847; Frederick Law Olmsted, *A Journey Through Texas*, 69.

Augustine University were unsuccessful. After both institutions collapsed in 1847, the remnants of the two were merged in the short-lived University of Eastern Texas. But this school was handicapped by administrative ineptitude, and San Augustine was losing its importance as the West lured away its best citizens. In addition, religious controversy had drained the vitality from the cause of education in the town.[20]

Yet in the early eighteen forties San Augustine had been notable not only for two praiseworthy educational ventures but also for the high cultural level of many of its citizens. Indeed, San Augustine of that day must provide a notable exception to any attempt to characterize the Republic of Texas as devoid of the best in the civilization of the period. Even now, a century later, something of the atmosphere of good taste still lingers in the fine, clear-cut lines of its old homes.

Nacogdoches was another East Texas town with a number of citizens of considerable intellectual attainments. Several of them, under the leadership of Dr. James H. Starr and Thomas J. Rusk, watched the progress of the San Augustine institutions with interest. In 1844 they decided that a propitious time had arrived for launching a school, and early in 1845 the representatives of their district piloted an act through Congress granting a charter to Nacogdoches University. It was reported that subscribers had pledged more than 20,000 acres of land to the school. A Presbyterian preacher, Rev. J. M. Becton, was appointed field agent, and the school was endorsed by the Presbytery of Brazos of the "Old School" Presbyterian Church.

The Reverend Mr. Montrose, former head of San Augustine University, was elected to the presidency. He developed an ambitious program which included a new three-story brick building, which would be heated by one stove on the ground floor and would be (he modestly stated) "the only convenient building on the continent, for literary purposes." He also added law, "military exercises and evolutions," and a "health" program to his "Electic

---

[20] Memorials and Petitions, File 64, No. 253; Crocket, *Two Centuries in East Texas,* 307–309; San Augustine *Red-Lander,* December 2, 1843, May 18, 1844, November 6, 1845.

System of Universal Education."[21] Early in 1846 Montrose resigned in the middle of a session and subsequently moved to another town. Nacogdoches University announced that he would be replaced by a new instructor, or preferably a gentleman and a lady, "as will give entire satisfaction to the patrons of the school."[22] Although Nacogdoches University continued in existence until the Civil War, Dr. James H. Starr, one of the leaders in its establishment, believed that "the name and university scheme, as provided for in the Charter, were not in accord with the moderate views of myself and some others of the active participants in the undertaking; but grander conceptions prevailed."[23]

The Reverend Mr. Montrose immediately became involved in still another controversy. As the end of the independent existence of the Republic of Texas approached, a group of preachers and other interested persons met at Houston in January, 1846, to consider the standardization of textbooks, the systematization of pedagogy, and the improvement of instruction of students who intended to become teachers. The "convention" was addressed by Rev. Chauncey Richardson, president of Rutersville College, who advocated that each college establish a department in which teachers "shall be prepared for their task, not only by a course of instruction designed for their personal improvement, but by teaching them how to instruct and educate." The Texas Literary Institute was organized at this meeting "to arouse public interest to the subject of general education in this state, influencing the Legislature to take some active and efficient plans for adopting a general system of education in Texas."[24] Montrose (who apparently was not present at Houston) disputed the institute's claim to have begun the

21 Marcus A. Montrose to James H. Starr, March 12, 1845, Starr Papers; San Augustine *Red-Lander*, November 30, 1844, September 11, December 18, 1845; New Orleans *Daily Picayune*, January 10, 1845; Minutes of the Presbytery of Brazos, 1840–45, 23, 26.

22 San Augustine *Red-Lander*, February 5, 1846; legal agreement between Montrose and Frost Thorn, president of the board of trustees, January 31, 1846, Montrose MS.

23 "Autobiography of Dr. James H. Starr," 47, Starr Papers.

24 Chauncey Richardson, *An Address on Education: Delivered before the Educational Convention of Texas, in the City of Houston, January, 1846*; Red, *History of the Presbyterian Church in Texas*, 224; Houston *Telegraph and Texas Register*, November 19, December 10, 1845; New Orleans *Daily Picayune*, December 7, 1845.

first movement in Texas for the concentration of public effort on the subject of education, and maintained that he had originated a movement of this kind at San Augustine in 1842. He came out flatly against sectarian schools and in favor of a state university, two or more normal schools, and a board of education. The historian of Texas Presbyterianism has pointed out that his views on a state-supported educational system eventually became the state's policy: "Montrose was thirty-five years ahead of his time."[25]

Although Rev. Chauncey Richardson did not include McKenzie College (also called McKenzie Institute) among the Texas colleges that had "either suitable buildings or a regular organization" in his address before the Houston educational convention in 1846, the Clarksville institution had begun a long and honorable history. Its founder and head was Rev. John Witherspoon Pettigrew McKenzie, widely known as "Old Master." Prior to the opening of his Clarksville school in 1841, he had had a variety of experiences as a teacher in Tennessee, as a missionary to the Choctaws, and as a Methodist circuit rider in a large area in northeastern Texas. McKenzie College was first conducted in a log cabin with sixteen pupils; but by 1854 it had more than three hundred students, nine faculty members, and four large three-story buildings.[26]

A series of letters descriptive of life in the frontier college, written by a student in McKenzie College in 1848 and 1849, has been preserved. Their suggestion of internal conflict in the matter of religious conviction was typical, because more than two-thirds of the students were converted while attending McKenzie. Illustrative excerpts from the letters follow:

[Mar. 5–12, 1848] The times are very dull here, especially on Saturdays and Sundays. I am getting on tolerably well in my Studies   I am reading in Caesar now and have been for about two weeks. . . . We are troubled with Cold very much here, the whooping-cough is also among

[25] Red, *History of the Presbyterian Church in Texas,* 225; Huntsville *Texas Presbyterian,* February 13, March 24, November 6, 1847.

[26] B. E. Masters, "A History of Early Education in Northeast Texas" (M. A. thesis, University of Texas), 20–52; Clarksville *Northern Standard,* August 6, 8, 1846; Macum Phelan, *History of Early Methodism in Texas, 1817–1866,* 187, 289, 405.

us, there are several of the little fellows who have it. . . . I have a bad cold myself, but otherwise am well. . . .

I have commenced studying astronomy And also the Greek language. . . .

I am the same fellow that I ever was Still without religion and I sometimes think that it ever will be So I believe I have never felt more careless than I do now And I cannot help it although I endeavor to reflect on the subject.

[April 1, 1848] I am in good health and in tolerably good Spirits, though for the last week or two I have felt extremely lazy and Sleepy all the time almost I suppose though it a natural consequence of the approach of Spring. . . . I am trying my best to learn to write but it look like a bad chance, but there are other things that are of more importance though I would very much like to write a good hand, but if I have a good Classical education I can get a place in Some good institution [as a teacher], which I sometimes think of trying to do, you remember I used to talk of being a lawyer, but then it was more than half in jest but now I really have a notion of that or of being a *Doctor* though perhaps I may be neither. . . .

I believe though there is more danger of my not exercising enough than two much, as it is not very often that I take any, but all I wish to take is just what my health demands. . . .

It is night and there is so much confusion that I scarcely know what I am writing. . . .

[April 29, 1848] You request me to write to you respecting the State of my mind as regards religion; now I Scarcely know what to Say about that, though I know I have not got religion, and although I believe I desire to have it as much as ever I did, yet I do not feel as much hope as I have [had], the thought of having sought so long in vain makes me almost despair of ever obtaining it—I find it the most difficult thing to keep my mind on any thing Solemn, even during the hour of preaching my mind is any where but there, on the Sermon.

. . . it is now but three months till the examination and I am anxious to make as great a proficiency in my Studies as possible: I am reading two Latin books Caesar and Sallust and I am kept tolerably busy. . . . [In later letters, he stated that he was reading Vergil and Greek and was studying "Mental Philosophy."]

[Oct. 15, 1848] Our debating Society met again on last friday night; it was my duty to address the Society which I did So to the best of my ability on the progress of freedom   it was Short (three pages of foolscap) and I will say nothing of the quality but I have it and you can See it if we Should ever meet again; I have a blank book in which I intend to write all my Speeches and compositions and other little odd affairs; they made me Secretary which is the only office I want in the Society.

[Nov. 4, 1848] Do you have any sons of temperance in your part of the world   I have never heard of any such a thing about there but to speak plainly they have a society in Clarksville that the[y] call the Sons of temperance   it is something on the order of masonry   there are a good many of the students have joined and last tuesday they initiated me after my petition had laid over for one week which is the law, I saw a heap of pretty sights but they are not lawful to be told   it is doubtless a good society, its motto is love, purity, and fidelity; which is no secret. The second article in the constitution is as follows, "no brother shall make buy sell or use as a beverage any Spirituous or malt liquors wine or cider["] but I think I shall send you the Constitution after awhile, this is called the, "Clarksville division No. 12 of the sons of temperance of the State of Texas"   most all the folks in Clarksville have joined it, there are a hundred members now and some join every meeting which is tuesday night.

5th   having been stopped yesterday I now again resume, we had a considerable snow last night and this morning we have had great fun at snow-balling   Old Master helped us some. There were several little wounds recieved [*sic*] but no damage done.

[Mar. 4, 1849] There has been a great revival of religion in the School, there have been about twenty professed religion, there were fifteen one evening   Two of the boys in my room are in the number. . . . You ask me my views on religion, and whether I have yet obtained it, I think I can answer that question in the affirmative, and indeed for several weeks before I acknowledged it I believe I had it, but it came so much easier than I ever expected that I could not believe it was religion although I felt some change.[27]

---

[27] All from letters from Malcolm H. Addison to Oscar M. Addison, Addison Papers.

Sessions of Texas colleges closed with public examinations and exercises of two or three days' duration. An examining committee of Wesleyan College reported in the summer of 1845 that "the class in Olmsted's Natural Philosophy, and Comstock's Natural Philosophy, and General History displayed a more thorough knowledge than we had witnessed on any previous occasion." The most advanced students read original compositions and delivered declamations on such subjects as "Ambition," "Ancient Greece," "Liberty," "Freedom," "Female Education," "Causes and Results of War," and "Varieties of Human Life." At Rutersville in the same year, the young ladies exhibited copybooks and herbariums as evidence of their proficiency in penmanship and botany, which must have been a soul-trying procedure to the instructor in the sciences, Charles Wright, a Yale graduate and competent naturalist. The climax of the exercises usually was an address by the president or possibly a visiting orator. An address by President Richardson, as reported by the examining committee, was "listened to with profound attention and thrilling interest."

Extracurricular activities in Texas colleges included meetings of literary and debating societies and the celebration of patriotic holidays. May Day was deemed an appropriate time for the young ladies of a college to hold a special celebration. On May 1, 1844, the young ladies of the University of San Augustine crowned the queen, Miss Almedia Thomas, before a packed house. At the opening of the exercises, the girls marched around a stage which was decorated with flowers and evergreens, "Madame Brichta being at the piano." The queen then took her place on the throne, while the maids of honor, cushion-bearer, and other attendants assumed appropriate positions. Several of the young ladies, including the queen, delivered original speeches; a song composed for the occasion was sung; and a procession formed and proceeded to a nearby home for a banquet. In her speech Almedia gave thanks for the honor that had been rendered her, praised the school, and gracefully ended her address with the following pulsating paragraph:

My Comrades, may you see the return of many a season of flowers —though storms may gather, the tempest roar, and the chilling winds of apathy freeze, yet remember this day and remember this institution.

Forget not to cultivate those graces of the heart, so often portrayed; drink deep of the Pierian Spring—then shall Orion, Arcturus and the Pleiad[e]s, speak of the ages they have glittered in yonder sky. The flowers of the field shall utter prophecies, and all nature shall open her lavish store for your admiration and your pleasure—by such literary efforts, our nation shall be great and the "Home of the Brave."[28]

Texas indeed had come a long way in school development between San Jacinto and Annexation. Before the Texas Revolution there was a mere handful of teachers among a population that increased to more than twenty-five thousand Anglo-Americans; in the succeeding ten years, the proportion of teachers to the rapidly increasing population became much larger, and a number of them were able educators. Furthermore, a few advanced students were reading Latin, Greek, and other languages and studying philosophy, botany, and calculus. This was no mean achievement in a country where the Mexicans and Indians were a constant threat, violence rampant, and business procedures disrupted by a disheartening depression. Many of the newly arrived immigrants were not financially able to support their sons and daughters at school, and some needed their labor services at home. Other parents either did not appreciate fully the value of an education, "perhaps from not having enjoyed its benefits," or they believed that instruction of their children by "self-recommended itinerant teachers" was sufficient. Jealousies existing between neighboring towns tended to prevent unified support of colleges. In view of difficulties of this sort, the Republic's educational effort was worthy of anything but scorn.

[28] San Augustine *Red-Lander*, May 18, 1844.

VII

"Tall Talk" and Cultural Ferment

"THE LITERATURE OF TEXAS is yet in its elementary condition"—this not precisely startling announcement was made by the editor of the Washington *Texas National Register* in the issue of December 7, 1844. Yet, in Texas as in other frontier regions, one of the origins of indigenous literature was appearing in the mythology of Western folk heroes, in "tall talk" and exaggerative humor. For the frontier, whatever else it might have been, was a land of storytellers. Their yarn-spinning was something rare and distinctive; their humor was lusty and often bucolic in contrast to the brittleness and prurience of much urban badinage today.

While some historians minimize the cultural contributions of the West to American life, it cannot be denied that the spirit of frontier humor and imagination fortunately pervades substantial segments of modern American literature. It is necessary to add, however, that Mark Twain, Josh Billings, and Artemus Ward pointed out the truism that much of the flavor of the frontier brand of humor lies in the manner of telling. Consequently the efforts of Western storytellers usually are not so effective in the written form as in the spoken. Yet Western lore has given a folk meaning to the New World adventure, and the subliterary prose of the frontier and the tales which have endured for generations provide a foundation for the literary efforts of many modern writers.

Texas had a part in laying this foundation for a distinctively American literature. The stories related before the firesides of Texas cabins and at meetings of the bar—legal or liquid—were literary materials in the raw. Every Texas village had its "loafer's log," where wits and tale-tellers found a ready audience. In the course of their discussions, they naturally enlarged upon the exploits of some of their contemporaries who possessed highly individualized personalities, such as Aylett C. ("Strap") Buckner and Davy Crockett.

Strap Buckner was a tempestuous individualist who fought with a number of the filibusterers who sought to liberate Mexico before Stephen F. Austin began to lead his colonists into Texas. As one of the earliest settlers on the Colorado River, he suffered heavily from Indian depredations. He evidently enjoyed fighting, and he took advantage of many opportunities for conflict with Indians and Mexicans. His fellow colonists knew him as a man who was both hospitable and quick tempered—a combination of characteristics that gave rise to many tales about him. Succeeding generations made him the mythological hero of the story of "The Devil and Strap Buckner," as told in N. A. Taylor's *The Coming Empire* (1877). He had not only "knocked down Austin's whole colony at least three times over," but he had bested a ferocious black bull and had fought a mighty battle with the Devil.

By 1939 Strap Buckner was nationally known. A writer in the July issue of *Harper's Magazine* grouped him with Paul Bunyan and Johnny Appleseed as "the three heroic figures of traditional America." The mythography of the three was depicted in ribald sculpture reliefs on the Theme Center Façade of the Medicine and Public Health Building at the New York World's Fair in 1939. Thus unfettered Texas individualism rough-cast the material for one of the imperishable legends of American folklore.

The fabulous Davy Crockett legend illustrates the epic and Gargantuan proportions that the exploits of many other frontier heroes stimulated in lesser degrees. In its final form, peerless Davy was commanding the whole Western world, and even the universe. He had not died at the Alamo; on the contrary, he had been shot by a silver bullet which made no wound and had merely feigned death as a means to escape. But most of the Crockett story had a tang of fanciful earthiness. There was Crockett's uncle, for example, who lived

at the jumping off part of the western country. He is celebrated in that part of the *world* for the following peculiarities: he shaves himself with sheet lightning, and eats pickled thunderbolts for his breakfast, and hail stone life pills when he's sick, picks [his] teeth with a pitch-fork, combs his hair with a rake, fans himself with a hurricane, wears a *cast iron* shirt, and drinks nothing but kreosote and aquafortis.[1]

Men who reached the top in public life rarely achieved substantial stature as mythical folk heroes. The failure of the Sam Houston legend to outstrip the facts concerning him resulted from the sheer difficulty in elaborating upon the startling truth. There was little common clay in the make-up of Mirabeau B. Lamar and of Stephen F. Austin, and the absence of a modern Austin legend also may be accounted for by a certain reserve in his personality that did not appeal to his generation as the stuff from which stories might be fabricated.

In other respects, Texans did more than their share of spreading misinformation. Artemus Ward once declared that "the trouble with Americans is that they know so many things that ain't so," and Mrs. Houstoun, a visiting Englishwoman, localized this idea when she wrote that the "bump of invention" was well developed by Texas imaginations.

The Texas tall tale sprang from the earth. It frequently was used to make light of the conflict of man with his environment: his attempts to subject the animals of the wilderness to his domination; his troubles in raising crops; and his experiences in love affairs in a land where women were scarce. Pioneer privations would have been much more difficult to bear if a saving leaven of humor often had not rendered them funny—for the roisterous laughter of the frontier was no great distance from grim experience, from harassment of the ordinary man by exploitation, and from maladies that medical science did not understand. One has to examine the frontiersman's personal letters, not his prose and verse publications, to find much of the contemporary evidence, and even the correspondence is dominated by the incurable optimism of the belief that present ills were precursors of substantial future wealth.

One of the earliest illustrations of Texas tall talk occurred in 1830 in a series of whimsical animal and fish tales that appeared in the San Felipe de Austin *Texas Gazette*. These fish, snake, crawfish, sea-serpent, flying-ox, and turkey-buzzard yarns gave Texas a place in the tall-tale literature that was just beginning to assume

1 *Fisher's Crockett Almanac. 1843*, [20].

Bullock's Hotel, a famous Austin hostelry of the 1840's

Reproduced from William S. Red, *A History of the Presbyterian Church in Texas*, 1936

The building that housed San Augustine University in the middle 1840's, built in 1839 by Sidney A. Sweet and sold to the university in 1843. From a sketch by Rev. G. L. Crocket.

Reproduced from William S. Red, *A History of the Presbyterian Church in Texas*, 1936

TELEGRAPH
AND TEXAS REGISTER.

VOL. II.—NO. 30.—WHOLE NO. 82. WE LABOR FOR OUR COUNTRY. HOUSTON, SATURDAY, AUGUST 12, 1837.

THE TELEGRAPH AND TEXAS REGISTER

Is published weekly, at the city of Houston, by CRUGER & MOORE, *proprietors.*

TERMS.—*Subscription,* five dollars a year, payable in advance.—*Advertising,* one dollar a square for the first insertion, and fifty cents for each continuance: seven lines, or less, is considered a square. Marriage and obituary notices, cards of passengers, and announcements of candidates for political offices, will be charged at the common rates of advertising.

☞All advertisements to be paid for in advance.

AGENTS FOR THE TELEGRAPH:—J. BRENT CLARK, New Orleans. BAILY, GAY & HOXEY, Washington. Col. Geo. W. Poe, Columbia. BENNETT & SHARP, Brazoria. W. W. SHEPARD, Montgomery, Lake creek. Judge CUNEX, Texana. E. T. BRANCH, Liberty. JOS. ROWE, San Augustine.

LAWS OF THE REPUBLIC OF TEXAS.

AN ACT

Establishing the county of Houston.

Be it enacted by the senate and house of representatives of the republic of Texas, in congress assembled, That all that portion of the county of Nacogdoches within the following limits, to wit: Beginning on the east bank of Trinity river, at a point two leagues above the mouth of Kickapoo creek, from thence in a north easterly direction to the Neches at the mouth of Big Pine creek; thence up the Neches to the 32d degree of north latitude; thence due west to the Trinity river; thence down the said river to the place of beginning, form a county to be called and known by the name of Houson county.

SEC. 2. *Be it further enacted,* That the citizens of said county be and are hereby authorized and required to elect seven commissioners, who, (a majority of them concurring,) shall select a site for the seat of justice of said county.

SEC. 3. *Be it further enacted,* That the president be, and he is hereby authorized to order an election for one representative, and all the officers of the county to take place on the 1st Monday of September next and also to appoint commissioners to hold said election.

B. T. ARCHER,
Speaker of the house of representatives.
JESSE GRIMES,
President pro tem. of the senate.

Approved, June 12th, 1837.

SAM. HOUSTON.

AN ACT

Supplementary to the act establishing the county of Houston.

Be it enacted by the senate and house of representatives of the republic of Texas, in congress assembled, That the county of Houston shall be included in the 1st judicial district of this republic and the district courts for said county, shall be holden on the last Mondays of February and August and can continue one week and no longer.

SEC. 2. *Be it further enacted, &c.,* That the county courts for said county shall be holden on the first Monday in January, April, July and October.

SEC. 3. *Be it further enacted,* That the said county shall be attached to the senatorial district of Nacogdoches.

B. T. ARCHER,
Speaker of the house of reps.
JESSE GRIMES,
President pro tem. of the Senate.

Approved, June 12, 1837.

SAM. HOUSTON.

JOINT RESOLUTION

Requiring the Auditor of public accounts to audit the accounts of J. Bryant and S. Francois.

Resolved by the senate and house of representatives of the republic of Texas in congress assembled, That the auditor of public accounts is hereby authorised and required to audit the accounts of John Bryant for three hundred and sixty-four dollars and also to audit the account of Sebastian Francois for the sum of two hundred and fifty nine dollars; and further, that said Bryant and Sebastian are entitled to twelve hundred and eighty acres land each, as bounty land for services rendered this republic as soldiers.

B. T. ARCHER,
Speaker of the house of representatives.
JESSE GRIMES,
President pro tem. of the senate.

Approved 7th June, 1837.

SAM. HOUSTON.

JOINT RESOLUTION

For the benefit of Texian Prisoners taken by the Mexicans.

Resolved, by the senate and house of representatives of the republic of Texas, in congress assembled, That the president be and he is hereby authorised and empowered to send a flag of truce to Matamoros or any other part of Mexico for the purpose of effecting an exchange of prisoners; and that he take all other means that he may deem expedient to procure the release of all citizens of Texas, the crew and other prisoners taken on board the Independence and Julius Cæsar and any other persons, who may be prisoners there connected with this government.

SEC. 2. *Resolved,* That the president be and he is hereby authorized to draw upon the secretary of the treasury for such an amount of money as may be necessary to carry the foregoing resolution into effect.

B. T. ARCHER,
Speaker of the house of representatives.
JESSE GRIMES,
President pro tem. of the senate.

Approved, 12th June, 1837.

SAM. HOUSTON.

JOINT RESOLUTION.

Requiring the Attorney General to report to the next session of congress.

Be it resolved by the senate and house of representatives of the republic of Texas, in congress assembled, That the attorney general is hereby required to report to the next session of congress such a system for the organization and direction of the different accounting officers of the government as is best adapted to the condition of the country.

B. T. ARCHER,
Speaker of the house of representatives.
JESSE GRIMES,
President of the senate pro tem.

Approved, 5th June, 1837.

SAM. HOUSTON.

JOINT RESOLUTION

Respecting fees of Attorneys.

Resolved by the senate and house of representatives of the republic of Texas, in congress assembled, That so much of "an act entitled an act estabilsuing the fees of office," as relates to the perquisites of the attorney general or district attornies shall be understood to enure to the use of the said attornies as perquisites of office, instead of to the use of the republic of Texas.

B. T. ARCHER,
Speaker of the house of representatives.
JESSE GRIMES,
President pro tem. of the senate.

Approved, June 7th, 1837.

SAM. HOUSTON.

JOINT RESOLUTION

For the relief of free persons of Color.

Resolved by the senate and house of representatives of the republic of Texas, in congress assembled, That all free Africans or the descendants of Africans, who were residing within the republic of Texas at the date of the declaration of Independence, and their natural issue, are hereby granted and allowed the privilege of remaining in any part of the republic as long as they choose; on the condition of performing all the duties required of them by law.

B. T. ARCHER,
Speaker of the house of representatives.
JESSE GRIMES,
President pro tem. of the senate.

Approved, 5th June, 1837.

SAM. HOUSTON.

MEXICO.

Translated from the Mercurio de Matamoros,

MEXICO, April 2, 1837.

In the session of the day before yesterday, the Ministers of Foreign Relations and of War appeared before congress, and the former announced that it appeared, from the *Bee* of New Orleans of the 13th of March, that the government of the United States had recognized the Independence of Texas, and has appointed a plenipotentiary to that new republic. That although these documents cannot be regarded as certainly official, not having been communicated as such, but appearing in a journal of the government of Louisiana, they may be considered as authentic; and that this being an act which unequivocally attacks and offends the sovereignty of the nation, the government was employed in preparing a protest against such a proceeding.

After the abovementioned documents were read, the MINISTER OF WAR said:

The national congress is informed, by the communications and documents which have been read by my colleague, the Minister of Foreign Relations, that the government of the United States has at length acknowledged the Independence of Texas. This event was skilfully arranged many years ago, and we have been witnesses of the intrigue and management (manejos) by which the United States have perseveringly endeavored to get possession of a portion of our territory, with the same Punic faith (*fe punica*) with which they took possession of the Floridas. In a time of profound peace, and of the most perfect harmony with the Mexican republic, which was assured by solemn treaties, armed expeditions were set on foot in the United States for the purpose of enabling the rebel colonists to throw off the government of the Mexican laws. Our vessels have been insulted. They have been carried into the ports of the United States, and there treated as pirates, whilst the real pirates displayed a new and unknown flag in the same ports, and received every kind of assistance and protection. The well timed and energetic remonstrances that were addressed directly by the government, or through its agents, to the cabinet at Washington, were scarcely considered as deserving even of an equivocal answer, which, it may be said, had no other object than to amuse and to gain time, whilst the wellknown design continued to be prosecuted. Under the pretext of carrying into effect the treaties subsisting between the two republics, the territory of the Mexican republic has been invaded, for the purpose, as it was said, of preventing hostile movements on the part of the Indians who had been expelled from the United States. It was considered as an insult for the Mexican Minister to protest against so obvious a violation of the faith of treaties, and which was a violation, also, of principles recognised among nations, and particularly of the obligations existing between the two republics.

Under these circumstances, there appeared a message of the president of the United States, in which it is expressly and definitely declared that that Government ought not to recognize the independence of Texas, until it was recognised by some other respectable Power, (*nacion de categoria,*) or unless the Mexican Government was unable to protect and to maintain her rights by force. But subsequently this declaration was contradicted by the message called the *Message of reprisals,* in which we are threatened with war, if we do not give immediate satisfaction for injuries which it is pretended we have done the United States; thus changing the satisfaction that we had a right to demand, into a grievous complaint, for the purpose of justifying before the civilized world the aggressions that were contemplated. The speculators in lands—and it must be recollected that among them are many persons exercising influence in the public affairs of the United States—have availed themselves of every occasion to hasten the catastrophe. They imagined that we were powerless in consequence of the unfortunate affair of San Jacinto, and flattered themselves that the Mexican republic would abandon the defence of her rights, for want of power to enforce them. Finally, the congress of the United States has attacked them, by recognising the independence of Texas, and has thus given offence to a nation distinguished for its complying disposition. In this deplorable state of things, the government declares, in the midst of the national representation, that the recognition of the Independence of Texas by the United States in no wise affects the rights of the nation, or impairs the vigor with which they will be maintained. Already the Mexican soldiers are prepared to tread with their feet this ungrateful soil; and we cherish the hope that the God of battles will secure to the nation the triumph of its cause, as it will be also the triumph of justice. If hereafter the responsibilities and dangers of the nation should be increased, it will not consider the relative strength of the parties; and the Mexicans, for whom glory and the national dignity are most sacred titles, will maintain their rights with energy and decision. The nation does not compromise itself, because compromises at the expense of honor are not noble. Hitherto we have preserved peace; and we will endeavor to preserve it, for it is the greatest blessing of nations: but if we are provoked into a war, we will not decline it. The government knows that, whatever may be the situation of the republic, she has, within herself, as all young nations have, a vital principle of energy that insures their safety; and she will imitate the illustrious examples that so many people have given of a sublime resignation under difficult circumstances. *Gentlemen, the Mexicans will conquer, or will cease to exist.*

PROTEST

Addressed to the government of the United States of America, by the Minister of Foreign Relations of Mexico.

To his Excellency the Secretary of Foreign Relations of the United States.

MEXICO, March 31, 1837.

The undersigned, acting Minister of Foreign Relations of the Mexican republic, has the honor of addressing himself to the honorable Secretary of the same department of the United States of America, for the purpose of expressing the well-grounded surprise with which his Excellency the president *ad interim* of this republic has seen it announced in the *Bee* of New Orleans, that the Independence proclaimed by the insurgents of Texas has been recognized by the Congress of those States, and of the appointment of Mr. Alcee Labranche, as their minister plenipotentiary near the new republic, as it is called.

The proceedings, which have been carried so far, have occasioned the more astonishment to the Mexican government, as there was no reason to fear that they would be adopted, whether we bear in mind the obligations annexed to the friendship existing between this republic and that, and which has been recognized by solemn treaties, or the assurances which have been given officially, by that government at various times, and of which the undersigned takes the liberty of citing the most recent and emphatical.

When, on the 24th of May, of the year last past, Senor Gorostiza, the Mexican Minister near that government, in consequence of the proposition in the Senate of those States, that the Independence of Texas should be acknowledged immediately after the reverse sustained by our troops, on the 21st of April, called the attention of that government to the rights of Mexico upon Texas, and her resources for making them available, the honorable John Forsyth, Secretary of Foreign Affairs, thought fit to declare in his reply to him on the 29th of the same month of May, (which reply the undersigned has now before him,) that he had received instructions from the president of those States, to assure him that no final action would be taken in relation to the question, unless founded upon the same rules and principles which were taken as the guide in the disputes between Spain and the Hispano-American States; and when all the facts should be known, and not before; after a perfect, diligent and impartial examination, and keeping always in mind what was due to the friendly relations subsisting between that republic and this, then it would be that that government would proceed to decide upon a question, which it considered, as well as the Mexican-Minister, of the greatest importance to its immediate relations and in its final results.

This is precisely the language used by the honorable Secretary in the last days of May, of last year, and immediately after the only victory obtained by the insurgents. Now let it be allowed the undersigned to ask: Has the condition of things described by Mr. Forsyth arrived? Are the Texians, with respect to Mexico, in the same position that the Mexicans were, with respect to Spain, when the United States acknowledged her independence? Is there one single circumstance of identity between a nation of more than six millions of inhabitants, who, by their unassisted efforts, threw off the yoke of oppression, after a bloody contest of eleven years, and drove the host of oppressors beyond the ocean, and a few thousand vagrant persons, without country, without religion, without laws, and threatened by a numerous army now on the march, and full of enthusiasm, to recover the laurels which capricious fortune denied it at San Jacinto? Can so atrocious a wrong be done to Mexico, as to consider her so weak, that, incapable of vindicating her rights over the territory usurped by these miserable adventurers, she will consent to the establishment of that ridiculous republic? If the undersigned should stop to furnish himself the solution of these questions, this note would become tiresome by its prolixity, and he would give offence to the well known intelligence of the minister whom he now addresses.

The undersigned has now before him another document, not less interesting than the one already mentioned. The honorable Secretary will easily know that I refer to the message of president Jackson, transmitted to the house of representatives on the 21st of December last, with extracts from the report of the agent that he had appointed and sent, for the purpose of ascertaining the civil, military, and political condition of Texas, in consequence of a resolution of congress, declaring that the independence of Texas ought to be recognised, when satisfactory information should be received that there existed a government capable of discharging the duties, and of fulfilling the obligations of an independent power.

This official document, founded upon the most solid basis of justice and equity, and in which are conspicuous the most sublime principles of international law, was published in the journals of those States, as an additional guaranty given to Mexico that her rights would be respected. Its whole contents are interesting, and give assurances of the neutrality of the United States in the question between Mexico and Texas. After establishing general principles, that document prescribes the act of recognising a new State as one of great delicacy and responsibility. It admits that a premature acknowledgment, if not considered as a justifiable cause of war, is always in danger of being regarded as a proof of a hostile feeling towards one of the belligerents. It assures us that every question relating to the governments of foreign nations has been regarded by the United States as very embarrassing, (*sediciosa,*) and that they have abstained from recognising them, until after obtaining the most satisfactory evidence to enable them not only to decide correctly, but to guard their decisions from every unworthy imputation.

Descending afterwards to particular cases, it reminds us of the prudence they observed in the controversy between Spain and her colonies, waiting not only until the capacity of the new States for self-government should be abundantly established, but until every probability that they would be again subjugated had entirely disappeared; and confining itself, in continuation, to the question of Texas, it describes the disaster which took place at San Jacinto, and its consequences; dwells upon the measures taken by the government to repair it, and expresses the opinion that until the results of the new expedition that was about to be taken should be known, the Independence (of Texas) should be considered as suspended. But why trespass any longer on the patience of the honorable Secretary, in narrating the contents of that official paper, which must be familiar to him, and which, besides, he has at hand, among his archives? It will be sufficient to remind him that, on that occasion, general Jackson believed that prudence dictated to the United States to look to the future, and to maintain their present position, if not until Mexico, or one of the great foreign powers, had acknowledged the

First page of the *Telegraph and Texas Register* for August 12, 1837

huge proportions all over that considerable part of the South still in the frontier stage. One story about turkey buzzards, "hereditary proprietors of the prairies of Texas," and their ability to strip the meat off a deer's bones in machinelike fashion, ended with a hunter's making long strides for his cabin in apprehension that they might relish "by way of dessert . . . the sweet *meat* that covered his own *joints.*" Another turkey-buzzard tale narrated that

A gentleman of this place, a few weeks ago, being in search of his horses, chanced to kill a fine large buck; and as the practice is, with hunters, in such cases, he suspended the deer between two trees with its lower extremity several feet from the ground. In this situation he left his game and came home. On his return, which was in about an hour and a half, he found the *bones* of his buck where he had left them, but they were completely stripped of hide, flesh, muscle and sinew—dry and smooth as "hickory pole with the bark off." The hide had fallen to the ground and was not materially injured. The buzzards, who had thus unceremoniously divested these bones of their outward covering, were seated quietly and contentedly on the branches of the neighboring trees, *picking their teeth,* and smiling.[2]

But the chief character of the tale often won in the conflict. Astounding exploits in the subjugation of wild horses were ascribed to Davy Crockett and other heroes. Captain Caldwell of the Rangers was reported to be superior in many respects to the well-known scout, Deaf Smith. "He caught a mustang stallion the other day [a contemporary letter states], & held him until his fellow hunter shot an other, & skinned a larriette to tie him . . . an exploit not surpassed by Gen. Putnam's wolf story."[3]

Lies about the astounding size and characteristics of crops and farm animals were a part of frontier humor. The sad fate of a hog in a neighboring state resulted in typical bragging on the part of one writer, who, in boasting of the fertility of his land, said:

I had a good sized sow killed in that same bottom land; the old thief stole an ear of corn and took it down to where she slept at night to eat;

---

[2] Both turkey-buzzard stories are in San Felipe de Austin *Texas Gazette,* February 27, 1830. For a crawfish story, see *ibid.,* April 24, 1830.

[3] James W. Robinson to M. B. Lamar, February 24, 1839, in Gulick *et al.* (eds.), *Lamar Papers,* II, 468.

well, she left a grain or two on the ground, and lay down on them; before morning the corn shot up, and the percussion killed her dead. I don't plant any more; natur intended Arkansas for a hunting ground, and I go according to natur.[4]

A more pretentious outlet for tall talk was oratory, which was popular because it furnished diversion and a means of expression for the turbulence of the eighteen forties. Speeches generally were interlarded with bombast and often were spiced with frontier saltiness as well as a smattering of burlesque. Texans had a penchant for organizations, ostensibly formed for a variety of purposes, but actually the chief function of most of them was listening to orations. The Philosophical Society of Texas, organized by a group of prominent men in 1837 "for the collection and diffusion of knowledge," spent most of its short existence in Houston and Austin listening to speeches, although it was claimed seriously that "the field of our researches is as boundless in its extent and as various in character, as the subjects of knowledge are numberless and diversified."[5]

The more serious-minded young men in towns and colleges organized "lyceums" or debating clubs. At their meetings forensic talents were exercised in verbal jousting concerning questions which interested the debaters as well as many of their elders. Among the most popular subjects were: "Ought the Texian government to have put Santa Anna to death in 1836?"; "Has the use of tobacco a more injurious tendency, morally and physically, on manhood than the use of ardent spirits?"; "Which is the stronger passion, love or hatred?"; and the ageless controversy, "Are the minds of females susceptible of as high cultivation as those of men?" The debating societies were chiefly training grounds for young politicians and embryo preachers, all of whom took their speech-making seriously. Noah Smithwick relates in his reminiscences of Austin's Colony that he heard a great noise one night, and on investigation found a boy of sixteen rehearsing the address of the Scythian ambassador to Alexander the Great by the light of the moon before an audience of one Negro boy.

[4] New Orleans *Weekly Picayune*, August 2, 1841 (quoting *Spirit of the Times*).
[5] Houston *Telegraph and Texas Register*, January 13, 1838.

A politician's most ambitious oratorical efforts were made at public dinners or barbecues arranged in his honor, or at holiday celebrations or funerals. The opening words of a funeral address delivered by David G. Burnet (who had been president of the provisional government in 1836) over the body of John A. Wharton still carry a vibrant ring:

Friends and Fellow-Citizens:

The keenest blade on the field of San Jacinto is broken!—the brave, the generous, the talented John A. Wharton is no more! His poor remains lie cold and senseless before you, wrapped in the habiliments of the grave, and awaiting your kind offices to convey them to the charnel-house appointed to all the living. A braver heart never died. A nobler soul, more deeply imbued with the pure and fervent spirit of patriotism, never passed its tenement of clay, to the more genial realms of immortality. He was young in years, and, as it were, at the very threshhold of his fame: and still it is a melancholy truth, to which every heart in this assembly will respond in painful accordance, that a mighty man has fallen amongst us. Many Princes of the earth have perished in their prime, surrounded with all the gorgeous splendors of wealth and power, and their country has suffered no damage. But surely it will be engraven on the tablets of our history, that Texas wept when Wharton died![6]

Not all speeches were well received, however, and even a statesman as eminent as former President Lamar once failed to evoke audible response from the supposedly sympathetic audience. On a very hot day in the summer of 1843, he was guest of honor at a public barbecue at La Grange. In accordance with elaborate preparations for his reception, a welcoming salute was fired at noon as Lamar and his entourage rode into town. Afterward a "venerable citizen" introduced the distinguished visitor to the crowd in a most laudatory manner. Lamar then delivered a speech in which he defended various acts of his administration, attacked the vindictiveness of the incumbent Houston administration, and concluded with some "very happy" compliments to the ladies in the audience. Immediately following the peroration, the gentleman who had introduced the speaker jumped up and called for "three

---

[6] *Ibid.,* December 22, 1838.

cheers for General Lamar." Embarrassingly enough, the listeners must have been singularly apathetic, for an Englishman who was present recorded that "whether it was the suffocating heat of the weather or any other cause, there was no response."[7]

Lesser politicians, including those running for militia-company offices, were expected to be somewhat less profound and grammatical in their harangues, and it was axiomatic that free whisky and tobacco provided admirable stimulants to the electorate's appreciation of their oratory. Speeches delivered under these conditions were not always completely serious. This was the period (according to a modern critic) when "serious oratory rose and fell in . . . cascades, but so far-reaching was the burlesque that it was often impossible to tell the one from the other without a wide context of knowledge as to the subject and the speakers. Popular declamation of the '30's and '40's has often been considered as bombast when it should be taken as comic mythology."[8] One rendition of a Texas speech, which probably was never delivered seriously, found its way into American newspapers:

The way some of the speechifiers in Texas use the English language is curious. Just read the winding up of a recruiting sergeant's harangue to his neighbors in an endeavor to enlist them against the Mexicans. After having launched out against the religion of the common enemy, in none of the mildest terms, our hero winds up with, "Corncrackers, Hoosiers, Pukes, Wolverines, and Suckers, if the voice of piety cannot move you to exterminate those cursed, cruel, Catholic yallar skinned, d———d illiterate Mexicans aforesaid, if the sacred voice of Texan liberty strikes no sympathetic chord in your bosom, if the cries of bleeding humanity cannot draw you to deliver the freemen of Texas from the unparalleled, unprecedented oppression of hard work, why, you are not the men I take you for, that's all. But no, I see the fire of patriotism gleam in your eyes, I see you rise indignantly *en masse* to resist interference of property, even to the blood of the cursed yaller skinned Mexican emancipators, I see the breath of Texan freedom animate you. Come then and rally round the standard of an insulted country, and fists clenched, and teeth set, swear to fight knee deep in blood for that con-

[7] Bollaert, "Notes on Texas, 1843–1844," 13.
[8] Constance Rourke, *American Humor,* 64.

stitution which was founded on the bones of your martyred countrymen, and cemented with the blood of expiring saints and heroes. 'Let's
liquor.' "[9]

The heroic aspects of the existence of Texas as an independent
republic had seriocomic relief in the affair of Count de Saligny,
the French chargé d'affaires, and the pigs of the Austin innkeeper,
Richard Bullock.

I have for a long time suffered [Saligny wrote to the Texas government in his complaint against Bullock and his pigs] . . . from the
many hogs with which this town [Austin] is infested. Every morning
one of my domestics spends two hours in putting up and nailing the
palings of the fence, which these animals threw down for the purpose
of eating the corn of my horses; one hundred and forty pounds of nails
have been used for this purpose. One day these hogs entered even to
my chamber, and ate my towels and destroyed my papers.

De Saligny charged specifically that pigs belonging to the owner
of the hotel had destroyed his garden, and that his servant, who
had killed a number of the invaders, had been attacked by Bullock
in reprisal. In this encounter (reported a New Orleans newspaper)
Bullock had fallen upon the "unlucky murderer" of the pigs,
"bunging up his eyes and phlabotomizing his nose in a manner to
appease the ghosts of the slaughtered innocents." Saligny neglected
to state in his complaint that Bullock's original grievance was the
French diplomat's refusal to pay a bill at the hotel, before he had
established himself next door.

According to the official government version of the pig controversy, published in 1841, the outraged French diplomat considered
that the honor of France had been traduced and demanded that
the hotel operator be punished in accordance with "the enormity
of the offence," which he denounced as "an odious violation of the
law of nations." Bullock's defense was that the Count should have
kept his fence in better repair. The Texas government, which had
had previous difficulties with de Saligny, properly refused to punish
Bullock without a trial. The French chargé, deeming it beneath his
official dignity to attend a hearing, demanded and received his pass-

[9] Camden (South Carolina) *Commercial Courier*, December 23, 1837.

ports.[10] Count de Saligny had other alleged grievances against the government of the frontier Republic, but used this incident as grounds for disruption of diplomatic relations. Meanwhile, many a frontiersman enjoyed a horselaugh at the spectacle of an aristocratic French whippersnapper receiving his "comeuppance" at the hands of an Austin hotel proprietor and his porkers.

Love-making, matrimony, and bachelors vied with barrooms and drunkards as subjects of newspaper levity. A love letter with which a northeastern Texas newspaper regaled its readers offers an excellent example of the tendency to burlesque romance:

My dear Ichabod. How I want to see your big grey eyes. O, how horror stricken am I at your long absence. I want to see you and feel your heart bump. Oh, sweet Ichabod, now do come out and let us get married if you love me. God bless you, if you are not sufficiently blest in being so sweet. Oh you marry-gold, you hollyhock, you tulip, you cabbage. Oh you sweet owl, do come and comfort your dying, sorrow smitten Caroline. Oh Ichabod, but how I do love your big red lips. Oh, you trim, tall fellow, full of manna of sweet love, how I do want to see you, you moddle of perfection. You have been gone this two months, and to me, poor me, it does seem like a hundred years. Your dear presence would to me be more than the cooling spring to the parched traveller of the desert; more than the green grass to the hungry ox; more than the pebbled pool to the wanton duck; yes more than a lump of sugar to a spoiled child! Why then, will you not come, yes, fly as swift as the lightening to kiss the tear from the dimpled cheeks of your mad love. Oh bleak and wild is the house, the garden, the woods, and the world without thee. Oh, yes, bless thee, my dumplin, my jewsharp, my all, my rooster, my gentleman.

Caroline[11]

Local news was occasionally treated in semihumorous style by the newspapers, but care had to be taken not to offend local pride. William D. Wallach, a Matagorda editor who was in a rival town during an Indian scare, was handicapped by no such restraint in his description of the raid in a series of articles entitled

---

[10] *Correspondence Relative to Difficulties with M. de Saligny, Chargé D'Affaires of France*, 11, 14, 26, 36; New Orleans *Bee*, April 24, 1841.

[11] Clarksville *Northern Standard*, July 8, 1846.

"Indians in Austin." One night (the editor wrote) he was in a well-known politician's Austin office, discussing "the shortest way of making every body rich without work, for that seems to be the upshot of most modern scheming on that subject." Their conversation was interrupted by the sound of rifle and pistol shooting, much vociferous swearing, and Colonel L. P. Cooke's cry that Indians "are here murdering my family." Editor Wallach was restrained from rushing to the rescue by the politician, who assured him that if he ran out, "you'll be sure to find drunken men enough to shoot you for an Indian." So they blew out the light, covered the fire, and remained quiet until a band of armed rescuers came rushing pell-mell up the street. The editor and the politician joined this war-like crew, who were engaged in loud threats against the Indians and in complacently honoring each other with military titles. "Now, General," they were saying, "Yes, Captain," "We'll make mince meat out of them, Major," and "Certainly, Colonel." (A contemporary letter written by another eyewitness states that a general panic prevailed while "the men ran through town like a gang of wild Mustangs," and that Captain Nicholson wounded Colonel Clendennen in the excitement.)

Soon it was evident, the story went on, that the few Indian marauders had fled into the woods and that deeds of valor were not to be required of the Texans that night. Wallach hurried back to the center of town, where most of the frontier capital's inhabitants were assembled in and around the yard of Bullock's Hotel.

There were frightened women [the editor related], yelping children and armed men in profusion, for the whole house and its ample court was overflowing. There was the graceful, nonchalant Major H———, whose mild, yet brilliant blue eye, and mouth which always smiles whether he will or not, looking so "devil may care" as he swaggered to and fro among the feminine, all bristling as he was with knives and pistols. His red sash, grey undress military jacket, and shining sombrero, gave his appearance a decided guerilla turn, and we thought as we gazed on him, what an admirable study he would have made for an artist, intending to portray a dashing, love-making, fire-eating, modern novel hero.

Leaving the Major to assure the ladies of their safety, we directed

our attention to other objects around us, and saw somebody whose . . .
astonishing nerves riveted our attention. . . . [He] was seated at the
piano, banging away most unconcernedly amid the din, which was
"confusion worse confounded." What a remarkable taste for music!
Mozart himself, who used to eat, drink, and sleep on it, would not
have been so completely absorbed by *"la douce passione,"* under such
circumstances; for the rattling tramp of three or four hundred armed
men, as they hurried to and fro—the crying of lots of children, not
knowing what to make of the muss—and the anxious clatter of fifty
or sixty female tongues, formed an accompaniment which appeared
to us, sufficient to drive all Italy mad.

We involuntarily turned our eyes from the piano to the various
groups formed in and about the house and yard.

Wallach saw all sorts of people in the crowd—soldiers, border
ruffians, government clerks, newspapermen, Mexican traders, "cow
drivers and ox drivers," and one man who kept shouting, "Hurrah
for Old Virginia!" Then the editor noticed that

some of the soldiery seeing the red men had escaped, had turned to
combatting another enemy, which, they, apparently with one consent,
conceived to be red enough for exercising on.

They were attacking brandy and its kindred allies. Attacking it—
some in squads of two or three, some in sections of five or six, some
in platoons of twelve or fourteen, and again, others by companies.

And they fought manfully indeed. They managed it upon the regular fire and fall back principle; for no sooner would one squad discharge their pieces, but another standing ready to take their places,
would advance heroically up to the breastwork, behind which, the
enemy were drawn up in perfect military order, and each selecting his
particular adversary, would, in the twinkling of an eye, toss him down.

For a long time the engagement was kept up on our side with great
spirit; until by the increase of noise and confusion it was plain to per-
ceive the battle was at its height. In a little while, however, a few of
our men, who, up to the middle of the engagement had manifested the
most vociferous heroism, began to show very evident signs of declining
prowess, more especially by reeling up to the charge out of their squad
or platoon's regular turn. . . . It was therefore not to be wondered at,
that these gallant fellows should give in, or rather give out. . . .

Some of our disabled might be seen laying helpless in the gutter—others sitting stupidly . . . one by one they withdrew from the field, leaving it in the enemy's possession.[12]

Newspaper humor often was inspired by current events. One news item was presented in this manner: *"Look out for squalls. Lately arrived in New Orleans—as we learn from the best authority—a boat load of cradles, labelled for 'Texas.'"* If such a play on words begets no spark of laughter, it should be remembered that immortal "terrible" jokes must be historically good since their variants have come down through the centuries. Newspapers of the day were given to even more egregious puns, such as "Why is the present administration worse than that of General Houston? Because it is *La*-mer." In addition, humorous poetry, such as "The Humbugged Husband" or "To an Aching Tooth," was attempted, and many of the advertisements, which occupied a substantial portion of newspaper space, were written in what purported to be a humorous vein.

Essays, poems, and editorials in the newspapers reflected something of the thoughts and aspirations of the literate. The editorials were chiefly devoted to politics and comments on various local happenings, but flourishes toward gentility were made in essays (usually extracted from United States newspapers and magazines) on such diverse topics as "Mozart," "The Sovereigns of the World," "The Character of George IV," "Indian Mounds," "The White Polar Bear," "Home," "A Sister's Love," and "Woman's Enduring Affection." Occasionally a religious contributor sent in an article intended to improve the moral tone of the community, but the most pretentious literary efforts of the newspapers were in printing large numbers of poems, one of the most commonly quoted poets being Mrs. Hemans.

Most of the native poetry that found its way into print appeared in newspapers. One exception was Hugh Kerr's ambitious *Poetical Description of Texas, and Narrative of Many Interesting Events in that Country* (1838), which was reputed to have been the occasion of an uncomplimentary couplet:

---

[12] Matagorda *Colorado Gazette and Advertiser*, March 27, April 3, 10, 17, 1841. The letter quoted is Jacob Snively to James H. Starr, February 23, 1841, Starr Papers.

O Kerr, Kerr, Kerr
What did you write these poems fur?

Texas poetry dealt with manifold aspects of human existence—the country, the frontier, romance, habits, and the settlers' philosophy. Nearly all of it was of doubtful literary merit, and was most disappointing in describing Indian life. Although there was a dearth of love verse until the early eighteen forties, a romantic and sentimental vein in the Southern style predominated in most of the poetry, regardless of subject matter. Mirabeau B. Lamar, who wrote verse both before and after his election to the presidency, Harry Richardson of San Augustine, and Reuben M. Potter probably were the best poets in the Republic. The opening lines of Lamar's "My Gem of Delight," written in 1845, furnishes ample illustration of his style:

> *Oh, bright is the maiden who wakens my sighs,*
> *No planet can equal the light of her eyes;*
> *Her form is elastic—her spirit elate—*
> *The spring of the willow is seen in her gait;*
> *The tones of her laughter are dulcimer-sounds,*
> *And gladness is scattered wherever she bounds.*[13]

On the other hand, some of the verse was warlike and anti-Mexican in tone, particularly in the early years of the Republic. One example was the poem, "To Santa Anna," the first and last verses of which follow:

> *Back, back to thy covert, thou blood-hound of death,*
> *There is woe in thy footstep, and guilt in thy breath;*
> *Thou warrest with women, thou curse of the brave,*
> *Thy pity is blood, and thy mercy the grave. . . .*
>
> *The aged shall curse thee, thou thirster for gore—*
> *The worm shall be sicken'd with gnawing thy core,*
> *The tombstone shall blush that points to thy grave,*
> *Thou scorn of the true, the wise, and the brave!*[14]

[13] Clarksville *Northern Standard,* January 15, 1853.
[14] Signed "J. E. D.," Washington, May 7, 1836, in Columbia *Telegraph and Texas Register,* August 16, 1836.

On the whole, serious newspaper poetry signally failed to reflect the spirit of the people and their environment. Texas was still too much a part of the South to break away from the prevailing Southern romanticism. The major concession to realism was afforded by humorous poetry on subjects such as the ague, love-making, bachelors, widows, and women's clothes. A humorous poem written in sentimental style was this:

THE WEEPING MAIDEN

I saw a fair maid weeping,
  Down by yon old oak tree,
One day when I was reaping—
  The cause I flew to see.
She turned as I approached her,
  Then blushing, dropped her head;
While I, in tones of kindness,
  Unto the maiden said:

"What grieveth thee, fair maiden?
  Ah, maiden, tell me true,
Can sorrow rest within the breast
  Of one so fair as you?"
"Yes! yes!" she cried, "Kind stranger,
  I've drunk of sorrow's cup—
Just now my ma, with ruthless hand,
  Cut my new bustle up!"[15]

While Texas newspapers frequently printed whole columns (copied from American newspapers and magazines) dealing with events, industries, and arts in foreign countries, local news was doled out in meager quantities. The facts concerning local events in the closely knit social fabric of frontier communities already had been relayed verbally from person to person. Adolphus Sterne, postmaster at Nacogdoches, made this entry concerning the newspaper of neighboring San Augustine in his diary: "the eastern mail came in nothing but Redlanders, hardly worth reading as all the news they contain has been known here for several days past." Very frequently both local and foreign news was copied from other

[15] Clarksville *Northern Standard*, November 4, 1843.

Texas newspapers. The Houston *Weekly Times of* April 30, 1840, took this characteristic thrust at one of its competitors: "We received a [Austin] Sentinel yesterday, the [Houston] Star is the echo of its columns to day."

The columns perused with most avid interest were those concerned with politics. Practically all newspapers aligned themselves with a political faction, and, particularly in the heated election year of 1841, they did not hesitate to go to extreme lengths in excoriating opposing politicians. The Austin *Texas Centinel* of July 5, 1841, which was supporting David G. Burnet for the presidency, stated that Sam Houston would *"blaspheme his God,* by the most horrible oaths, that ever fell from the lips of man." On the other hand, the *Houstonian* of August 18, 1841, had the following to say to Burnet (in a diatribe written by Houston under the pen name "TRUTH") : "You prate about the faults of other men, *while the blot of foul unmitigated treason rests upon you.* You political brawler and canting hypocrite, whom the waters of Jordan could never cleanse from your political and moral leprosy."

Some of the choicest editorial adjectives were saved for opposition editors. The following editorial under the heading "Ourselves" was written by Charles DeMorse, one of the Republic's leading editors, about an East Texas rival:

We learn that during our absence at the west, a personal attack upon our integrity, of the vilest and dirtiest character, has been made by the editor of the Red Lander. We have not yet seen the article, having been unable so far, to find the paper. What motive the contemptible scoundrel had, in making such base and villainous charges against us . . . we do not know, but . . . a cowhide will settle the matter, the first time we lay our eyes upon him. . . . The article, we shall make one answer to. . . . and shall after that pay no attention to either it, or its author, who we are informed, is a low blackguard, utterly destitute of character. . . .[16]

A suspicion is reasonable, however, that some of the abuse heaped upon opposition editors' heads was feigned and written for the amusement of readers. If so, a part of newspaper brawls

[16] *Ibid.,* December 3, 1842.

and jibing must be classified with burlesque oratory as a form of humor. The following statement about a Matagorda newspaper editor made by the editor of the Austin *City Gazette,* on July 5, 1841, might not have been entirely serious:

The "Fat Boy," alias W. D. Wallach, the slick-haired, silly-pated, *gum-elastic*-conscience editor of the Colorado Gazette . . . is beginning to whistle to his patrons for better support.

The little chap is hard pushed these hard times, and is fast finding that the "gum-*glory*" of abusing and villifying honest men is not quite so profitable as he had thought. He, therefore, turns into downright plain cheating of the government. He closes his doleful appeal for *money,* by assuring his patrons, good easy souls, that any Post Master will frank a letter inclosing their subscription.

Quere.—Is the Fat Boy a very small rogue, or very great simpleton —or are the two delectable characteristics about equally blended in his composition? We opine to the latter conclusion.

Quere.—What right has any Post Master to frank the Fat Boy's letters?

Another editor found that his rival was far too imaginative:

The Editor of the "Richmond Telescope" is certainly a *"genius"* of no ordinary kind. He says he has no doubt a machine may be constructed by means of which communications may be made by word of mouth from one end of the earth to the other. This goes ahead of the moon story all hollow.[17]

Meanwhile, a few Texans were attempting to write something more edifying than editorial vilification. Many of them turned for encouragement to the second President of the Republic, Mirabeau B. Lamar, who "was almost the only patron of the arts in that broad land" and himself a poet whose literary labors had been interrupted by his cognizance of the doubt expressed by some of his critics that a poet might also be a statesman.[18] His correspond-

[17] Houston *Morning Star,* August 23, 1839. Even such an enlightened publication as the New Orleans *Daily Picayune* in its issue of May 23, 1843, placed "aerial steam carriages" in the same category as "Miller absurdities" and "Mormon humbugs."

[18] Philip Graham, *Life and Poems of Mirabeau B. Lamar,* 71, 90.

ence contains a number of "poeticals" sent to him for criticism.

Lamar's influence also was pronounced in the field of history. His confidential secretary, Edward Fontaine, at one time contemplated writing a history of Texas on the basis of information obtained directly from him as well as from government records in Austin. Henry S. Foote (later governor of Mississippi) wrote to Lamar in 1840 that his history of Texas would soon be published and that he had taken Lamar's advice to devote "more care to style of composition than I at first designed."[19] Lamar himself did much historical research, including interviews with participants in contemporary events. In 1837, when he was vice president, he began to collect source materials for a biography of Stephen F. Austin and a detailed history of Texas. He had much to do with preserving two of the richest collections of historical data for the period 1820–45, which have been published in modern times as the *Papers of Mirabeau Buonaparte Lamar* and the *Austin Papers*. Meanwhile, he wrote an introduction to his projected history in which he emphasized the necessity for saving contemporary records from destruction lest "a chaotic jumble of falsehood and truth is transmitted to futurity as the early history of the Country." Although Mirabeau B. Lamar never actually wrote either of his projected books, his services to the historians of the future and their readers were notable.

The spectacle of an independent republic existing on the American-Mexican frontier stimulated the writing of books, pamphlets, and articles in the United States, Great Britain, France, and Germany. Many of these publications contained a statement of the historical background of the Republic. Here again Lamar's advice frequently was sought. He encouraged Mrs. Mary Austin Holley to publish her second volume on Texas in 1836, and Henry Thompson wrote to Lamar from Philadelphia and New York and William Kennedy from London concerning their publications about Texas.

Kennedy's *Texas: the Rise, Progress, and Prospects of the Re-*

19 Foote to Lamar, April 25, 1840, in Gulick *et al.* (eds.), *Lamar Papers*, III, 379. Lamar wrote most of Chapter X of Foote's history and allowed him access to historical materials that he had collected.—Foote, *Texas and the Texans*, I, 197–98.

public of Texas (1841) was designed chiefly to promote amicability of Texan-British relations, and was based on a considerable amount of research as well as the author's first-hand observations as a British diplomat in Texas. Although such anti-Texas journals in England as the London *Atlas* thought that another Englishman, N. Doran Maillard, had written a more accurate history of the Republic, Kennedy's flavorsome work has retained a place, in some respects, as a standard and authoritative account. It was one of the two outstanding writings about Texas prior to 1850, the other being the travel and geological account of the German scientist, Ferdinand Roemer. These books, and most other cognate works of importance, were written for propaganda purposes or as guides to emigrants. Among the guides, Edward Stiff's *The Texan Emigrant* (1840) ranks high in reading interest. Its style has been characterized by J. Frank Dobie as "worse than abominable . . . both turgid and prolix." Yet the very pomposity and lack of restraint of its phraseology is intriguing.

Several other contemporary accounts of the Republic of Texas written by foreigners deserve consideration. Charles Hooton, an English novelist and essayist, lived at Galveston for several months during 1841, and six years later published *St. Louis' Isle, or Texiana,* in England. The book is generally unfavorable to Texas, which he found to be a "refuge for rascality and criminality of all kinds." The author wrote most of *St. Louis' Isle* while sick-abed, in the hope, he said, of deterring English emigrants from following in his "fatal footsteps" to Texas. Although six years had elapsed since his observations were made, yet, he wrote, "there still remain the same sun, the same brick-burned earth, the same pestilent, sweltering bayous, in which the fish that cannot escape get cooked (though not literally boiled) to death, as before."[20] Despite the unreliability of many of Hooton's stories and the bias of a person obviously unfitted for frontier life, *St. Louis' Isle* was written in a vigorous and facile style. As an antidote, one may read Mrs. Matilda C. F. Houstoun's *Texas and the Gulf of Mexico,* which generally de-

[20] Hooton, *St. Louis' Isle, or Texiana, viii–ix,* 15; obituary notices in *New Monthly Magazine,* Vol. LXXIX, No. 315 (March, 1847), 397–98, and *Gentleman's Magazine,* New Series, Vol. XXVII, No. [4] (April, 1847), 442–43; biographical sketch in *Dictionary of National Biography,* IX, 1202.

fends the Texans and their revolution. This genial English traveler first visited Galveston and Houston in 1843–44. While she thought many frontier crudities were deplorable, she was agreeably impressed with the Texas scene as a whole. But it must be remembered that she traveled with her husband on a 219-ton, 100-foot "schooner yacht," which carried a crew of eleven, while Hooton evidently was poor and never completely recovered from an attack of "ague and fever," which "in that savage country . . . is appropriately termed 'The Shakes.' "

Although all of these books were written by persons who had been in Texas, not one of the authors was in any sense a Texan. The citizens of the Republic produced no substantial body of literature of their own. Aside from contributions to newspapers, their writing efforts were confined chiefly to the publication of political pamphlets and accounts of various expeditions against the Mexicans. In 1844 George Wilkins Kendall, an editor of the New Orleans *Daily Picayune,* published the *Narrative of the Texan Santa Fé Expedition,* a work of real distinction and a best seller for its time. The author's interest in Texas was so lively that his book can be regarded with justification as a native product.

In the early eighteen forties Kendall had published in the *Daily Picayune* a number of well-written and realistic stories about Texas and adjoining territories. Products of trips to the Republic and his participation in the ill-fated expedition to Santa Fé by a body of Texans, Kendall's sketches contained some of the most vigorous and sympathetic indigenous writing about the frontier Republic and its borders. Some of his accounts of aspects of the Santa Fé expedition were incorporated into Captain Frederick Marryat's *The Travels and Adventures of Monsieur Violet, in California, Sonora, and Western Texas,* the publication of which in Europe in 1843 provoked vigorous controversy in both England and Texas.

The most realistic section of Marryat's book was plagiarized from newspaper stories by Kendall and Josiah Gregg, both of whom wrote with considerable authority, but it also contained many contumelious and absurd statements, such as the description of the Comanche Indians as remarkable for their intelligence and refinement. Sharpest cut of all, Marryat's "Monsieur Violet" impugned Texan hospitality. This was particularly galling to Texans,

178

because they readily identified "Monsieur Violet" as one "Count de Narbonne," a shrewd adventurer, who in 1842 had swindled gullible citizens throughout the frontier Republic. Texas newspapers exposed the book; and Dr. Ashbel Smith, who was Texan minister to England and France, assailed it in the London press.[21] Later the book was parodied in the Texas press: on July 20, 1844, the Matagorda *Weekly Despatch* began the "Journal of the Seeings, Sayings, and Doings, of the Count de *Gnaw-Bone,* in the Prairies and Bottoms of Texas . . . Being a Sequel to 'Monsieur Violet.' " Tall tales about the frontier did not originate solely in Western imaginations.

Painting and sculpture languished in the United States during this period. This was the era of the portrait painters, a few of whom gained precarious livelihoods in Texas. One such artist, Charles Kneass, appeared at Brazoria as early as the summer of 1835, and offered to paint portraits, "likeness warranted," for a minimum price of twelve dollars. Shortly after the Texas Revolution, Major J. Strange attempted to create likenesses of the Mexican leaders, Santa Anna, Almonte, and Cos. Under the auspices of President Houston, a portrait and miniature painter named Jefferson Wright became the semiofficial artist of the Republic and his "gallery of *National Portraits*" hung for a period in the capitol at Houston. He produced at least two pictures of his patron, whose penchant for posing in all sorts of costumes made him one of the most painted and photographed individuals in ante-bellum public life. Wright's paintings were on exhibition at various times from 1837 through 1842, and possibly longer.[22] Although there were a few portrait painters in the coastal towns in the early

---

21 Ashbel Smith to Sam Houston, October 20, 1843 (letter-book MS), Ashbel Smith Papers; London (England) *Morning Herald,* November 3, 1843; *Civilian and Galveston Gazette,* December 9, 1843, January 24, 1844; Copeland, *Kendall of the Picayune,* 59–115 *passim.*

22 Houston *Telegraph and Texas Register,* May 9, June 3, October 7, 1837, February 17, 1838, June 2, 1841; Houston *Morning Star,* January 6, 1840; Houston *Weekly Times,* April 30, 1840; [Sam Houston] to Anna Raguet, February 1, 1838, in Williams and Barker (eds.), *Writings of Sam Houston,* II, 190; Mrs. Mary Austin Holley to Mrs. William M. Brand, December 30, 1837, Holley Papers; William Bollaert, Private Journals, entry for June 16, 1842.

eighteen forties, the demand for their work was lessened after 1843 by the recently improved daguerreotype pictures. At the same time, the newly established French and German communities boasted a few professionally trained artists and craftsmen.

Misguided patriotism led one sculptor to finish an artistic production which later generations of Texans, who have become eager to preserve their historic sites, must necessarily regret. Late in 1843 a man named Cox was preparing to exhibit in New Orleans "a beautiful monument, the production of which has cost him two years' labor. It is constructed of white stone taken from the ruins of the Alamo." The inscription on this memorial ended with the rallying cry which orators for a hundred years have found effective: "Thermopylae had her messenger of defeat, but the Alamo had none." A friendly New Orleans newspaper urged that every Texan and friend of Texas should inspect the monument, and that the government of Texas should purchase it, "as we believe the Government is now aiming to do."[23]

The frontier social environment was not one to nurture scientific work of a high order. Scientists such as Jean Louis Berlandier and Charles Wright passed practically unnoticed by the people among whom they worked, and their achievements were recognized by only a few enlightened colleagues in Eastern seaboard and European intellectual centers. One exception was William P. Huff of San Felipe, and even his forte apparently was commercial showmanship rather than science, at which he was no more than a talented amateur. In 1845 he was exhibiting his "noble and wonderful collection" of extinct mammals—including the remains of a mastadon and a Pleistocene elephant—in Houston. Huff made a business of showing his Brazos River finds to the curious for more than twelve years, first in San Felipe, and later in Houston, Galveston, and New Orleans.[24] The Huff collection eventually was

[23] New Orleans *Daily Picayune*, December 2, 1843.

[24] Houston *Telegraph and Texas Register*, September 9, 1837, April 15, October 14, 1840, November 26, 1845; *Civilian and Galveston Gazette*, December 10, 1845; William Bollaert, *Observations on the Geography of Texas*, 115; Carl Solms-Braunfels, *Texas, 1844–1845*, 66; Samuel W. Geiser, "Audubon in Texas," *Southwest Review*, Vol. XVI, No. 1 (October, 1930), 132.

deposited in the British Museum and described in scientific publications. Several other sets of fossil remains also were discovered in the Colorado River watershed, near Bastrop.

Ironically enough, the Republic of Texas paid more attention to the contemporary pseudo science of phrenology than to the work of a number of able naturalists. Their worth was not to be brought to the attention of the public until, a century later, Samuel W. Geiser set them to stalking realistically through the pages of his magnificent book, *Naturalists of the Frontier* (1937). In the late eighteen thirties the "science" of phrenology was generally accepted in the United States, though not without skepticism in some quarters. Its converts included such well-known individuals as Nicholas Biddle, Henry Schoolcraft, Horace Mann, Joseph Smith, Clara Barton, and Black Hawk. In Texas, one of the striking cases of the practice of phrenology occurred in March, 1838, at Houston. Four men, including two doctors, went to the near-by execution grounds and cut off the heads of two convicted murderers who had been hanged, in order to dissect and examine their heads. The examination fully substantiated their belief in the validity of the science, because the heads of both murderers allegedly showed why they had gone to their doom. One, in particular, had "a very bad head—all moral powers very deficient—the bumps of distinctiveness and firmness remarkably large—no reverence, veneration, and but little perception with no comparison or ideality—his animal organs well developed."[25]

In the closing years of the Republic's independent existence, lecturers on phrenology appeared in Texas. In 1844 the Reverend Levi Chase spoke in several East and South Texas towns, combining with his mission as a Universalist minister a series of "scientific lectures on Phrenology and Physiognomy," for each of which he charged an admission fee of twenty-five cents. In the following year Dr. A. Crane, "a gentleman eminently distinguished as a professor of the science of Phrenology," lectured in most of the larger towns in Texas. If newspaper accounts can be given credence, the Republic received his message with gracious earnestness. Though the Houston *Morning Star* previously had defined phrenology as

[25] Herndon, Diary, 1837–38, 59–60.

"the *science* of raising the wind by itinerant lecturing," that newspaper now succumbed to the spell cast by the personality of Dr. Crane. The editor of the Washington *Texas National Register* urged that the professor be given substantial financial support, for the reason that "much information may be thus obtained of the highest value to all who would assist in directing and moulding the intellectual elements of society so as to insure its present and lasting happiness." In Houston the man of science spoke to a "large and delighted auditory" at the Methodist Church. A few days later, after he had satisfactorily demonstrated a correlation between the heads and characters of dozens of Texans, including President Anson Jones, a subscription was raised to induce him to deliver a few lectures apart from his regular series.[26] Even as our generation has been known to place its faith in pseudopsychological theories of equal plausibility, Republican Texas had little skepticism about the scientific merits of phrenology. While the genuine scientists worked in the dim background, the charlatans received the plaudits of the crowds.

The Republic of Texas was a singing country. Neither special talent nor great array of instruments was required for the common man to give musical vent to robust spirits, while his vocal chords were in working order. Yet along the musical frontier in Austin's Colony were found German harps, a piano or two, and several guitars, flutes, and fiddles; by 1846 nearly every settlement had at least one piano and other instruments, and instances were not unknown where the mahogany legs of pianos rested on the dirt floors of log cabins. The majority of pianos were in the homes of the coastal planters or of the affluent residents of coastal towns such as General Thomas Jefferson Green of Velasco, S. Rhoads Fisher of Matagorda, and Michel B. Menard of Galveston. But fiddles (infrequently called violins) were the characteristic and most common musical instrument.

All forms of music were welcomed. The popular songs of the day (including many with a definite frontier flavor, such as "Rosin

[26] Galveston *Daily Galvestonian,* April 4, 1840 (quoting Houston *Morning Star*); Washington *Texas National Register,* May 15, 1845; Houston *Morning Star,* July 8, 12, 1845; Houston *Telegraph and Texas Register,* July 9, 1845.

the Bow") were whistled and sung. At a higher level, musical education was made available in all of the female seminaries and colleges and by a few professional music teachers in the towns. The Houston theaters had their own orchestras, and in 1840 there was an "amateur band" at Austin. In some of the towns visiting actresses and semiprofessional songsters gave concerts, and local groups occasionally presented public song programs. A Galveston public song concert, in which two of the performers were a German musician (who was also a militia colonel) and his wife, was described in a manuscript written by a third participant:

Readers pardon me—for now I am obliged to speak somewhat directly of myself. I was invited to take part with the professionals! on the occasion & solicited to sing a Spanish song or two there being several families from San Antonio (where Spanish is spoken), who intended to patronize the concert—which was held at the Tremont Hotel. The Audience arrived when it was first treated to the tuning of what had been once a piano, but more appropriately now might be called a collection of tin kettles. The German Colonel's wife was the only prima donna and the opening piece, a quartette; before it was concluded there was a regular break down. Never was so indulgent an audience, & rounds of applause followed. The Colonel now had to give the "Largo al Factotum," but what with the tinkling tones of the piano, & his own tremulous (husky) voice, having had a severe fit of the ague in the morning, he made, to use a common expression, a missifit. Still he came in for his share of applause.

According to the program it was my turn. A Spanish song was given at the end of which "Bueno, Bueno, mui bonita" from the Spaniards—but from the Texan citizens resounded "Give us a song from the old country." I gave them one breathing as much of Trumpets, drums, powder & shot &c . . . encore'd of course. Amongst other protestations of . . . everlasting friendship, were the following: "Now if that Stranger wants a Town lot here, I'll give him one," "If he stops in the Country and will run for Congress he has my vote," "They say he's a lawyer, why we'll make him a Judge ere long."

It was now suggested that as the Piano was in such "a fix" another should be sent for, & in the interim, audience and singers should retire to the Bar of the Hotel and "take a drink." This, however, only extended to the mob part of the Audience (& I may here mention that during the considerable time I was in Texas I never saw a woman in the Bar room of an Inn or Hotel, or one in any way under the influence of liquor). The second piano arrived, when after much ... thumping, it was pronounced to be tuned, when a flute solo by a violent tempered Irishman, with piano accompaniment was announced—it commenced—went on a few bars—they tried back—if anything the second piano was worse than the first. Our Nicholson became infuriated and he cursed the piano. Up jumped the Lady performer horror stricken at the imprecations. He rushed out of the room swearing that he "would be d———d if he would be made a fool of by any such piano on that side of the Atlantic." This of course produced roars of laughter & more amusement than any vocal or instrumental display by us possibly could have done.

The Concert was soon brought to a close when the fair sex retired to the "Ladies parlour" of the Hotel to which they invited ... [the performers] to supper after which Singing & music commenced & this in fact was the real concert, when we were favoured amongst others, with many Lyrical compositions, including some real & original negro melodies. These enlivened the hours of night.[27]

The varying attitudes of different religious denominations concerning the propriety of using musical instruments in church worship did little to hinder participation and interest in music. It is true that, late in 1838, the Mississippi Conference of the Methodist church, which assigned missionaries to Texas, passed a resolution that "the introduction of instrumental music into public worship" and "the conducting of the music in our churches by choirs" were "injurious to the spirituality of singing" and "inconsistent with the directions of our Discipline." It is likewise certain that many Baptist congregations concurred in these sentiments. But it must be borne in mind that while the Methodists and Baptists were the largest denominations in Texas, they had not yet reached their periods of strongest influence; and dancing still remained a widely practiced pastime among all classes. Furthermore, congregations of these denominations made the backwoods ring with hymns; the Methodist "sister" who sang the following must have had a cer-

27 William Bollaert, "Texas in 1842," 2–4.

tain amount of music in her soul:

> *A Methodist it is my name,*
> *I hope to live and die the same,*
> *And when I die I'll go to rest*
> *And live among the Methodist.*
> *The devil hates the Methodist*
> *Because they sing and shout the best.*

The singing at Methodist and Baptist church services and camp meetings was certainly fervent though unaccompanied. It is also worthy of note that Rutersville College and Wesleyan College, both Texas Methodist institutions, offered instruction in piano. Then, too, the Presbyterian and Episcopal churches fostered musical activities. Indeed, a Presbyterian minister, Rev. William Y. Allen, took part in the sacred-music concerts in Houston in 1838, and probably was instrumental in the formation of the Sacred Music Society in the following year. On one occasion, when he preached at the dedication of a church at Houston, in 1842, a choir of twenty-five or thirty persons sang, accompanied by an orchestra consisting of two bass viols, a violin, a flute, and a clarinet.[28] And on January 20, 1844, the *Civilian and Galveston Gazette* proudly announced that "a fine-toned organ" had arrived from Antwerp, and would be used on the following Sunday in the services of the Episcopal Church.

The contributions of European settlers and Mexicans to Texas music must be gauged from scattered evidence. Many German immigrants had been trained to appreciate, play, and sing both classical and folk music, and a number of families brought pianos and other musical instruments with them. A group of Germans "sang in concert" at Galveston in 1837, and several German musicians and music teachers appeared in the early eighteen forties. At Houston, in 1840, a Mr. Heerbrugger gave a number of concerts, featuring German and Swiss airs, and was lauded by the local press as the ablest musician who had come to the Republic. In the eighteen

---

[28] William S. Red (ed.), "Extracts from the Diary of W. Y. Allen," *Southwestern Historical Quarterly,* Vol. XVII, No. 1 (July, 1913), 47; Red (ed.), "Allen's Reminiscences of Texas," *ibid.,* Vol. XVIII, No. 3 (January, 1915), 294; Houston *Morning Star,* September 26, 1839.

forties group singing was a part of German celebrations and organization meetings, and in the next decade German singing societies became active in many communities. Spanish and French contributions to Texas music are outlined in Mrs. Lota Spell's study of *Music in Texas*. The soft cadences of Mexican voices doubtless were heard many times in San Antonio and elsewhere; and the French priest, Emanuel Domenech, heard several French songs sung by his countrymen in and near that town.

It is impossible to reach definite conclusions concerning reading habits and literacy as well as that somewhat nebulous imponderable called "culture." Bernard DeVoto very rightly says that "the social historian practices the most precarious kind of history, and his job is at its most precarious when he tries to say something usable about literary culture, reading habits, and the conditions of literary taste. He ends by falling back on individual experience, hoping that many minute dots may sometime be brought together in a half-tone of the whole." This statement is especially applicable to any consideration of general reading habits on the frontier, where even the type of statistical data that indicates the number and kinds of books purchased—whether read or not—is not available. One sensitive army surgeon, who found his Texas environment too sordid to endure, wrote: "all this I could bear, had I Books to read but there is not one I presume within twenty miles of us."[29] On the other hand, a young Easterner was gratified to find that Robert Mills, Brazoria commission merchant and planter, had "quite an extensive historical library."[30] Between these extremes, an impressionistic conclusion—obviously based on very incomplete data—about the intervening truth may be attempted.

A few men—such as Thomas J. Rusk and Charles S. Taylor of Nacogdoches, Rev. James Russell of San Augustine University, William H. Wharton of Eagle Island Plantation (near Velasco), and possibly Dr. Pleasant Rose of Staffords Point—had libraries of several hundred volumes. If a library of any size was assembled, it usually represented a wide variety of interests—law, mathematics,

[29] T. F. Anderson to Ashbel Smith, June 12, 1838, Ashbel Smith Papers.
[30] S. M. Westervelt to "Dear David," March 15, 1842, Westervelt Papers.

Greek, Latin, oratory, history, poetry (especially the English classics), and military tactics. The advantages and curses of the age of specialization had not yet seriously affected man's intellectual development. The list of authors in the library of Willis Alston of Brazoria County, for example, included Scott, Byron, Irving, Jefferson, Shakespeare, Dryden, Pope, Burns, Mrs. Hemans, Paley, Goldsmith, Kames, Plutarch, and Josephus. Various works dealing with philosophy, history, geography, algebra, and oratory, as well as the Koran, Milman's *History of the Jews,* and "Demonology & Witchcraft," were also among those books sold at the auction of his effects.[31] But the mere possession of wealth by an individual did not mean that he had acquired a library. Kelsey H. Douglass, a Nacogdoches merchant, congressman, and military leader, died with a sixty-thousand-dollar estate which included only twenty-five books appraised at approximately ten dollars.[32]

The best library in the Republic of Texas probably was owned by Dr. Ashbel Smith of Houston and Galveston, a man of varied literary interests. In addition to the usual English poets and essayists and a large number of medical works, his books included the writings of Voltaire (forty-one volumes), Racine, Corneille, Mme de Staël, Plato, Homer, Seneca, Sallust, Spinoza, Descartes, and Confucius, as well as volumes dealing with international law, phrenology, and military tactics. He was also a subscriber to the best American and English literary journals and the sporting, humor, and literary magazine, the *Spirit of the Times.*[33] Smith's passion for books was so great that one friend warned him "for old friendship sake" not to buy any more. Few modern Texans can match Ashbel Smith in catholicity of literary taste.

Reading figured prominently in the life of Ira Ingram, an educated and well-to-do Vermonter who settled with his brother about thirty miles from the Gulf of Mexico on the San Bernard River. In a letter to a cousin he described his daily routine in 1827:

[31] Brazoria County Probate Records, A, 563.

[32] Nacogdoches County Probate Inventories, A, 1–33, 67–68, 126–27.

[33] "Legation de la Republique du Texas ce 25 Nov. 1844"; C. W. Pennock to Smith, February 26, 1838; Henry Barnard to Smith, March 29, 1838; Jesse Kincaid to Smith, May 11, 25, 1838; George A. Smith to Ashbel Smith, July 26, 1840—all in Ashbel Smith Papers.

My time is passed entirely in moderate exercise in my garden, with my dog & gun, hunting the deer & turkies, and in visiting my neighbors. I might here add too, in reading—but that is one of my principal "enjoyments." We have a well selected library of between three and four hundred volumes of books, and with them, I pass a great proportion of my time. It embraces a very valuable collection of maps & atlases, a full and complete circle of an. modern, & ecclesiastical history, most of the English classics, and almost every American production of any note. . . . How do you approve of this kind of life? . . . By a removal here, I have removed also, from a thousand artificial wants, and have acquired in exchange, many substantial, and if you will excuse the metaphor, perennial comforts.[34]

In the eighteen forties booksellers operated in Houston, Galveston, and Matagorda. Their advertisements offered the public several of the magazines and newspapers of the period—*Godey's Lady's Book, Graham's Magazine, The Lady's Magazine, The Columbian, Youth's Gazette, Sargent's Magazine, Brother Jonathan,* the New York *Mirror,* and the New York *Herald.* The "facts of life" were available in such volumes as *A Whisper to a Newly Married Pair; Manhood, the Causes of its Premature Decline;* and *Midwifery* by Dewees. Novels by Cooper and Bulwer were imported, too; Bulwer's *Zanoni* was a favorite in 1842 in Galveston and elsewhere in Texas. *Jack Hinton, Handy Andy, Harry Larroquer, Robinson Crusoe, The Mysteries of Paris* and its numerous sequels, *The Two Flirts, Able Parsons, or the Brother's Revenge,* and histories of Texas, the United States, and European countries also were offered for sale. But it is doubtful that the existence of a few bookstores and circulating libraries in the towns greatly affected public reading habits. Indeed, some persons believed that the influence of novel reading was deleterious: one writer claimed that his mind had been ruined by this practice and he had been rendered unfit for any useful or profitable employment. Furthermore, he thought that a

parent should never permit his child to peruse a work of fiction, as long as he has any regard for his mind, his morals, or his happiness. Novels,

[34] Ira Ingram to Mrs. M. B. West, February 19, 1827, Ingram Papers (Library of Congress).

in my opinion [he continued], are the most fruitful source of unhappiness and discontent in the world. Even drunkenness, with all its sickness and loathesome horrors, does not engender more pure and unmitigated misery. They portray unreal and overwrought images of perfection, and inspire wishes in our bosoms which can never be realized. Consequently, we are disappointed and uneasy. They clothe vice and immorality in the hues of the rain-bow. . . . Finally, they create a distempered fancy, and morbid sensibility, which renders us totally unfit for collision with the cold and uncharitable world.[35]

Texas undoubtedly had at least its share of educated men and women. Ferdinand Roemer, the German geologist, expressed surprise that well-bred, educated men could endure the simplicity and even crudeness of frontier life. One explanation was given by Francis R. Lubbock: "It was a time of brightness in my life that was not surpassed by any other period. In truth, society in Houston at that early day, mixed though it was with some rough characters, and without the sheen of later day finery, was just glorious; and I was young." Perhaps some of the cultured persons managed to endure by virtue of association with a few men of similar tastes. A number of the inhabitants of Clarksville, Matagorda, San Augustine, and certain German settlements evidently were above the normal cultural level.

But what of the "common man"? While the evidence is inconclusive, it is clear that the possession of a few dozen books must have marked an individual as exceptional in that respect. The inventories of hundreds of deceased Texans' effects show that most of them possessed only a very few volumes, and those of doubtful literary quality. In regard to literacy, Bugbee's study of Austin's first colonists, "The Old Three Hundred," revealed that only four of those concerning whom evidence was available were unable to write, and one early Texan asserted that two-thirds of the settlers after 1833 could read and write. Pro-Texas propagandists often claimed that the cultural level of the citizenry was generally high, but, wrote Dr. John Washington Lockhart:

Comfort is a great civilizing power . . .

[35] Washington *Texas National Register,* May 1, 1845.

See a man in a little log cabin, with a family of little children gathered around him; barefooted and bareheaded, and his wife in pretty much the same fix.

They are seated at the table, breakfasting, dining and supping on corn-cake, a little fried beef, and a cup of black coffee; and at night going to rest on a scaffold covered with ox-hide, and a few bed-clothes.

Think you there is much chance for elevation in that family?[36]

The possibilities for elevation were not so remote as modern critics of the crude frontier allege. The Republic had acquired a group of leaders who would have been remarkable in any age, most of them evidencing a thoroughgoing determination to give the common man opportunities to "go ahead." The lack of material comforts for the ordinary settler was counterbalanced by his belief that economic betterment was an imminent possibility, by his knowledge that he was living in a country with a fighting tradition in the making, by folk humor and imagination, and by freedom from a restraining and deadening uniformity of culture. All classes were imbued with pride in their notable experiment in self-government; variations of the phrase "this young, rising, and interesting Republic" recur throughout the records of the period. Then, as now, Texans were proud of Texas.

[36] Wallis and Hill (eds.), *Sixty Years on the Brazos,* 223.

~~~ VIII ~~~

Fighting the Devil on His Own Ground

•

ABOUT FIFTEEN YEARS before Stephen F. Austin began to bring
colonists from the United States into Texas, a United States
Army officer named Zebulon M. Pike had passed through
the province and reported that its religion was "Catholic, but much
relaxed." The Anglo-American settlers' brand of Catholicism was
even more relaxed, although until March 26, 1834, they legally were
required to subscribe to the established religion. Doubt whether
Texas authorities would "wink at liberty of conscience" eliminated
an undeterminable number of prospective Protestant immigrants
to whom deprivation of religious services of their own choosing
would have been a sharp personal loss. In practice, however, neither Protestant nor Catholic clergymen often labored among the
early colonists, "and, so far as one may judge from the documents
that have come down to us, they reconciled themselves to the situation with very little complaint."[1] The legal device of marriage
by bond removed one of the most urgent needs for clergymen. In
fact, some Texans positively approved of the nonsectarian atmosphere. Ira Ingram, a prominent settler, wrote:

The constitution . . . exempts us entirely from the shameless strifes
and animosities, too often the offspring of a well-meant zeal for the
cause of true religion, and invariably the handmaid of intolerant fanati-
cism.

We hear no ravings, and see no rompings, or indecorous and inde-
cent exhibitions under the cloak of a religious assemblage, either by

[1] Eugene C. Barker, *The Life of Stephen F. Austin,* 147, 260; Samuel H. Lowrie,
Culture Conflict in Texas, 1821–1835, 138. The thesis of William S. Red, *The Texas
Colonists and Religion, 1821–1836,* is that denominational religious interests were
prominent in the early colonists' lives, but a study of contemporary evidence has led
the writer to agree with the conclusions reached by Barker and Lowrie, as cited
above.

night or by day, no san[c]tuary's are polluted by unholy intrusions and desires; for we have no sanctuaries but private ones, and here, all are perfectly free to worship as they please.[2]

As a means of avoiding conflict with the Mexican government, and in expectation of eventually securing open toleration for all religious faiths, Austin forbade the few Protestant preachers who ventured into the province before 1834 to continue preaching—a restriction which his antipathy to "the Methodist excitement" doubtless enabled him to enforce with few twinges of conscience. However, the somewhat ambiguous law granting religious toleration, passed in 1834, apparently was interpreted as legalizing Protestant preaching. Early the following year Ingram noted that several itinerant clergymen were preaching when they desired; and a few organized churches were in existence in Texas in the three years preceding the Texas Revolution. But formal religious services were rare events before the separation from Mexico.

Thus many of the children of the early settlers who became of age while Texas was independent had little or no knowledge of formal religion. Nor had many of their elders heard sermons for several years, and Rev. Chester Newell, who was in the Republic in its formative years, concluded that the populace, with few exceptions, apparently were not very anxious for the establishment of "the institutions of Christianity." He added that they were "far from being generally Atheists and scoffers at religion," which was charitable of him in view of the meager four votes that he received in a House of Representatives election of a chaplain in which fourteen were cast for a Presbyterian minister and "seven by way of burlesque for an apostate Catholic priest of San Antonio."[3] Downright skepticism was most prevalent among the lawyers and doctors, but many individuals who formerly had been active church members found it difficult to maintain their piety in Texas. In 1839 Rev. Abel Stevens, a Methodist minister, reported to the New York

[2] Ira Ingram to Roswell Ingram, May 29, 1830, Ingram Papers (University of Texas Library).

[3] Chester Newell, *History of the Revolution in Texas,* 193; "Jottings from the Old Journal of Littleton Fowler," *Quarterly of the Texas State Historical Association,* Vol. II, No. 1 (July, 1898), 81; Red (ed.), "Extracts from the Diary of W. Y. Allen," *Southwestern Historical Quarterly,* Vol. XVII, No. 1 (July, 1913), 45.

Christian Advocate and Journal that "backslidden" members of his denomination (among them many former church leaders and even preachers) were scattered over the whole settled extent of the new country. He ascribed their spiritual decline to the general failure to observe the Sabbath, the lack of religious teachers, and the distances which precluded religious intercourse with brethren of similar persuasion. In fact, the minister had heard one Methodist state that he had been in Texas five years before he saw "a professor of religion."

The lack of intercourse with fellow religious votaries, the excesses of frontier boom towns, and the license-provoking aftermath of a recent war were not the only antireligious forces at work. With all of its immense power for good, denominational religion, bolstered by dogmatic authority, tended to offer certainty and provide a refuge for the fearsome—qualities that did not attract many self-reliant frontier individualists, so resentful of authority. On the other hand, the principle that economic advancement accompanies the establishment and growth of churches was not forgotten. The suspicion is permissible that William Barret Travis had such a thought in mind when, in 1835, he sent his often quoted appeal for Methodist preachers to come to Texas. Certainly his diary of the two preceding years shows that he would have had to change his habits before they would have been worthy of emulation by the pious.

Failure to observe the Sabbath was the general rule; in 1843 this was listed among "the national sins" by the Protestant Episcopal minister, Rev. Charles Gillett. One exception to the rule, a religious carpenter in Galveston, found it possible in 1845 to attend a Sunday school and three preaching services in one day, in addition to three or four prayer meetings (with one auction for relaxation) on week nights. However, the four church buildings which this young man could see from his boardinghouse window comprised a view not likely to be duplicated elsewhere in Texas, because church buildings were scarce. Most church services were held in rude log buildings, schoolhouses, private homes, or the open air. During 1838 three small Methodist churches were erected in the Republic, but both Houston and Matagorda boasted theaters before the completion of their first church buildings, and the sole church in Austin was a frame structure completed in 1841. The most handsome Protestant houses of worship were erected by the Protestant Episcopal churches at Galveston and Matagorda.

By the end of 1845 not more than one-eighth of the white population were either active or nominal members of Texas churches, and Protestantism dominated the religious scene, such as it was. The churches in the order of their numerical strength were the Methodist, Baptist, Presbyterian, Catholic, and Protestant Episcopal, followed by minor sects. Since detailed studies of the history of the most important of these groups have been made by denominational historians, their growth will be sketched hereinafter only in broad outlines.

The Methodists led all the rest, claiming more than half of all church members. Texas was described as "a great, beautiful, dry, windy, cotton, cattle, Methodist, live-oak State," and the Methodists had strong grounds for considering the Republic peculiarly their province. Not only were many of the settlers of that spiritual persuasion—though admittedly a goodly proportion were "backslidden"—but also the Methodist system of using itinerant circuit riders, exhorters, local preachers, and "class leaders" was especially adaptable to the needs of the people and "their immature state." The entry for January 16, 1843, in the diary of one of their ministers reads: "The backwoodsman has gone into the forest, and the panther is scarcely more keen scented for his blood than the Methodist preacher is for his soul."[4]

In 1837 three eager missionaries came to Texas, all of whom ultimately were important in the history of Texas Methodism. They were appointed by the bishop in charge of Methodist Episcopal home missionary work, on the recommendation of the Mississippi Conference. Rev. Martin Ruter was made superintendent of the Texas Mission, which also included Rev. Robert Alexander of the Mississippi Conference and Rev. Littleton Fowler of the Tennessee Conference. This was merely the beginning. Methodist circuit riders began to appear in every hamlet, following the expanding edge of settlement. A Methodist itinerant was in the Dallas–

4 Quotation from the diary of Rev. Josiah W. Whipple in Frank Brown, "Annals of Travis County," X, 65.

North Texas region soon after settlement began in 1842–43. In 1845 another preacher was at Brownsville, on the Rio Grande, while in the following year Rev. John Haynie was preaching in a theater in the army town of Corpus Christi, where he "attacked the enemy on his own ground."[5] A rival sectarian tartly observed that "the Methodist preacher is far in advance of even the Yankee Clock Peddler."[6]

By 1840 the Texas Mission of the Methodists was so flourishing that the General Conference considered it expedient to order the organization of the Texas Conference. After the presentation of a petition by Rev. B. M. Drake of the Mississippi Conference, and a favorable recommendation by the Committee on Boundaries, the general body adopted a resolution that the Texas Conference should comprise the Republic, "except what is embraced in the Red River District, Arkansas Conference."[7] The new conference was organized officially on December 25, 1840, with eighteen traveling and twenty-five local preachers ministering to a membership of nearly nineteen hundred persons. At the end of 1844 the membership had increased to more than six thousand and Methodism was firmly established in the Republic,[8] a fact evidenced further by the division of the Texas organization into the Eastern and Western conferences.

The pastoral address delivered at the 1843 annual conference enjoined members to read the Scriptures and conduct family prayer to respect the Sabbath and aid "the Sabbath School"; to give children a common school education and "a knowledge of the higher branches if convenient"; to beware of debt and to avoid tale-bearing; and to "be punctual at love feasts, class and prayer-meet-

[5] In a letter dated February 15, 1846, printed in *Southwestern Christian Advocate* and reprinted in Phelan, *History of Early Methodism in Texas,* 264. Variations of this phrase often were used in letters written by Methodist preachers. For Haynie's presence in Corpus Christi, see New Orleans *Daily Delta,* February 18, 1846.

[6] John Stamps, writing from Washington County, Texas, November 7, 1849, in *Millenial Harbinger,* Third Series, Vol. VII, No. 3 (March, 1850), 174.

[7] "Journal of the General Conference of the Methodist Episcopal Church, Held in the City of Baltimore, 1840," 20, 80, in *Journals of the General Conference of the Methodist Episcopal Church,* II.

[8] *Minutes of the Annual Conferences of the Methodist Episcopal Church,* III, 120, 554–55, 603.

ing."[9] Three years later the Missionary Society of the Methodist Episcopal church, South, reported: "It has been well said, that 'the success of our missionary labors in Texas is unparalleled in the history of Christian Missions.' "[10]

Both Methodist conferences adhered to the newly organized Methodist Episcopal church, South, formed as the result of the division of the Methodist church in 1844–46 over the slavery question. Since 1820 this dread subject had been lurking in the background at each meeting of the General Conference, which had withdrawn from subordinate conferences the power to regulate slaveholding among the membership. With very few exceptions, Texas Methodism supported the Southern point of view when division finally came.

The Texas representatives at the General Conference of 1844 were Rev. Littleton Fowler and Rev. John Clark. Fowler wrote to his wife from the Conference at New York: *"My firm conviction is that in this meeting our beloved Methodism will be snapped in twain.*... My poor heart is almost sunk within me, which is partially relieved at times by giving away to tears. There is much excitement among the members, and it is daily increasing with fearful apprehensions to all concerned."[11] The specific question which split the General Conference was whether Bishop James O. Andrew should be retained in office while he owned slaves, or was the husband of a wife who owned them. On the final vote the Texas delegation split. Fowler favored his continuance in office, but Clark voted to suspend the bishop.[12]

Rev. John Clark never returned to Texas—because of sickness in his family, he said. Whatever the reason, his failure to reappear in the Republic prevented the development of a violent squabble. Texas Methodism considered that he had violated his trust by his vote, and Rev. Robert Alexander wrote that he did not think the

[9] Matagorda *Weekly Despatch,* March 16, 1844.

[10] *First Annual Report of the Missionary Society of the Methodist Episcopal Church, South,* 45.

[11] Littleton Fowler to Mrs. Missouri M. Fowler, May 8, 1844, Fowler Papers.

[12] "Journal of the General Conference of the Methodist Episcopal Church, Held in the City of New-York, 1844," 36, in *Journals of the General Conference of the Methodist Episcopal Church,* II; *Debates of the General Conference of the M. E. Church, May, 1844,* 279; B. M. Hall, *Life of Rev. John Clark,* 224–30.

erstwhile delegate could travel through the western counties without being mobbed. Meanwhile, the Eastern Texas Conference voted unanimously that "the church has nothing to do with the relation that exists between slave and master." The Republic's leading newspaper summed up the situation with a prophetic comment: "So the Methodist Union is dissolved, on the fearful question which will in all probability at no distant day dissolve the Union of the confederated States! The devil, it strikes us, has more of a hand in this deeply agitating blow of abolitionism, than the spirit and religion of the Saviour."[13]

Although Texas Methodists endorsed "the peculiar institution," no inconsistency was felt in extending Christian fellowship to slaves. On the contrary, Methodists and Baptists took the lead in admitting Negroes to membership in white churches and occasionally allowed them to form churches of their own, usually under a white pastor. Two Methodist missionaries "to colored people" were appointed in East Texas, and in 1844 Texas Methodist churches reported an incomplete total of more than one thousand colored members, an increase of about eight hundred since 1840.[14] Moreover, one slave achieved a high place in Texas Methodism: "Uncle Mark," a Washington County Negro, preached to both whites and Negroes, and (according to one source) was later purchased by a Masonic lodge and repurchased by a Texas Methodist annual conference in order that he might have complete freedom in preaching.[15]

Baptist beginnings in Texas have been traced back to the early eighteen twenties, but intense denominational activity did not start until after independence was achieved. In 1835 Rev. Z. N. Morrell

[13] Houston *Telegraph and Texas Register*, July 17, 1844.

[14] MS signed by Rev. Littleton Fowler, presiding elder of Lake Soda District, October 21, 1843, Fowler Papers; *First Annual Report of the Missionary Society of the Methodist Episcopal Church, South*, 34; "Autobiography of Rev. Francis A. Wilson," 86, 91; *Minutes of the Annual Conferences of the Methodist Episcopal Church*, III, 120, 554–55, 603.

[15] "Rev. John Mark (Colored)," MS, probably written by Rev. Oscar M. Addison, Addison Papers. Wallis and Hill (eds.), *Sixty Years on the Brazos*, 54, states that he was able to purchase his freedom with contributions given him by white people.

of Mississippi began the long and effective Texas ministry described in his sprightly *Flowers and Fruits from the Wilderness.* He was followed by other preachers, including two notable missionaries, Rev. James Huckins and Rev. William M. Tryon. The first association was the Union Baptist Association, founded on October 8, 1840, with three ministers, three churches, and forty-five communicants. By 1846 this organization had grown to include ten preachers, nineteen churches, and approximately six hundred members. The Sabine Baptist Association was organized in November, 1843, and almost three years later had seven ministers, sixteen churches, and about five hundred communicants, while two smaller associations were reported to have eight ministers, fifteen churches, and a membership of more than three hundred souls.[16]

Meanwhile, the Union Association of Regular Predestinarian Baptists—a group that was violently "antimissionary" in belief—had been formed on October 11, 1840, under the leadership of Elder Daniel Parker, the famous exponent of the "Two-Seed-in-the-Spirit" doctrine. Elder Parker's home congregation, the Pilgrim Church, had been brought from Illinois in 1833 and had constituted the first organized Protestant church in Texas. In 1840 the Predestinarian Baptist Association claimed less than 100 members in Texas, and five years later there were 215 members in ten churches. The antimission doctrine dominated in at least a dozen additional churches in East Texas, some of which belonged to a small "Predestinarian" association that spanned the Louisiana border.[17]

Including the memberships of a few "Hard-Shell" Baptist congregations which were unattached to any association, the aggregate

---

[16] *Minutes of the Seventh Annual Meeting of the Union Baptist Association,* 16–17; William M. Tryon, "Texas," *The Baptist,* New Series, Vol. I, No. 16 (December, 1844), 254; "Texas Associations," *ibid.,* Vol. I, No. 34 (April, 1845), 531–32; J. W. D. Creath, "Texas Associations," *The Tennessee Baptist,* Vol. VII, No. 44 (July, 1851), [p. 4]; San Augustine *Red-Lander,* October 23, 1845.

[17] "Records of an Early Texas Baptist Church," *Quarterly of the Texas State Historical Association,* Vol. XI, No. 2 (October, 1907), 85–156, and Vol. XII, No. 1 (July, 1908), 1–60; "Minutes of the Fifth Annual Meeting of the Union Association of Regular Baptists," October 11, 1845, in San Augustine *Red-Lander,* November 6, 1845; Morrell, *Flowers and Fruits from the Wilderness,* 190; James M. Carroll, *History of Texas Baptists,* 116. By 1845 the Parker antimission group had dropped the word "Predestinarian" from the title of the association.

of all Baptist membership in the Republic was less than two thousand, even when full credence is given to the figures furnished by the churches.

The first Presbyterian group to become active in Texas was the Cumberland Presbyterian church, which had separated from the mother Presbyterian church amid the frontier revivalism of the early eighteen hundreds. In 1825 Sumner Bacon, former soldier and surveyor, was converted in Arkansas, and before 1830 arrived in Texas with the endorsement of a Tennessee presbytery. In 1834 he became an agent of the American Bible Society in Texas. Although he did not secure a license to preach until 1835, he previously had begun to deliver "publik addresses or Exhortations" (which amounted to sermons) among the colonists, some of whom objected to his efforts on the ground that they were unlawful. A man of small literary attainments but forceful character, he lived to become the first moderator of the Texas Presbytery, which was organized at San Augustine on November 27, 1837, as well as the first moderator of the Texas Synod, organized in 1843 with seven preachers present. By 1847 this synod had twenty-nine ordained preachers, thirty-seven congregations, and more than thirteen hundred communicants.[18]

One of the most effective Cumberland Presbyterian preachers was Rev. Sam Corley, who served northeastern Texas with Clarksville as his home. Sam Corley's singing gave him the name of the "Sweet Singer of Israel," and one of his contemporaries wrote that "a nobler man never lived." It was largely through his efforts that Cumberland Presbyterianism secured a firm foothold in northeastern Texas.

Corley himself was very intelligent and facile in expression, yet a part of the success of his church must be attributed to the common touch possessed by a poorly educated ministry. The methods of the Cumberland preachers were adapted to the demands of the frontier, while the doctrine of their church was very advanced. Indeed, many frontiersmen preferred the liberalism of Cumberland

[18] Minutes of the Texas Presbytery of the Cumberland Presbyterian Church, 1837–39, entry for November 27, 1837; Minutes of the Texas Synod of the Cumberland Presbyterian Church, 1843–68, 35, 47.

THE TEXAS REPUBLIC

Presbyterianism to the rigid polity and doctrine of the "Old School" Presbyterian church, in which "every innovation to meet the peculiar needs or problems of a new country were [sic] always strongly opposed."[19] Under the impulse of the revival spirit, the Cumberland Presbyterians put more stress on the recognition of "extraordinary cases" of conversions. Furthermore, they dissented from the "Old School" Presbyterian Calvinism of the Westminster Confession of Faith by denying the doctrine of election and the damnation of nonelect deceased infants. Finally, the Cumberland Presbyterian preachers, some of whom were assigned to circuits, traveled more than the divines of the older Presbyterian group. In this, as in the use of local church leaders in holding congregations together and in preaching a democratic gospel, the Cumberland system was akin to the successful Methodist technique in ministering to the frontier.

The "Old School" division of the Presbyterian church sent an educated ministry to Texas.[20] In 1837 the Board of Domestic Missions began its work in Texas, under the patronage of the Synod of Mississippi; but this synod, organized only recently, was none too strong. Furthermore, there was some doubt whether Texas was the proper province of the Board of Domestic Missions or the Board of Foreign Missions, and for a period representatives of both bodies functioned there. Finally, in 1843, "since the Domestic Board had done nothing in Texas for three and one-half years," the General Assembly transferred all work in the Republic of Texas to the Board of Foreign Missions.[21]

Meanwhile, on April 3, 1840, the Texas Presbytery (later the Presbytery of Brazos) was organized by Rev. William Y. Allen, Rev. Hugh Wilson, Rev. John McCullough, and Elder John McFarland. This new group manifested remarkable independence

19 William W. Sweet, *The Story of Religion in America,* 312.

20 After the "Old School"–"New School" division took place in 1837–38, Texas Presbyterianism, with few exceptions, adhered to the "Old School." The only active exponent of the "New School" doctrine in Texas was Rev. Henry Reid, who was a member of an "Old School" presbytery in the United States but was denied fellowship with the Presbytery of Brazos.

21 Red, *History of the Presbyterian Church in Texas,* 50; *Seventh Annual Report of the Board of Foreign Missions of the Presbyterian Church, in the United States of America,* 8; "Texas," *Missionary Chronicle,* Vol. XI, No. 25 (July, 1843), 213.

by antagonizing both the Board of Domestic Missions and the Synod of Mississippi by neglecting to apply for admission to the Mississippi group (which had authorized the formation of the Presbytery) until late in 1843. The Presbytery of Brazos continued its independent course until the spring of 1846, when admission to the Synod of Mississippi formally was announced. It had increased its enrollment of seventy-eight members, six churches, and three ministers in 1840 to more than two hundred members, thirteen churches, eight ministers, and four prospective ministers.[22] In effectiveness on the Texas frontier, the "Mother Church" lagged far behind the Cumberland branch, yet the preaching and activities of the "Old School" Presbyterian and Protestant Episcopal churches helped preserve interest in religion and education among the literate.

The Protestant Episcopal church had churches in Matagorda, Galveston, and Houston. In 1838 Rev. Caleb S. Ives began his ministry at Matagorda, where six years later he still presided over "the most western and southern Protestant Episcopal Church in North America" and "stood as a sentinel upon the outer wall."[23]

Rev. R. M. Chapman's labors at Houston and Galveston also began in 1838, but he returned to "the States" in June of the following year. Rev. Benjamin Eaton's work at Galveston was started early in 1841, and about two years later Rev. Charles Gillett took charge of the church at Houston. Eaton received a severe setback on the night of September 18–19, 1842, when the beautiful, recently finished Trinity Church at Galveston was destroyed by a storm. The pastor immediately began to raise funds in the United States for rebuilding, and in less than a year the church was restored. The Protestant Episcopal cause also was encouraged by visits of Bishops Leonidas Polk and George W. Freeman, who doubtless strengthened the resolution of the small band of ministers. Despite such encouragement, Gillett, who presided over a Houston membership

22 Minutes of the Presbytery of Brazos, 1840–45, 1, 7, 10; Minutes of the Presbytery of Brazos, 1846–54, 5, 12–13. See also Washington *Texas National Register*, May 22, 1845; and *Minutes of the General Assembly of the Presbyterian Church in the United States of America*, IX, 351.

23 Matagorda *Weekly Despatch*, March 2, 1844.

of about thirty in 1844, wrote that the "poetry of Missionary life consists of sitting quietly at home and talking and writing about it; for when it comes to the real plain matter of fact, the romance vanishes."[24]

Minor religious sects also were scattered throughout the Republic. The Disciples of Christ, who were gaining momentum in the United States under the inspiring direction of Alexander Campbell, had several dozen adherents in Texas but lacked effective leadership. Prominent laymen from Washington, Harris, and San Augustine counties appealed to Campbell to send out "teaching brethren" or "proclaimers," lest the Disciples continue as sheep astray without shepherds.[25] A number of small congregations of the Independent Evangelical Church were organized among the German settlers. Then, too, the prospectus of a monthly journal to be called *The Nazarene Advocate* to revive "The Sect of the Nazarenes" was published in 1837 in a Matagorda newspaper. Moreover at least one Universalist, Rev. Levi Chase, visited several Texas towns, at Washington on the Brazos announcing in his sermon that the Devil was dead. Whereupon a public meeting passed resolutions sympathizing with the speaker on the death of his venerable father and appointed a local worthy as administrator of Satan's estate. In addition, the Mormons had a small community near Austin; the sect gained a victory over the first Baptist minister in Texas, Rev. Joseph L. Bays, by inducing his wife to leave her husband and espouse the Mormon faith. A few Texas Millerites, looking to an early millennium, muddled the ecclesiastical scene.

The lingering effects of the Catholicism to which the early settlers had been committed were very slight. Father Miguel Muldoon, a jovial and liberal priest who had remained in Texas for less than a year in the early eighteen thirties, reappeared for a brief period in 1839. He had not relinquished his claim to spiritual guidance of Texas Catholics, and on March 18 he performed a marriage ceremony at Houston as "D. D. Vicar General of the Catholic

---

[24] Letter from Rev. Charles Gillett, dated March 18, 1844, in "Texas," *Spirit of Missions,* Vol. IX, No. 5 (May, 1844), 156.

[25] *Millenial Harbinger,* New Series, Vol. V, No. 8 (August, 1841), 381; Third Series, Vol. IV, No. 3 (March, 1847), 173; Third Series, Vol. IV, No. 8 (August, 1847), 480; Third Series, Vol. IV, No. 9 (September, 1847), 534.

Communities of the free & Independent Republic of Texas." But he soon returned to Mexico, where he was imprisoned, apparently because of his friendliness to the Texans.

In the early part of 1839 a new order in Texas Catholicism was presaged by the appearance of the Very Reverend Father John Timon, a visitor of the Lazarists. Sent to Texas by the Bishop of New Orleans, after the prelate's attention had been directed to the barren state of Texas Catholicism, Timon was appointed prefect after his return to the United States, and his first important act was to appoint the Reverend Jean Marie Odin as vice-prefect apostolic. In 1840 Odin began his Texas ministry, which ultimately stimulated sharply the reorganization of the Catholic church. A man of ingratiating personality and kindly spirit, he traveled throughout the Republic, and under his diligent supervision, Catholicism began to rebuild on sound beginnings.[26] After his appointment as bishop, he traveled in the United States and Europe in the interests of the Texas Mission, and gradually gathered around him a corps of competent priests to replace the two renegade priests at San Antonio whom he had found it necessary to depose. Particular attention was paid to the Irish, German, and French settlers. The two Catholic strongholds in the Republic were San Antonio and Galveston.

A surprising lack of overt antagonism existed among the representatives of various Protestant denominations. The number of preachers was so small and the Lord's work so vast that hostility remained submerged until strong congregations were established. In 1841 a member of the Disciples of Christ wrote from Washington County: "There is scarcely any dissensions among the various sects here, owing, I think, to their weakness."[27] In 1838–39, when Houston presented a challenging picture of grogshops and gambling houses to ministers of the Gospel, they co-operated in preach-

[26] Houston *Telegraph and Texas Register*, March 23, 1842; Roemer, *Texas*, 213; Solms, *Texas*, 54; Bollaert, "Personal Narrative, 1840–1844," 219; New Orleans *Weekly Picayune*, August 16, 1841; New Orleans *Daily Picayune*, December 4, 1844; E. Domenech, *Journal d'un Missionaire au Texas et au Mexique, 1846–1852*, 27.

[27] *Millenial Harbinger*, New Series, Vol. V, No. 8 (August, 1841), 381.

ing services. The Reverend William Y. Allen, a Presbyterian, shared his room and bed with an Episcopalian preacher for several months, and at another time boarded with a "Baptist brother." In 1843 a part of the ceremonies dedicating the Methodist Church at Houston were held in the Presbyterian Church. At Washington on the Brazos in 1838, Methodist, Baptist, and Cumberland Presbyterian preachers united in overcoming the opposition of gamblers and drunkards who attempted to prevent them from holding services in a vacant billiard room. Furthermore, preachers of different denominations often co-operated at camp meetings, and it was not until the country became more settled that many Protestants began to regard each other malignantly, convinced that the Devil was stoking his fires for the wayward neighbor who persisted in listening to the wrong preaching.

Even in this early period, however, Methodists and Baptists did not always regard each other with amity. The correspondence of Rev. Oscar M. Addison, Methodist circuit rider, contains many references to his conflicts with the "watery tribe" and his resentment of their attempts to persuade "Methodists to join them and be Burried-alive!!" with water. The Baptist attitude toward other denominations was expressed in an official statement that Baptists held an attitude of sincerest affection for other evangelical denominations and that they preached and labored together for the spread of the Gospel. However, the statement further set forth that Baptists could not go to the Lord's table with members of other denominations because they had not complied with the essential preliminary duty of *"regeneration* and *baptism."*[28]

The most virulent quarrels took place within denominations as a result of internal dissension and division. The "Old School" Texas Presbytery (later Presbytery of Brazos) of the Presbyterian church refused membership to a minister of "New School" leanings, who replied with a vigorous counterattack. There was likewise internal discord among the Cumberland Presbyterian brethren in Texas. Moreover, the "Missionary" Baptists constantly had to contend with antimissionism, both within their own ranks and in that of the rival Predestinarian Baptist organization, the leader

[28] *Minutes of the Ninth Anniversary of the Union Baptist Association,* 4.

of which was Elder Daniel Parker, "arch enemy of missions on the frontier."

Before 1833, when Parker led his congregation to Texas, he had fought very successfully against the cause of Baptist missions in Tennessee, Indiana, and Illinois. He had been in the forefront of the frontier movement against missions which split Baptists throughout the Western states. Baptist antimissionists objected to any tendency toward centralization of church authority, opposed a paid and educated ministry, and believed that missionary societies and other "man-made" religious organizations were unscriptural. In 1826 Parker had promulgated an extreme statement of the ultra-Calvinist antimission theology in a pamphlet setting forth his "Two-Seed-in-the-Spirit" doctrine, which presented a variation of ancient dualism. According to the Elder, God planted a seed emanating from himself in his creations, Adam and Eve, but after man fell, the "seed of the serpent" also was planted in Eve and all her daughters. It follows, then, that "all children born of the divine seed are the children of God, while all children born of the evil seed are children of the devil. Those children begotten of the devil are his bona fide children, and to their father they would and ought to go." Hence, Parker reasoned, it was inexcusable and wicked folly to preach the Gospel or give Bibles to the nonelect who had the misfortune to be born of the "seed of the serpent." Therefore he violently opposed missionary and Bible societies.[29]

According to the historian of Texas Baptists, Daniel Parker probably left a "deeper or more nearly ineradicable impress on the theology" of East Texas than any other preacher in its history.[30] In the eighteen forties a number of churches in his region were rent with dissension on the question of missions, and the influence of his group was largely responsible for the dissolution of the Sabine Baptist Association—nominally associated with the missionists—after five years of bitter controversy. Even in recent years, some of the issues he raised have been very much alive in Texas.

Meanwhile, the majority of Texas Baptists adopted a course of action sharply divergent from that advocated by Elder Parker.

[29] William W. Sweet, *Religion on the American Frontier: the Baptists, 1783–1830,* 75, 67.
[30] Carroll, *History of Texas Baptists,* 116.

At the first meeting (in 1840) of the strongest Baptist group, the Union Association, it took a tolerant view of the principal moot issue: "Each member shall forever have a full and free right to exercise his or her discretion" in regard "to the support of missions, general benevolence, &c., and in other matters that may not lead to immorality." Yet at its next meeting, the Association excluded its moderator, Rev. T. W. Cox, after a long and unpleasant trial, chiefly because of his heterodox predilection for the principles advocated by Alexander Campbell (then an antimissionist in the sense that he opposed organized missions). Soon afterward the Union Baptist Association was firmly supporting both missions and an educational policy that led to the establishment of Baylor University. Finally, in the middle eighteen forties, the association was deploring the fact that only a very few preachers could spend most of their time in the work of the ministry and it adopted the Biblical principle that "the laborer is worthy of his hire!" Baptists were admonished to "say to your Preachers, leave your School Houses! Leave your Farms! Give yourselves to study! Give yourselves wholly to the Ministry of the Word. You shall suffer no loss. Your families *shall be sustained.*"[31]

Privations and poverty, loneliness, conflict with an unconquered wilderness and with ribald degenerates—such was the lot of the frontier preacher. That he was sincere there can be no doubt. For sincerity based on deep conviction must have been the motivation that sent him on long rides across rough country, swimming swollen streams and running the risk of Indian ambush. In 1838 a Methodist bishop wrote to the presiding elder of the Texas Mission: "We have sent you Brother Sneed [Rev. J. P. Sneed], a man who is not afraid to die or sleep in the woods."[32] While other men were laying the foundations of potential fortunes, the preacher had to depend for a livelihood chiefly upon the benevolence of his scattered parishioners and on the yield of his own part-time farming. The journal kept in 1838–40 by Rev. Jesse Hord, the Methodist pathfinder in the coastal country, is a saga of quiet heroism and

31 *Minutes of the Eighth Annual Meeting of the Union Baptist Association,* 10–12; *Minutes of the Sixth Annual Meeting of the Union Baptist Association,* 5.
32 T. A. Morris to Littleton Fowler, December 13, 1838, Fowler Papers.

hardship. He was able to "thank God for sleep" and to "thank God for a horse" that enabled him to traverse a prairie that "nothing but a duck or a goose ever crossed." The annals of early Texas preachers and priests are filled with similar accounts. One additional illustration will suffice. The Reverend Francis A. Wilson, an East Texas Methodist, recorded in his autobiography: "I have traveled 150,000 miles and preached 7,000 sermons; have lived and worked hard most of the time, and received small allowance for my support."

Among the most trying experiences that frontier soldiers of the cross had to undergo was "fighting the Devil on his own ground." In 1840 gentlemanly Rev. Caleb S. Ives of Matagorda offered an Episcopalian prayer book to a drunken visitor whose curiosity had led him to attend Sunday school. The visitor informed the preacher that he already had a box full of books but would accept the gift. And he added in a loud voice, as he staggered about, making "Grecian bends": "I don't like you Episcopalians. You have too much form about you. You are too much like the Masons—I don't like you."[33]

A rebuff such as this was mild compared with the reception of preachers who held a meeting at Washington on the Brazos. The town gamblers and rowdies stood outside the meetinghouse, holding a chicken by the neck while the preacher who was leading the singing "lined out" the words of the songs. When the congregation sang, the chicken's neck was released so that the bird might emit a protesting squawk. The service was disturbed further by a large Negro who had been placed on the front porch in a crowd of about twenty partly intoxicated hecklers. The slave was ordered to stick his neck in the window at intervals and yell, "Glory to God." Whereupon his fellow tormentors on the porch would respond, "Amen and amen!" One of the the preachers, Rev. Z. N. Morrell, stated that his "bosom heaved with holy indignation." He took a hickory walking cane and struck the black man on the forehead, scarring him for life. After the service was concluded, the band of mockers followed the preachers and "barked at them like dogs." But the next day a community indignation meeting condemned the actions of "this wicked crew," and services continued.[34]

33 "Autobiography of James Norman Smith," III, 138.
34 Morrell, *Flowers and Fruits from the Wilderness*, 82–85.

Another preacher, the Presbyterian John McCullough, narrowly escaped death when a drunken gambler rode into the house in which he was staying and fired two bullets through the minister's hat as he opened the door of his room.

In 1839 Rev. J. P. Sneed, a well-known Methodist circuit rider, accompanied a sick preacher on a steamboat trip from Houston to Galveston. A group of noisy inebriates began to dance, sing, shout, and curse. Brother Sneed tried to quiet the revelers by telling them about the condition of his companion. But this only furnished the carousers with a rallying cry, and they began to shout: "Jonah's aboard! Jonah's aboard! We'll go to the bottom tonight." This jocular prophecy came close to fulfillment, for a storm arose soon after midnight. The boat rolled and tumbled, while the wind howled "and the thunder roared amid the frantic glare of the lightning. Within, the scene was equally indescribable. Some uttered yells of despair, some, exclamations of lost! lost! others were thrown into spasms, while others prayed, as for life."[35] Though the boat steamed safely into Galveston harbor on the following morning, a severe chastening had been administered by Nature—or the Lord.

The opposition or indifference of the faithless was doubtless lessened by the preachers' use of anecdotes and the idiom of their listeners in sermons. In 1844 a preaching service conducted by Rev. Z. N. Morrell at Huntsville was disturbed by a number of men outside the building who were growing uproarious in appreciation of stories told by several of their group. Whereupon they were challenged by the preacher to a contest in taletelling—the loser to listen thereafter to the winner—and the yarn spinners agreed. After Morrell had finished his story of the Anglo-American "Tories" who shouted for Santa Anna before he lost the Battle of San Jacinto, and then even louder for Sam Houston after the Texans were victorious, the rowdies agreed that he had won and listened quietly to the sermon. About two years later Morrell reached the frontier village of Springfield, which was preparing for a season of racing. When about fifty of the gambling gentry appeared at the service (after they had been drinking at the "grocery"), Morrell launched

35 O. M. Addison, "Life and Times of Rev. Joseph P. Sneed," 105–106, Addison Papers.

into a sermon replete with race-track illustrations. He announced his text to be Hebrews, XII, 1, 2: "Wherefore, seeing we also are compassed about with so great a cloud of witnesses, let us lay aside every weight and the sin which doth so easily beset us, and let us run with patience the race that is set before us, looking unto Jesus, the author and finisher of our faith." This text was expounded at length in racing terminology. Finally, he entered "the *white horse* of the *gospel*" in the race for happiness against Satan's silver-mounted steeds—riches, honor, pleasure, and passion. Morrell asserted that the white horse never had lost a race in all of the years that men had been "risking their all" on him. And he warned that all who ran "on any other track than that which is stained with Jesus' blood" would lose everything and gain nothing.[36]

Among the tribulations that beset the ministry were the presence and conduct of a number of pulpiteers who falsely claimed to be regularly accredited preachers. In the absence of ministers, frontier laymen without licenses read one of Wesley's sermons or a similar dissertation to small groups of the pious. There was no objection to this procedure, but lack of strong denominational governing bodies also made the frontier a happy hunting ground for evangelical charlatans.

At Velasco, "Daddy Spraggins," who professed to be a "Hard-Shell" Baptist, visited the saloons before preaching in search of inspiration and afterward for recuperation. "When this man preaches," wrote the Baptist preacher James Huckins, "drunkards, blacklegs, and the vile of every description are sure to attend . . . and applaud by clapping their hands and stamping their feet. . . . O Lord! how long shall Thy precious cause bleed by our being allied in name to such men?" Huckins also wrote that a minister bearing genuine credentials had brought into the country two boxes filled with cards and "Hoyles Games," containing, "as he said his library."[37] So many bogus preachers appeared that in 1837 "The Ecclesiastical Committee of Vigilance for Texas" was organized at Houston by a group of Methodist, Baptist, and Presby-

[36] Morrell, *Flowers and Fruits from the Wilderness*, 202–205, 242–52.

[37] Carroll, *History of Texas Baptists*, 151, 155; Red (ed.), "Allen's Reminiscences of Texas," *Southwestern Historical Quarterly*, Vol. XVIII, No. 3 (January, 1915), 292.

terian ministers. The purpose of this interdenominational group was to expose the pretenders who did not have the proper denominational credentials. Two years later the Quarterly Conference of the Methodist Episcopal church, Washington Circuit, issued a warning against two impostors who claimed to be Methodist preachers. One was a bricklayer, who was "remarkably *boisterous* in reading hymns and preaching," and another was a bigamist with a fraudulent license to preach. "The church in Texas has bled," stated the conference, "and still bleeds at . . . the conduct of hypocritical impostors."[38]

The activities of spurious preachers undoubtedly provided many frontiersmen with one of their chief excuses for regarding ministers as slightly comical figures. A humorous sally that appeared in several newspapers illustrates this point:

Queer Estate for a Preacher to Leave

A preacher who recently died up in the Red River country, is said to have left the following singular effects: a Bible, two collars, a Bowie-knife, a psalm-book, a deck of cards somewhat used, Bunyan's Pilgrim's Progress, nearly new, a pocket flask or "tickler," a collection of sacred music, a quarter nag with saddle and bridle, a pair of pistols, and a copy of Hoyles Games.

The most spectacular phase of frontier religious life occurred in camp meetings, which had been typically Southern since the Great Revival had swept the United States in the early eighteen hundreds. The results of revival meetings were more pronounced among the poor and the uneducated, although some more richly endowed with worldly goods occasionally were affected. In Texas the meetings were conducted chiefly by Methodists, with Cumberland Presbyterians and other denominations sometimes taking part. They did not reach their point of greatest influence in Texas until after entrance into the Union was effected, yet they combined with the circuit-riding system to furnish two causes for Methodist predominance in the Republic.

The success of camp meetings can be explained in part by the opportunity they afforded for social intercourse among "neighbors"

[38] Houston *Telegraph and Texas Register,* April 6, 1839.

who lived many miles apart. Many families traveled forty to fifty miles to attend, bringing with them pots, kettles, and other cooking utensils for open-air cooking. They slept in tents or wagons or even on the ground. For a brief span of four to ten days people found companionship in community living at the encampment.

A camp meeting customarily began on Thursday and worked up to a climax on the following Sunday, or if it continued throughout another week, fervor gradually increased until the second Sunday. The services were held in a forest clearing, in which a pulpit stand, brush arbor, and log benches had been set up. Assembly was called by blasts on a ram's horn, in remembrance of the horns used before Jericho, or, if none were available, on an ordinary cow's horn. Services were held from three to five times during a twenty-four hour period, but the daytime sessions were only preparatory for the night meeting, when the assembly place was illuminated by torches, lamps, and bonfires. In this favorable setting, the preachers put forth their most strenuous exertions. "The stillness of the night, the serenity of the heavens, the assembly of decorous worshippers, all wrapped in deep attention, the pointed and sincere manner of the preacher, produced solemn sensations in the minds of the listeners."[39]

Sermons were preceded and followed by singing and praying. A preacher "lined out" a hymn, two lines at a time, and a layman with a lusty voice "raised the tune" by pitching the key and leading the singing of the lines by the congregation. Often the preacher interspersed comment on the words of the hymn.

Camp-meeting sermons usually emphasized the crying need of every soul to accept the Saviour in order to avoid the torments of hell-fire. The frontiersman's religion was not the modern one of social service. It emphasized the future rather than the present, just as his economic life looked toward another though not so distant future.

To a boy attending his first camp meeting, Brother McKenzie, a Methodist preacher in the pulpit, "seemed to be as restless as though he stood on embers, running first to one end of the box [the pulpit] and then to the other, as though he wanted to get out

[39] Brown, "Annals of Travis County," III, 51.

of the box. He was talking loudly and his gestures were of the most violent character. At once I concluded that for some cause they had him confined in the box so that he could not get out, or that he feared to come out."[40]

At the climax of a successful camp meeting sermon

a low wailing could be heard from some old sister in the congregation [Dr. John Washington Lockhart wrote]. As the sound penetrated the ears of the audience others would take it up, and it seemed as the sighing of maddened winds off the desert of despair. Others would be affected in a more vehement manner. The shout of "Glory! Glory!" would follow, and still others of "Glory! Hallelujah! Blessed be the name of God!" and then the clapping of hands. At this juncture the younger sisters would approach the old ones, loosen their bonnet strings and proceed to fan them, and administer words of consolation, the best at their command. Nor was the amen corner of the old brethren silent, for they would shout with much unction, "Amen! Amen!" and perhaps break into a holy laugh, which would resound with a rasping noise throughout the whole congregation. The preachers, seeing their vantage ground gained, would commence one of those good old chorus songs which ran thus:

"Jesus, my all, to heaven is gone
And I want to go there too;
His tracks I see and I'll pursue,
And I want to go there, too."

This with the aid of good voices from the Congregation, would create a panic that nothing could resist. When the call for mourners was made, an indiscriminate scramble would be made for the altar, and in the twinkling of an eye every place would be filled with beseeching mourners, who by their prayers and importunities would almost open the very gates of heaven. Have I overdrawn this picture? I ask all candid old men to speak.[41]

One of the hardest-working and most effective Methodist preachers in the Southwest was Rev. Francis A. Wilson, who made

[40] "Autobiography of Andrew Davis," *Southwestern Historical Quarterly,* Vol. XLIII, No. 3 (January, 1940), 338.
[41] Wallis and Hill (eds.), *Sixty Years on the Brazos,* 154.

San Augustine his center of operations. He was noted for the fervor and intensity of his pulpiteering. One night, after the persons attending a camp meeting near Little Cow Creek in the Sabine River border region had retired to sleep, the encampment was startled by a series of loud horn blasts. The people gathered together at this call, and found Wilson in the pulpit attired in a long flowing robe, with his hair disheveled, and a Bible in his hand. After an admonition to silence he delivered a fiery and tremendously effective sermon on the Last Judgment.

Wilson had a nervous disease which made it necessary that he travel in the company of someone who could care for him if he were attacked by his affliction. Lucifer was a real force to him and sometimes gave evidence of being almost physically present. Here is Wilson's description of how his Satanic Majesty was put to rout at a East Texas camp meeting:

There was energetic preaching, powerful prayers, and some conversions, yet nothing much. . . . I delivered a kind of war speech and called on all the friends of religion to engage in a powerful effort of prayer. . . . and the mighty effort continued all night. Ah, what a poor creature is man! I never felt such power from beneath. The air was dark with the infernal beings. Sometimes it seemed that they would prevail. We made the best fight. After four o'clock in the morning while the preachers were engaged in mighty prayer in the tents, one of them began to plead the suffering of Christ, and to demand if the Saviour did not meet all the demands of the law, and why suffer his poor servants to be overpowered by the power of darkness, and now for the sake of Christ give victory. And while this was pleading I heard a sound of a rushing in the southwest corner of the tents. I heard a strange noise of something. It proceeded until it came under the bed in the room where I lay. Then it made a strange noise and then it moved out of the house, and a horse that was tied near where the noise was heard . . . appeared alarmed almost to death, and after making several powerful efforts he broke loose and ran as if the devil was after him, and with that the shouts commenced in the tents all over the camp ground, and from thence on to the close of the meeting there was victory on the Lord's side.

Nor did Brother Wilson pull his punches in dealing with human representatives of the Devil. He closed a meeting in feud-ridden Shelby County with this prayer:

Now Lord again we got the victory over hell and the wicked. Now Lord hear our prayer that we make for this people. If any Regulators & Moderators ever make an effort to revive their disturbance of hell either religiously or particularly, curse him with the loss of eyes, destroy his limbs that he may never be able to walk, curse him when he sits down to eat within his house, curse his fields, and if this will not stop his hellish career then kill him & send him to his own place where he ought to have been long ago. In the end may God grant this. Amen.[42]

The slaves who were allowed to attend camp meetings were especially susceptible to attacks of hysteria under the stress of intense religious feeling. On one occasion, Brother Wilson put the fear of the Lord into a Negro girl with his description of eternal death as something that had ten thousand heads; every head had ten thousand bodies; every body had ten thousand tails; every tail had ten thousand stings; and every sting emitted ten thousand deaths. The terrified girl became hysterical and was taken from the meeting, yelling that the big black man who was carrying her out was the Devil taking her to hell. At another Methodist meeting a Negro girl began to cry for mercy, and the preachers were unable to help her receive an answer to her supplications. An old Negro woman finally asked and received the presiding elder's permission to use different tactics on the sinner. She went up to the girl, seized her by the shoulders, and vehemently shook her. Then she told the girl: "You gal! What dat you doin'? Just shet up your mouth and open your heart; and hasn't the Saviour said, 'I will come in dare?' Now just try it." Soon the supplicant was "happy in the knowledge of sins forgiven."[43]

A special idiom for different phases of the process whereby an individual was "converted" and became "a professor of religion" was in use. A person who sought "to get religion" was "a seeker" who might occupy "the anxious seat" for some time, while those who had "backslidden" sought to be "pardoned." In getting religion, a few Texas seekers experienced the ecstatic loss of muscular

---

[42] "Autobiography of Rev. Francis A. Wilson," 80, 89.
[43] *Ibid.*, 86; Hall, *Life of Rev. John Clark,* 223.

control called "the jerks" in the early revivals east of the Mississippi River, and a great many participants in camp meetings had deeply emotional experiences.

A few Methodist preachers were beginning to discourage conversions under emotional stress. A contemporary letter describes a Methodist camp meeting at which the presiding elder discouraged "people getting religion under an excitement. He wanted them to come up coolly and deliberately." The half-dozen preachers who were co-operating with the elder in conducting the services were not at all pleased by this state of affairs, for although "several very warm sermons" and "exhortations" were delivered, there was only one conversion in four days. On the fifth night, after Rev. J. P. Sneed preached "a very warm feeling sermon," the presiding elder got up and told all listeners who had made up their minds "to get religion" to come forward without any excitement of any kind, since he did not like to see people "scared into religion." "Now just come along," he said, "without any persuasion or singing." At this point, one of the other preachers arose and called out, "Let us sing that good old song, 'Come ye Sinners poor and needy.' " As this invitation hymn was sung, a number of mourners came forward, and the presiding elder lost control of the meeting. The work of exhortation and singing then began in earnest, and before the meeting broke up at two forty-five A.M., eight "seekers" professed to have obtained "the pearl of great price."[44]

The year of 1843 marked the rise of the camp meeting to an important place in the promotion of Methodism in Texas. Notable meetings were held near Egypt, in the Chappell Hill community, at Cedar Creek, and in a number of places in East Texas. Although camp-meeting converts often did not remain within the fold, some churches undoubtedly were strengthened by the revivals in both the rural areas and the towns. This was certainly true of the meetings held in 1845 and 1846 at Houston, which had been a stronghold of the unrighteous for a decade.

Camp meetings in the country and the correctly named "protracted meetings" in the towns were regarded with favor by the

---

[44] J. H. Addison to O. M. Addison, July 8, 1846, Addison Papers. See also Mrs. Sarah Addison to O. M. Addison, July 10, 1846, *ibid*.

ardent religionists and frowned upon by the critical. A correspondent reported a Houston meeting in the *Southwestern Christian Advocate* as follows: "The Lord is doing a good work for us in our city. We have had a protracted meeting in our church for the last twenty days, and it is now in progress. . . . I believe that I have never seen a greater excitement in religion. In every group of men, from the church to the grog shop, their conversation is on religious subjects." But the conversation probably was not always of the type implied by the pious brother. Witness the description of a Houston meeting in the fall of 1845 as given in a personal letter:

The Methodists of this town are in a state of horrible—of frightful excitement—which has lasted already eight or ten days and attracts crowds of spectators. No pen or tongue could give you an adequate description of these riotous scenes—a person must see & hear in order to be convinced of their mad extravagancies & I fancy most will distrust the evidence of their senses. They call it a revival.[45]

A camp meeting in 1841 near Independence was described in the following pithy sentence: "They had rather singular doings; all that I saw were preaching, praying, or shouting, but one old woman, & she had fits."[46] This was mild criticism compared with other reports. Though most of the adverse criticism was by persons who could have been expected to look askance on camp meeting and revival activities, it is worthy of note that the phrase "camp-meeting babies" still persists in East Texas. As many as one thousand to fifteen hundred souls often were reported in attendance at camp meetings, and it is undoubtedly true that many were present as a result of curiosity or other nonreligious motives.

The interrelationship between education and religion was evident in the organization of Sunday schools. Secular school teachers often were leaders in forming them and continuing their work. School teacher Thomas J. Pilgrim inaugurated the Texas Sunday-school movement in 1829 with an organization in a crude log cabin at San Felipe; and afterward was instrumental in building up

45 John W. Bauer to Ashbel Smith, September 3, 184[5], Ashbel Smith Papers.
46 Statement by Alexander Chalmers, as reported in Edward Fontaine to M. B. Lamar, October 20, 1841, in Gulick *et al.* (eds.), *Lamar Papers*, V, 494.

strong Sunday schools at Houston, Austin, and Gonzales. Though he was a Baptist, he often worked outside of denominational traces. In like manner, in 1840, school teacher James N. ("Uncle Jimmy") Smith organized the first Sunday school on the Guadalupe River, at the Cuero Creek settlement. Few women became Sunday-school teachers, for it was believed that instruction of the young in religious matters could be handled best by men who had steeped themselves in knowledge of the Bible.

As early as the spring of 1838 Sunday schools were in existence at Houston, San Augustine, Nacogdoches, and Washington on the Brazos. The Houston group was organized by the Presbyterian minister, Rev. William Y. Allen. A correspondent of a local newspaper observed: "Wherever the enterprising spirit of the Anglo-Saxon race has reached, *there* is to be found children gathered together on each returning Sabbath, to receive instruction at the hands of their benevolent teachers."[47] In time, auxiliaries of the American Sunday School Union and other American Sunday-school organizations were formed at Brazoria, Austin, and elsewhere. By the end of 1843, twenty Sunday schools and three Bible classes were reported to have been organized among the Methodists. But on the whole, the observation of William Kennedy, an English diplomat, was an understatement: "Texas has Temperance and Bible Societies, and Sunday Schools, but there is ample room for the extension of these and kindred institutions."

A number of Masonic lodges were established during the days of the Republic. Representatives of lodges at Houston, Nacogdoches, and San Augustine organized the Grand Lodge of Texas in 1837, and before Texas was annexed by the United States, twenty-four subordinate lodges were chartered. The order exerted a strong influence as a social institution, and the establishment of a lodge in a town or settlement usually indicated that it was increasing in prosperity and population. The Independent Order of Odd Fellows also was established in the Republic, but it did not achieve a strong foothold until a later period.

[47] Houston *Telegraph and Texas Register,* May 30, June 2, 1838; Red (ed.), "Extracts from the Diary of W. Y. Allen," *Southwestern Historical Quarterly,* Vol. XVII, No. 1 (July, 1913), 48. See also Abner S. McDonald to "Bro. John," March 11, 1838, in *ibid.,* Vol. XIV, No. 4 (April, 1911), 335.

The advance of Protestantism also was forwarded by the distribution of Bibles and religious tracts. This work was done chiefly by the American Bible Society, acting through its agents or through resident preachers of the leading Protestant denominations. In 1832 the society sent seventy-five Bibles and one hundred Testaments, some of which were printed in Spanish, to Texas. In the following year, Rev. Benjamin Chase, a Mississippi Presbyterian who was acting as the society's agent in Mississippi, Louisiana, and Arkansas, brought a few more Bibles to the Mexican province across the Sabine River. As a result of his visit, Sumner Bacon, a Cumberland Presbyterian of Texas, offered his services as agent. In the jurisdiction of Nacogdoches, Bacon wrote, there were six hundred American and three hundred Spanish families, and "the households, destitute of the Bible are as nine to one." And the proportion was even greater in the interior. Bacon received his appointment and, as a representative of the society, in 1834 organized the first Bible society in Texas at San Augustine. Another was formed in the Columbia jurisdiction in the following year.[48]

After the Texas Revolution the American Bible Society resumed its activities in Texas. In 1837 it forwarded four hundred Bibles, which were supplemented by a collection of religious pamphlets sent by benevolent citizens of Natchez to the "chivalrous, but morally destitute" people of Texas.[49] In the fall of 1838, Rev. Schuyler Hoes, representing the American Bible Society, appeared at Houston and on November 11 organized the Texas Bible Society, with a pious politician, David G. Burnet, as president. Among the speeches made at the organization meeting was a scholarly address on the Bible by a well-known lawyer, William H. Wharton. Though he was skeptical of the divine inspiration of the Holy Scriptures, Wharton did not mention his doubts in his speech and was elected one of the vice presidents. Dr. Ashbel Smith also was selected as a vice president, although he feared that the society

[48] *Seventeenth Annual Report of the American Bible Society*, 36; *Eighteenth Annual Report of the American Bible Society*, 31; *Nineteenth Annual Report of the American Bible Society*, 18.

[49] *Twenty-second Annual Report of the American Bible Society*, 49; Columbia *Telegraph and Texas Register*, February 21, 1837; *Mississippi Free Trader and Natchez Gazette*, December 16, 1836.

would have no appreciable influence, because at times he believed "that there is not now existing in this community a sufficient regard for virtue, in which religion and a well based morality can take root and attain a permanent stand."[50] Reverend Mr. Hoes spent several months traveling over Texas, organizing a number of local Bible societies as auxiliaries to the national group.

The Texas Bible Society held two annual meetings in Austin, but after the capital was removed from that town and Mexican aggression disturbed the country in 1842, Bible societies in Texas became "well nigh extinct." In the summer of 1845, however, the Texas Bible Society was revived under the leadership of Rev. Chauncey Richardson, president of Rutersville College. After addresses by several lawyers and preachers of various denominations, the society passed a resolution that an attempt would be made to supply every family in Texas with a copy of the Holy Scriptures, "so that emigrants who may desire to cast their lots among us may know that they are coming to a land of Bibles."[51] In the same year Rev. James H. Kain, an agent of the American Bible Society, stimulated societies at Brazoria, Galveston, San Augustine, and Nacogdoches, while his organization sent nearly twenty-four hundred Bibles to Texas. Meanwhile, a colporteur of the American Tract Society arrived to distribute additional Bibles and pamphlets to the citizens of Texas.

In the words of the Texas preacher, Rev. Sam Corley, the cause of temperance in drinking was "religion's handmaid." The organization of a temperance society at the capital heralded the opening of a movement against drinking, though not its success. Early in 1839 Rev. William Y. Allen made a temperance speech amid the shavings in a workroom in the Tremont Hotel at Galveston. Shortly afterward, on February 18, he assisted in founding the Texas

---

[50] Journal, November 25, 1838, Ashbel Smith Papers; Red (ed.), "Extracts from the Diary of W. Y. Allen," *Southwestern Historical Quarterly*, Vol. XVII, No. 1 (July, 1913), 58; Houston *Telegraph and Texas Register*, November 24, December 1, 1838; *Twenty-third Annual Report of the American Bible Society*, 42.

[51] San Augustine *Red-Lander*, February 5, 1846; Houston *Telegraph and Texas Register*, August 6, 1845; Washington *Texas National Register*, May 1, May 29, 1845; Clarksville *Northern Standard*, June 28, 1845.

Temperance Society at Houston. A meeting was called at the insti-
gation of former President Sam Houston who addressed the audience with "a grand speech," in which he used his own experiences
as an illustration and admonished his hearers "to do as he advised,
and not as he had done." He spoke at such length that a visiting
preacher, who also was scheduled to harangue the listeners, did
not have time to give his speech and had to wait until the following
night. The society was formed as the result of the passage of a
resolution introduced by the principal speaker; and many signed
"the pledge."[52] But Houston did not indicate his willingness to
become an abstainer, possibly because he did not trust himself.
Early in the previous year he had made a wager of a suit of clothes
worth five hundred dollars that he would abstain from the use of
intoxicants until the end of 1838, but in November he had been
"nearly all the time drunk."[53]

Politicians frequently placed themselves in the forefront of the
temperance movement, and Sam Houston was no exception.
Whether or not he was sincere in his efforts to persuade his fellow
men to abstain from following the path that he had lighted so
luridly, he continued to make temperance speeches. In the summer
of 1839 the favorable impression made by his anti-alcohol addresses
in Mississippi was reported to be dissipated somewhat by his actions shortly thereafter while allegedly intoxicated. Six years later
he was rallying the temperance forces in Galveston. His speech
before the temperance society there was reported by a local newspaper in glowing terms: "The whole discourse was chaste and
appropriate and many passages were eloquent and thrilling." A
few days later he delivered another temperance lecture at a meeting of "The Order of the Star of Temperance" in a New Orleans
Methodist church. A correspondent of a Natchez newspaper, po-
litically hostile to Houston, wrote that the New Orleans speech
was a failure, and that "the only unusual sentiment he uttered

---

52 Red (ed.), "Allen's Reminiscences of Texas," *Southwestern Historical Quarterly,* Vol. XVII, No. 3 (January, 1914), 287–88; Houston *Telegraph and Texas
Register,* February 20, April 10, 1839; Houston *Morning Star,* April 27, 1839.

53 A. C. Allen and Sam Houston, "A Prohibition Wager," January 7, 1838, in
Williams and Barker (eds.), *Writings of Sam Houston,* II, 180; Thomas F. Mc-
Kinney to Samuel M. Williams, November 3, 1838, Williams Papers.

that no victory or military success had ever been achieved by an army whose commander was a drunkard seemed to wither all the laurels of San Jacinto."[54]

Foremost among the few antidrinking newspaper editors was Dr. Francis Moore, Jr., self-appointed director of several humanitarian movements. In his Houston newspaper, he admonished the young men of the country to forswear indolence, which might soon lead them to *"grogshops, which in the low country of Texas, are but the portals to the grave."* He frequently edified his readers with homilies based on his personal observations; among them he cited the instance of the physician who had cautioned the man of wealth against drink, only to see him become "a poor, degraded, homeless, penniless, bloated drunkard, despised, and pitied." He also inveighed against Congress because the tariff duties on books had not been removed while ice, which was useful in drinking, was placed on the free list, and during his terms as mayor of Houston, he was quick to impose fines on rowdy drunkards. Other Texas newspaper editors printed very few articles depicting the horrors resulting from drinking, though there were some exceptions. The Clarksville *Northern Standard* occasionally pointed out the evils of intemperance; while the Matagorda *Weekly Despatch* of February 10, 1844, reprinted an editorial on liquor from the La Grange *Intelligencer,* which called it

a poison, more deadly than the fatal Upas of Java, or the seducing eye of the great Boa of South America. The first destroys by its shade; the latter brings the fierce tiger within its reach by that glare which he cannot escape. . . . But the drinking of this cursed liquor is still more dreadful; it gradually burns up that fuel which is the foundation of intellect and reason; it gives to its victim an idea of bliss . . . until the day of retribution arrives; the poor being becomes a madman and a devil,—feelings too horrid to depict are upon his brain,—he is a lunatic; all decency, self demeanor, and even death, are set at defiance, while his hand is raised against the friend of years, his parents, his children, and against her whom he swore to cherish. . . . To those morals which the future may generate, there is a hope that the use of liquor may be

---

[54] Houston *Telegraph and Texas Register,* June 4, 1845 (quoting *Civilian and Galveston Gazette*); *Mississippi Free Trader and Natchez Gazette,* June 7, 1845.

abolished. And trusting to the talents of the minister of the gospel, and the school-master, this age may yet see that brilliant epoch.

Although few temperance groups had been organized in Texas by 1840, the succeeding years saw the movement gain headway— at least in the formation of societies in a number of towns. All adopted a constitution, drew up a roll to be signed by both men and women, and set about soliciting pledges of abstinence.

Preachers took the lead in forming these organizations. The first session of the Union Baptist Association recommended "to the members of the various Baptist Churches throughout the land, the formation of Temperance Societies in their neighborhoods, so that the stream of liquid fire which has devastated other countries, may not blast and wither the rising prospects of this young and interesting Republic." And invitations to "take the pledge" were a regular part of camp meetings and revival services. As a practical expression of the attitude of churches, members sometimes were disciplined for selling liquor and drinking, and the Union Baptist Association recommended that church members who had been twice convicted by a church of drunkenness (within a short space of time) should be excommunicated.[55]

A typical temperance rally was held at Corsicana on July 4, 1842. After an Independence Day celebration in the morning and a dinner in the open at noon, the Sons of Temperance met at their hall and formed a procession which marched to the local tavern where it was joined by "the Ladies." All then went "to the stand, preceded by the Bible and Banner." The first part of the program consisted of a prayer by a preacher, the singing of "the teetotallers song," the presentation of the banner to "the Division," and a response to the presentation speech by another preacher. "The Division" was then presented with a Bible by a woman speaker, who in the course of her remarks made "an animated appeal to the sons in behalf of the wives, widows and orphans of the inebriate, which was heartily responded to by Rev. Jas. H. Addison."[56]

[55] *Minutes of the First Session of the Union Baptist Association,* 5; *Minutes of the Fifth Anniversary Meeting of the Union Baptist Association,* 12.

[56] James H. Addison to J. W. Addison, July 12, 1842, Addison Papers. In this letter, the addressee was requested to send the writer a copy of "Here we come with pure cold water," a song which doubtless had its uses at temperance meetings.

Temperance speeches followed a general pattern. The address delivered in 1843 by James W. Latimer at a camp-ground near Clarksville contained many of the points usually made by temperance speakers:

I would to God, my own country was an exception. . . . I would to God Texas had never been cursed with men reckless of their moral obligation. But unfortunately its awful ravages are but too apparent, its traces but too visible. There is scarcely to be found a man of distinction, scarcely an individual holding offices of honor, who is not a *slave,* more or less, to intemperance. Yes, some of the first officers of government are "confirmed sots and worn out debauchers."

I am aware that people are beginning to open their eyes to this subject; and I already descry through the mist of futurity, the dawn of better days, when we will have no more judges *sleeping* upon the bench from intoxication—no more reeling presidents at the helm of state—no more congressional representatives *wallowing* in the streets of our capital. . . .

[To the ladies:] Act not unworthily of your sex. Recollect that the influence of one woman involved Greece in a ten year's war. . . . I tell you your influence on man's every action is almost omnipotent. Use it then in a noble cause, and add, if possible, another ray to the glittering diadem of your unpresumptious fame.[57]

As indicated by the speaker, the victories gained by the temperance forces in the Republic had been sporadic and had caused few interruptions in the reign of King Whisky.

Though hindered by the turbulence of the raw frontier and by intradenominational jealousies, the beginnings of the social power of the church and its ministry thus were discernible. Preachers were in the forefront of temperance and education movements, and community religious meetings met a pressing social need. The churches were responsive to many public attitudes at the same time that they combated the most virulent contemporary evils, and the circuit riders in particular were both an integral part of frontier life and a corps of militant leaders in the uneven struggle to subdue the unruly legions of Satan.

[57] Clarksville *Northern Standard,* December 23, 1843.

These Racking Fever Chills

THE WIDESPREAD PREVALENCE of malaria, one of the chief deterrents to the development of the Texas wilderness, was a more consistently pressing problem than Indian and Mexican depredations. Most new arrivals, especially those from the northern United States and Germany, found it necessary to experience suffering from malarial fevers, or at least loss of energy and weight, during habituation to a new climate. As one man wrote, "Could this be deferred, till the newcomer has time to make a crop or two; shelter himself comfortably from the weather, and see around himself the comforts of life, his sufferings would no doubt be greatly [a]meliorated." But acclimation with its accompanying chills and "shakes" and general debility usually occurred in the first warm season the newcomer spent in Texas.

A contemporary poem under the title "Chills and Fever" described the results of an attack by this ravening and persistent enemy:

> *Did you ever? No I never!*
> *Have the racking chills and fever?*
> *Then you surely cannot know*
> *All the pangs of human woe!*
> *Fever like hot lava ranging,*
> *Sanity at once estranging,*
> *Rushing through the blood with ire,*
> *Like a never ending fire,*
> *Chills that set your bones to aching,*
> *Giving you an earthquake shaking,*
> *Causing every tooth to chatter*
> *Like bones shaken on a platter;*
> *Twisting all your thews about*

These Racking Fever Chills

With a wrench that makes you shout,
Climax of all earthly ills
Are these racking fever-chills.

Frontier conditions in a southern area rendered settlers particularly susceptible to malaria and typhoid. Heavy rainfall and long seasons of hot weather "encouraged insect life associated with malaria, yellow fever, dengue, and typhoid," and enhanced difficulties of preserving food and maintaining even the rudimentary sanitation of the day. Yet the comparatively unhealthy lowlands were preferred as areas of settlements, except by a few individuals who sought localities which had reputations for healthfulness; among these few was Samuel A. Maverick of San Antonio whose father once advised him: "Of what use is all the lands in Texas or the figurs on a Bank book to a dead man."[1] Many townsites were laid out on river banks, and settlers sought river bottom lands because of their fertility and access to actual or prospective water transportation facilities.

In the spring of 1842 a young New Yorker wrote the following comment on the women of Brazoria County, where he had been working a short time: "I can't say that I admire their looks generally their complexion being mostly of a sallow hue, and wanting that rich mixture of red and white so common at the north." This was typical of comments of Northern travelers on the pallor of Texas faces attributable to that prevailing curse of the South—malaria, referred to in its various forms as intermittent fever (tertian or quartan malaria), remittent fever (estivo-autumnal malaria), country fever, or ague and "ager." Intermittent and remittent fevers were often bilious in character, and frequently were referred to as "bilious" fever. In Texas, malarial and "bilious" fevers as a matter of course were expected to ravage the settlements every summer, though newcomers and persons in "the low country" were subject to the most severe attacks. A common opinion developed that the healthfulness of Texas increased fairly regularly as one proceeded from east to west. The comparative scarcity of trees in the western counties, with a corresponding increase in open country and wind, was believed to "dissipate miasmata, or whatever are the causes of

[1] Samuel Maverick to Samuel A. Maverick, December 12, 1841, **Maverick Papers.**

intermittents and remittents." If the journey could be afforded, settlers attempted to avoid "the fevers" in the summer by repairing to "the mountains" or to San Antonio or to certain places on the coast "until the heats were over."

Although malarial fevers were expected every summer, certain years brought more sickness than others. The summer and fall of 1843 were particularly difficult for the settlers along the Brazos, Guadalupe, Colorado, and Trinity rivers, and even the Indians were reported to be seriously afflicted. In August, 1843, Samuel A. Maverick wrote from La Grange that his "eldest son & eldest daughter have been at the point of death from the billious fever which has this year in consequence of heavy & constant rains prevailed here (on the Colorado) to an extent which has never been known before since the first settlement."[2] "Bilious" fevers were thought to cause excessive secretions of bile and were extremely dangerous. Ferdinand Roemer, the German geologist, observed that the disease required immediate attention because it often proved fatal during the first two days of the attack.

Some observers believed that, by 1850, malarial fevers had grown less severe in their attacks; the types characterized by chills and intense congestion supposedly gave way to one which was less virulent and debilitating. Dr. Ashbel Smith decided that perhaps increased comfort in living was one cause for the change, but in searching for more fundamental causes, he stated that he knew "nothing better than to take refuge in the old 'constitutional state of the air' having changed." At any rate, by 1850 he was able to use saline purgatives, especially Epsom salts, which he said had been "formerly prescribed as almost fatal."

The most commonly held theory of the causes of malarial fevers was that they resulted from "miasma of marshes"—infectious material and noxious effluvia supposedly arising from stagnant water or vegetable decomposition in the lowlands. This theory found expression in the term *malaria,* literally "bad air." Some ascribed the malarial fevers to overexertion, exposure to the sun, and unwholesome food. Exposure to the sun also was supposedly the cause of "congestive" fever, which sometimes began with chills. The follow-

2 Maverick to R. N. Wier, August 15, 1843, *ibid.*

The city hospital at Galveston in the early 1840's

Reproduced from Charles Hooton, *St. Louis' Isle, or Texiana,* 1847

ESSAY

ON THE

PARTICULAR INFLUENCE

OF

PREJUDICES IN MEDICINE,

OVER THE

Treatment of the Disease most common in Texas,

Intermittent Fever;

PRECEDED BY A FEW

GENERAL OBSERVATIONS ON MEDICAL THEORIES.

BY THEODORE LEGER, M. D.

LATE PROFESSOR OF MIDWIFERY OF THE FACULTY OF PARIS,
MEMBER OF THE MEDICAL COLLEGE OF MEXICO,
AND EX-VICE PRESIDENT OF THE MEDICAL
SOCIETY OF NEW ORLEANS.

1838 :

PEOPLE PRESS—BRAZORIA, TEXAS.

Title page of Dr. Leger's pamphlet on one form of malaria

ing theory was advanced, apparently in all seriousness, by a Houston newspaper: "It has generally been noticed that fevers are most frequent just after the excitement of the September election. We hope all will bear this in mind, and endeavor to avoid all unnecessary excitement; neither giving way to passion nor intemperance."[3]

The routine Texas diet of corn bread, beef, bacon, and potatoes and the ravages of overindulgence in intoxicating liquors of inferior quality also were thought to be among the real causes of fevers and other diseases among whites as well as Negroes. Although there is no conclusive evidence on the subject, scurvy and rickets must have been prevalent as a result of an inadequate diet in which vegetables and milk often were sadly lacking. Amusingly enough, Dr. Francis Moore, Jr., of the Houston *Telegraph and Texas Register* warned travelers to be particularly wary of tavern food:

The ill-cooked, unwholesome food which is so often furnished at our taverns is a fruitful source of disease. The heavy sodden dough-balls, which in the shape of "hot rolls" are served so plentifully at the hotels, are of themselves sufficient to create the worst of remittent fever, and should be shunned by the hungry traveller as he would shun a charge of grape-shot; indeed, we believe the grape-shot of the Mexicans have committed less havoc among our citizens than these vile dough-balls.[4]

But Roemer, the German scientist, observed that malarial fevers sometimes occurred in the higher sections of the country, where not all the conditions commonly attributed as their cause were present. Mosquitoes—one genus of which is now known to be responsible for spreading malaria—were noted, but they were regarded chiefly as an intolerable nuisance, along with the flies which infested the unscreened houses. In 1831 Henry Austin wrote that the insects had "operated upon me . . . like a perpetual blister" at Bolivar, his Brazos River home. And fleas and mosquitoes moved a young man to write his mother from Galveston:

You sometimes *think* you are troubled with fleas, but you have no

[3] Houston *Morning Star,* August 29, 1843.

[4] Houston *Telegraph and Texas Register,* July 1, 1840.

227

cause for complaint, and were you to spend a few nights in Galveston you would be presented with the fact in a most demonstrable light. They are dreadful troublesome—to me—I had almost said to the good citizens—but they are not so easily troubled, they have become used to the anoyance and are apparently indifferent to their severe attacks they prevail universal throughout the City—no place is exempt from their ravages—but I am getting *hardened* & dont mind them much now. The musquitoes however are more formidable, and the poor fellow who has to sleep without a "bar" is indeed in a "bad fix" & realy is entitled to sympathy—[5]

Some individuals fortunately were able to afford mosquito nets. For those who did not have this protection, a Texas newspaper in 1836 recommended attaching a piece of flannel saturated with "camphorated spirits" to the bedstead, "and the musquitoes will leave the room."

In 1833–34 Asiatic cholera was epidemic in certain parts of Texas. This dreaded disease was rightly called "the scourge of nations." Long known and feared in India, it had been pandemic in Asia between 1816 and 1830, and then, following trade routes the world over, spread through Russia and entered Germany, the British Isles, and France. In 1832 it appeared in Canada, New York, and other regions along the Atlantic coast, and in October reached New Orleans, where it took a tremendous toll. The colonists in Texas were not spared. Early in April, 1833, cholera appeared at the mouth of the Brazos River, where it practically depopulated the town of Velasco, and then moved up the river to Brazoria, causing most of the citizens to take flight. (Two doctors who were at Columbia, on the Brazos, stated in later life that the cholera was accompanied by yellow fever.) Early in August the fearful malady was raging at San Felipe de Austin, and the Matagorda vicinity also received visitations of both cholera and malignant fevers, which in many instances proved fatal. The pestilence was accompanied by the Great Overflow of 1833 in the spring and a very wet summer, both of which added materially to human suffering and economic loss. The cholera disappeared by the end of October, leav-

[5] O. M. Addison to Mrs. I. S. Addison, April 25, 1845, Addison Papers. (First part of letter is dated April 20, 1845.)

ing in its wake a list of deaths which included many of the staunch-
est citizens of Austin's Colony; and the survivors were seriously
weakened and bereaved by loss of relatives and friends.

Although cholera did not attack the Mexican settlements of
Texas (which had prepared against the plague) in 1833, it wrought
havoc south of the Rio Grande at Monclova. In the following year
it caused a wholesale desertion of San Antonio, as well as much
loss of life at Goliad and Victoria. The scourge also recurred in
San Felipe, and the ranks of Irish immigrants on the San Antonio
River were depleted. The epidemic of 1833–34, and the accompanying fevers and crop losses of those years, afford adequate explanation of the lull in Anglo-American activity following the political
and military disturbances of 1832–33. This furnishes support for
the point of view of the not inconsiderable number of students who
have concluded that the Texas Revolution had its real beginnings
in 1832—not in 1835–36.

The only other exotic epidemics prior to annexation occurred
in 1839 and 1844, when Galveston and Houston were subjected to
attacks of yellow fever—which periodically invaded many other
American seaport towns, especially those on the Gulf of Mexico.
The disease first appeared on Strand Street in Galveston late in
September, 1839, and soon broke out in Houston. Considerable
excitement prevailed in both towns. In Galveston, large property
holders endeavored to conceal existence of the disease for fear of
damaging the value of their holdings. Dr. Ashbel Smith wrote
that they "declared war against me—I set them at defiance." In
Houston an average of five to seven persons—including "the most
abstemious"—died each day for several weeks; newspaper editors
were criticized for withholding from the public information about
the real nature of the epidemic; and the citizens were reported to
"appear to be much frightened."

Although business in both towns was paralyzed, the invasion
of the disease in Galveston was confined to streets near the harbor,
and a severe "norther" early in November brought relief. By November 21 Dr. Smith was able to refer to the epidemic as "a little
flourish of Yellow fever here" and to state that "accounts . . . have
been greatly exaggerated." Nevertheless, this ambitious and sci-
entifically minded physician utilized his experiences to publish a

pamphlet on yellow fever in Galveston, a study based principally on cases which had come under his observation and on autopsies of victims. He promised to send copies to his "medical friends" in the United States and England, and offered to mail a specimen of *"genuine black vomit"*—the chief positive sign of the disease—to one of them.[6] But throughout the whole epidemic he continued to proclaim that Texas (and Galveston in particular) was an extremely healthy region, especially for persons with weak lungs. He pointed out the indubitable fact that aside from the yellow-fever area, the remainder of the country had suffered comparatively little sickness. On the whole, 1839 was a healthy year for Texas.

In July, 1844, yellow fever again appeared in Galveston. The epidemic raged until about the middle of August, when it began to abate. Among the several hundred fatalities were two United States diplomats, a newspaper editor, and several prominent lawyers. The population of Houston was also subjected to attacks by the pestilence, but one sufferer testified: "It has been very sickly this Summer in Houston and Galveston with the Yelow Fever. It happened that my family were in the country and Escaped. I had it very severe and like to have died There were few deaths in Houston compared with Galveston . . . no one escaped being sick who had not been sick before with the yellow fever."

Yellow-fever epidemics called attention to the pressing need for improvements in sanitation in Houston and Galveston, where there was constant danger of contagious diseases following in the wake of an influx of immigrants and a large number of transients who were willing to endure filth temporarily. In the summer of 1839, a grand jury had denounced the Houston jail as "not only injurious to the inmates, but . . . very liable to become a source of malignant disease to persons residing in its vicinity. The effluvia now environing the jail for some feet about it, are so potent as to

6 Smith to "Pennock," November 29, 1839 (letter-book MS), Ashbel Smith Papers; Smith, *An Account of the Yellow Fever which Appeared in the City of Galveston, Republic of Texas, in the Autumn of 1839*. See Smith to Pennock, October 21, 1839 (letter-book MS), Ashbel Smith Papers, for a description of the interiors of the yellow fever victims upon whom he had performed autopsies; and William McCraven, "On the Yellow Fever of Houston, Texas, in 1847," *New Orleans Medical and Surgical Journal*, Vol. V, No. [2] (September, 1848), 231, 234, for brief discussions of the 1839 and 1844 attacks of yellow fever in Houston.

sicken the stoutest stomach." In October, when yellow fever caused
the death of a number of Houstonians, a local newspaper blamed
the board of health for the streets that had "remained unattended
to, and consequently horridly filthy," for the carrion that "has
been suffered to lay unremoved in our vicinity, so near as to im-
pregnate the atmosphere with its putridity," and for permitting
"the washings of the kitchens and back yards of the whole city
... to be thrown into the streets and gutters, there to rot and emit
a stench disgusting and poisonous in the extreme." Thereafter the
board was more active.

Although smallpox caused much terror, its attacks were short-
lived and localized. An epidemic prevailed in various parts of
Mexico in 1830, and probably in a mild form at San Antonio, where
the local government, aided by private contributions, furnished
vaccine to the people. This disease appeared later at Brazoria in
1835, at San Antonio and Houston in 1840, and in Austin County
in 1844, but it was never a serious problem.

Although there are scattered references to gonorrhea in contemporary records, even an approximation of the extent of venereal
diseases is impossible. Until 1838 syphilis and gonorrhea were
thought by medical science to be one disease, and the relation of
syphilis to apparently unrelated diseases was not understood until
many years later. Furthermore, no vital statistics were kept. Perhaps venereal diseases sometimes may have had a connection with
the "purulent op[h]thalmia" which Dr. Joseph E. Field found
"considerably frequent, though not epidemic" in Texas.[7]

The real dangers to health lay in the recurrent and more common maladies—malarial fevers, intestinal diseases, respiratory diseases, and probably typhoid fevers which were known under other
names. Dysentery—often called diarrhea, bloody flux, or summer
complaint—was a malignant and prevalent ailment. In the cold
season, settlers frequently were attacked by pneumonia, pleurisy,
diphtheria, or colds, although medical science was not yet able to
discriminate accurately among them. One doctor wrote: "In the
winter, *pneumonia typhoides,* or bastard pleurisy, is most common." One form of severe pneumonia was called "bilious pleurisy"

[7] Field, *Three Years in Texas,* 37.

or "head pleurisy." Croup and whooping cough also were frequently encountered. The open construction of houses, in which glass panes were luxuries, doubtless left many individuals susceptible to attacks of throat ailments. It was reported that, at Washington on the Brazos in January, 1845, "influenza has prevailed among men, and not any among women." This was the first appearance of this infectious disease in Texas, and it spread rapidly with disastrous results particularly apparent in Brazos County.[8] And in the following spring whooping cough became "prevalent in many parts of the country."

The treatment of practically all diseases, especially those of which fever was a symptom, began with the employment of purgatives and emetics. Tartar emetic, ipecac, and Dover's powders (containing ipecac and opium) were used as emetics and to increase perspiration. Purgation was stimulated by the use of calomel, blue pills (prepared mercury), and castor oil, and less often by jalap, rhubarb, senna, or Seidlitz powders.[9]

The most common treatment for malaria involved the traditional "puke, purge, and bleeding"—heroic treatments which were supposed to reduce "irregular or convulsive wrong action" by "depletion" but actually sometimes killed the patient or often left him so debilitated that he fell victim to other diseases. In 1838 Dr. Theodore Leger of Columbia published a pamphlet in which he attacked this merciless regimen when it was used in treating intermittent fever: "Do we not see our self-styled Doctors hurry to pour down their incendiary drugs, to administer purgatives, vomitives, bleeding and cupping, and to bring into play all the resources

[8] The quotation is from Mrs. S. J. Allen to Mrs. Isabella H. Gordon, January 20, 1845, Gordon Papers. For an analysis of symptoms in this epidemic, see Thomas J. Heard, "Medical History of Texas," 2–4.

[9] The account book of Dr. James H. Starr of Nacogdoches for 1841 shows that he prescribed or sold the following: rhubarb, calomel, prepared charcoal, "Blue Mass," aloes, blue pills, morphine, quinine, "S. Arabic," sweet oil, "G. arabic," laudanum, "spts. nitre," "Pill Hyd," "Elix Vit," sugar of lead, peppermint, "Pl Mustard," paregoric, "Cream Tart.," snakeroot, magnesia, "Ext Pink root," Seidlitz powders, Cook's Pills, "Empl vesic [?]," "solut caustic," ipecac, "Nitro muriatic acid," salts, "Hardamans pills [?]," and "Batmans drops."—Starr Papers. Cook's Pills, Lee's Pills, and Rush's Pills appeared frequently in contemporary prescriptions.

of their pharmaceutick arsenal? Calomel and Blue-pills form their heavy artillery; then advance, in second rank, Jalap and Rhubarb; Epsom-salts and Castor oil bring up the rear."[10] This was a period when excessive bloodletting and use of calomel were under attack, but still commonly prescribed for a wide variety of ailments by all except the most advanced practitioners. Bad teeth were thought by some observers to be among the results of the overuse of calomel in childhood.

In many Texas houses there were no feminine hands to concoct homemade remedies or soothe the fevered brows of bachelors or widowers. Among the latter was Colonel James Morgan of New Washington, who unburdened himself in 1841 of the following discourse on his recent illness:

For the first time since I have been in Texas, now *ten years,* have had to Call in Medical Aid! My indisposition was of short duration but the d——d Doctor came near Physicking me to death. He poured it into me at *both ends* for 24 hours without cessation—making an apothecary shop of my abdomen. . . . I had fever but three days but long enough to prostrate me for several weeks with debility. O! my, dear Sir, how I miss my wife . . . never so much before—And if I Could *forget her* I would have another as soon as I could get one—There is no one around a Sick bed like a wife or mother and I am so lonely without somebody near to console and . . . sympathise. But I believe I am a widower for life.[11]

Another presumably indispensable treatment was "bleeding," usually from the arm. This practice grew less frequent during the period of the Republic and "cupping" often was substituted. "It called forth that instrument of torture, the 'scarifactor,' which tore ten to twelve holes in a man's skin at one blow." The openings were covered with a heated cup, which would fill with blood. Though even the most competent practitioners thought it necessary at times to relieve their patients of blood, they did so with increasing reluctance. Yet in 1850 patients suffering attacks of the type of pneumonia formerly called "bilious pleurisy" recovered

[10] Leger, *Essay on the Particular Influence of Prejudices in Medicine, Over the Treatment of the Disease Most Common in Texas, Intermittent Fever,* 17.

[11] Morgan to Samuel Swartwout, November 6, 1841, Morgan Papers.

"under the use of the lancet in moderation, with tartarized antimony."

The chief advance in medical practice in Texas during this period was the gradual substitution of quinine for Peruvian bark, which medical authorities disliked because uniform dosage was difficult and because it upset the patients' stomachs. Among the favorite forms of quinine medication were Dr. Champion's Pills, Dr. Thruston's Unrivalled Antifever Pills, and Dr. Sappington's Anti-Fever Pills. Although quinine came into general use before 1846, "atrocious adulterations" tended to lessen the value of the new medicine,[12] and the cause of malaria was yet undiscovered. "Chills and fever" patients also were given small doses of champagne, other wines, or Godfrey's Cordial, or they might be rubbed with camphorated oil or red pepper and brandy.

Cholera was a mysterious disease. Its origin and efficacious treatment baffled medical authorities, who debated interminably whether the plague was caused by filth or contagion. Many absurd and peculiar methods of treatment were used in the South and in Texas, as elsewhere in the world. In addition to the hopeless bafflement resulting from ignorance concerning the proper treatment, terror and panic were precipitated by the sudden incidence of the disease and its horrible effects. Cramps, internal pains, excessive evacuation, and vomiting were among the symptoms. At Velasco in 1833 Thomas Drummond, the Scottish naturalist, managed to relieve the violent cramps in his legs with opium, but reported that "all the cases terminated fatally except mine, and always in ten or twelve hours, save one person, who lingered a few days."[13] While opium, blisters, bleeding, and astringents were used, calomel probably was prescribed most often by doctors.

The administration of bleeding, vomitives, plasters, blisters, and mustard, onion, and flaxseed poultices in severe cases were the

---

[12] Smith, "On the Climate, Etc., of a Portion of Texas," *Southern Medical Reports,* II, 455. Bollaert, "Notes on Texas, 1843–1844," 43, warned against "Dr Vancouvers powders," composed of powdered Peruvian bark, cayenne pepper, and magnesia. Quinine was extracted from Peruvian bark (cinchona bark).

[13] Thomas Drummond to William Jackson Hooker, May 14, 1833, quoted in Geiser, *Naturalists of the Frontier,* 78. See also J. Villasana Haggard, "Epidemic Cholera in Texas, 1833–1834," *Southwestern Historical Quarterly,* Vol. XL, No. 3 (January, 1937), 216–30.

methods most often used in the treatment of chest and throat ailments. Sometimes a piece of fat meat to which pepper had been applied was tied around the neck of the patient. Powdered alum and a mixture of camphor, brandy, and sugar were among remedies suggested for home preparation, and before 1850 doctors were applying nitrate of silver to swollen parts.

Doctors often were community leaders. Although frequently they were not informed of the latest scientific developments in their profession, they gained general respect by attention to duty and by long and difficult trips over bad roads. They added to their incomes by selling drugs and occasionally nonmedicinal items such as "perfumery" and "rectified perfumed bear's oil" for the hair. Physicians also practiced law, farmed, preached, became proprietors of general stores, edited newspapers, accepted political appointments, and ran for offices, and at New Braunfels a doctor served as apothecary and baker. Dr. William P. Smith was a soldier, politician, Methodist preacher, farmer, and newspaper editor. One Houston doctor went into partnership with a barber; their advertisement offered shaving at six and one-quarter cents and haircutting at twenty-five cents, as well as services in "tooth-drawing, bleeding, cupping, and other surgical operations."

A few Texas doctors had excellent backgrounds in education and training. Dr. Ashbel Smith had been educated at Yale and in Paris and had practiced in North Carolina. Dr. Alexander Ewing, who was Dr. Smith's predecessor as surgeon general of the army, had obtained his M.D. degree from the University of Edinburgh in 1815 and ten years later had attended a course of lectures on the theory and practice of surgery sponsored by the Royal College of Surgeons of Ireland. For the most part, however, the apprentice system of "reading medicine" under the supervision of a doctor, followed in some cases by attendance on lectures at a medical school (perhaps for one winter only), was in vogue in the United States. This was essentially the training that had been received by Dr. Thomas J. Heard, a widely respected doctor of Washington on the Brazos and later of Galveston, and by Dr. Anson Jones of Brazoria, who supervised the professional education of at least two Texas neophytes who later were associated with him.

However, in the absence of satisfactory evidence on the subject, it is a distinct probability that Texas doctors as a group were not even as well qualified as their professional colleagues in the United States. With few exceptions the frontier practitioners did not have access to the medical journals of the period; and the estate records of doctors who died in Texas during the period of the Republic indicate that their medical libraries were very small, usually including "Hamilton on purgatives," "Hunter on the blood," and works by Eberle and Cooper.

"Impostors" were able to acquire "the *honorable* title of doctor merely by the simple process of emigration." A few well-known doctors even advertised that they possessed degrees from medical institutions whose records now fail to substantiate their claims. Certainly there was nothing to prevent any person who imagined himself competent from hanging out his shingle, because no effective organization of physicians was formed and the efforts of the Texas national government to restrict the practice of medicine to qualified practitioners were abortive and ineffectual. The amount of actual malpractice by untrained doctors, judged by the standards of the time, is difficult to determine. In 1838 Dr. Leger of Columbia assailed "the quacks who abound in Texas," and on June 24, 1837, the Houston *Telegraph and Texas Register* contained an editorial denunciation of quackery, using as its chief illustration a Texas doctor who recently had been a shoemaker in Tennessee:

We may be styled goose, gosling, or *quack, quack, quack,* but we shall certainly prescribe a remedy for a species of vermin which infests our country, distinguished by the *once* august title of Doctor. These pseudo "M.Ds" or "Drs" are, we sincerely believe more dangerous than the hostile Indians; and not considerably less numerous. . . . We had rather at any time see a company of armed Mexicans in battle array, than a squad of these *grave* gentry, parading with their "Pandora boxes" in the shape of pill bags—which are seldom opened without entailing on the community disease and death. . . .

A few doctors were "Thomsonians," a medical sect whose "botanic system" was based on the theory that vegetable remedies and "steam doctoring" provided the heat necessary to cure all diseases. The development of this sect—which was strongly opposed by "regular" doctors—was a part of the revolt against bloodletting and the inordinate use of calomel. In the Republic of Texas several doctors used both herb remedies and conventional medicines: Dr. W. F. T. Hart, a well-known Clarksville doctor, advertised that he "embraced the theory and practice of the Botanic system blended with the regular practice"; and although Dr. James H. Starr of Nacogdoches was a graduate of a Thomsonian medical school, his account book for 1841 indicates that his prescriptions usually were in accordance with the customary practice of physicians.

Before final judgment is passed upon practitioners on the Texas frontier, it must be remembered that standards of medical education in the United States generally were low in the eighteen thirties and forties and that medical science was in a semichaotic condition.[14] Provincialism and mediocrity flourished in American medicine, and quacks and charlatans were in public favor on both sides of the Atlantic. This was the period when a Philadelphia newspaper poked fun at New York doctors in the following gibe:

Doctors. The Philadelphia Sentinel says that N. York has a greater variety of physicians than any other city in the world. The Sentinel enumerates them thus:—

Regulars, irregulars, Broussaisans, Sangradoarians, Morrissonians, Brandrethians, Beechitarians, botanics, regular botanics, Thomsonians, reformed Thomsonians, theoretical, practical, experimental, dogmatical, emblematical, magnetical, electical, electrical, diplomatical, homeopathians, rootists, herbists, florists and quacks.[15]

The Congress of the Republic established a board of medical censors to examine persons who wished to practice medicine. This body consisted of one physician, who held a diploma or degree, from each senatorial district. But there was no meeting of the board in 1839, and in the following spring the most prominent member asserted that "it operates a serious inconvenience without the smallest advantage."[16] Although undoubtedly there were medical

14 Richard H. Shryock, *Development of Modern Medicine,* 251; Thomas L. Nichols, *Forty Years of American Life, 1821–1861,* 227; William F. Norwood, *Medical Education in the United States Before the Civil War,* 385, 421–22, 431–43.

15 *Niles' Weekly Register,* Vol. LI, No. 7 (October 15, 1836), 112.

16 Ashbel Smith to David Scott, March 1840 (letter-book MS), Ashbel Smith

charlatans in the Republic, the court records may be searched in vain for evidence that they were prosecuted—either for incompetence or practicing without a license.

In 1838 the "Medical & Surgical Society of Houston" set a standard scale of charges for services—one of few instances of attempted self-regulation by the profession. Whether that body passed on the nice point in medical ethics that occurred in Houston, when a friend of a dying man called in a second physician after Dr. Ashbel Smith had given up the case, is doubtful. Smith threatened to cane the friend, a local merchant.

During the period of the Republic, doctors' fees usually were five dollars per call (doubled after nine P.M.); cupping, five dollars; bleeding, two dollars; consultation, fifteen dollars; midwifery, thirty to forty dollars; and detention (per hour), one dollar. But occasionally a doctor advertised reduced rates. When patients died, doctors often presented unitemized bills for sums ranging from ten to three hundred dollars, and the charges usually were allowed by the executors of the estates without question by the probate courts. Bills for medical attention, however, were as difficult to collect as in later times, and medical fees are not a safe guide to determination of doctors' incomes.

The financial rewards of the practice of medicine generally were disappointing for ordinary practitioners. Warnings occasionally were sounded that the country had its share of members of the medical profession, that Texas was an agricultural country and needed farmers. The boom towns, particularly Houston, attracted many lawyers and doctors, some of whom found little practice. The prospects in Austin in the spring of 1841 likewise were discouraging; a medical man wrote from that place that "I find that should we [he and his partner] get all the practice in this Section, that it would but poorley pay a hungry son of Aesculapius!"[17] The doctor who had an estate valued at more than $2,500 was rare, and often the bills which his patients had neglected to pay constituted the major portion.

Papers. In colonial Texas, local governmental agencies had attempted to limit the practice of medicine to trained physicians, and in 1835 a meeting of the "Medical and Philosophical Society of Texas" was called to convene at Brazoria.

17 W. K. Cooke to James H. Starr, March 2, 1841, Starr Papers.

The difficulties of settling accounts for services rendered were partially remedied by doctors' acceptances of cows, horses, pigs, cotton, corn, or land. In 1831 a doctor received a cow in payment for one five-mile trip and a consultation, thus showing "the scarcity of medical science in the country, and the abundance of beef." This type of compensation was satisfactory because many physicians were acquiring land and developing farms. Among these was Dr. T. F. L. Parrott of Fort Bend County whose $6,000 estate in 1839 included six slaves and several thousand acres of land.

A few doctors developed practices that yielded adequate returns. Among these were Dr. James H. Starr of Nacogdoches, Dr. Anson Jones of Brazoria, and Dr. Ashbel Smith of Houston and Galveston. All three became prominent in the political life of the Republic; and in the early eighteen forties, Dr. Starr gave up his medical practice and went into a more lucrative land-agency business. Since both Jones and Smith truthfully stated that they were in the lead of their competitors in their respective communities, they must be regarded as exceptional cases. At the end of 1834, Jones had a practice which he estimated as worth $5,000 a year, while Smith made even more money in the early years of the existence of the Republic. In 1837 he averaged twenty-five to thirty-five dollars per day in private practice, in addition to the returns from his position as surgeon general which he valued at nearly four thousand dollars per annum. He stated that he would clear more above his expenses in one year than he could in six years in North Carolina, and he believed that his investments in Houston property and in lands would eventually provide him with a large fortune. Two years later he estimated that his Texas estate was worth between $30,000 and $40,000. In addition to his investments, he had supplemented his income by selling medicine (including quinine at 500 per cent profit), magazines, paper, and clocks, and by hiring out a slave at three to five dollars per day. Dr. Smith's success may be ascribed to indubitable competence and energy and an ability to maintain friendly connections with leading figures on both sides of a political fence.

Although there were a few dentists in the Republic, teeth were generally treated or pulled by untrained relatives or by family physicians. Doctors often advertised that along with their medical and surgical practice, they also would extract teeth—usually for two dollars per tooth. The following advertisement appearing in a Galveston paper indicates that at least one dentist took advantage of his position to sell an early precursor of modern oral hygiene mixtures: "Dr. J. J. Davis has resumed the practice of Surgeon Dentistry.... He has on hand a good assortment of Porcelain teeth &c. Also tooth powder a superior article for preserving the teeth, correcting or sweetning the breath, &c."[18] But a far more impressive instance of enterprise on the part of a dentist occurred on San Jacinto battlefield. John J. Linn arrived there shortly after the historic engagement and saw "the ghastly spectacle of six hundred Mexican corpses festering in the sun." The clothes of all of them had been thoroughly searched for plunder. But a dentist was obtaining the final fruits of victory by extracting the teeth—"these valuable adjuncts of his trade"—from the dead bodies.[19]

A number of Texas doctors were competent surgeons, but, in the absence of anesthetics, operations must have been harrowing experiences for patients who often were tied or held down. In emergencies, when trained surgical assistance was not immediately available, laymen treated patients and even operated. One East Texan related his efforts on behalf of Henry Strickland, a Shelby County desperado:

On this man I got to test my skill in surgery. Hansford Hicks plunged an old rusty dirk in Strickland's right breast, and when I got to him he was spitting up clots of blood and had a high fever. I got from my private medicine box rhubarb and alum, took some padding and screwed it into the hole, made a large slippery elm poultice that went all around his body, kept his bowels regular and dieted him. I cooked his food, pulled him through in ten days and had him on his feet again. He was the most grateful man I ever saw.[20]

18 *Civilian and Galveston Gazette,* September 24, 1842. A small notebook in the Burnet Papers contains various recipes and prescriptions, including "Tincture for Toothache," "Tooth Paste (Gums)," and "Tooth Powder." The latter is a mixture of "prepared chalk," "cuttle fish powder," "root powder," and "rose pink." For a zinc and silver cure for the toothache, see Clarksville *Northern Standard,* November 7, 1846.

19 Linn, *Reminiscences of Fifty Years in Texas,* 263; Stiff, *Texan Emigrant,* 103.

20 Eph M. Daggett, "Recollections of the War of the Moderators and Regu-

Such heroic measures did not always save lives. One of the most harrowing accounts of an unsuccessful operation by a layman is given in the reminiscences of Capt. Jesse Burnam:

You ask me to tell you about taking the man's leg off. I was living on the Colorado at that time. His name was Parker, and he lived on the opposite side of the river. His leg was terribly diseased, and he begged us to cut it off two months before we consented. One day he sent for me. I went over, and he took hold of my hand with both of his and said, "Oh, have you come to take my leg off?" I said, "Yes, I have come to do anything you want me to do." "That is right," he said. "If I die I don't want to take it with me." So Tom Williams, Kuykendall, Bostick, and I undertook the job with a dull saw and shoe knife, the only tools we had. I heated and bent a needle to take up the arteries with. I was to have the management of it and hold the flesh back, Tom Williams was to do the cutting of the flesh, Bostick to saw the bone, and Kuykendall to do the sewing. I took his suspenders off and bandaged the leg just above where we wanted to cut. I put a hair rope over the bandage, put a stick in it, and twisted it just as long as I could; then I was ready to begin operations. When Mr. Kuykendall began to sew it he trembled, so I took the needle and finished it. Parker rested easy for several days; but the third day he complained of his heel hurting on the other leg, and the eleventh day he died.[21]

The existence of a few crude hospitals did little to relieve human suffering. The Texas Army provided rudimentary hospital service for its soldiers, and city hospitals were operated at Houston and Galveston. For several years the small tax on all incoming passengers from foreign ports was the source of support for the Galveston hospital, described by an Englishman as "that shell of misery, that great coffin of the unburied dead." In the summer of 1843 a court ruled that there was no provision for the tax in the city charter and that consequently it was illegal. In commenting on the finding of the court, a local editor wrote: "The burthen must now fall upon the charity of the people. There are four or five poor fel-

lators," 12. For treatment by laymen of a compound fracture of a leg, see Mary Austin Holley, *Texas* (1836), 172.

[21] *Quarterly of the Texas State Historical Association,* Vol. V, No. 1 (July, 1901), 14–15.

lows in the Hospital now, confined with dropsy, scurvy and other chronic diseases, who have no dependence against starvation except the assistance of the generous and humane."[22] It was not until early in 1845 that Congress passed a special act authorizing the levying of the tax.

A few private philanthropic societies were organized to care for the sick, aged, or impoverished, but these societies and the poverty-stricken county governments were unable to care for a large proportion of the needy and the sick. A number of unfortunates were reduced to despair by sickness, financial misfortune, or nostalgia. One Texas doctor wrote that he often "had cause to yearn over them, when broken down in body and mind, without a cent or a friend, and sick unto death, they would say 'I wish I could see them at home.' "[23]

The stores offered a variety of patent medicines, some of which advanced extravagant claims. At Matagorda, in 1837, the local newspaper sold Burnham's Drops of Medicine for fever. In other towns the following remedies could be purchased: Moffat's Vegetable Life Pills, Dr. Frank's Pills, Gridley's Life Pills, Lee's Billious Pills, Morrison's Hygeian Pills, Hooper's Female Pills, Rowan's Tonic Mixture, Balsam of Columbia (for baldness), Dr. Hull's Worm Lozenges, Dalby's Carminative, Godfrey's Cordial, Dr. Taylor's Balsam of Liver-Wort, headache pills, Dalley's Magical Pain Extractor Salve (for burns, scalds, eyes, and piles), and Indian Vegetable Elixer and Nerve and Bone Liniment—which carried an ironclad guarantee: "Rheumatism and Lameness positively cured, and all shrivelled muscles and limbs are restored."

In addition to taking such dubious bottled and packaged nostrums, laymen frequently became adept in bleeding, blistering, and the application of poultices. In accordance with the practice of most doctors, a patient was given calomel at the first sign of fever. Though amateur treatment was not always effective, some intelligent mothers were able to buy the most highly recommended medicines for their families. In 1845 Mrs. Mary A. Maverick of San An-

[22] *Civilian and Galveston Gazette,* July 15, 1843.
[23] Heard, "The Medical History of Texas," 1.

tonio addressed a letter to her husband, who was in New Orleans, asking him to bring a list of medicines: "A vial of Ipicac, or some vomit in case of croup. A little quinine, & smelling-salts—sal volatile. Vaccine virus. A pound or 2 of salts. 25cts worth of gum of camphor ... Something good for baby's colic—if harmless—A plaster of Burgundy pitch, for weakness of the back, as large as your hand."[24]

Medical advice occasionally was obtained by correspondence, but this method was slow and uncertain. In 1840 Dr. Francis Moore, Jr., a Houston newspaper editor who had some medical training before he came to the Republic, learned on a visit to the interior that many settlers were unable to secure the services of a physician. Dr. Moore thereupon published detailed instructions for treating malarial fevers in their various stages in the *Telegraph and Texas Register*. His suggestions included the use of calomel, mustard-seed poultices, a blister on the stomach, castor oil or salts and senna, quinine, and abstinence from eating fruit or uncooked vegetables in favor of a diet of mush and molasses and rice.

Among the remedies prepared by women in the homes—and used before doctors were called—were pills made of flour mixed with the boiled inner bark of ash trees for action on the liver and bowels; willow bark prepared in the same manner for use as a tonic; and a brew from green gourds as an emetic. "If any in these sophisticated days doubt the efficacy of the latter remedy," wrote Dr. John Washington Lockhart many years later, "try it once, and be convinced." The same doctor testified that household remedies and herb cures, including "tansy roots and yarrow and catnip, and camphor roots, and rue and balm and a host of other bitter yarbs— ˮs they were called" did much to relieve suffering.[25] Among the ꞁumerable antidotes for snake bite were tobacco juice, gunꞁwder and vinegar, brandy and salt, alum, and a drink made from the bark of the black ash tree. A German settler noted that medicinal plants included the "wonder tree" (castor-oil plant), sassafras,

24 Mrs. Maverick to Samuel A. Maverick, November 16, 1845, Maverick Papers.

25 Wallis and Hill (eds.), *Sixty Years on the Brazos,* 172, 175. Dr. J. O. Dyer listed a large number of home remedies in his series of articles under the general title, "The Pioneer Texas Farmer," in Galveston *Daily News,* April 1, 8, September 2, 9, 16, 23, 30, 1923.

rhatany, locust, elder, sumac, sage, mint, and "many kinds of tea herbs." In this connection, Mrs. Mary Austin Holley boosted Texas as a region abounding in "valuable medicinal herbs and roots. Every *old woman,* at least, knows how desirable such a natural pharmacopia is to a frontier family, far distant perhaps from the shops of the druggist and the physician, where every man, in time of sickness, becomes a *'botanical quack* and *steam doctor,'* and practices upon his own *'patent.'* "

In a region where many healthy people believed that the hanging of a snake would bring rain, the sickly were even more inclined to place faith in mysterious incantations. Doctors, therefore, had to assume more knowledge than they actually possessed, and some of them endowed bread pills and colored water with Latin names in order to reassure the weak and depressed. Slaves frequently had to be forced to take calomel and castor oil, their reluctance arising from their belief that calomel was composed of the bones of dead persons ground to powder, and that castor oil was extracted from their bodies. In an effort to attack the popular dread of night air, at least one newspaper occasionally printed long discussions of the importance of fresh air in sleeping. Home treatments with plant remedies were necessary and effected cures, yet their use often was connected with erroneous ideas and superstitions. Among them was the idea that parts of the mandrake, which received its name from its resemblance to the human form, would be useful in treating the corresponding afflicted parts of a sick person's body. On the whole, however, ordinary persons were not far behind the majority of doctors, for both suffered from the backwardness of medical science.

~✽~ X ~✽~

Curses on the Law's Delay

A CONTEMPORARY SOUTHERN LAWYER observed that every state "has its peculiar tone or physiognomy . . . of jurisprudence imparted to it . . . by the character and temper of its bar."[1] In the Republic of Texas, a variety of historical and geographical influences were added to the welter of judicial processes in the courts. From these processes emerged the initial interpretations of the legal syncretism which is modern Texas law. The Spanish civil law, the Code Napoleon as interpreted in Louisiana, the English common law with its various American revisions, the limitations and definitions of the constitution and statutes of the Republic— all were being blended into Texas jurisprudence.

During the period of the Republic, the Texas legal system was removed from Spanish influences—with certain notable exceptions. After the adoption of the constitution of 1836, Texas continued under the Spanish civil law for a few years; and cases pending on the dockets of the Mexican alcalde courts were transferred to the newly created district courts. A modern lawyer and historian has noted that "twenty-seven million acres of our lands were granted by Spain and Mexico and every title and every transaction with reference thereto, prior to 1840, must to this day and throughout the ages to come be measured by the laws of the fallen sovereign."[2]

In 1840 the Congress of the Republic adopted the common law of England, so far as consistent with the constitution and laws then in effect, and repealed all Mexican laws "in force in this Republic" prior to September 1, 1836, except those relating to land grants, colonization, and minerals. This carried out the provision of the constitution of 1836 that required Congress to introduce by statute,

[1] Baldwin, *The Flush Times of Alabama and Mississippi*, 239.

[2] Clarence Wharton, "Early Judicial History of Texas," *Texas Law Review*, Vol. XII, No. 3 (April, 1934), 324.

as soon as practicable, the English common law, with such modifications as might seem necessary, and made it at once the rule of decision in all criminal cases. But the act of 1840 also adopted, as an exception from the application of the rules of common law, an important feature of Spanish civil law—the community system of property rights of husband and wife. A wife also retained sole ownership of all lands, slaves, and other chattels which were her property at the time of marriage—thus placing Texas among the first American jurisdictions that allowed a wife to remain a legal entity. The same Congress passed another act that, contrary to the common-law procedure, established the system of petition and answer for pleading in civil suits. Moreover, the sweeping homestead-exemption law, passed by the Mexican state legislature in 1829, continued in effect until 1839, when it was superseded by another homestead act passed by the Texas Congress. The principles of all of these elements of civil law still exist to reflect the influence of the period on modern Texas jurisprudence.[3]

The problems posed by this changing and diversified system of law confronted the legal profession at a time when its general standards of training and practice were low. In the fall of 1838 a well-informed Texas doctor wrote to a lawyer in the United States who was contemplating moving to the Republic: "Although there are many practicing Law, competent Lawyers are, in my opinion, in very great demand."[4] This appraisal of the legal profession was substantially correct. Lawyers were flocking to the new country, where the insecurity of many land titles gave promise of lucrative litigation, and expectations of increments in land values stimulated hopes for wealth. While the rolls of bar members included a pro-

[3] Gammel, *Laws of Texas*, I, 1074, 1077, 1255; II, 125, 177–78, 262, 1294; *Texas Jurisprudence*, I, *li*. In making contracts, however, practically all of a married woman's disabilities, as they existed under common law, were fastened upon her.—D. Edward Greer, "A Legal Anachronism: The Married Woman's Separate Acknowledgment to Deeds," *Texas Law Review*, Vol. I, No. 4 (June, 1923), 409. For a contemporary Supreme Court decision which cited Spanish civil law in the settlement of a case involving community property of man and wife, see James W. Dallam (comp.), *Opinions of the Supreme Court of Texas from 1840 to 1844 Inclusive*, 551.

[4] Ashbel Smith to J. A. King, October 8, 1838 (letter-book MS), Ashbel Smith Papers.

ficient minority, among whom were a few who approached emi-
nence, many undoubtedly deserved the contemporary epithet
"cornstalk lawyer"—a designation that was about as opprobrious as
"quack doctor." On the whole, however, the law was a highly regarded profession which might be used to gain community influence and possibly serve as a springboard to political and even military success. "High aspirations were at that early day freely indulged in by men who had acquired in some of the older States
the smallest degree of distinction at the bar, or from some petty
office," wrote an intelligent Baptist preacher. "Such men easily
worked themselves up to the belief that in this new country in a
very short time, they could become generals or statesmen."[5]

Financial returns from the practice of law were moderate at
best, and in the depression-ridden early eighteen forties they became extremely meager. In 1840 J. Pinckney Henderson was preparing to settle at San Augustine in East Texas, where there was
"more law business . . . than [in] any other section of the Republic." Henderson's prospects were excellent, he thought, because
"the Gentleman who had the best practice in that region has been
appointed Judge and solicits me to take charge of his practice which
he assures me was worth to him last year ten thousand dollars in
good money."[6] Five years later, Thomas J. Rusk, who had been
Henderson's partner in one of the best law firms in Texas, testified
that the practice of law would "barely support a man, owing to
the poverty of our people caused by our disturbances with Mexico
and the overstock of young men in the profession."[7] It is not surprising, therefore, that few lawyers engaged exclusively in legal
work. The successful held a majority of the important political positions, often operated plantations, and acquired land in large quantities. The mediocre and the novices did all sorts of work outside
the courtroom. They taught school, preached, edited newspapers,
promoted town developments, farmed, and kept inns. Two of them
became barbers, and announced their new calling in the following
advertisement:

[5] Morrell, *Flowers and Fruits from the Wilderness*, 31.

[6] Henderson to "My Dear Brother," February 25, 1840, Henderson Papers.

[7] Rusk to Edward Harden, September 16, 1845, Harden Papers. See also Rusk
to John T. Mason, December 28, 1847, Rusk Papers (University of Texas Library).

TO THE PUBLIC
LEAGUE & AINSWORTH

(formerly Attorn-eys at Law) being a second time "choked off" from the practice of their profession beg leave to inform their friends that they have modelled their Law Office into a Barbers Shop, and having a plentiful supply of Scissors & Razors, are prepared to execute all work in the line of their new calling, in a *Barber-ous* manner—Their patrons may rest assured that if they call, they will be *clipped* and *shaved* to their hearts content.[8]

The presence of a large number of "that species of pragmatical mortality known as lawyers" (as they were described by Mirabeau B. Lamar) resulted in part from the lax requirements for gaining bar membership in the Republic. The nucleus of the important Brazoria County Bar was formed by persons who had practiced in Texas prior to June 1, 1835, or could exhibit a license from "any court of Record in the United States"—neither qualification guaranteeing vast legal knowledge. One example of a lawyer who automatically was included as a member of the bar because of a few previous appearances in Texas courts was Henry Austin. He was intelligent but virtually self-taught, possessed no detailed knowledge of law, and had very little professional experience. Yet Austin was on the first committee appointed to examine aspirants for admission to the Brazoria County Bar.[9]

The committees appointed in the various courts to ascertain the fitness of applicants set the minimum standards for training, and —in view of the general lack of legal background of many of the lawyers already practicing—could not have expected the examinees to possess more than elementary learning. The comment of a Southern lawyer on the admission of candidates to the bar in Mississippi (which had been the training ground for many Texas lawyers) was equally applicable to the bar of the frontier Republic: "Practising law, like shinplaster banking or a fight, was pretty much a free thing; but the statute required a certain formula to be

[8] Brazoria *Texas Republican,* July 18, 1835.

[9] Brazoria County District Court Minutes, A, 2. See also by the writer, "Henry Austin," *Southwestern Historical Quarterly,* Vol. XXXVII, No. 3 (January, 1934), 185–214.

gone through, which was an examination of the candidate by the Court, or under its direction."[10]

The customary procedure, in Texas as in the United States, in preparing for a bar examination was to apprentice oneself to an established lawyer. In the spring of 1834 William Barret Travis contracted with J. H. Kuykendall "with approbation of his father to live with me three years—& study law & help me in my office—& I to find him every thing." Three days later young Kuykendall moved his personal effects into the Travis lodgings at San Felipe de Austin, and Travis arranged for him to board at "Connell's at $15 per month." Various entries in Travis's diary show that he bought clothes and shoes for the apprentice and on one occasion employed a doctor "to cure H. Kuykendall's mouth."[11]

During the period of the Republic the lawyer did not always agree "to find him everything," and the period of study was usually less than three years. The apprentice read his patron's law books and paid for this privilege, as well as for those of associating with members of the profession and learning how to write legal documents, by acting as office clerk and janitor. This arrangement often enabled the counselor to spend more time promoting good will in his favorite tavern. After several months of study, the applicant was examined by a committee of three members of the bar appointed by a district court judge. The committee almost invariably reported that the candidate was of "good moral character" and sufficiently learned in the law to warrant the issuance of a license. Thereupon the court ordered the clerk to issue the license after the licensee had paid a five-dollar fee and had taken a solemn oath to conduct himself "with all good fidelity" to the court, to serve his clients according to the best of his skill and ability, and to support the constitution and laws of the Republic.

On rare occasions an examining committee recommended postponement of the admission of a candidate. In 1842 the Harris County committee appointed to examine William C. Bevens reported: "We find Mr. Bevens to be a man of good moral character, of studious habits and better qualified than many who are admitted

[10] Baldwin, *The Flush Times of Alabama and Mississippi,* 324; Gammel, *Laws of Texas,* II, 137, 336.
[11] Travis, Diary, 1833–34, 107–10, 116–17, Starr Papers.

to practice in this Country; but the Committee, being desirous to elevate the standard of qualification for admission to the Bar, have advised him to postpone his application until the next term of the Court, to which he, being desirous to aid in promoting the object desired, readily consented."[12]

A Montgomery County committee found one Aaron Ketchell qualified, but in view of rumors of an occurrence in Georgia "highly prejudicial to his Character," thought that, since the legal profession should be "Above Suspicion," the application should be postponed. The examiners subsequently reported that, about 1835, the applicant had been seized illegally by "Sundry respectable citizens" of Georgia who proceeded to try him on a charge of being an abolitionist and to punish him. The committee could not determine whether the charges were true but believed he could not have done much harm as an abolitionist in Georgia. Since Ketchell apparently had lived a reputable life for eight or ten years thereafter, the examiners expressed willingness to have him admitted.[13]

Surprisingly few lawyers conducted themselves in a manner that brought serious reflection on their profession, and even the sins of the few usually were viewed with tolerance. Perhaps the darkest among the records of Texas lawyers was that of A. M. Tomkins, for several years incumbent of the district attorneyship of the judicial district which included Houston—a position called "the most profitable office in the nation." The Chief Justice of Harrisburg County reported to the President that Tomkins was "a man destitute of all moral principle, a spendthrift, a gambler and a *debaucher,* or one in the habit of taking too much *steam* aboard . . . a man who instead of aiding to execute the laws is known oftener to violate them than probably any other man in our county."[14] After his term expired, Tomkins was indicted several times for gambling, and in 1840 for allegedly aiding his brother in killing a well-known local official in a riot at Galveston.[15]

[12] Harris Country District Court Minutes, C, 326.

[13] Montgomery County District Court Minutes, B–2, 220, 237–38.

[14] Andrew Briscoe to M. B. Lamar, February 12, 1839, in Gulick *et al.* (eds.), *Lamar Papers,* II, 451. See also "Notes on Texas," *Hesperian,* Vol. II, No. 6 (April, 1839), 420.

[15] Brazoria *Brazos Courier,* October 27, 1840; New Orleans *Daily Picayune,*

Other derelictions were less sensational. In 1841 Colonel Josiah Crosby of the Montgomery County Bar was indicted for swindling, but a bar investigation held that the indictment was unwarranted.[16] John E. Jeffers, admitted to the Galveston County Bar in the spring of 1839, was indicted for taking unlawful fines as justice of the peace, removed from office, and ruled "incapable of holding it."[17] Amos Morrill of the Red River County Bar, who became chief justice of the Supreme Court of Texas during the Reconstruction period and later a federal district judge, was suspended from practice, but eventually was reinstated. Judge John T. Mills used the case to admonish the "members of the Bar to let their walk be upright, let their acts be open, bold and determined, and the petty slanders which are retailed by the ignorant and the vulgar against the profession will in a short time cease."[18] On the whole, lawyers followed this advice. Although in some quarters there had been violent denunciations of them as a group in pre-Republic days, critics of the profession were comparatively temperate after independence was achieved. Furthermore, lawyers shared with doctors the domination of the political life of the country, and some were very active in cultural affairs.

In consequence of the lack of extensive training of the ordinary lawyer and the inadequacy of legal libraries, extensive research was not a part of his work. Even the fortunate owner of a few-score law books probably did not have most of them available when they were most needed, because successive terms of district courts were held in various county seats, and it was customary for the entire bar to stuff only the most urgently needed volumes into saddlebags and ride from county to county. As a result, arguments and decisions (even of the Supreme Court) were based more often on common sense than on citations.

It was quite possible for a lawyer or minor judge to be fairly successful and possess only a small number of law books. A chief justice of Brazoria County who spent considerable sums on clothes

October 20, 1840; James Love to M. B. Lamar, September 21, 1840, in Gulick *et al.* (eds.), *Lamar Papers,* III, 452; Galveston County District Court Minutes, B, 45.

[16] Montgomery County District Court Minutes, B-2, 37.

[17] Galveston County District Court Minutes, A, 150; B, 87.

[18] Red River County District Court Minutes, A, 388, 392, 420, 434–36.

and liquor owned only two law books at the time of his death. The estate of a respected young Houston lawyer, president of the Franklin Debating Society, consisted almost entirely of a library of seventy-four volumes, of which twenty-six were law books.[19] The inventory of the effects of a Matagorda County lawyer, who died in 1843, showed that he had accumulated a $14,000 estate—including only eighty-three books, mostly legal works.[20]

A few private law libraries were more substantial in size. One of the largest was that of Thomas J. Rusk, who served as chief justice and attorney general for brief periods. Chief Justice James Collinsworth assembled a library of 175 volumes. Most of them were law books, and included "Chitty on Pleading," "Stephen on Pleading," "Coke's Institutes," "Kent's Commentaries," "Civil Code Louisiana," and "Martin's Law of Nations."[21] The library of William Fairfax Gray of Houston numbered 267 volumes, consisting largely of law books which included various state codes and standard works by Chitty, Vattel, Wheaton, and Blackstone. Among the individual volumes listed in the Gray library were "Angell on Water Courses," "Reeve on descents," "Peak's evidence," "Brown's Civil Laws," "Stone's Coms. on Pleading," and "Stone's Coms. on Bailments," and eight sets of the "Laws of Texas."[22]

While many poorly educated lawyers were allowed to practice, the leadership of the Texas bar included some very talented individuals and a few with genuine claims to distinction. Thomas J. Rusk of Nacogdoches and his partners, J. Pinckney Henderson and Kenneth L. Anderson of San Augustine, were very able and rendered signal services to the Republic. Judge George W. Terrell had been attorney general of Tennessee, while two other San Augustinians who became judges, William B. Ochiltree and Royall T. Wheeler, were recognized as possessing acumen in legal matters. Indeed, "the Temple Bar of the young Republic" at San Augustine probably had the highest level of legal talent in Texas. The Brazoria Bar was perhaps next in professional rank. It was headed

[19] Harris County Probate Court Minutes, A, 263; Houston *Telegraph and Texas Register,* October 1, 1837.

[20] Matagorda County Probate Records, Inventory Book, B, 1.

[21] MSS, Brazoria County Probate Records, Case No. 79.

[22] Harris County Probate Court Minutes, C, 562.

by the important firm of John A. Wharton, John W. Harris, and E. M. Pease (who later became governor). Other noted lawyers in the Republic were James Collinsworth, John Birdsall, John C. Watrous, Peter W. Grayson, John Hemphill, William H. Jack, and James Webb.

The judiciary, established in 1837, was a simple framework of courts very similar to that in existence in Tennessee and certain other Southern states. At the head of the system was the Supreme Court, presided over by the chief justice elected by joint vote of both houses of Congress. The remaining members were the judges of the district courts (also elected by Congress), with a majority constituting a working quorum. The powers of the Supreme Court —all appellate in nature—resembled those usually invested in courts of final resort in "the States." The district courts had original jurisdiction in all civil cases wherein real or personal property to the value of one hundred dollars or more was involved, and in prosecutions for treason, murder, and "other felonies, crimes, and misdemeanors," except those exclusively cognizable in a lower court, and in admiralty and maritime cases. Seven district courts, in addition to the more numerous county and justice courts, eventually were established.

A chief justice and associate justices (district judges) were appointed in 1837, but the first session of the Supreme Court was not held until January, 1840. Although modern legal historians point out that the court's decisions contain a paucity of references to authorities, they commend the vigor of its decisions. They likewise acclaim Chief Justice John Hemphill (who presided over the court most of the time from late in 1840 to 1858) as a brilliant jurist, though contemporary lawyers certainly did not always venerate him or the court in which he presided. In 1845 one of the associate justices wrote as follows:

I am told by some of the Southern bar that there are cases now undecided in the Sup. Court which have been argued two three & four times—I suspect that the Ch. J. [John Hemphill] has at length concocted some learned opinions with which he is pregnant & which he is desirous to promulgate before the expiration of the Republic. . . .

Besides from the respect accorded to the decisions of our Sup. Court, it [is] doubtful how far they will be regarded as settling any thin[g]. The bar south and west entertain a very moderate respect for Judge Hemphill & are extremely averse to see him retained upon the bench— ... I hope he is entitled to more credit for talents & learning than he receives—Ochiltree thinks well of him—But Gillespie says it was his custom after a session of the Sup. Court absolutely to box up his books & lie about the places appropriated for loafers in Washington in a perfect state of torpor (like a lizzard in the winter) until the next Sup. Court.[23]

Prime agencies in the administration of Texas justice were the district courts, which not only were the scene of the most important litigation, but also were the centers of a certain amount of social life. While they were in session, litigants, witnesses, prospective jurors, friends of persons on trial, spectators, gamblers, and an occasional peddler crowded courtroom, grogshops, and streets. Gambling games flourished in the shady back rooms of stores and grogshops. At night the barristers engaged in storytelling in which they not only enlarged upon the comic incidents of current and past trials, but also told anecdotes of hunters, preachers, schoolmasters, gamblers, and swindlers. Sharp observers and magnificent storytellers, the veterans of the bench and bar created whole cycles of stories about frontier types as well as about themselves. Doubtless the best of these tales were related at suppers at which the lawyers sometimes got drunk en masse. Indeed, court week furnished one enthralling substitute for formalized amusements.

The unsettled conditions of the country demanded that the district judges be firm and tactful, if not always erudite. In 1839 the Speaker of the House of Representatives testified that most of the district judges were not well qualified for the office. This may have been true of some of them in regard to knowledge of the law, but the problems in human relations confronting the judges required far more that they be rugged, sensible, and not too insistent upon formality than that they be versed in legal technicalities.

These jurists inspired many an anecdote and legend. One tale about Judge William B. Ochiltree may have been true. During a

---

[23] Royall T. Wheeler to O. M. Roberts, November 21, 1845, Roberts Papers.

period of public unrest in East Texas, he allegedly ascended the bench, though he had seen a piece of artillery pointed at the courthouse. Calmly he laid his pistols before him and surprised his enemies by ordering the sheriff to remove the cannon and arrest anyone who dared resist his authority. Another story was told of a jurist's advisory opinion in announcing to a district court the news of the passage of the joint resolution annexing Texas by the Congress of the United States. The learned judge adjourned court until the next morning so that a celebration might be held and stated that the rule in order would be that ascribed to Chief Justice Marshall: "No man should be considered drunk on Independence Day so long as he could pronounce the word 'Epsom.' " Still another yarn found its way into at least one newspaper in the United States:

A very learned and compassionate judge in Texas, on passing sentence on one John Jones, who had been convicted of murder, concluded his remarks as follows:—

"The fact is, Jones, that the court did not intend to order you to be executed before next spring, but the weather is very cold—our jail, unfortunately, is in a very bad condition—much of the glass in the windows is broken—the chimneys are in such a delapidated state that no fire can be made to render your apartments comfortable; besides, owing to the great number of prisoners, not more than one blanket can be allowed to each; to sleep soundly and comfortably, therefore, will be out of the question. In consideration of these circumstances, and wishing to lessen your sufferings as much as possible, the Court, in the exercise of its humanity and compassion, do hereby order you to be executed tomorrow morning, as soon after breakfast as may be convenient to the Sheriff and agreeable to you."[24]

That the judicial system was not immediately systematized became evident in a communication that appeared in the Houston *Telegraph and Texas Register* near the end of 1840:

[24] *Mississippi Free Trader and Natchez Gazette,* January 11, 1843. This was only one of several versions of this tale, which apparently was largely folklore arising from the circumstances under which David Jones and John C. Quick were sentenced to death at Houston and executed in 1838. Neither the newspaper accounts of the judge's sentence nor the official court records confirm this story.

Mr. Editor—May we [be] permitted to ask if in the approaching sixth year of a Supreme Court and a Chief Justice, with all of their imposing concomitants of profit and honor, we may look for the adoption of sufficient Court Rules, and the definite settlement thereby of a system of practice at Common Law, in Equity, and of Admiralty, for all the Courts of the Republic? It would seem to be time that there was some concert of action between the different courts, at least of similar jurisdiction;—some practical and uniform lines of demarcation for the government of all the courts of the country, as yet almost as confused, irregular, and unharmonious as at their first organization.

HOUSTON[25]

In 1842 the Supreme Court ruled that allowance was to be made for irregularities in judicial proceedings that took place in the early years of the Republic's existence.[26] Even in the eighteen forties William Bollaert, an intelligent Englishman who generally was friendly to Texas, was somewhat shocked at the lack of decorum in the courts. He saw a Galveston judge "chewing his quid" and resting his feet on his desk, while the district attorney and the legal talent, "ready of speech and loads of references—from Magna Charta upwards," chewed, smoked, and whittled.[27] Elementary courtroom manners made necessary the rule in the district court at Galveston "that any Attorney entering the Court room in a state of inebriety shall be stricken from the Roll"; and other courts had to prohibit the exhibition of arms in the courtroom and immediate vicinity. In 1838 a visitor in Houston recorded in his diary that sessions of the district court were conducted with "great irregularity" and that the bar "gave a Supper to the Grand Jury—high meeting, some gloriously drunk."[28] Fines for contempt of court frequently were imposed, and one individual's conduct in the district court at Houston was so unruly that he was fined ten thousand dollars (Texas money?) and sentenced to prison for twelve months.

[25] Houston *Telegraph and Texas Register,* December 30, 1840.

[26] Dallam (comp.), *Opinions of the Supreme Court of Texas from 1840 to 1844 Inclusive,* 452.

[27] Bollaert, "Personal Narrative, 1840–1844," 191.

[28] Herndon, Diary, 1837–38, 47, 51.

District judges often had to deal with obstreperous young lawyers. The actions of one of them in conducting a case in 1840 caused him to be fined and subjected to a strong reproof from the bench:

The Court would remark, that this is not the first instance of several that its opinions have been impugned and treated Contemptuously by this young man, who has just entered his probationary career in the science of law, who is yet in his horn Booke, and his remarks after this subject was noticed from the Bench were even more Contemptuous than his former. He got up and observed that he blenched before no power, he had been here three years, that his character was too well Known to sustain any injury here from any Course the Court might think it proper to pursue, thus setting [at] defience the power of the Law sustaining the Court.[29]

Similar forthrightness on the part of an attorney confronted the Honorable George W. Terrell, presiding in 1840 over the district court at San Augustine. Attorney William C. Duffield had been indicted for forgery in a case involving the alleged alteration of election returns, and also had been made the defendant in a suit brought by Sam Houston, "an attorney of record at this bar," who had moved that the court suspend Duffield as attorney and counselor. J. Pinckney Henderson prosecuted the forgery case, and aroused Duffield's ire. He maintained that one of Henderson's requests for the admission of certain evidence "was one of the tricks of the Gentleman of which he was habitually and perhaps Constitutionally Guilty." The judge stopped Duffield and reminded him that it was "a rule of this Court that no gentleman of the bar was permitted to cast imputations upon another." Duffield replied that he gladly placed himself within the restriction of the court, "but that neither this Court nor any other Court short of the Court of heaven should rule him down from resenting an insult or protecting his rights when infringed upon." For using this language, Judge Terrell ruled that he was in contempt of court and imposed a fine of five hundred dollars on Duffield, who replied, "You may say a thousand dollars." The judge did say so, and in addition or-

[29] Harris County District Court Minutes, B, 429.

dered the sheriff to take the lawyer to jail and keep him in close confinement until released by order of the court.[30]

In 1838 Judge James W. Robinson took "under advisement" some cases tried before the district court at Matagorda. One was reported to be of "great magnitude and much importance to the interests of the city of Matagorda." The local newspaper was informed "on good authority" that the decisions would be made some distance from Matagorda. "Did the gentleman fear personal violence," inquired the editor, "as the result of an open declaration of his Judgments?" If so, "we feel indignant at such an . . . imputation."[31]

Indians and Mexicans also caused interruptions of the labors of the judiciary. In September, 1842, General Adrian Woll led an invading Mexican force in a surprise attack on San Antonio, and captured the district court then in session; in consequence, lawyers were scarce in San Antonio for a period. During the ensuing months the threat of Mexican invasion prevented at least four other courts in western counties from convening. The records of the district courts in other years also show that judges occasionally failed to arrive, probably because of sickness or the difficulties of transportation.

Moreover, in 1836–38, there were no court actions in the settlements along Red River, in northeastern Texas, with the possible exception of a few cases which the inhabitants may have entered in the courts of Miller County, Arkansas. Even after courts were established, a murderer was amenable to legal action only when the motive was robbery or the murder was done in cold blood.[32]

Suits to establish titles and to collect debts predominated in the civil dockets of the courts, and many lawyers specialized in land practice. The diary (1833–34) of William Barret Travis of Austin's Colony shows that he was employed in several probate cases and that he drew up the necessary papers for the establishment of titles

30 San Augustine County District Court Minutes, B, 162–63. See also *ibid.*, *passim,* and C, 18.

31 Matagorda *Bulletin,* April 27, 1838.

32 Rex W. Strickland, "Anglo-American Activities in Northeastern Texas, 1803–1845" (Ph.D. thesis, University of Texas), 382, 389.

TEXICAN JUDGES AND JURY, AND MEXICAN SOLDIERY.

TEXAS AGAIN INVADED.—CAPTURE OF SAN ANTONIO.

(From the *New Orleans Bulletin*, Sept. 27.)

By the politeness of Captain Boylan, of the steam-packet Merchant, we have full files of Galveston, Houston, Matagorda, and Austin papers to the latest dates. The news from Texas is of a startling and important character, if we may place full credence in the following extract from the *Galveston* (extra) *Times* of the 20th. That paper says:—" We stop the extra to give the following information, but this moment received from a gentleman who has just arrived, and met the express the other side of Oyster Creek. San Antonio was completely surprised on the 11th instant, by 1300 Mexicans under General Wall. Fifty-three of the principal citizens taken."

When San Antonio was taken, the circuit court was in session, and the judge and the officers of the court were made prisoners— lawyers, clients, and all. It seems strange that the vigilant Texans should have allowed themselves to be " come over " so handsomely. A few months ago they took the alarm, and prepared for defence. But the immediate danger having soon passed away, the militia were discharged, and affairs were suffered to go on as if in the midst of a profound peace. Never since the declaration of independence was Texas more unprepared for a vigorous contest than at this moment. Her army is disbanded; her ships of war lie idle at New Orleans for want of funds, when their presence is urgently needed on the coast of Texas and Yucatan ; her credit is utterly prostrate, and money she has none. Still, she has brave hearts and strong hands, and, when the crisis comes, we trust she will be found equal to it.

This story of the capture of the district court at San Antonio by a Mexican army appeared in the *Illustrated London News*, November 5, 1842.

Mrs. Mary Austin Holley, first cousin of
Stephen F. Austin

Courtesy University of Texas Library

General Sam Houston, twice president of
the Republic of Texas

Courtesy Rosenberg Library, Galveston

Mirabeau B. Lamar, poet, soldier, and
president of Texas, 1838–1841

Courtesy Rosenberg Library, Galveston

Samuel L. Williams, merchant, banker,
and a founder of Galveston

Courtesy Rosenberg Library, Galveston

(his fee was thirty dollars each) and for the execution of deeds, bills of sale, powers of attorney, and wills. He took his pay in any convenient form—in one case, a league of land. The extensive papers of Benjamin C. Franklin, who was a lawyer and district judge in the courts of the Republic, indicate that he handled Texas land business for persons in various parts of the frontier commonwealth and in a number of Southern states besides. But the collection of debts was an extremely irksome business. In 1839 a well-known lawyer wrote from Houston to a friend: "I knew that many employed against me would do any thing for delay, yea that so base & grovelling are they, they would have gone to Hell itself & dragged up a plea for the purpose of defeating the payment of an honest debt. . . . I have brought suits here to the amount of 109,000$ & have no expectation of getting any fees for years. Curses on the law's delay."[33]

Practically all lawyers handled criminal as well as civil practice, and the court records reveal their consistent success in obtaining entries of nolle prosequi, quashed indictments, hung juries, case continuances (often until witnesses or accused left the country), and acquittals. In defense against a charge of murder or assault with intent to kill, the first step toward success was that of obtaining a sympathetic jury. Then perhaps the barbaric tyranny of the rules of British law might be attacked, and a plea of self-defense advanced. As in other Southern states, "almost anything made out a case of self-defence—a threat—a quarrel—an insult—going armed, as almost all the wild fellows did—shooting from behind a corner, or out of a store door, in front or from behind—it was all self-defence."[34] Then "the apostolic twelve" in the jury box were reduced adroitly to tears or at least to render a favorable verdict.

There were a number of shrewd and effective pleaders among Texas advocates, and the courtrooms rang with vigorous pleas such as the one which began: "May it please the Court and Gentlemen of the Jury: In all prosecutions by the Commonwealth or otherwise, it is indeed a pleasing task to be engaged for the defence; to plead the cause of Mercy and frail Humanity; to defend our fellow man against the vigor and Severity of harsh laws, and

---

[33] James Reily to James H. Starr, December 6, 1839, Starr Papers.
[34] Baldwin, *The Flush Times of Alabama and Mississippi*, 58.

the malicious and revengeful prosecution by wicked or designing persons."[35] Ineffective though such phrases might be now, they were quite typical of the type of pleading at the bar that won the hearts and verdicts of juries. The "wind-sellers" in the courtrooms won most of their cases by appealing to the unwritten code of personal independence and honor, under which individuals settled differences with pistols or fists, provided all participants had a fair chance in the encounter. Accordingly criminal lawyers as a group were cast in the role of public benefactors, and their community standing was high.

Texans commonly settled differences by personal encounters, whether by fighting, shooting, stabbing, or dueling. More than two-thirds of the total number of indictments in the district courts were for the crimes of assault and battery, affray, assault with intent to kill, or murder. About 60 per cent of the assault and battery (usually fist fighting) cases resulted in convictions, but sentences were light—ordinarily five or ten dollars and costs. Prosecutors in trials for more serious offenses encountered great difficulty in obtaining convictions because juries tended to give serious consideration to pleas of self-defense, the extenuation of unbearable provocation, or the severity of punishments prescribed by law. A minister's point of view was expressed in a sermon delivered by Rev. Charles Gillett at Houston in June, 1843:

God has said *Thou shalt do no murder.* This people have reversed the command. I do not here speak of that fashionable mode of taking life, according to an imperious code of *self-styled* honor. But I speak of *wanton, barbarous outrages,* in violation of all law human and divine, which find among this people, not simply apologists, but everywhere, bold defenders. Go through this land, and point me to a single town, which has not been the scene of some deadly affray— . . . and then tell me of an instance where the murderer has been arraigned by the proper authorities, and made to suffer the penalty due to his crime. Nay, men swear each other's death, and that too openly—and from day to day walk the streets with deadly weapons, and no effort is made by the public authorities to put a stop to their murderous intentions—and

[35] San Augustine County Miscellaneous MSS.

when at last one has fallen, how often is heard the comment—"It is all right, he ought to have died long ago."[36]

The preacher added a revealing footnote to the published account of his sermon: "The Author has been informed since the delivery of this sermon, that during the existence of the Republic, *two men* have been convicted of murder, and hung."

The executions referred to by the clergyman doubtless were those of John C. Quick and David Jones at Houston on March 28, 1838. One hundred and forty men were deputized to escort these criminals to the gallows. An eyewitness recorded in his journal: "A concourse of from 2000 to 3000 persons on the ground and among the whole not a single sympathetic tear was droped." The rarity of such a sight in early Texas perhaps attracted as many persons as morbid interest. Though violent deaths were frequent, the law exacted society's most severe punishment in less than a dozen cases.

The court records of the Republic reveal that more indictments for gambling were returned than for any other crime. The prevalence of gambling and the ineffectuality of the laws to suppress it are attested by plentifulness of evidence, both in and outside the court records; less than 15 per cent of the indictments resulted in conviction, and even after conviction, the penalty was customarily only a fine of twenty-five or fifty dollars and costs—by no means a strong deterrent to frequenters of gambling houses. Professional gamblers were numerous in some of the towns, and the gambling tables over which they presided were the scene of many altercations.

A Texas doctor wrote that "the killing of a fellow was looked upon with greater leniency than theft," a crime comparatively rare except for the depredations of bands of horse and cattle thieves. The frontier aversion to any kind of theft was reflected in the harshness of the provisions of the criminal code which prescribed death for horse theft (in 1839–40), death for robbery and burglary (before 1840), and whipping and branding as partial punishments for larceny—depending upon the gravity of the offense. In 1838 three men convicted in Harrisburg County of the theft of a hog worth fifty dollars were sentenced to pay for the stolen animal, bear the

[36] Houston *Telegraph and Texas Register,* June 28, 1843.

costs of the suit, and receive thirty-nine lashes. Petit larceny (theft of property with a value of less than twenty dollars) usually was expiated by five to twenty lashes. In 1843 one John Owen was held by a Galveston County jury to be guilty of stealing "one finger ring and one breast pin . . . of the value of nine dollars—But in consequence of his youth and services in the navy of the Country, without compensation; recommend him to the mercy of the Court"; the judge decided that twelve lashes would be a fair sentence.

No less than fourteen offenses were punishable by death under acts of Congress passed late in 1836, but the crimes for which prison sentences of more than one year were prescribed were very few. Why did the criminal code place emphasis on death sentences and the administration of lashings rather than on prison sentences? A part of the answer lies in the absence or insecurity of jails—a state of affairs typical of frontier regions. But it also should be remembered that flogging was, in this period, still a common method of punishment for many crimes in Southern states.

Some mitigation in severity came in 1840, when all laws defining theft, forgery, and counterfeiting as capital offenses were superseded by one under which these crimes were punishable by thirty-nine lashes and one to five years imprisonment. A few punishments by branding occurred before 1840 and aroused journalistic opposition. In 1842 a Houston paper summed up the popular attitude toward severe punishments and the results: "The laws that have heretofore been in operation for the punishment of crime, were of so sanguinary a character that they defeated the very object for which they were intended, and criminals were permitted to escape unpunished because those laws were considered too severe."

Laxity of law enforcement gave rise to the organization of vigilance committees and occasional instances of lynchings. In an editorial on the prevalence of lynch law in Shelby County and elsewhere in the Republic, a Houston newspaper editor wrote in 1841: "The press of our country have been too long silent upon this subject. The laws have been violated in repeated instances." He then cited five instances of mob action that had occurred during the year. In the same year, Josiah Gregg noted that "the people of this vicinity (Clarksville) have been endeavoring lately to strike terror to the miscreants of the country, by the exercise of Lynch's law—

whipping some and hanging some three or four others." The out-standing case of mob rule also occurred in 1841, when Colonel Willis Alston was lynched near Brazoria in December. Alston had killed a well-known and popular physician, Dr. John McNeill Stewart, who had publicly condemned him for the manner in which he had killed General Leigh Read in Florida. Such intense local excitement was aroused against the wounded survivor of the "difficulty" that a mob finally took him out to be hanged. According to one of several versions of the incident, a pistol exploded among the crowd and wounded one of its members. In the resulting melee, Alston was shot down on the spot.

Gangs of robbers and desperadoes occasionally defied established authority, but their period of dominance in any single area usually was short. Early in 1836 it was reported that "an organized desperate set . . . formed a league" in Matagorda County "to assist each other and give protection under all circumstances right or wrong." They were accused of being "a murdering, plundering lawless Band." But this condition was soon remedied and the region became more peaceful. In 1839 the *"band of Brothers"* was reported stealing cattle from both Mexicans and Anglo-Americans in the Victoria–Goliad area. Two years later parties of robbers were still active there, while at the same time "a Gang of desperadoes" was terrorizing the sector around Corpus Christi, and traders en route between San Antonio and the Rio Grande often were robbed by armed horsemen. But the far western frontier was not the scene of the most ruthless disregard of legal authority. That distinction was reserved for a section of the Sabine River country on the eastern border.

In the early eighteen forties a whole region in East Texas, centering in Shelby County, was plunged into virtual anarchy by the "Regulator-Moderator War." This large-scale feud arose from the lawlessness that long had prevailed in Shelby and neighboring counties. Since the days of the Neutral Ground agreement between Spanish and United States military commanders, the international border had attracted the dregs of society—murderers, horse thieves, gamblers, forgers, counterfeiters, and land thieves. A number of these desperadoes and fugitives from justice drifted across the Texas border and settled among the respectable citizenry north of the principal east-west highway. Here they continued their nefarious activities, and during the early years of the Republic they quietly gained control of the Shelby County local government and consequent immunity from prosecution by the courts.

Co-operation between the "land pirates" and local officialdom was so effective that the security of titles in several East Texas counties became very questionable. In 1840 Dr. James H. Starr of Nacogdoches wrote President Lamar urging care in the appointment of a district attorney and judge for the judicial district that included Nacogdoches County and adjacent counties. He feared that "great efforts will be made to secure the appointment of some corrupt man" as judge, for the "land thieves and others who have so long reigned supreme in the adjoining Counties feel that their power is passing from them, and will make a desperate effort to secure the appointment of a corrupt Judge."[37]

A dispute that culminated in murder was all that was needed to set guns blazing throughout Shelby County. In 1839 Charles W. Jackson, who had established a criminal record while a steamboat captain on Red River, killed Joseph Goodbread in Shelbyville after a quarrel over the sale of a Negro for a fraudulent land certificate. A special term of district court convened in Harrison County for Jackson's trial, concerning which there was much ill feeling. Finally, Judge John M. Hansford was forced to adjourn court and leave town. He explained his action in an order to the sheriff of Harrison County: "Sir, Being unwilling to risk my Person in the Court House any longer where I see Myself Surrounded by Bravoes and Hired Assassins and no longer left free to Preside as an impartial Judge at the Special Term of the Court Called for the Trial of Charles W. Jackson, I order you to adjourn Court." The judge addressed a similar communication to the clerk in which he stated that he took this action "to avoid the mockery of holding a court under the Government and Controle of hired Assassins, and to secure the safety of his Person."[38] Hansford afterward lost his life in the conflict that began to rage.

37 James H. Starr to M. B. Lamar, April 16, 1840, in Gulick et al. (eds.), Lamar Papers, III, 374. See also Morrell, Flowers and Fruits from the Wilderness, 186.

38 Harrison County District Court Minutes, A, 63–66.

Shortly thereafter friends of Jackson and Goodbread formed two lawless armed gangs called the Regulators and the Moderators, both ostensibly organized to suppress crime. Actually they took turns in waylaying individual enemies or burning their houses. In the first phase of the struggle, the Regulators under the superior leadership of Watt Moorman gained control of the town of Shelbyville. Moorman, who was a man of commanding appearance, became so certain of his power that he even envisioned the overthrow of the Texan national government. But when he openly sentenced twenty-five of the leading citizens of Shelby County to exile or death, the more respectable elements of the citizenry revived the Moderator organization under the headship of a Colonel Cravens. Both Regulators and Moderators then obtained reinforcements from neighboring counties so that each group had at least one hundred and fifty men under arms.

Eventually practically every man in Shelby County, and many in Sabine, Harrison, and San Augustine counties, as well as in Louisiana, took sides. One fairly impartial account states that "a reign of terror and dread of impending evil spread themselves like a nightmare over the land." From ambushings, hangings, and house-burnings, the "war" moved into a phase of armed camps and general engagements, none of which were decisive. Finally, in August, 1844, President Houston proclaimed martial law, and sent a body of six hundred militia from neighboring counties into the region. Both factions were dispersed, and their leaders were arrested. A district court convened at Shelbyville under the protection of the militia and worked out a peace plan, but smoldering animosities and uncertainty concerning land titles continued for several years.

The "Regulator-Moderator War" served to enhance the reputation for lack of law and order which Texas had enjoyed since the early eighteen twenties, a reputation which gave rise to an often quoted contemporary couplet:

> *When every other land rejects us,*
> *Here is a land which freely takes us (Texas).*[39]

[39] William Bollaert, *Notes on the Coast Region of the Texan Territory*, 234. For a variant of this couplet, see Dobie, *The Flavor of Texas*, 6.

Many of the tales stressing this theme originated with persons whose unsuitability for frontier life had subjected them to unhappy experiences in colonial Texas or the Republic. Two of the most bitterly anti-Texas contemporary books were written by Englishmen after short residences in the Republic—N. Doran Maillard, *The History of the Republic of Texas,* and Charles Hooton, *St. Louis' Isle, or Texiana.* On the basis of his experience in 1841, Hooton reported that "Texas generally may with safety be regarded as a place of refuge for rascality and criminality of all kinds," and that "human life is held at the least possible value."[40] Many persons in the United States had heard similar reports. When some of them actually emigrated to Texas, what did they find? Let one of them give a fairly typical answer: "The many tales you have heard of the uncivilized state of the inhabitants of Texas are all false. There are a great many roagues murderers & rascals &C tis true but the majority of them are as respectable people as are in the world."[41]

This testimony was closer to the truth. The human "scum that waves of advancing civilization bore before them" undeniably were present in Texas. But the desperadoes, the gamblers, and the gun-bearing rowdies tended to swarm together in boom towns such as Houston and in areas favorable for their operations, particularly Shelby County. Furthermore, unbridled lawlessness (as distinguished from the necessity to "shoot it out" imposed upon the normally law-abiding individualists) was far greater in the period immediately following the Texas Revolution, when the war spirit still ran high, and the organs of legal authority were in the process of growth; when bars to immigration were nonexistent, and all sorts of individuals left the United States for Texas. Nevertheless, the great majority of the newcomers were sturdy homemakers who were an essentially law-abiding people.

[40] Hooton, *St. Louis' Isle,* 15, 16; Maillard, *The History of the Republic of Texas, passim.* For English defenses of Texas in this regard, see Houstoun, *Texas and the Gulf of Mexico,* II, 98–103, and Arthur Ikin, *Texas,* 74.

[41] James P. McKinney to Walker Austin, June 2, 1837, James P. McKinney Papers.

XI

Rampant Individualism

THE REPUBLIC OF TEXAS gave exuberant expression to the spirit described by Walt Whitman as "the American contempt for statutes and ceremonies, the boundless impatience of restraint." This temper characterized many American frontiers, yet for more than a century pronounced individualism has marked Texas as a region apart, even in the West. Phrases such as "those traditional and genuine individualists, the Texans" constantly recur in the writings of respected moderns.

The exact beginnings of a trait attributed to a region must remain among the insolvable problems of history. Perhaps this one germinated in the uniqueness of the establishment of the Republic and the maintenance of its independence. Certainly the frontier commonwealth attracted a group of unconformable leaders, headed by coruscating Sam Houston, and the whole country reflected—and still reflects—their characteristics. If a key to the nature of William Barret Travis, who led his men to patriotic suicide at the Alamo, is to be found anywhere, it appears in his diary in the entry for March 9, 1834: "Started to Mill Creek waters all swimming & prairie so boggy—could not go—*The first time I ever turned back in my life.*"[1] It is also true that the Texas reputation for toughness in the eighteen thirties and forties, whether deserved or not, repelled timid prospective immigrants, and many were rejected in the usual process of frontier selectivity. As one man wrote shortly after his arrival in 1839: "This country is full of enterprising and persevering people. The timid and the lazy generaly return to the States."[2] In 1846 a visitor found an economic basis for Texas independence, and concluded that "the Texans are the most inde-

[1] William B. Travis, Diary, 1833–34, 84, Starr Papers.
[2] James Nicholson to Mrs. James Nicholson, June 6, 1839, Nicholson Papers.

pendant people under the whole canopy of heaven the wealthey of the old states not excepted."[3]

Individualism manifested itself among all classes, in all types of activity. In religion it was reflected in a report on the prospects of the Disciples of Christ in Texas which was made to Alexander Campbell: "There is a kind of manly independence among them here (all denominations) that you do not see in the United States."[4] That it existed among the doctors as late as 1850 was the belief of Dr. Ashbel Smith, who wrote: "We have, so far as I am aware, no medical organization in our State; nor is there such prospect of any change. Each member of the faculty [the medical profession] is a separate independancy, and sometimes adopts a sort of armed neutrality system."[5] In law the common man was made a king in his own domain by the homestead acts of 1829 and 1839. Among other manifestations of individualism were resentment of encroachments on personal "rights" and a concomitant readiness by some persons who were "a law unto themselves" to settle disputes without adjudication; a democratic willingness to accept any person regardless of his past record; and a state of affairs wherein tough-fibered women like Mrs. Pamelia Mann could come to the forefront, economically and otherwise. The whole pattern of "freedom" and unrestricted individual profits made inevitable the beginnings of irrevocable sacrifices of grasslands, forests, and wildlife, but destruction of these resources occurring in the pioneer period was not serious.

Cultural individualism in the raw was present in the realm of imaginative, exaggerative humor. Texans made striking contributions to the tall tales of the period. From yarns about the unprecedented size and ferocity of crawfish and turkey buzzards, those "hereditary proprietors of the prairies of Texas," it was but a step to the assertion of the superiority of all things Texan. "An Old Kentuckian" claimed that he could raise ten calves in Texas

---

[3] [Moore?], "Reconnoissance of Texas in 1846," *Southwestern Historical Quarterly*, Vol. XXX, No. 4 (April, 1927), 271.

[4] John Stamps, writing from Gay Hill, Washington County, Texas, April 25, 1841, in *Millenial Harbinger*, New Series, Vol. V, No. 8 (August, 1841), 381.

[5] Smith, "On the Climate, Etc., of a Portion of Texas," *Southern Medical Reports*, II, 458.

with less trouble than one in Kentucky. Then came the "Munch-hausen-like idea of Texan prowess" which a Virginia lawyer observed was possessed by most Texans. And by 1846 it even was reported that Texas children "can make more noise with impunity than any other children on the face of God's earth."

Swearing was another widely practiced "art," which required highly individualized creative imaginations in its most sublime demonstrations. Charles Hooton, the English author whose Texas experiences left him misanthropic, wrote that Texas oaths were "of a character so entirely new and diabolical, that one would be apt to imagine the genius of Depravity herself had tasked her utmost powers to produce them for the especial use of this rising State."[6] One candidate for the title of most talented practitioner of this "art" was Dr. Branch T. Archer ("The Old Roman")—secretary of war and holder of other important offices—who justified himself by asserting that he meant to honor God by his lack of verbal inhibitions. Another candidate was Watt Moorman, leader of the Regulators in the East Texas "Regulator-Moderator War" of the early eighteen forties, who claimed to have "invented more oaths than any other man in the world." Such word-mongering was one indication of a widespread passion for freedom of speech, which the motto of the Matagorda *Colorado Herald* further exemplified: "Give me liberty to know, to utter, and to argue freely, above all liberties." But most liberties have attendant penalties. Unbridled talk contributed to the frequency of fights and, to a lesser extent, of duels.

Chief among those who fought with sheer gusto was James B. ("Brit") Bailey of Brazoria, one of the hardy group that settled in Texas before Stephen F. Austin began to lead other Anglo-Americans across the Sabine in the early eighteen twenties. Though lame and hoarse, he had salt in his soul and was by no means a weakling. He had a quaint habit (according to family tradition) of joining in fist fights, whether personally concerned or not, yelling "Free fight, boys" as he began throwing punches. Countless tales—true and untrue—have been told about this eccentric individualist. In

[6] Hooton, *St. Louis' Isle*, 23. See also *Texas in 1840*, 235; Houstoun, *Texas and the Gulf of Mexico*, II, 110; and Houston *Telegraph and Texas Register*, June 28, 1843.

the early eighteen thirties his frame house near Brazoria was painted red, presenting "a very novel appearance for Texas." It is legally recorded that his will particularly enjoined his friends and executors "to have my remains inter'd erect with my face fronting the west—." Legend tells that Brit requested that his coffin be further ornamented by his rifle, powder horn, bullets, and whisky jug. Though Bailey's past record and his early movements in Texas were subject to suspicion, he lived to acquire the appreciation of his fellow colonists as well as a respectable estate, including one of the first brick houses erected in Austin's Colony. It is a reflection on machine-age progress that few of his kind walk the earth today, even in Texas.

The modern tradition associating Texas with blood and violence has definite antecedents in the early years of the Republic. A. A. Parker observed before 1836 that fighting was no more common among the Anglo-American colonists than in the United States. But with the inauguration of the powder-stained Republic, turbulence prevailed in many places. A large majority of the indictments in the district courts presented charges of assault and battery, affray, assault with intent to kill, or murder. Furthermore, many fights naturally were not made the subjects of legal action.

Many bloody brawls occurred in the streets, saloons, and houses of prostitution of booming Houston in the late eighteen thirties. On March 25, 1838, a visitor found the following unusual circumstance worthy of an entry in his diary: "No affray on this day"; but he also recorded that one man had caned another. Four days before, Mrs. Mary Austin Holley had written to her daughter from Texas that Houston "by its sudden growth, & the influx of foreigners, without comforts, or even a lodging place for half who arrive there, presents to the newcomer a scene of vice greater, I suppose, than can be found elsewhere in the same compass." This, however, was not an unmixed evil. "If it keeps off some honest folk who lack enterprise & perseverance to penetrate to the good of the land, it concentrates the rascals, with the Government and its hangers-on & leaves the rest of the people in peace." Fourteen months later a local newspaper suggested that the law-abiding portion of the citizenry should form a vigilance committee similar to the Galveston committee whose services had been accepted by the city council and almost had eliminated "fights and riots" there. "It was well remarked by a person who visited our city, that it appeared that a large portion of the citizens of Houston never slept—had he added, they permitted no one else to sleep, he would have been about right."[7] Other towns were subjected to similar disturbances, ranging from the rowdyism of the Austin pranksters who threw rocks at the capitol and filled up one of the protecting cannon with stones, to the "most disgraceful drunken frolic" in Nacogdoches which resulted in one of the brawlers being tried for assault with intent to kill.

Men of all classes appear to have participated in fights. Court records show that a number of respected citizens were involved in altercations, sometimes through no fault of their own. Among them were John S. Ford, William Barret Travis, Judge John M. Hansford, Alexander Horton, and Kenneth L. Anderson. In 1838 Jefferson Wright and George W. Bonnell had two fistic encounters, following Bonnell's insinuations that Wright was a coward and had "resigned his Indian Agency from fear." Our informant reported that Wright acted "very properly & spirited," and that "he dared Bonnell to a 3d contest before more than 300 people & abused him in the strongest manner."[8]

At least five fights disturbed the dubious dignity of the Congress of the Republic, and many others were threatened. After a pistol shooting "almost within the portals of the house" had disordered a meeting of the first session of the House of Representatives, that body voted to arrest the offenders. Another noteworthy embroilment took place in the spring of 1838 between Comptroller Francis R. Lubbock and one-legged Colonel Thomas W. Ward, "a passionate man" (according to his opponent). Following a disagreement concerning a business transaction, Lubbock "abused him publicly." Thereupon the colonel challenged him, but Lubbock refused to fight under the Code Duello because the challenger was already under obligation to meet a friend. "A sort of brawl" ensued. On April 14, shortly after the adjournment of a joint session of

---

[7] Houston *Morning Star*, May 29, 1839. See also *ibid.*, July 5, September 23, 1839.

[8] James Reily to Henry Raguet, November 20, 1838, Raguet Papers. Yet Reily was a vehement opponent of dueling.

Congress, Ward attacked the Comptroller with a stick "in the gallery of the capitol, in view of the Senate." Lubbock drew a derringer and fired, but a bystander struck the pistol upward, and no one was injured. Both combatants were arrested and brought before the Senate on the charge of contempt; Lubbock was discharged, and Ward was reprimanded.[9]

A third breach of the Congressional peace occurred early the following year when Surgeon General Ashbel Smith attacked Senator S. H. Everitt in the chamber of the Senate during a recess. In the course of a conversation "respecting some matters not of an official nature," wrote Smith, "he contradicted me in an insulting manner; whereupon as in duty bound I struck him with my buggy whip . . . and I continued to repeat the blows." A "right severe fight" followed, the sprightly physician claiming that "it is allowed on all hands that I had the best of the affair." Testimony showed that Smith, in accordance with common practice, also had a knife and a pistol available. The Senate considered that he had violated its dignity, and passed a resolution urging the President to impose a fine and remove him from office. Though the President refused, the Surgeon General resigned.[10]

In 1842 the Congressmen were treated to a fourth clash. It followed a speech on a judiciary bill made on the floor of the House of Representatives by James S. Mayfield, who mentioned David S. Kaufman, former speaker, "in a very Severe manner Calling him by name." After the adjournment of the House that evening, Kaufman was waiting with a cane. But Mayfield also was prepared and, after an acrimonious verbal interchange, shot Kaufman twice. The second shot lodged on "the rite Side directly under the Suspender button."[11] On January 19, the Houston *Telegraph and Texas Reg-*

[9] Lubbock, *Six Decades in Texas*, 75–77; Red (ed.), "Extracts from the Diary of W. Y. Allen," *Southwestern Historical Quarterly*, Vol. XVII, No. 1 (July, 1913), 45.

[10] Smith to "My dear Cousin," January 29, 1839 (letter-book MS); Smith to I. W. Burton, January 9, 1839 (letter-book MS)—both in Ashbel Smith Papers; Houston *Telegraph and Texas Register*, January 9, 12, 1839; Houston *Morning Star*, July 25, 1839. See also Smith to I. W. Burton, January 10, 1839, in Gulick *et al.* (eds.), *Lamar Papers*, II, 407.

[11] Kenneth L. Anderson to Thomas J. Rusk or James H. Starr, January 7, 1842, Starr Papers; Austin *City Gazette*, January 12, 1842; Natchez (Miss.) *Daily Courier*, January 31, 1842 (quoting "*Austin Bulletin*, Jan 7").

ister deplored this incident and other recent affrays: "We shall be rejoiced when our unhappy republic shall cease to be the arena of private feuds and disgraceful brawls, that tend alike to degrade those who engage in them, and to fasten opprobrium upon the national character."

On another occasion, during President Lamar's administration, A. C. Horton supposedly instigated a severe personal attack against Judge Edwin Waller. Afterward the judge attacked Horton in front of the capitol. Congress recessed "to witness the 'row,' a sight which then as now, appealed to the deepest emotions of the Texas character . . . the congressmen stood around shouting riotously and boisterously, encouraging first one gladiator and then the other." Lamar rushed out and unsuccessfully attempted to persuade the statesmen to separate the contestants. Later, as his friend Waller began to best Horton, he "brandished his hat fiercely in the air and shouted lustily, 'Do not interrupt them, let them fight.' "[12]

Many encounters resulted from the custom of wearing bowie knives and pistols. As the country became more settled, this practice became less general, although it was not abandoned entirely by all classes for many years. A penetrative analysis of the situation appears in a contemporary letter written by a prominent East Texan:

When will a proper estimate be set upon human life? or rather when will our community individually and collectively *properly* reflect upon the commission of that crime whereby, one of its members is frequently on slight provocation, and sometimes without shadow of cause deprived of life; since my return from the army, two men have been killed in Town, one the day before yesterday, and wantonly so killed, but some will say it can't be stopped—it can be stopped, and almost effectually; let it be made a penal offence to carry arms in any town . . . for but few desperadoes are to be found in any one settlement or Town, and if they were placed under heavy restrictions, many who now bear arms under pretence of self defence would be induced to lay aside the practice; if the Public will, it can be done.[13]

[12] P. E. Peareson, "Reminiscences of Judge Edwin Waller," *Quarterly of the Texas State Historical Association,* Vol. IV, No. 1 (July, 1900), 49–50.

[13] Charles S. Taylor to James H. Starr, August 23, 1839, Starr Papers.

Some shooting affrays naturally ended in fatalities. The lack of effective law-enforcement agencies combined with the presence of pot-valiant ruffians to draw into fights persons who normally never would have been involved. Public reaction to an outright murder by a "bad man" was considerably different from that to an encounter in which an individual, ordinarily law-abiding, was forced to defend himself. When a cutthroat died in a clash with a reputable citizen, the general feeling was that justice had been meted out, however informally, and the survivor usually was vindicated triumphantly by jury investigation and trial. Less than 10 per cent of the murder and assault-with-intent-to-kill cases culminated in convictions. Who could have blamed a Texas statesman for defending himself when confronted with this problem: "The Senator from Sabine is in hot water he has to leave this City in two days or suffer the penalty of death. The man killer Lewis from Sabine has given him that length of time. I believe he will leave. If he does not there will be hell to pay."[14] In a personal letter, one of the Republic's ablest lawyers and diplomats, J. Pinckney Henderson of San Augustine, described his feelings about having killed a man:

I had been annoyed for more than a year by a desparado named N. B. Garner whom I was at last forced to Slay a few weeks since. He had often threatened to kill me and twice when I was unarmed attempted to assassinate me. I had a great abhorance to the sheding of human blood in a street fight and laboured to avoid it as it never in my estimation adds to a mans reputation—A few days before I killed Garner he waylaid me with a double barreled gun to assassinate me as I passed but I learned his movements & avoided him—from that time I *marked* him as my own. He was preparing to shoot me when I shot him and was closely watching an opportunity to take some advantage of me for he was a coward and would not attack me with pistols when I was similarly armed or on the look out. I regret that the *beast forced* me to do that which some ruffian ought to have done but I shall never regret that I killed him as I am sure he then would have killed me if I had not slain him. . . . I demanded an investigation of the affaire after I killed Garner & the court of inquiry declared me fully justified.[15]

[14] K. H. Muse to James H. Starr, December 15, 1841, *ibid.*

That Henderson's position in society was not endangered by his deed is shown by his election as first governor of Texas under the United States. Yet one wonders how his cultured and well-educated wife felt about her husband's act. At least she did not hear him called "murderer"; for the society of her day "made a distinction at once fine and blunt" between a murder and a "killing" or a "difficulty."[16] The word "difficulty"—a masterpiece of tactful understatement—referred to gun, pistol, and knife fights, or duels. And a horse thief or counterfeiter was lower socially than a murderer. Even forthright frontier individualism had its subtleties.

Very few duels were fought in Texas in the decade and a half preceding independence. The most significant meeting on the field of honor—it occurred in 1834 between William T. Austin and John A. Wharton—had a twofold background: factional jealousy and a property dispute. Stephen F. Austin was in Mexico at the time of a Texas dinner, at which Wharton gave a toast: "The Austins; may their bones burn in hell." Wharton was challenged by William T. Austin, who felt obligated to defend the family name. Because of his inexperience in pistol shooting, the challenger went into training under the supervision of Colonel W. D. C. Hall. In the ensuing duel Wharton was wounded in his right arm, and the honor of both participants was deemed to have been satisfied. Though hostility between the families was not ended immediately, they later were thoroughly reconciled.

Another challenge had a less fortunate result. In 1830 Seth Ingram—a highly respected colonist—killed John G. Holtham in a street fight, after Holtham had refused to withdraw notices denouncing Seth's brother, Ira, for declining to fight a duel.

Other duels were averted by colonists. Aylett C. ("Strap") Buckner's choler several times led him to issue challenges (in one of which rifles at ten paces were proposed), but his prospective opponents usually laughed him out of his hostile intentions. Threatened duels between John W. Moore and J. G. Wright, as well as between Wyly Martin and Thomas F. McKinney, never reached

15 J. Pinckney Henderson to Ashbel Smith, November 25, 1842, Ashbel Smith Papers. Numerous entries in the San Augustine County District Court Minutes indicate the correctness of Henderson's estimate of Garner.

16 Dobie, *The Flavor of Texas,* 61.

the critical stage. In 1833 the Martin-McKinney misunderstanding was referred for settlement to a board of honor, consisting of Stephen F. Austin, Branch T. Archer, William H. Wharton, and Sam Houston—all influential in the colony and acquainted with the Code.

A prospective duel between Ira R. Lewis and William H. Jack, members of opposing factions striving for control at San Felipe de Austin, was settled in what was called "a Texas fight" by mutual agreement of the seconds. Lewis had no great liking for "this vulgar mode of fighting" but was induced to participate by his seconds, one of whom explained his own attitude in crisp language: "In this vile community [wrote T. McQueen] a boxing match is the prettiest way in the world of settling a difficulty; a victory does not draw the persecution of a party, and a defeat is soon forgotten. Chivalry has not yet found entrance in Texas."[17]

After the Texas Revolution, both fighting and dueling were more frequent and in some instances more brutal. Witness the following description of a bowie-knife duel in feud-ridden Shelby County:

Henry [Strickland, "the bully of the Tenaha"] was cut to pieces in a bowie duel with Riproaring Jim Forsyth . . . a very resolute man. He . . . walked into a ring with Henry Strickland, both having knives. All hands were asked if they were ready, and both answered "ready." "Then turn loose" was the word given and neither flinched. They swung forward and both struck a chopping lick as their hands met. Forsyth struck Strickland's right a little above the knuckles, cleaned all the flesh off of four fingers clear to the bone, and lodged against his knuckles. Strickland's knife fell and he was at the mercy of Forsyth who only hacked Strickland on his arms, cleaving the flesh to the elbow on both arms. . . . He struck him on both arms with a downward lick, calling it trimming his marble. . . . Strickland turned and ran, but Forsyth followed and cut his shoulder blade in two. . . .

17 T. McQueen to "Madam ———," August 9, 1832, Lewis Papers; James Whiteside to Anthony Butler, August 2, 1832, in Barker (ed.), *Austin Papers,* II, 830–31. Mrs. Hally Bryan Perry of Houston, who is a granddaughter of William H. Jack, states that, according to "family history," the reason why no duel occurred was that Jack proposed shotguns across a table as terms. Jack was extremely near-sighted and would have been at a distinct disadvantage in a regular duel.

He then let him go, declaring that Henry was in good condition to behave himself and repent of his evil ways. . . . I thought that a generous act on Forsyth's part. . . . Forsyth told me he could have killed him but only wanted to cripple him in order to make a pious man out of a rogue, a sponger, a horse thief, and a peace disturber.[18]

Several contemporary visitors wrote that a savage brawl was the Texan mode of managing a duel. Another half-calumny was credited to General Zachary Taylor, who was reported to have expressed an opinion that Texans were neither cowards nor gentlemen. But if adherence to the principles of the Code of Honor was a criterion, many individuals in the Republic of Texas—especially persons in military and political life—deserved to be called gentlemen. The relationship of frontier conditions to dueling was expressed in a letter written in 1840 by a Texan concerning a young friend who was returning to the United States:

I think it a proper subject of congratulation that he has mingled so freely in the affairs of Texas without any of those disputes which terminate in personal combat, and which are so easily provoked by the hot blood of young men particularly in a new country and in the camp. For had circumstances appeared to require it I feel sure that R[adcliffe Hudson] would have yielded obedience to what is styled the Code of Honor.[19]

Dueling reached its height in 1837–38. It was most common among the motley group of rampant spirits who sped to Texas to assemble in the army and in the vicinity of the capital, Houston, which had a specifically designated dueling ground.

The duel that caused the greatest amount of contemporary furor and had the most effect in arousing public opinion against the practice was the Goodrich-Laurens meeting of June 25, 1837. Dr.

18 Daggett, "Recollections of the War of the Moderators and Regulators," 12, 32. This quotation is a composite of two paragraphs on the pages cited which obviously refer to the same duel. In the region between San Antonio and the Rio Grande, knife or dagger duels between men whose left hands had been lashed together came to be known as "Mexican fights" or "Helena duels," from the name of the town in which many such meetings occurred.—J. Frank Dobie, "Bowie and the Bowie Knife," *Southwest Review*, Vol. XVI, No. 3 (April, 1931), 364.

19 Ashbel Smith to Henry Hudson, January 11, 1840 (letter-book MS), Ashbel Smith Papers.

Chauncey Goodrich, a truculent Mississippian, was a surgeon in the Texas Army; young Levi Laurens was the reporter of the proceedings of the House of Representatives and a protégé of M. M. Noah, New York newspaper publisher, critic, and playwright. The duel resulted from a misunderstanding. Several men, including Laurens and Goodrich, were quartered in the same room in the Mansion House in Houston—not an unusual circumstance in the crowded Texas hotels. During the night of June 23, a $1,000 bill was stolen from Goodrich. On the following morning the physician accused Laurens, "a suspicion utterly false [according to Goodrich's superior, Dr. Ashbel Smith] & groundless and gratuitous as it was false and infamous—and it is so deemed by every person here, by Dr. G. himself now [after the duel] equally with others." The prevailing conception of honor forced Laurens to demand a retraction of the accusation. Upon Goodrich's refusal to withdraw his statement, Laurens challenged the doctor. Rifles at twenty yards at six A.M. were the terms. The young journalist fell with both thighs pierced before the first fire of his experienced opponent. He died forty-seven hours later, his physician testifying that "the wound of the spirit was more fatal than that of the body."

At a public meeting, the young men of the city passed resolutions of regret and agreed to wear the customary badges of mourning for thirty days. Editor Francis Moore, Jr., carried the Laurens death story in a column outlined in black, in the manner commonly reserved to report the demise of front-rank politicians, and wrote a white-hot editorial against dueling, "one of the most fiendish, foulest practices that ever disgraced a civilized society." The laws, he charged, were of no effect; public opinion was against dueling, yet "our rulers" suffered the practice to continue. "Let them answer for this to their God."[20] Though his worldly possessions in Texas were valued at less than fifty dollars, Laurens had earned the friendship of many influential individuals and his death was not without compensatory effects for it gave the opponents of dueling an unanswerable argument.

A sort of ironic justice marked the future course of two of the living participants in this deadly affair. Dr. Goodrich found it con-

[20] Houston *Telegraph and Texas Register,* July 1, 1837.

venient to attend to business in other parts of Texas. Though apparently he had repented, in a fashion, because of the outcome of the duel, he still had plenty of truculence when, a few days later, he sent the following communication to Dr. Smith:

I trust and believe that you will see justice done me in my unfortunate matter in Houston, I fear from what I heard from Mrs. Mann the night I left that Dr. Moore [editor of the *Telegraph and Texas Register*] may do me injustice in his paper. *He must not* he cannot without being noticed in due form *with the Cow hide*, Col°. Patton stands by and says he will go further. His Ears Shall be the forfeit, the publick good, does not require that any thing should be said on the subject—I trust and pray you to prevent anything being said in the Telegraph, as, we want no more quarreling among citizens of our late adopted Country. . . . We . . . wish the matter to drop and never! O never to be heard of again. "Tell it not in Gath" Tell it not to our children.[21]

Early in August Goodrich arrived in San Antonio, where he remained about six weeks before he had an affray with a gambler named Allen. Shortly afterward, Allen killed the duelist in his bed by plunging a bowie knife through him so as to pin him to the mattress. The *Telegraph and Texas Register* trumpeted: *"Whoso sheddeth man's Blood, by Man shall his Blood be shed."*[22]

But the *Telegraph* had not found the real villain. One of the men who had spent the night in the hotel room with Laurens and Goodrich was young Marcus Cicero Stanley. Though a member of a prominent North Carolina family, he was one of those persons whom Nature produces in its less resolute moments. He appeared in the role of a Laurens sympathizer by acting as one of his seconds in the duel. But circumstantial evidence later developed that it was he who stole the $1,000 note. Stanley's past and later record, at any rate, branded him in the words of a New Orleans newspaper as *"an unmitigated scoundrel."* In 1839 he was arrested for stealing

[21] Goodrich to Smith, June 30, 1837, Ashbel Smith Papers. This quotation has been edited by the addition of capitalization and the omission of numerous periods.

[22] Houston *Telegraph and Texas Register,* September 16, 1837; New Orleans *Daily Picayune,* November 2, 1837; Smith to H. L. B. Lewis, October 31, 1837 (letter-book MS), Ashbel Smith Papers.

five hundred dollars from a Texas friend, but managed to procure bail and left for England where "he was sent to the House of Correction in London for robbing Mr. Catlin at his Indian Portrait Gallery." In reviewing the evidence concerning Stanley's theft from Goodrich, the *Civilian and Galveston Gazette* pronounced him probably guilty of "cold-blooded villainy and depravity seldom equalled, and of a character at once sorrowful and revolting."[23]

The post–San Jacinto army of the Republic had a number of officers who were continually bickering and fighting, and occasionally dueling. One of the chief "hell raisers" of Brigadier General Thomas Jefferson Green's brigade was a Colonel Milroy, who frequently quarreled with fellow officers. After a disagreement with Lieutenant Colonel Thomas W. Ward in August, 1836, he accused H. Moscross of reporting that he had apologized to Ward. Brandishing a brace of pistols, he demanded instant denial or satisfaction. Moscross refused to make denial before he learned the source of Milroy's information, and accepted a pistol from the infuriated Colonel with the intention of going outside the lines immediately and settling the matter "honorably." Fortunately, another officer intervened. Six days later Milroy had a fracas with Captain William R. Hays, in which the Captain's sword belt was dented by a sword thrust and his face was scratched. But Hays had the satisfaction of reporting that Milroy eventually begged for mercy. During the following month, discipline of the enlisted men in General Green's brigade was good, but the officers were "quite the reverse—on the 23[rd of September] there was not less than three fist fights."[24] In the same year two army captains fought on Galveston Island over the question of precedence in choosing cuts of beef for their respective companies; cavalry officer Stanley went to his death with a bullet in his head inflicted by the fire of a Captain Graham. In March, 1837, a Texas Army sergeant died from a wound received in dueling with a lieutenant; the decedent's father

[23] New Orleans *Daily Picayune,* January 5, 1841; *Civilian and Galveston Gazette,* May 17, 1839.

[24] This paragraph to this point is based on the following: H. Moscross to Green, August 26, 1836; Green to Thomas J. Rusk, August 23, 1836; Green to Milroy, August 25, 1836; Hays to Green, August 30, 1836; and Leon Dyer to Green, September 26, 1836–all in Green Papers.

claimed that his death resulted from inhumane treatment and improper care, but a War Department investigation exonerated all concerned. In December of the same year, Major Stiles Leroy was killed by Major James W. Tinsley in a duel over a horse. In the spring of 1840 both Colonel Lysander Wells of the First Cavalry Regiment and Captain William D. Redd of the First Infantry Regiment died after meeting on a field of honor near San Antonio.

One dispute between officers was about to end in shooting when Albert Sidney Johnston came riding by on his horse and jerked a pistol out of "Major V———" 's hand "with a tremendous grab." A second "difference" which resulted in a semblance of a duel was related by Johnston. As he rested on his blanket one day, a colonel stepped up, with a cocked pistol in his hand, and asked him to see that the settlement of a quarrel with another officer was entirely fair. "Before he could rise to expostulate, one of the duellists gave the word, 'Are you ready?' The other replied, 'Ready.' Both fired, and one fell severely wounded."

Though army regulations strictly forbade dueling, adherence to the rules could not be expected when the two ranking officers fought a duel in which one was seriously wounded. An issue arose over Albert Sidney Johnston's right to the commandership of the Texas Army—a position to which Lamar and Green had unsuccessfully aspired. On December 21, 1836, the nomination of Felix Huston as junior brigadier general was approved by the Senate. Since the Senate also refused to confirm President Sam Houston's nomination for senior brigadier general and Thomas J. Rusk had resigned as commander-in-chief, Felix Huston was temporarily in command. Huston was a swashbuckling Mississippian—planter, lawyer, former slave-trader, and soldier—who had brought a troop of volunteer soldiers to Texas in July, 1836. He controlled the army by his personal magnetism and was possessed of an overweening desire to march against Mexico. Poignantly offended by the appointment of Johnston to a position of seniority, Huston considered that an attempt had been made "to ruin my reputation and inflict a stigma on my character." Accordingly, on February 4, he challenged Johnston, for whom he professed high personal regard, as the representative of the President and the Senate. The duel was fought near the Lavaca River early on the following morning.

Johnston chose pistols in the face of his opponent's well-known proficiency in pistol shooting as contrasted with his own inexperience. After several fires, General Johnston fell with a ball through his hip. The future Confederate general lingered near death for several days. He never resented Huston's actions and, though personally opposed to dueling, met his opponent "as a public duty." He could not have held the command "if he had shown the least hesitation in meeting General Huston's challenge." The President and the Secretary of War reprimanded Johnston in perfunctory manner, but also assured him of their complete confidence and esteem. Perhaps the outcome of the duel was the best possible under the circumstances, for mutiny probably would have ensued if Huston had fallen. As it turned out, the army was united in ardently hoping for a brave man's recovery.[25]

After 1840 dueling was not often used in the settlement of disputes. The most notable duel in the 1841–46 period occurred at La Grange on the day that delegates were elected to the convention that accepted annexation to the United States. Augustus W. Williams killed a former sheriff of Fayette County, and was indicted for manslaughter and dueling.

In 1840 the Congress of the Republic passed a stringent law against the practice. It was chiefly the work of Dr. Francis Moore, Jr., editor of the Houston *Telegraph and Texas Register.* In 1837 he had begun to fulminate against the defects of the existing law against dueling, demanding that it be amended to exclude both principals and seconds from public office and service on juries. The general act to punish crimes and misdemeanors (1836) made the survivor in a fatal duel guilty of murder and subject to the death penalty; it also provided that persons assisting in a duel might be fined and imprisoned. But court records clearly indicate that indictments and convictions under this law were practically non-existent, and the district court at San Augustine held that sending a challenge was "insufficient in point of *law* to maintain an Action."

Moore crusaded zealously, often reminding the public of the

[25] The last quotation in the above paragraph is from William Preston Johnston, *The Life of Albert Sidney Johnston,* 80. The account of the duel is based chiefly on *ibid.,* 69–80, and Samuel E. Asbury (contributor), "Extracts from the Reminiscences of General George W. Morgan," *Southwestern Historical Quarterly,* Vol.

death of "the lamented Laurens." One of his philippics stigmatizing duelists stated that

There is no person more dangerous to society, none more deserving of the scorn, contempt, and abhorrence of all respectable and moral citizens, than the professed duellist. We had rather at any time see twenty branded thieves sneaking at large in a community, than a single person of this description. Such men are ever ready to quarrel about trifles, and are, therefore, invariably blackguards; yet they lay claims to respectability, and obtrude themselves upon gentlemen who secretly despise them, and barely from courtesy tolerate their company. . . .

We look forward with pleasure to the day, when the ladies of our country, whose pure minds are imbued with everything which is virtuous, refined, and noble, shall exert that mighty influence which is truly angelic, and with that delicacy which is the characteristic of innocence, shall refuse, in the ball room and at the social board, to permit their snowy fingers or rosy lips to meet the polluting touch of the foul and loathsome wretch whose hands have been thus defiled with one of the most horrid of human crimes.[26]

In addition to his own efforts, Moore printed articles written by authors such as the one who called himself "Society" and began his essay: "Duellist! go to the grave of your fallen foe, and ask your conscience if it envies him not the silence of his home." He used reprints of editorials against the "foul practice" appearing in other newspapers, notably the Matagorda *Bulletin* and various American journals; and reported addresses of grand juries against dueling. The attitude of contemporary grand juries usually was similar to that of Harris County, which in December, 1841, stated that dueling, gambling, and intemperance were "three of the most pernicious vices that ever befell the human family, the great springs from which all other vices flow."

Finally, Editor Moore was elected to the Texas Senate, where he was able to prosecute successfully his campaign for a more effective dueling law. His first step was to introduce an act to prevent dueling. In one of the resultant debates Senator Oliver Jones "urged

XXX, No. 3 (January, 1927), 187–94. See *ibid.*, 202, for another duel between army officers.

[26] Houston *Telegraph and Register,* April 21, 1838.

with great zeal, the utter impracticability of suppressing a custom so strongly justified by every chivalrous and independent sentiment, as not to be effected unless by public opinion." But Senator Moore could not believe that the bill would be rejected: "Sir [said he], shall Texas, the youngest republic in the world, which has sprung into existence, like Minerva from the head of Jupiter, all clad in armor—sir, shall she go back and, regardless of all circumstances, set an example so degraded and so childish?"[27] Though Moore's proposed statute ran into difficulties, he piloted a similar bill, passed meanwhile by the House of Representatives, to final enactment by the upper house. The strong efforts of Senator Jones to weaken the act failed but are worthy of note: He moved that the caption of the bill be changed to "An Act for the Protection of Cowards," and he later moved to strike out the provision disqualifying duelists from office. Both motions failed, however, and in 1840 Congress passed the law. Its provision excluding duelists from becoming officeholders was later incorporated into the constitution of 1845 and was a part of the basic law of Texas for many years. Prior to January 1, 1939, all state officials were required to take oaths that they had never taken part in a duel.

A fair estimate of the dueling spirit must take into consideration the large number of challenges that failed to result in combat. Not all of the more than forty cartels sent in Houston alone in the three years ending in 1840 brought about meetings on the field of honor. Furthermore, in view of the pungent language currently used in both private and public statements about political rivals, it is surprising that more formal declarations were not issued.

Especially during the years immediately following independence, dueling was both deprecated and condoned. Few men were willing to brave the possibility of being branded as cowards after a direct refusal to fight. But a duel might be averted in several ways, most of them satisfying the honor of both parties. The so-called Code of Honor may have implicated many reluctant persons in quarrels not of their own choosing, but its intricacies also prevented encounters—and a strong suspicion is permissible that many Texas politicians were well aware of that comforting fact.

27 Austin *City Gazette*, January 29, 1840.

Some duels were prevented by the mediation of friends. A notable instance arose in the proposed meeting between former President Lamar and General Memucan Hunt, one-time secretary of navy in Lamar's cabinet. Two articles appearing in rival Austin newspapers contained assertions that both Lamar and Hunt believed to be untrue. Hunt held Lamar responsible for certain of the statements, particularly one to the effect that Hunt had attempted to have J. Pinckney Henderson recalled as minister to France with the view of securing the appointment for himself. This Hunt categorically denied. When Lamar reasserted the truth of the affirmation and also referred to his adversary's introduction into the discussion of "a great deal of irrevalent matter & much personal abuse, which I shall suffer to pass unnoticed as the eminations of a . . . weak & vulgar mind," Hunt immediately challenged the former President.[28] Lamar denied the right of the General to issue the invitation, yet he said that he could not "allow the call which is made upon his chivalry to go unresponded to," and therefore agreed to fight. Then a group of five men, headed by General Albert Sidney Johnston, intervened and made a tactful adjustment of the controversy on the ground that it had resulted from "a misconception of the facts, which would be very natural under the circumstances."[29]

Three near-duels between James Collinsworth on the one hand and Dr. Anson Jones, General Thomas Jefferson Green, and Colonel Henry Millard on the other were all averted.

Another prospective duel between two prominent Texans failed to materialize because one of the parties had "conscientious scruples." In 1837 General Thomas Jefferson Chambers challenged David G. Burnet, who had been president of the *ad interim* government in the previous year. When Burnet refused to fight and continued to attack Chambers in public prints, the General replied in a pamphlet statement which amounted to a "posting" of the politician. Chambers charged that Burnet's "alleging conscientious

[28] [M. B. Lamar] to Memucan Hunt, May 4, 1842 (draft), in Gulick *et al.* (eds.), *Lamar Papers*, IV, pt. I, 14. For other letters concerning this dispute as outlined above, see *ibid.*, 1–14.

[29] Albert Sidney Johnston *et al.* to James S. Mayfield, May 9, 1842, in *ibid.*, 17–18.

scruples upon the subject" gave proof that "he is as mean spirited
and cowardly, as he is false hearted and vindictive."[30]

Other means of avoiding duels were used. The managers of a
"Cotillion Party," held at Matagorda in the fall of 1838, excluded
the name of a certain woman, "a person of doubted reputation,"
from the invitation list. The promoters were challenged by friends
of the uninvited woman. Ira R. Lewis challenged on the grounds
that the lady's intimacy with his family was sufficient guarantee of
her respectability and the managers' action an affront to himself
and his family. But a public meeting, presided over by pious Silas
Dinsmore, passed a resolution that it considered the matter "not
coming within the code of honor."[31]

A man might also ascertain whether his prospective opponent
were a gentleman before accepting or sending a challenge, while
another honor-satisfying method of refraining from taking part in
a duel was to claim that one of the parties was already obligated
to fight a third person. This type of lawyerlike interpretation of
the Code of Honor occurred in the quarrel between Colonel William H. Wharton and Colonel A. C. Horton, both senators. On
December 14, 1837, Horton made a speech on the floor of the Senate in which he was quoted as stating that "I would thank God if
the President [Sam Houston] were dead." On the following day
the speaker was asked by Wharton to explain this "unparliamen-
tary" and "malicious" remark. When Horton refused to explain,
Wharton gave notice that he would challenge when a gentleman
and a friend, former Secretary of the Navy S. Rhoads Fisher, who
had priority, received proper redress. But Horton asserted that
Wharton had first claim, which Fisher denied. Nothing occurred
beyond a three-cornered exchange of verbal barrages.[32]

Though duels were often evaded without loss of social standing,
ignoring a summons to a formal engagement usually was thought
to stamp a man with the stigma of cowardice. In 1841 a Dr. Watson

[30] *Reply of Major-General T. Jefferson Chambers, T. A. to the Newspaper Attack Made Against Him, by David G. Burnet, Late President* Ad Interim *of the Republic of Texas,* 81; Houston *Houstonian,* August 18, 1841.

[31] Matagorda *Bulletin,* December 6, 1838; Ira R. Lewis to the "Managers of
the Ball of 26th instant," November 27, 1838, Lewis Papers; and two subsequent
letters from Lewis to the "Managers," undated, *ibid.*

[32] Matagorda *Bulletin,* April 11, 1838.

challenged a young man named Gillett who failed to answer. Six days later Watson "posted him" as a coward. Captain R. Hudson, acting as a friend of Gillett, pulled down two of the notices. Hudson explained: "This I did expecting that Gillette [probably H. F. Gillett] would notice it on Monday.—but he with great philosophy and *Christian* forbearance would say or do nothing—Had I know[n] that the posting was of so little conciquence to him—I am certain that I should have let them remain for ever.—As it is—Watson when drunk—I think will attack Gillette."[33]

Many rumors of duels arose in the bitter strife of politics. According to Francis R. Lubbock, the Republic had no Democrats and Whigs in a party sense, but merely the "Houston Party" and the "Anti-Houston Party." The last six months of Sam Houston's first administration (which ended in December, 1838) found him opposed by a hostile Congress and a number of impetuous fire-eaters, including General Felix Huston, whose ambitions had been deflated by the President's action in furloughing most of the army. Shortly before the inauguration of Mirabeau B. Lamar as second president, a lawyer at the capital wrote to a friend: "Congress is decidedly Anti-Houston. I hope this remarkable man may escape our country without her limits being disgraced by the attacks which are now meditated against him. Dr Archer has challenged & the two Fishers & Felix Hueston intend so to do. I am no Houston man, yet I trust he will refuse to accept any of their offers to fight."[34]

Biographers of Sam Houston have accepted the statement that he was challenged by Albert Sidney Johnston, Mirabeau B. Lamar, Commodore Edwin W. Moore, David G. Burnet, and others. It is also a certainty that in 1841 reports were circulated by partisan newspapers that Burnet had challenged Houston and had been refused the right to fight. This was the year of the most vitriolic, name-calling campaign in Texas history. Political tempers were not sweetened by the virtual bankruptcy of the government and most of the citizens. Vice President Burnet, who was acting chief executive for several months in 1840 and 1841, aspired to prevent

[33] R. Hudson to Ashbel Smith, March 1, 1841, Ashbel Smith Papers.

[34] James Reily to Henry Raguet, November 20, 1838, Raguet Papers. But Felix Huston and Sam Houston soon adjusted their difficulties.—David S. Kaufman to Raguet, January 29, 1839, *ibid.*

Houston from returning to the presidency. Burnet generally was reputed to have called Houston a half-Indian, and the latter to have reported that "Wetumpka"—the name which Houston often called Burnet in derision—was a hog thief. Then came the challenge by Burnet, who had been publicly accused of claiming that conscientious scruples prevented him from meeting General Chambers. At the beginning of the election year Colonel James Morgan summed up the attitude of many Texans in picturesque verbiage:

We have a bad state of affairs here now—Lamar the poor imbecile could not hold out and had to give up the helm of State to Burnet— who is even more worthless— . . . Old Sam H. with all his faults appears to be the only man for Texas—He is still unsteady—*intemperate* but drunk in a ditch is worth a thousand of Lamar and Burnet. . . . Burnet has rendered himself supremely [?] ridiculous is so much disliked & being naturally [of] turbulent . . . disposition that he has become as snarlish as a half starved dog dealing forth anathemas aga'st everybody. . . . Report says He challenged Genl Houston because H intimated . . . that B was a *Hog thief!* [Houston's supposed reply is unprintable.][35]

A frequently cited authority for the allegation that Houston was challenged by several prominent men in his opposition is the recollections of that hero written by A. W. Terrell. He stated that Houston once handed his secretary a written challenge, with the instructions: "This is number twenty-four. The angry gentleman must wait his turn."[36] On the other hand, in 1854 Houston denied in a speech in the United States Senate that he had had correspondence on dueling with Burnet, Archer, Moore, or Lamar. "To be sure," he said, "they did not like me, but that was their fault, not mine. . . . I would not fight a duel." One of the gentlemen (whom he had previously identified as Burnet) sent him a verbal challenge on a Saturday night. But, he continued:

I objected to it, first, on the ground that we were to have but one

[35] Morgan to J. W. Webb, January 29, 1841, Morgan Papers. See also James Armstrong to Mirabeau B. Lamar, June 12, 1841, in Gulick *et al.* (eds.), *Lamar Papers,* III, 537; and Linn, *Reminiscences,* 346.

[36] "Recollections of General Sam Houston," *Southwestern Historical Quarterly,* Vol. XVI, No. 2 (October, 1912), 129.

second, and that was the man who brought the challenge. Another objection was, that we were to meet on Sunday morning, and that I did not think anything was to be made by fighting on that day. The third objection was, that he was a good Christian, and had had his child baptised the Sunday before. The fourth was, that I never fought down hill, and I never would. [Laughter.] I must, at least, make character, if I did not lose my life; and therefore I notified him in that way. He seemed to be satisfied with this good-humored answer, and it is the only challenge I have ever received in Texas.[37]

In the absence of direct evidence to the contrary, it seems likely that Houston was telling the truth, however facetiously, about the number of challenges he had received in Texas.

Why did dueling become far less prevalent after 1840? Notwithstanding the stagnation of credit and the lack of stable currency that followed the Panic of 1837, a fever of speculation in Texas townsites and lands reached epidemic proportions in the late eighteen thirties. As the full impact of the depression shortly after the end of the decade suddenly sent economic temperatures tumbling below normal, tension among individuals lessened. There was a sharp decrease in the number of rash adventurers who were rushing in "to fight for their rights" by marching against Mexico, help the Republic maintain independence, and share in speculative profits. "Gentlemen loafers"—many of whom had been only too ready to avenge fancied insults—returned to the United States, moved on to new frontiers, died of drunkenness, or went to work. After the election of 1841, sober contemplation of bedrock reality was imperative; for when and how to eat was a graver problem than the preservation of punctilios of "honor." Too, the campaigns of the Houston *Telegraph and Texas Register* and Matagorda *Bulletin* (using the Laurens-Goodrich duel as a telling argument) and the sturdy example of Sam Houston's reputed refusals to accept challenges were influential in developing opposition to dueling. In addition, the law passed in 1840 to suppress "the inhumane

---

[37] *Congressional Globe,* 33 Cong., 1 sess., Appendix, 1086. See also Houston *Houstonian,* August 18, 1841. Houston's opposition to dueling was publicly expressed after his duel in 1827 with General William A. White.—*Niles' Weekly Register,* Vol. XXXII, No. 14 (June 2, 1827), 229; *ibid.,* No. 25 (August 18, 1827), 413.

and detestable practice . . . this vice, the relic of an ignorant and barbarous age" was more effective than the previous statute. The new enactment reduced the classification of the crime of killing an opponent in a duel from first-degree murder to manslaughter, thereby increasing the probability of punishment. Convictions under either law were rare, but after 1840 court records show more willingness on the part of grand juries to return indictments. The law also held other potent threats. Convicted challengers, accepters of challenges, and persons consenting to act as seconds in a duel were penalized one thousand dollars, with imprisonment for twelve months, and incapacity to hold office. Since running for office or promoting a friend for a public position was a major sport in the Republic, debarment from seeking governmental jobs would have been calamitous for many individuals. Though Francis R. Lubbock, who was in the thick of politics and later became governor, admitted that "a challenge from a proper party could not be safely declined," he testified that the law effectually broke up the practice of dueling. None of the leaders in the Republic's political or military life took part in duels after the passage of the law. Like "Fighting Bob" Acres in Sheridan's play *The Rivals,* they doubtless bore their disappointments "like a Christian."

XII

Final Inspection

IN FEBRUARY, 1846, when Dr. Anson Jones performed his last official act as president of the Republic of Texas, an old settler could look back upon a decade of partial frustration and disillusion in his economic affairs. To be sure, many changes had occurred. The population of the country had more than quadrupled since 1836. Cotton production was perhaps ten times as great. The line of settlement had been pushed west of the modern cities of Dallas, Waco, Austin, and San Antonio in the face of possible Indian raids and Mexican invasions. Schools, newspapers, and incipient industries had been established. Striking contrasts between the crude and the luxurious had appeared in some of the towns. But these changes did not mean that the ordinary Texan had profited greatly. On the contrary, sound economic growth of his country had been seriously retarded first by a convulsion of speculation and then by the ravages of a devastating financial depression. Immediately following the end of the false boom in lands and townsites, both the government and its citizenry in 1840 had found themselves "land poor" and cruelly afflicted with a disorganized monetary system. The collapse of unsound real-estate values had coincided roughly with governmental issuance of large quantities of paper money, which promptly had undergone violent depreciation. Even in the towns there had been a widespread reversion to barter, which never had been wholly abandoned, as the method of exchange. In the summer of 1842 a leading newspaper had dolefully confessed: "A general gloom seems to rest over every section of the Republic, and doubt and sorrow are depicted on almost every brow."

Aside from dependence on selling land, the Republic's hopes for immediate economic salvation rested upon the exportation of cotton, some cattle, and a few hides. Texas was inescapably an agricultural country; the river valleys and the prairies contained very fertile cotton lands, and cattle were easily raised. But the expectations of most farmers were thwarted in several directions. Though the opinion was widely held that Negro slaves were needed for success in cotton culture, a large majority of Texas farmers were not able to buy even one. In addition to suffering the handicap of an inadequate labor force, they relearned the age-old lesson that farming was an uncertain undertaking which provided no assurance of reasonable returns; some Texas cotton drew the lowest prices in a low-price era because it was found difficult to prepare it properly for the market under frontier conditions, and in the early eighteen forties cotton and corn crops partially failed in two successive seasons. Finally, transporting the staple to shipping points was a time-consuming and onerous task.

Oxen still pulled a large part of Texas cotton to export centers through the mire of unimproved roads. A few steamboats and keelboats negotiated the often obstreperous, snag-blocked rivers, but the inland waterways were largely a failure as a medium of transportation. Although there was much talk of constructing highways, railroads, and canals, few internal improvements resulted. This failure to develop more advanced transportation facilities not only tended to accentuate sectional differences between the eastern and western counties but made stress upon cotton production almost inevitable. More perishable farm products could not have been as safely hauled and stored, and markets for them had not been developed.

Thus the Republic of Texas in the early eighteen forties was virtually impoverished. Its internal transportation system still was largely primitive. Many of its plans for achieving rapid economic maturity came to nothing. What, then, held it together?

Texans felt that their country had struck bottom during the depression years, that any buffeting that the future might bring could not be worse than what had gone before. Like frontiersmen everywhere, most of them were people of unhesitant faith, and their materialism was always tinged with visions of things hoped for in a world that was not only competitive but adventurous and quickly changing. Even new inventions, such as the Colt revolver, were reaching the frontier more rapidly than in an earlier day.

Meanwhile, settlers of both sexes were practicing the art of roughhewing civilization in a semiwooded wilderness, an art that had been almost perfected by past pioneer generations. Many of the women were vigorous products of one or more generations of frontier life, they had been trained from childhood to do their jobs, and they were able to bear hardships. The evidence is strong that most women were both busy and happy, and that they rarely voiced the complaints which some modern historians chivalrously assume that they often made. Even in an economic depression, participation in the process of creating a new country tended to produce resilient spirits and strong muscles.

The poverty of the frontier family undoubtedly differed from the abject poverty of the poorly paid urban artisan of the eastern seaboard. The possessions in a cabin might be few, but they had been fashioned on the adamantine anvil of experience, and they were cherished and owned in a very real sense. Shelter, food, and clothing could always be obtained. Life could be sustained regardless of the price of cotton, and hopes that the future would bring increased security and added value to landholdings were never abandoned.

The broad distribution of land ownership—an inheritance from the liberal policy of the Mexican regime, reinforced by the typically Western demand for free land—did much to alleviate the pain of the depression years, because ownership of land in this period of American history was viewed as "the key to happiness." The chief source of agrarian discontent arose from uncertainty concerning land titles, and in this matter the government took vigorous steps to rectify an alarming situation.

Although professional speculators partially succeeded in withholding some of the best lands from immediate settlement, their activities in the Republic were hampered by several circumstances. Since the national government, which controlled the public domain, was close to the people, the antispeculation sentiment of the "real cultivators"—who constituted the mass of the electorate—was sufficiently strong not only to secure constitutional guarantees but also to force any politician to think twice before openly associating himself with a land-grabbing scheme. The antispeculation sections of the Republic's constitution, including one which specifically prohibited aliens from acquiring land titles except directly from the government, dealt a blow to rapacious moneyed interests in the United States who hoped to achieve extraordinary returns from unearned increment in Texas land ventures. Thereafter, any attempted land grab involving any group of politicians within the Republic also was subject to condemnation by an opposition group, although neither might be wholly blameless. Moreover, the monetary tightness of the early eighteen forties forced many of the resident "land sharks" to sell their lands. The depression also combined with antagonistic public opinion to cause the Texas Rail-Road, Navigation and Banking Company—considered "the biggest steal ever attempted in Texas" by one historian—to fold up before it began operations.

Large-scale land speculation, commonly condemned by historians of the American West, was not an unmixed evil in the Republic of Texas. Although McKinney, Williams and Company of Galveston and the Allen brothers of Houston acquired thousands of acres of land, they also contributed largely to the development of two important towns, started industries, operated steamboats, set up credit facilities, and established channels for the inflow of productive capital. Matthew Cartwright of San Augustine eventually realized a fortune from land purchases, but he was also a prominent and highly respected merchant who supported many worthwhile local causes. Merchandise firms in nearly every town acquired land at the same time that they combined the functions of banker, shipper, middleman, and retailer. The Mills brothers of Brazoria carried on all of these activities and also became large-scale cotton producers, while members of two leading San Augustine firms, I. D. Thomas and Blount and Price, operated plantations. Regardless of the extensive land acquisitions of some of these firms, they constituted the backbone of the financial and commercial structure of the country.

The public-land system furnished one of the original mainsprings of the intense Texas nationalism that has never subsided. Whereas frontier titles elsewhere emanated from a distant federal government in Washington, free land was obtained in the Republic of Texas from a national government that was close at hand. Most citizens, moreover, were proud that their Republic had shown ability to maintain itself in the face of staggering obstacles, that their laboratory experiment in self-government was proving workable. A sense of participation in the task of "helping to rear up our infant republic" permeated the thinking of all classes. Whether the first professional theater was being opened or the first rail was being laid in a prospective railroad, the orator of the occasion or the local newspaper editor invariably dramatized the event in terms of historical beginnings. This was a popular note, for Texans believed that there was a certain admirable singularity about their frontier commonwealth and that they themselves were a part of history in the making.

While citizens of the Republic demanded that their government see that "all start fair," they were perfectly willing to maintain freedom on a competitive basis, and the pressures of potential insecurity were never so great that they drove the people to any form of collectivism or utopian experiment. On the other hand, co-operative action freely taken by individuals was common. Newly arrived immigrants were aided by houseraisings and similar neighborly frolics. When the Indians or Mexicans threatened, the exodus of volunteers who hurried to join the ranks left whole towns without able-bodied males. Local meetings occasionally expressed community sentiment in regard to political or economic questions, and important political decisions were made by conventions which were proving to be an effective cross between pure democracy and representative government. In the field of religion, camp meetings met both spiritual and social needs. Participation in all of these enterprises was entirely voluntary.

While distance from centers of traditional culture was a handicap, many persons found compensation in the simplicity and freedom of the social mechanism and in the prevailing equalitarian standards that tended to provide broad bases for future development. Cabins were reflections of the personalities of the builders—strong, angular, and open. Both food and clothing usually were rough; refinements in the latter were occasionally seen, but class distinctions in dress were tending to disappear. The chief amusements were square dancing, horse racing and gambling, carousing, practical joking, and yarn swapping—all reflections of a hardy civilization. Imaginative, exaggerative humor aided in withstanding the rigors of frontier life at the same time that malaria, an unbalanced diet, and economic misfortune made life burdensome. The leaders among the lawyers, the doctors, and the teachers were men of ability, but charlatans flourished in all of the professions and standards of apprentice training were low. In the field of education, two achievements that were not petty in a frontier society were recorded: Instruction rose above the secondary level in a few church "colleges," and the substructure of a future educational system for "the whole people" was firmly fixed both in law and in public opinion.

Methodist and "Old School" Presbyterian preachers took the lead in providing facilities for education, and the Methodists, Baptists, and Cumberland Presbyterians dominated the religious scene. In spite of the pertinacity of the indomitable circuit riders, not more than one-eighth of the population were enrolled as church members. Strong forces opposed to the spread of formal religion included postwar social ferment, the riotousness of boom towns, frontier resentment of dogmatic authority, and intradenominational struggles. The religious atmosphere of the Republic was congenial to the skeptics occasionally found among the doctors and lawyers, to those who sought their religion in the open spaces, and to the persons who were repelled by the emotionalism of camp meetings. But the churches were largely responsible for the maintenance of mass moral standards that were conservative in aim, if not always in practice.

Most heads of families were men who sought a productive farm and future comfort for themselves and their families. Every community also had young men who hoped to achieve a more rapid rise in the legal and medical professions and in politics than would be possible in older communities. The most successful among the lawyers and doctors tended to blend into the small planter class, while many others were versatile enough to shift from their professions to other occupations as the occasion demanded. In the larger towns the diversity of occupations was surprising for towns so recently established. On the streets of Houston and Galveston, farmers, small planters, slaves, doctors, and lawyers touched elbows with merchants, clerks, boat crews, actors, barbers, auctioneers, tanners, carpenters, blacksmiths, tailors, teamsters, an occasional friendly Indian, a long-haired scout or two, possibly a group of Germans, rowdies, and loafers.

A small segment of the population gave Texas a reputation for sharp dealing and lawlessness. In the last half of the eighteen thirties the frontier Republic attracted a number of adventure-craving Southern hotheads as well as canny, land-seeking gentlemen who were not overly particular concerning the methods they used to attain an estate. Land frauds by a handful of swindlers were the key factor in igniting the Regulator-Moderator War, which for a time transformed a region centering in Shelby County into an area of law defiance and bloodshed. Some immigrants were shiftless, others had come to Texas to avoid the consequences of discreditable actions, and a few had criminal records. Professional gamblers gravitated to the towns that offered opportunities for the exercise of their special talents. Communities which fortunately failed to attract large numbers of these elements were comparatively peaceful, but individuals everywhere were forced to maintain a hair-trigger regard for their "rights."

The period of the Texas Revolution and the republic which emerged from it bred a temper peculiarly Texan—or "Texian" as it was often spelled in those days. The defense of the Alamo, recently called "the high mark of all time for fearless behavior," the massacre at Goliad, and the subsequent defeat of the Mexicans at San Jacinto gave Texan men at arms rallying cries and a tradition that have persisted for a century. Their fighting spirit arose not alone from national compulsion but also from individual necessity. In the years immediately following the Texas Revolution, law enforcement agencies were still in the process of organization precisely at the time that the country was in a state of postwar unrest and in the grip of a paroxysm of speculation. Disputes between persons with upper-class backgrounds were settled by resort to the Code Duello, and men of all classes engaged in other forms of personal conflict. Indians, Mexicans, desperadoes, drunken ruffians, gamblers, trigger-quick duelists who sought to have their honor offended—any of these might assail normally peaceable citizens. Hence they learned to defend themselves and, if necessary, take the offensive. Their confidence in their ability to look any man in the eye gave them a feeling of strength in their own opinions.

In a society which required strength and self-reliance both in acquiring the necessities of life and in social relationships, everyone was inclined to be self-assertive and restive under restraint. Theoretically one man was as good as another on the frontier, and a feeling of equality prevailed. Although the energy and leadership of business and professional men generally enabled them to exercise dominance, they rarely assumed attitudes of social superiority. The plain people elected few demagogues to high office, but politics was a rough-and-tumble spectacle. In 1838 two candidates for president committed suicide, and the campaign of 1841 was featured by vituperative charges of cowardice, dishonesty, and habitual drunkenness against the candidates.

The Republic was fortunate in its choice of leaders. Houston, Austin, Travis, Lamar, Rusk, Hemphill, Burleson, Burnet, Jones, Ashbel Smith, the Whartons, Henderson—these names only top a long list. The repercussions of the revolution they led and the republic they helped establish have not yet spent themselves, for their actions have impressed themselves indelibly on the consciousness of every Texan to this day. Houston responded to his elevation to the presidency by rising in stature from his former position of speculation-minded adventurer to one of real statesmanship, while Lamar's interest in intellectual matters is still felt in Texas.

So there arose a Texan way of life that still exists, even in the face of all the mass promotion and standardization of machine civilization. Stamina, individualism, "go-ahead" initiative, pride in everything Texan—these were and still are, in varying degrees, among the ingredients of the Texas spirit. Bitter courage, wry or raucous laughter, and kindliness stood out amidst the drabness and coarseness of frontier life. An astonishing number of urbane and intelligent men found a satisfying freedom from compulsion. Indeed, the Republic of Texas worked a curious alchemy with its citizenry, educated and untutored alike. It took the sons and daughters of Tennessee, the Carolinas, Georgia, Mississippi, New York, France, and Germany and set its own ineffaceable stamp on their souls. The same process is still working in Texas today.

Bibliography

MANUSCRIPTS:

PERSONAL, BUSINESS, AND ORGANIZATION

(Unless otherwise indicated, all manuscripts of these types are in the University of Texas Library Archives, Austin.)

Addison (Oscar M., and Family) Papers, 1835–49.

Adriance (John) Papers, 1832–41.

Arnett (William W.) Papers, 1841–85.

Asbury (Samuel E.) Collection, 1810–1935.

Ashcraft, Levi H. "Thrilling Scenes in Texas." Asbury Collection.

Austin (Henry) Papers, 1831–52.

Austin (Stephen F.) Papers, 1820–36. Unpublished.

"Autobiography of B. F. Hall."

"Autobiography of James Norman Smith."

"Autobiography of Rev. Francis A. Wilson, 1810–1846."

"Autobiographical Sketch of the Life of S. F. Sparks."

Barrett (D. C.) Papers, 1836.

Barry (James B.) Papers, 1841–1900.

Billingsley (Jesse) Papers, 1835–40.

Blake (R. B.) Collection, 1830–50. Stephen F. Austin Teachers College Library, Nacogdoches, Texas.

Bollaert, William. "Cherokee Memos . . . For an Article on the Cherokees, 1843." Ayer Collection, Newberry Library, Chicago.

Bollaert (William) Diary, April 20–July 2, 1844. Ayer Collection, Newberry Library, Chicago.

Bollaert (William) Miscellaneous Notes Concerning Texas. Ayer Collection, Newberry Library, Chicago.

Bollaert (William) Notes and Memoranda, 1837–38. Ayer Collection, Newberry Library, Chicago.

Bollaert, William. "Notes and View of Galveston Island." Ayer Collection, Newberry Library, Chicago.

Bollaert, William. "Notes for a life of William Kennedy." Ayer Collection, Newberry Library, Chicago.

Bollaert, William. "Notes on Texas, 1843–1844." Ayer Collection, Newberry Library, Chicago.

Bollaert, William. "Personal Narrative of a Residence & Travels in the Republic of Texas by W. B. During the years 1840–2 & 3–4." Ayer Collection, Newberry Library, Chicago.

Bollaert (William) Private Journals, 1841–49. Ayer Collection, Newberry Library, Chicago.

Bollaert, William. "Texas in 1842—by a Traveller." Ayer Collection, Newberry Library, Chicago.

Brazos and Galveston Rail-road Company Papers, 1839–40.

Brigham (Asa) Papers, 1832–36.

Brown, Frank. "Annals of Travis County."

Bryan (Guy M.) Papers, 1843–55.

Bull (Pleasant M.) Papers, 1832–58. In private possession.

Burnet (David G.) Papers, 1821–69. Rosenberg Library, Galveston, Texas.

Burnet (David G.) Papers, 1836–90.

Cartwright (Matthew) Papers, 1830–59. In private possession.

Clay (Nestor) Papers, 1802–32.

Clay (Nestor) Papers, 1830–32. In private possession.

Cochran (R. E.) Papers, 1838–46.

"Constitution of the Philosophical Society of Texas."

Crane (William Carey) Papers, 1832–86.

Daggett, Eph M. "Recollections of the War of the Moderators and Regulators." Asbury Collection.

Diary of James Weston Miller, D.D., 1844–49.

Dinsmore (Silas) letter to R. L. Crawford, 1844.

Douglass (Kelsey H.) Papers, 1837–40.

Ellis (T. C. W., and Family) Papers, 1847–53. Louisiana State University Department of Archives, Baton Rouge.

Erskine, Blucher Haynes (ed.). "The Diary and Letters of Michael Erskine."

Ewing (Alexander) Papers, 1825–46. Texas State Library Archives, Austin.

Ewing (Alexander) Papers, 1825–26.

Fisher (S. Rhoads) Papers, 1836–99.

Fontaine (W. W.) Papers, 1785–1846.

Fowler (Littleton) Papers, 1833–46. In private possession.

Franklin (Benjamin C.) Papers, 1832–50.

Fulmore (Z. T.) Papers, 1826–68.

Fulton (J. C. and G. W.) Papers, 1836–46.

Galveston Chamber of Commerce, Charter of, 1845. Rosenberg Library, Galveston, Texas.

Galveston Hussar Company Papers, 1842. Rosenberg Library, Galveston, Texas.

Gordon (Isabella H.) Papers, 1825–45. In possession of Miss Mary M. Clark, Clarksville, Texas.

Green (Thomas Jefferson) Papers, 1834–45. University of North Carolina Library Archives, Chapel Hill.

Grover (Walter R.) Papers, 1840–82. Rosenberg Library, Galveston, Texas.

Hanrick (Edward) Papers, 1831–45.

Harden (Edward) Papers, 1845. Duke University Library Archives, Durham, N. C.

Hardin (Sarah) Papers, 1832.

Heard, Thomas J. "The Medical History of Texas," 1876.

Henderson (J. Pinckney) Papers, 1837–47. In private possession.

Herndon (J. H.) Diary, 1837–38.

Histories and Muster Rolls of the Galveston Artillery Company, Galveston Fusileers, Lone Star Rifles, Hermitage Guards, Houston Light Guards, Sealy Rifles, and Island City Rifles, 1840–75. Rosenberg Library, Galveston, Texas.

Holley (Mary Austin) Papers, 1829–46.

Houston, Texas, Christ Church Burial, Marriage, and Baptismal Records, 1843–73.

Independence, Texas, Presbyterian Church Records, 1839–86.

Ingram (Ira) Papers, 1824–37. Library of Congress, Division of Manuscripts.

Ingram (Ira) Papers, 1830–35.

Jenkins, John H. "Personal Reminiscences of Texas History Relating to Bastrop County."

Jones (John Rice) Papers, 1835–40.

Kuykendall (James Hampton and William) Papers, 1822–97.

Labadie (N. D.) Papers, 1824–40. Rosenberg Library, Galveston, Texas.

Lake (Mary Daggett) Papers, 1843–48.

Lamar (Rebecca Ann) Journal, 1838. San Jacinto Memorial Museum, Houston, Texas.

Lamar (Rebecca Ann) Papers, 1840–41.

Lewis (Ira R.) Papers, 1813–73.

"Life of John Haynie."

Lincecum (Gideon) Papers, 1838–70.

THE TEXAS REPUBLIC

Lockhart (John W.) Papers, 1830–1918. Rosenberg Library, Galveston, Texas.
McKinney (James P.) Papers, 1790–1865.
McKinney (Thomas F.) Papers, 1835–73.
McKinney (William C.) MS concerning Ben Milam, 1874. In private possession.
Maverick (Samuel A.) Papers, 1830–46.
"Memoirs of John S. Ford."
Menefee (John S.) Papers, 1831–46.
Minutes of the Presbytery of Brazos, 1840–45, 1846–54.
Minutes of the Texas Presbytery of the Cumberland Presbyterian Church, 1837–39. Archives of Bethel College, McKenzie, Tenn., and the papers collected by the late Rev. B. A. Hodges, Waxahachie, Texas, in possession of his widow.
Minutes of the Texas Synod of the Cumberland Presbyterian Church, 1843–68.
Mitchell (Asa) Papers, 1836–39.
Montrose (Marcus A.) MS, legal agreement between Montrose and Frost Thorn, president of the Board of Trustees, Nacogdoches University, 1846. In possession of R. B. Blake, Nacogdoches, Texas.
Morgan (H. S.) letter to "Dear Brother," 1837. In possession of Garland Miller, Bastrop, Texas.
Morgan (James)Papers, 1809–64. Rosenberg Library, Galveston, Texas.
Nicholson (James) Papers, 1826–46.
Perry (James F.) Plantation Papers, 1810–75.
Raguet (Henry) Papers, 1833–50.
Rawlins (William) Papers, 1846. In private possession.
Read (Richmond) Papers, 1837–40. In private possession.
"Recollections of James Monroe Hill, 1897."
Reding (W. R.) Papers, 1837–46.
Reily (James) Papers, 1830–49.
Rice, Edwin B. "Biographical Sketch of Rev. Benjamin Eaton." Rosenberg Library, Galveston, Texas.
Roberts (O. M.) Papers, 1843–50.
Ross (John E.) Papers, 1838–41. In private possession.
Rusk (Thomas Jefferson) Papers, 1823–54.
Rusk (Thomas Jefferson) Papers, 1836–47. Duke University Library Archives, Durham, N. C.
Sharp (W. G.) Collection, 1825–35. San Augustine, Texas.
Sheridan (Francis C.) Diary, 1839–40.
Sherman (Sidney) Papers, 1837–46. In private possession.

Sinks, Mrs. Julia Lee. "Texas Reminiscences."

Smith (Ashbel) Papers, 1830–50.

Smith (Henry) Papers, 1822–46.

Smyth (George W.) Papers, 1819–92.

Starr (James H.) Papers, 1830–50.

Swartwout (Samuel) Papers, 1834–1902.

Taylor (Calvin, and Family) Papers, 1847. Louisiana State University Department of Archives, Baton Rouge.

Trask (Judith) Papers, 1835–39. In possession of Miss Emma R. Totman, Norwell, Mass.

Travis (William B.) Diary, 1833–34. Starr Papers.

Victoria, Texas, Presbyterian Church Records, 1841–72.

Watkins, Richard Overton, "Life of Rev. Richard Overton Watkins," 1876.

Weeks (David) Papers, 1839. Louisiana State University Department of Archives, Baton Rouge.

West (George W.) Papers, 1840–55. Duke University Library Archives, Durham, N. C.

Westervelt (S. M.) Papers, 1841–42. In possession of Carlos Masterson, Angleton, Texas.

Wheelock (E. L. R.) Papers, 1833–47.

Williams (Samuel May) Papers, 1830–46. Rosenberg Library, Galveston, Texas.

Willich (George, Jr.) Papers, 1834. In possession of Willich & Co., New York.

Wood (H. A.) Papers, 1832–65. Rosenberg Library, Galveston, Texas.

Wright (George Travis) Family Papers, 1824–1917.

MANUSCRIPTS: GOVERNMENTAL RECORDS

(Unless otherwise indicated, all governmental records are in Texas.)

Bexar Archives, 1820–35. University of Texas Library Archives, Austin.

Colonization Papers, 1829–45. Texas State Library Archives, Austin.

County Records and District Court Records in following counties: Austin, Bastrop, Bexar, Brazoria, Brazos, Colorado, Fannin, Fayette, Fort Bend, Galveston, Goliad, Gonzales, Harris, Harrison, Jefferson, Matagorda, Montgomery, Nacogdoches, Red River, Robertson, San Augustine, San Patricio, Travis, and Victoria.

County Tax Rolls, 1837–45. 24 vols. State Comptroller's Office, Austin.

Galveston Customs House Records, 1835–44. Rosenberg Library, Galveston.

General Land Office Records. Austin.

Goliad Minutes of Common Council, 1841–46. Goliad.

Houston City Council Minutes, Vol. A. Houston.
Leon County Deed Records, Vol. E. Tallahassee, Florida.
Matagorda Corporation Treasury Accounts, 1838–43. Bay City.
Matagorda Minutes of Meetings of Proprietors, 1830–38. Bay City.
Memorials and Petitions to the Congress of the Republic of Texas and the Legislature of the State of Texas, 1835–52. Texas State Library Archives, Austin.
Nacogdoches Archives, 1820–36. Typed copies. University of Texas Library Archives, Austin.
State Department Archives (Post Office Department), Republic of Texas. Texas State Library Archives, Austin.
Treasury Department Archives, Republic of Texas. Texas State Library Archives, Austin.
U. S. Customs Service Records, Port of New Orleans, 1826–46. New Orleans, Louisiana.
Washington County Court Minutes, 1837–43 (civil cases). University of Texas Library Archives, Austin.

NEWSPAPERS

(Unless otherwise indicated, all newspapers listed were published in Texas.)
Austin *City Gazette,* 1839–42.
Austin *Daily Bulletin,* 1842.
Austin *Daily Texian,* 1841–42.
Austin *Texas Democrat,* 1846.
Austin *Texas Sentinel,* 1840–41. (Variant title: Austin *Texas Centinel.*)
Austin *Texas State Gazette,* 1849.
Austin *Weekly Texian,* 1841–42.
Austin *Western Advocate,* 1843.
Bonham *Daily Favorite,* 1935.
Brazoria *Advocate of the People's Rights,* 1834.
Brazoria *Brazos Courier,* 1839–40.
Brazoria *Constitutional Advocate and Texas Public Advertiser,* 1832–33.
Brazoria *Texas Republican,* 1834–36.
Brazoria *The People,* 1838.
Camden (South Carolina) *Commercial Courier,* 1837.
Canton *Van Zandt Enterprise,* 1906.
Centerville *Leon Pioneer,* 1852.
Cincinnati (Ohio) *Chronicle,* 1840.
Civilian and Galveston Gazette, 1838–40, 1842–45. (Variant title: *Civilian and Galveston City Gazette.*)

Clarksville *Northern Standard*, 1842–53.
Columbia *Planter*, 1843–44.
Columbus (Mississippi) *Democrat*, 1837–41.
Galveston *Commercial Intelligencer*, 1838.
Galveston *Daily Advertiser*, 1842.
Galveston *Daily Galvestonian*, 1840–41.
Galveston *Daily News*, 1842.
Galveston *Daily News*, 1918, 1923.
Galveston *Galvestonian*, 1839.
Galveston *Texas Times*, 1842–43.
Galveston *Weekly Galvestonian*, 1841.
Gazette de Baton Rouge (Louisiana), 1844.
Houston *Houstonian*, 1841.
Houston *Morning Star*, 1839–46.
Houston *Musquito*, 1841.
Houston *National Banner*, 1838.
Houston *National Intelligencer*, 1839.
Houston *Telegraph and Texas Register*, 1837–46. (Previously published at San Felipe de Austin, Harrisburg, and Columbia, 1835–37.)
Houston *Texian Democrat*, 1844.
Houston *Weekly Houstonian*, 1841.
Houston *Weekly Times*, 1840.
Huntsville *Patriot*, 1846.
Huntsville *Texas Banner*, 1846.
Huntsville *Texas Presbyterian*, 1847.
Illustrated London News (England), 1842–46.
La Grange *Intelligencer*, 1844–46.
London (England) *Atlas*, 1841–42.
London (England) *Globe and Traveller*, 1843.
London (England) *Morning Herald*, 1843.
Matagorda *Bulletin*, 1837–39.
Matagorda *Colorado Gazette and Advertiser*, 1839–42.
Matagorda *Colorado Herald*, 1846.
Matagorda *Weekly Despatch*, 1844.
Mississippi Free Trader and Natchez Gazette, 1836–45.
Natchez (Mississippi) *Daily Courier*, 1842.
New Orleans (Louisiana) *Bee*, 1841, 1843.
New Orleans (Louisiana) *Commercial Bulletin*, 1838–41.
New Orleans (Louisiana) *Daily Delta*, 1845–46.
New Orleans (Louisiana) *Daily Picayune*, 1837–50.
New Orleans (Louisiana) *Le Courrier de la Louisiane*, 1836.

New Orleans (Louisiana) *Morning Advertiser,* 1841.

New Orleans (Louisiana) *Weekly Picayune,* 1838–49.

Pendleton (South Carolina) *Messenger,* 1839–40.

Richmond *Telescope,* 1839–40. (Variant titles: Richmond *Telescope and Register* and Richmond *Telescope and Texas Literary Register.*)

San Antonio *Texas Evangel,* 1938.

San Augustine *Journal and Advertiser,* 1840–41.

San Augustine *Red-Lander,* 1841–46.

San Felipe de Austin *Mexican Citizen,* 1831.

San Felipe de Austin *Texas Gazette,* 1829–31, 1831–32.

San Luis *Advocate,* 1840–41.

Shreveport (Louisiana) *Caddo Gazette and De-Soto Intelligencer,* 1843–45. (Variant title: Shreveport *Caddo Gazette.*)

Washington *National Vindicator,* 1843–44.

Washington *Texas National Register,* 1844–45.

Washington *Texian and Brazos Farmer,* 1842–43.

BOOKS AND PAMPHLETS

Abstract of Land Claims, Compiled From the Records of the General Land Office of the State of Texas, and Published Under the Superintendence of the Comptroller. Galveston, 1852.

An Abstract of the Original Titles of Record in the General Land Office. Houston, 1838.

Acheson, Sam. *35,000 Days in Texas; a History of the Dallas News and Its Forbears.* New York, 1938.

Address of Major James Reily, on the Occasion of Laying the Corner Stone of the Houston and Brazos Rail Road. Houston, 1840.

Address to the Reader of the Documents Relating to the Galveston Bay & Texas Land Company, Which Are Contained in the Appendix. New York, 1831.

American Bible Society *Annual Reports* (Seventeenth Through Thirtieth). New York, 1833–46.

Andrews, J. O. *Miscellanies.* Louisville, 1854.

Annual Report of the Board of Foreign Missions of the Presbyterian Church in the United States of America. New York, 1838.

[Arrington, Alfred W.]. *The Rangers and Regulators of the Tanaha; or Life among the Lawless. A Tale of the Republic of Texas. By Charles Summerfield* [pseud.]. New York [*c.* 1856].

Arthur, Mrs. James J. (ed.). *Annals of the Fowler Family.* Austin, 1901.

Atkinson, Mary J. *The Texas Indians.* San Antonio, 1935.

Baker, D. W. C. (comp.). *A Texas Scrap-Book.* New York, 1875.

Baker, William M. *The Life and Labours of the Rev. Daniel Baker, D.D.* Philadelphia, 1858.

Baldwin, Joseph G. *The Flush Times of Alabama and Mississippi.* Americus, Ga., 1853.

Barker, Eugene C. (ed.). *The Austin Papers.* 3 vols. Vol. I, in two parts, published as Vol. II of the *Annual Report of the American Historical Association for the Year 1919;* Washington, 1924. Vol. II, published as the *Annual Report of the American Historical Association for the Year 1922;* Washington, 1928. Vol. III; Austin, 1927.

————. *The Life of Stephen F. Austin, Founder of Texas, 1793–1836.* Nashville and Dallas, 1925.

————. *Mexico and Texas, 1821–1835.* Dallas, 1928.

————. *Texas History for High Schools and Colleges.* Dallas, 1929.

————, and Ernest W. Winkler (eds.). *A History of Texas and Texans by Frank W. Johnson.* 5 vols. Chicago and New York, 1914.

Biesele, Rudolph L. *The History of the German Settlements in Texas, 1831–1861.* Austin, 1930.

Binkley, William C. *The Expansionist Movement in Texas, 1836–1850.* Berkeley, Calif., 1925.

———— (ed.). *Official Correspondence of the Texan Revolution, 1835–1836.* 2 vols. New York, 1936.

Biographical Encyclopedia of Texas. New York, 1880.

Bollaert, William. *Notes on the Coast Region of the Texan Territory.* Separatum originally published in *Journal of the Royal Geographical Society of London,* XIII (London, 1844), 226–44.

————. *Observations on the Geography of Texas.* Separatum originally published in *Journal of the Royal Geographical Society of London,* XX (London, 1851), 113–35.

Bonnell, George William. *Topographical Description of Texas.* Austin, 1840.

Bracht, Viktor. *Texas in 1848.* Translation from German by Charles Frank Schmidt. San Antonio, 1931; originally published in Elberfeld, 1849.

Brown, John Henry. *Indian Wars and Pioneers of Texas.* Austin [n.d.].

————. *Life and Times of Henry Smith, the First American Governor of Texas.* Dallas, 1887.

————, and William S. Speer (eds.). *Encyclopedia of the New West.* 2 vols. Marshall, Texas, 1881.

Campbell, Thomas H. *History of the Cumberland Presbyterian Church in Texas.* Nashville, 1936.

Carlson, Avery L. *A Monetary and Banking History of Texas.* Fort Worth, 1930.

Carroll, James M. *A History of Texas Baptists.* Dallas, 1923.

Chandler, B. O., and J. E. Howe. *History of Texarkana and Bowie and Miller Counties.* Texarkana, Texas, 1939.

Clark, Pat B. *The History of Clarksville and Old Red River County.* Dallas, 1937.

Cobb, Berry B. *A History of Dallas Lawyers, 1840–1890.* Dallas, 1934.

Cochran, John H. *Dallas County.* Dallas, 1928.

Cohen, Henry. "Settlement of the Jews in Texas," in *Publications of the American Jewish Historical Society,* No. 2, pp. 139–56. Baltimore, 1894.

Col. Crockett's Exploits and Adventures in Texas. Philadelphia, 1836.

[Coleman, R. M.?]. *Houston Displayed; or, Who Won the Battle of San Jacinto? By a Farmer in the Army.* Velasco, Texas, 1837.

Congressional Globe, 25 Congress, 3 session. Washington, 1839.

Congressional Globe, 33 Congress, 1 session. Washington, 1854.

Copeland, Fayette. *Kendall of the Picayune.* Norman, Okla., 1943.

Correspondence Relative to Difficulties with M. de Saligny, Chargé D'Affaires of France. Austin, 1841.

Crane, William C. *Life and Select Literary Remains of Sam Houston.* Philadelphia, 1884.

Crocket, George L. *Two Centuries in East Texas.* Dallas, 1932.

Cushing, S. W. *Wild Oats Sowings; or, the Autobiography of an Adventurer.* New York, 1857.

Dallam, James W. (comp.). *Opinions of the Supreme Court of Texas from 1840 to 1844 Inclusive.* St. Paul, 1883; reprinted from 1845 edition.

Debates of the General Conferences of the M. E. Church, May, 1844. New York, 1845.

De Bow, J. D. B. *The Seventh Census of the United States: 1850.* Washington, 1853.

——. *Statistical View of the United States . . . a Compendium of the Seventh Census.* Washington, 1854.

De Cordova, Jacob. *Texas: Her Resources and Her Public Men.* Philadelphia, 1858.

De Shields, James T. *Border Wars of Texas.* Tioga, Texas, 1912.

Dewees, William B. *Letters from an Early Settler of Texas.* Compiled by Cara Cardelle [pseud.]. Louisville, 1852.

Dictionary of National Biography. Vol. IX. London, 1922.

Dixon, S. H., and L. W. Kemp. *The Heroes of San Jacinto.* Houston, 1932.

Dobie, J. Frank. *The Flavor of Texas.* Dallas, 1936.

————. *Guide to the Life and Literature of the Southwest.* Austin, 1943.

————. *The Longhorns.* Boston, 1941.

Domenech, E. *Journal d'un Missionaire au Texas et au Mexique, 1846–1852.* Paris, 1857. Translated into English under the title *Missionary Adventures in Texas and Mexico, a Personal Narrative of Six Years Sojourn in Those Regions.* London, 1858.

Dowell, Greensville. *Yellow Fever and Malarial Diseases Embracing a History of the Epidemics of Yellow Fever in Texas.* Philadelphia, 1876.

Duval, John C. *The Adventures of Big-Foot Wallace.* [Macon, Ga.] 1870.

————. *Early Times in Texas.* Austin, 1892.

Eby, Frederick. *The Development of Education in Texas.* New York, 1925.

———— (comp.). *Education in Texas.* Austin, 1918.

Edward, David B. *The History of Texas; or, the Emigrant's, Farmer's, and Politician's Guide to the Character, Climate, Soil, and Productions of that Country.* Cincinnati, 1836.

Ehrenberg, Hermann. *Texas und seine Revolution.* Leipzig, 1843.

————. *With Milam and Fannin.* Abridged translation. Dallas, 1935.

Eighteenth Annual Report of the Missionary Society of the M. E. Church. New York, 1837.

Falconer, Thomas. *Notes of a Journey Through Texas and New Mexico, in the Years 1841 and 1842.* Separatum originally published in *Journal of the Royal Geographical Society of London,* XIII (London, 1844), 199–226.

Field, Joseph E. *Three Years in Texas.* Greenfield, Mass., 1836.

[*First*] *Annual Report of the Board of Foreign Missions of the Presbyterian Church, in the United States of America.* New York, 1838.

First Annual Report of the Missionary Society of the Methodist Episcopal Church, South. Louisville, 1846.

First Semi-Annual Report of the Public Schools of Galveston. Galveston, 1847.

Fish, Carl R. *The Rise of the Common Man, 1830–1850.* New York, 1927.

Fisher's Crockett Almanac. 1843. New York [1843?].

[Fiske?]. *A Visit to Texas.* New York, 1836.

Fitzmorris, M. A. *Four Decades of Catholicism in Texas, 1820–1860*. Washington, 1926.

Foote, Henry Stuart. *Texas and the Texans*. 2 vols. Philadelphia, 1841.

Franks, J. M. *Seventy Years in Texas*. Gatesville, Texas, 1924.

Fulton, Maurice G. (ed.). *Diary and Letters of Josiah Gregg; Southwestern Enterprises, 1840–1847*. Norman, Okla., 1941.

Gammel, H. P. N. (comp.). *The Laws of Texas, 1822–1897*. Vols. I–III. Austin, 1898.

Garrison, George P. (ed.). *Diplomatic Correspondence of the Republic of Texas*. 3 vols. Vol. I published as Vol. II of the *Report of the American Historical Association for the Year 1907;* Washington, 1907. Vols. II and III published as Vol. II of the *Report of the American Historical Association for the Year 1908*, in two parts; Washington, 1908.

Geiser, Samuel W. *Horticulture and Horticulturists in Early Texas*. Dallas, 1945.

——. *Naturalists of the Frontier*. Dallas, 1937.

Gouge, William M. *The Fiscal History of Texas*. Philadelphia, 1852.

Graham, Philip (ed.). *Early Texas Verse*. Austin, 1936.

——. *The Life and Poems of Mirabeau B. Lamar*. Chapel Hill, N. C., 1938.

Gray, William F. *From Virginia to Texas, 1835. Diary of Col. Wm. F. Gray Giving Details of His Journey to Texas and Return in 1835–36 and Second Journey to Texas in 1837*. Houston, 1909.

Green, Rena Maverick (ed.). *Memoirs of Mary A. Maverick*. San Antonio, 1921.

—— (ed.). *The Swisher Memoirs*. San Antonio, 1932.

Green, Thomas J. *Journal of the Texian Expedition Against Mier*. New York, 1845.

Greer, James K. (ed.). *A Texas Ranger and Frontiersman; the Days of Buck Barry in Texas, 1845–1906*. Dallas, 1932.

Gulick, Charles A., Jr., *et al.* (eds.). *The Papers of Mirabeau Buonaparte Lamar*. 6 vols. Austin, 1920–27.

Hall, B. M. *The Life of Rev. John Clark*. New York, 1857.

Hall, Ida B. "Pioneer Children's Games," in *Texian Stomping Grounds,* 141–51. *Texas Folk-Lore Society Publications*, XVII. Austin, 1941.

[Hammett, Samuel A.]. *Piney Woods Tavern; or, Sam Slick in Texas*. Philadelphia [*c.* 1858].

Hatcher, Mattie Austin. *Letters of an Early American Traveller, Mary Austin Holley; Her Life and Her Works, 1784–1846*. Dallas, 1933.

Heard, Thomas J. "Remarks on Yellow Fever," in *Transactions of the*

Texas State Medical Association: Sixth Annual Session, 1874, pp. 168–74. Houston, 1874.

Helm, Mrs. Mary S. *Scraps of Early Texas History.* Austin, 1884.

Henry, W. S. *Campaign Sketches of the War with Mexico.* New York, 1847.

Hill, Jim Dan. *The Texas Navy.* Chicago, 1937.

Holley, Mary Austin. *Texas.* Baltimore, 1833.

———. *Texas.* Lexington, Ky., 1836.

Hooton, Charles. *St. Louis' Isle, or Texiana.* London, 1847.

House of Representatives Executive Documents, 27 Congress, 2 session, Washington, 1841.

Houstoun, Mrs. [Matilda C. F.]. *Texas and the Gulf of Mexico; or, Yachting in the New World.* 2 vols. London, 1844.

Hudson, Estelle. *Czech Pioneers of the Southwest.* Dallas, 1934.

Hulbert, Archer B. *Soil; its Influence on the History of the United States, with Special Reference to Migration and the Scientific Study of Local History.* New Haven, 1930.

Hunt, Richard S., and Jesse F. Randel. *Guide to the Republic of Texas.* New York, 1839.

———. *A New Guide to Texas.* New York, 1845.

Hunter, Robert H. *Narrative of Robert Hancock Hunter, 1813–1902.* Austin, 1936.

Ikin, Arthur. *Texas: its History, Topography, Agriculture, Commerce and General Statistics.* London, 1841.

Indianola Scrap Book. Victoria, Texas, 1936.

Jackson, George. *Sixty Years in Texas.* Dallas, 1908.

James, Joshua. *A Journal of a Tour in Texas.* [Wilmington?] N. C., 1835.

James, Marquis. *Andrew Jackson: Portrait of a President.* Indianapolis, 1937.

———. *The Raven; a Biography of Sam Houston.* Indianapolis, 1929.

Jefferson, Joseph. *The Autobiography of Joseph Jefferson.* New York, 1889.

Johnston, William Preston. *The Life of General Albert Sidney Johnston.* New York, 1878.

Jones, Anson. *Memoranda and Official Correspondence Relating to the Republic of Texas, its History and Annexation, Including a Brief Autobiography of The Author.* New York, 1859.

Jones, John G. *A Complete History of Methodism as Connected with the Mississippi Conference of the Methodist Episcopal Church, South.* Vol. II. Nashville, 1908.

Jones, Margaret Belle. *Bastrop*. Bastrop, Texas, 1936.

Journals of the General Conference of the Methodist Episcopal Church. Vol. II (1840–44). New York, 1855.

Journals of the House of Representatives of the Republic of Texas, 1836–1845. 10 vols. Title and place of publication varies, 1838–45.

Journals of the Senate of the Republic of Texas, 1836–1845. 10 vols. Title and place of publication varies, 1836–45.

Kemp, L. W. *The Signers of the Texas Declaration of Independence.* Houston, 1944.

Kendall, George Wilkins. *Narrative of the Texan Santa Fé Expedition.* 2 vols. New York, 1844.

Kennedy, William. *Texas: its Geography, Natural History, and Topography.* New York, 1844.

———. *Texas: the Rise, Progress, and Prospects of the Republic of Texas.* 2 vols. London, 1841.

Kerr, Hugh. *A Poetical Description of Texas, and Narrative of Many Interesting Events in That Country.* New York, 1838.

Konwiser, Harry M. *Texas Republic Postal System.* New York, 1933.

Laws and Decrees of the State of Coahuila and Texas. Houston, 1839.

Laws Passed by the Second Legislature of the State of Texas. Vol. II. Houston, 1848.

Leger, Theodore. *Essay on the Particular Influence of Prejudices in Medicine, Over the Treatment of the Disease Most Common in Texas, Intermittent Fever.* Brazoria, Texas, 1838.

Lide, A. A. *Robert Alexander and the Early Methodist Church in Texas.* La Grange, Texas, 1935.

Lincecum, Gideon. "Autobiography of Gideon Lincecum," in *Publications of the Mississippi Historical Society,* VIII, 443–519. Oxford, 1904.

Linn, John J. *Reminiscences of Fifty Years in Texas.* New York, 1883.

Love, Annie Carpenter. *History of Navarro County.* Dallas, 1933.

Lowrie, Samuel H. *Culture Conflict in Texas, 1821–1835.* New York, 1932.

Lubbock, Francis R. *Six Decades in Texas; or, Memoirs of Francis Richard Lubbock, Governor of Texas in War-Time, 1861–63.* Edited by C. W. Raines. Austin, 1900.

[Lundy, Benjamin]. *The Life, Travels, and Opinions of Benjamin Lundy, Including His Journeys to Texas and Mexico; with a Sketch of Contemporary Events, and a Notice of the Revolution in Hayti.* Philadelphia, 1847.

Lyell, Charles. *A Second Visit to the United States of North America.* New York, 1849.

Lynch, James D. *The Bench and Bar of Texas.* St. Louis, 1885.

McCalla, W[illiam] L. *Adventures in Texas, Chiefly in the Spring and Summer of 1840 . . . Accompanied by an Appendix, Containing an Humble Attempt to Aid in Establishing and Conducting Literary and Ecclesiastical Institutions.* Philadelphia, 1841.

McCampbell, Coleman. *Saga of a Frontier Seaport.* Dallas, 1934.

McDanield, H. F., and N. A. Taylor. *The Coming Empire; or, Two Thousand Miles in Texas on Horseback.* New York, 1877.

McDonnold, B. W. *History of the Cumberland Presbyterian Church.* Nashville, 1888.

McKinstry, William C. *The Colorado Navigator.* Matagorda, Texas, 1840.

McKitrick, Reuben. *The Public Land System of Texas, 1823–1910.* Madison, 1918.

McLean, John H. *Reminiscences of Rev. Jno. H. McLean.* Nashville, 1918.

Maillard, N. Doran. *The History of the Republic of Texas.* London, 1842.

Marlay, John F. *The Life of Rev. Thomas A. Morris, D.D.* Cincinnati, 1875.

Marryat, Frederick. *The Travels and Adventures of Monsieur Violet, in California, Sonora, and Western Texas.* London and New York [1843?].

Middleton, John W. *History of the Regulators and Moderators and the Shelby County War in 1841 and 1842, in the Republic of Texas.* Fort Worth, 1883.

Miller, E. T. *A Financial History of Texas.* Austin, 1916.

Minutes of the Annual Conferences of the Methodist Episcopal Church. Vol. II; New York, 1840. Vol. III; New York [n.d.].

Minutes of a Called Session of the United Baptist Association . . . 1842. Washington, Texas, 1843.

Minutes of the Eighth Annual Meeting of the Union Baptist Association. [n.p., 1847?]

Minutes of the Fifth Anniversary Meeting of the Union Baptist Association. Washington, Texas, 1844.

Minutes of the First Session of the Union Baptist Association. Houston, 1840.

Minutes of the Fourth Anniversary Meeting of the Union Baptist Association. Washington, Texas, 1844.

313

Minutes of the General Assembly of the Presbyterian Church in the United States of America. Vol. IX. Philadelphia, 1846.

Minutes of the Ninth Anniversary of the Union Baptist Association. [n.p., 1848?]

Minutes of the Second Session of the Union Baptist Association . . . 1841. [Title page missing.]

Minutes of the Seventh Annual Meeting of the Union Baptist Association . . . 1846. [Title page missing.]

Minutes of the Sixth Annual Meeting of the Union Baptist Association. La Grange, Texas, 1845.

Mitchell, S. A. *Accompaniment to Mitchell's New Map of Texas, Oregon, and California, With the Regions Adjoining.* Philadelphia, 1846.

Moore, Francis, Jr. *Map and Description of Texas.* Philadelphia, 1840.

Morphis, J. M. *History of Texas, From Its Discovery and Settlement, With a Description of Its Principal Cities and Counties, and the Agricultural, Mineral, and Material Resources of the State.* New York, 1874.

Morrell, Z. N. *Flowers and Fruits from the Wilderness; or, Thirty-Six Years in Texas and Two Winters in Honduras.* Boston, 1872.

Morris, T. A. *Miscellany.* Cincinnati, 1852.

Murphy, DuBose. *A Short History of the Protestant Episcopal Church in Texas.* Dallas [c. 1935].

Neville, A. W. *The History of Lamar County, Texas.* Paris [c. 1937].

Newell, Chester. *History of the Revolution in Texas . . . With the Latest Geographical, Topographical, and Statistical Accounts of the Country.* New York, 1838.

Newman, John B. *Texas and Mexico, in 1846; Comprising the History of Both Countries, With an Account of the Soil, Climate, and Productions of Each.* New York, 1846.

Nichols, Thomas Low. *Forty Years of American Life, 1821–1861.* New York, 1937. A reprint of the 1874 edition of a volume first published in 1864.

Nixon, P. I. *A Century of Medicine in San Antonio.* San Antonio, 1936.

Norwood, William F. *Medical Education in the United States Before the Civil War.* Philadelphia, 1944.

Olmsted, Frederick Law. *A Journey Through Texas; or, a Saddle-Trip on the Southwestern Frontier.* New York, 1857.

Owens, William A. *Swing and Turn; Texas Play-Party Games.* Dallas, 1936.

[Page, F. B.]. *Prairiedom; Rambles and Scrambles in Texas or New Estrémadura.* New York, 1845.

314

Parisot, P. F., and C. J. Smith (eds.). *History of the Catholic Church in the Diocese of San Antonio*. San Antonio, 1897.

Parker, A[mos] A[ndrew]. *Trip to the West and Texas*. Concord, 1835.

Parker, James W. *Narrative of the Perilous Adventures, Miraculous Escapes and Sufferings of Rev. James W. Parker . . . With an Impartial Geographical Description of . . . Texas; Written By Himself. To Which is Appended a Narrative of the Capture and Subsequent Sufferings of Mrs. Rachel Plummer . . . Written By Herself*. Louisville, 1844.

Phelan, Macum. *A History of Early Methodism in Texas, 1817–1866*. Nashville, 1924.

Pickrell, Annie Doom. *Pioneer Women in Texas*. Austin, 1929.

Pickett, Arlene. *Historic Liberty County*. Dallas, 1936.

Polk, W. M. *Leonidas Polk, Bishop and General*. 2 vols. New York, 1915.

Potts, Charles S. *Railroad Transportation in Texas*. Austin, 1909.

Rankin, Melinda. *Texas in 1850*. Boston, 1850.

Red, Mrs. G. P. *The Medicine Man in Texas*. Houston, 1930.

Red, William S. *A History of the Presbyterian Church in Texas*. Austin, 1936.

———. *The Texas Colonists and Religion, 1821–1836*. Austin, 1924.

Reed, S. G. *A History of the Texas Railroads and of Transportation Conditions under Spain and Mexico and the Republic and the State*. Houston, 1941.

Reid, Samuel C. *Scouting Expeditions of McCulloch's Texas Rangers*. Philadelphia, 1847.

Reply of Major-General T. Jefferson Chambers, T. A. to the Newspaper Attack Made Against Him, by David G. Burnet, Late President Ad Interim of the Republic of Texas. Houston, 1837.

Richardson, Chauncey. *An Address on Education: Delivered Before the Educational Convention of Texas, in the City of Houston, January, 1846*. [Houston, 1846?]

Richardson, Rupert N. *The Comanche Barrier to South Plains Settlement: a Century and a Half of Savage Resistance to the Advancing White Frontier*. Glendale, Cal., 1933.

———. *Texas, the Lone Star State*. New York, 1943.

Roemer, Ferdinand. *Texas*. Translation from German by Oswald Mueller. San Antonio, 1935; originally published in Bonn, 1849.

Rourke, Constance. *American Humor*. New York, 1931.

———. *Davy Crockett*. New York, 1934.

Ruthven, A. S. (comp.). *Proceedings of the Grand Lodge of Texas . . . 1837 . . . to . . . 1857.* Vol. I. Galveston, 1857.

Sayles, E. B. *An Archaeological Survey of Texas.* Globe, Arizona, 1935.

Scherpf, G. A. *Entstehungsgeschichte und gegenwärtiger Zustand des neuen, unabhängigen, americanischen Staates Texas.* Augsburg, 1841.

Schmitz, Joseph William. *Thus They Lived.* San Antonio, 1935.

———. *Texan Statecraft, 1836–1845.* San Antonio, 1941.

Sealsfield, Charles. *The Cabin Book; or, Sketches of Life in Texas.* New York, 1844. Translated from the German by C. F. Mersch.

Second Annual Catalogue of Rutersville College. Austin, 1842.

Seventh Annual Report of the Board of Foreign Missions of the Presbyterian Church, in the United States of America. New York, 1844.

Shryock, Richard H. *The Development of Modern Medicine.* Philadelphia, 1936.

Smith, Ashbel. *An Account of the Yellow Fever which Appeared in the City of Galveston, Republic of Texas, in the Autumn of 1839.* Galveston, 1839.

Smith, Edward. *Account of a Journey through North-Eastern Texas.* London, 1849.

Smither, Harriet (ed.). *Journals of the Fourth Congress of the Republic of Texas.* 3 vols. Austin, 1929–31.

Smithwick, Noah. *The Evolution of a State.* Austin, 1900.

Solms-Braunfels, Carl. *Texas, 1844–1845.* Houston, 1936; translation of a work first published in Frankfurt am Main, 1846.

Southern Medical Reports. Vols. I and II. New Orleans, 1850–51.

Sowell, A. J. *Early Settlers and Indian Fighters of Southwest Texas.* Austin, 1900.

———. *History of Fort Bend County.* Houston, 1904.

Spell, Lota M. *Music in Texas.* Austin, 1936.

Stanley, Oma. *The Speech of East Texas.* New York, 1937.

Stiff, Edward. *The Texan Emigrant.* Cincinnati, 1840.

Stratton, Florence. *The Story of Beaumont.* Houston [*c.* 1925].

Strobel, Abner J. *The Old Plantations and Their Owners of Brazoria County, Texas.* Houston, 1930.

Sweet, William W. *Religion on the American Frontier: the Baptists, 1783–1830.* New York, 1931.

———. *Religion on the American Frontier: the Presbyterians, 1783–1840.* New York, 1936.

———. *The Story of Religion in America.* New York, 1939.

Taylor, Ira T. *The Cavalcade of Jackson County.* San Antonio, 1938.

Taylor, Paul Schuster. *An American-Mexican Frontier, Nueces County, Texas.* Chapel Hill, N. C., 1934.

Templeton, S. M. *A Paper on Early Cumberland Presbyterian History in Texas.* Fort Worth [1931?].

Texas in 1840; or, the Emigrant's Guide to the New Republic. New York, 1840.

Texas Jurisprudence. Vol. I. San Francisco, 1929.

[Thompson, Henry]. *Texas. Sketches of Characters; Moral and Political Condition of the Republic; The Judiciary, &c.* Philadelphia, 1839.

Thorson, P. E. "Some Facts Regarding the Early History of Norwegians and the Church in Central Texas," in *Lutheran Almanac, 1934,* pp. 45–54. Minneapolis [1934?].

Thrall, Homer S. *History of Methodism in Texas.* Houston, 1872.

———. *A Pictorial History of Texas.* St. Louis, 1879.

Turner, Frederick Jackson. *The United States, 1830–1850; the Nation and its Sections.* New York, 1935.

Tyler, George W. *The History of Bell County.* Edited by Charles W. Ramsdell. San Antonio, 1936.

Wallace, Ernest. *Charles DeMorse; Pioneer Editor and Statesman.* Lubbock, Texas, 1943.

Wallis, J. L., and L. L. Hill (eds.). *Sixty Years on the Brazos; the Life and Letters of Dr. John Washington Lockhart, 1824–1900.* Los Angeles, 1930.

Waugh, Julia Nott. *Castroville and Henry Castro, Empresario.* San Antonio, 1934.

Webb, Walter P. *The Great Plains.* Boston, 1931.

———. *The Texas Rangers.* Boston, 1935.

Weyand, Leonie R., and Houston Wade. *An Early History of Fayette County.* La Grange, Texas, 1936.

Wharton, Clarence R. *Gail Borden, Pioneer.* San Antonio, 1941.

———. *Wharton's History of Fort Bend County.* San Antonio, 1939.

Wilbarger, J. W. *Indian Depredations in Texas.* Austin, 1889.

Williams, Alfred M. *Sam Houston and the War of Independence in Texas.* Boston, 1893.

Williams, Amelia W., and Eugene C. Barker (eds.). *The Writings of Sam Houston, 1813–1863.* 8 vols. Austin, 1938–43.

Winkler, Ernest W. (ed.). *Secret Journals of the Senate, Republic of Texas, 1836–1845.* Austin, 1911.

Woodman, David, Jr. *Guide to Texas Emigrants.* Boston, 1835.

Wooten, Dudley G. (ed.). *A Comprehensive History of Texas, 1685–1897.* 2 vols. Dallas, 1898.

Ziegler, Jesse A. *Wave of the Gulf.* San Antonio, 1938.

PERIODICALS

"Agricultural Development in Texas," *De Bow's Review,* Vol. IX, No. 4 (October, 1850), 426–27.

American Turf Register and Sporting Magazine, Vol. VIII, No. 1 (September, 1836)–Vol. IX, No. 12 (December, 1838).

Arthur, Dora F. "The Reverend Littleton Fowler," *Texas Methodist Historical Quarterly,* Vol. I, No. 2 (October, 1909), 117–38.

Asbury, Samuel E. "The Amateur Historian," *Southwestern Historical Quarterly,* Vol. XXVIII, No. 2 (October, 1924), 87–97. (The first fifteen volumes of this publication appeared under the title *Quarterly of the Texas State Historical Association.*)

———(contributor). "Extracts from the Reminiscences of General George W. Morgan," *ibid.,* Vol. XXX, No. 3 (January, 1927), 178–205.

"Autobiography of Andrew Davis," *Southwestern Historical Quarterly,* Vol. XLIII, No. 2 (October, 1939), 158–75; Vol. XLIII, No. 3 (January, 1940), 323–41.

Barker, Eugene C. "The Government of Austin's Colony, 1821–1831," *Southwestern Historical Quarterly,* Vol. XXI, No. 3 (January, 1918), 223–52.

———. "Land Speculation as a Cause of the Texas Revolution," *Quarterly of the Texas State Historical Association,* Vol. X, No. 1 (July, 1906), 76–95.

———. "Minutes of the Ayuntamiento of San Felipe de Austin, 1828–1832," *Southwestern Historical Quarterly,* Vol. XXI, No. 3 (January, 1918)–Vol. XXIV, No. 2 (October, 1920).

———. "The Influence of Slavery in the Colonization of Texas," *ibid.,* Vol. XXVIII, No. 1 (July, 1924), 1–33.

Bertleth, Rosa G. "Jared Ellison Groce," *Southwestern Historical Quarterly,* Vol. XX, No. 4 (April, 1917), 358–68.

Blair, Walter. "Six Davy Crocketts," *Southwest Review,* Vol. XXV, No. 4 (July, 1940), 443–62.

Blount, Lois F. "A Brief Study of Thomas J. Rusk, Based on His Letters to His Brother, David, 1835–1856," *Southwestern Historical Quarterly,* Vol. XXXIV, No. 3 (January, 1931), 181–202; Vol. XXXIV, No. 4 (April, 1931), 271–92.

Briscoe, P. "The First Texas Railroad," *Quarterly of the Texas State Historical Association,* Vol. VII, No. 4 (April, 1904), 279–85.

Bibliography

Bugbee, Lester W. "The Old Three Hundred," *Quarterly of the Texas State Historical Association,* Vol. I, No. 2 (October, 1897), 108–17.

Bywaters, Jerry. "More About Southwestern Architecture," *Southwest Review,* Vol. XVIII, No. 3 (April, 1933), 234–64.

Castañeda, Carlos E. (tr.). "A Trip to Texas in 1828: José María Sánchez," *Southwestern Historical Quarterly,* Vol. XXIX, No. 4 (April, 1926), 249–88.

———(tr.). "Statistical Report on Texas by Juan N. Almonte," *ibid.,* Vol. XXVIII, No. 3 (January, 1925), 177–222.

Cauley, T. J. "Early Meat Packing Plants in Texas," *Southwestern Political and Social Science Quarterly,* Vol. IX, No. 4 (March, 1929), 464–78.

"Church in the Republic of Texas, The," *Historical Magazine of the Protestant Episcopal Church,* Vol. II, No. 2 (June, 1933), 34–46.

"Clopper Correspondence, 1834–1838, The," *Quarterly of the Texas State Historical Association,* Vol. XIII, No. 2 (October, 1909), 128–44.

Creath, J. W. D. "Texas Associations," *The Tennessee Baptist,* Vol. VII, No. 44 (July, 1851), [p. 4].

Curlee, Abigail. "The History of a Texas Slave Plantation, 1831–63," *Southwestern Historical Quarterly,* Vol. XXVI, No. 2 (October, 1922), 79–127.

DeWitt, Roscoe. "After Indigenous Architecture, What?," *Southwest Review,* Vol. XVI, No. 3 (April, 1931), 314–24.

Dienst, Alex. "Contemporary Poetry of the Texas Revolution," *Southwestern Historical Quarterly,* Vol. XXI, No. 2 (October, 1917), 156–84.

Dobie, J. Frank. "Bowie and the Bowie Knife," *Southwest Review,* Vol. XVI, No. 3 (April, 1931), 351–68.

———. "The First Cattle in Texas and the Southwest Progenitors of the Longhorns," *Southwestern Historical Quarterly,* Vol. XLII, No. 3 (January, 1939), 171–97.

Eagleton, Nancy E. "The Mercer Colony in Texas, 1844–1883," *Southwestern Historical Quarterly,* Vol. XXXIX, No. 4 (April, 1936), 275–91; Vol. XL, No. 1 (July, 1936), 35–57; Vol. XL, No. 2 (October, 1936), 114–44.

Erath, Lucy A. (ed.). "Memoirs of Major George Bernard Erath," *Southwestern Historical Quarterly,* Vol. XXVI, No. 3 (January, 1923), 207–33; Vol. XXVI, No. 4 (April, 1923), 255–79.

Estill, Harry F. "The Old Town of Huntsville," *Quarterly of the Texas State Historical Association,* Vol. III, No. 4 (April, 1900), 265–78.

Gambrell, Herbert. "Anson Jones. I. A Wandering Physician," *Southwest Review,* Vol. XVIII, No. 2 (January, 1933), 139–68.

Garver, Lois. "Benjamin Rush Milam," *Southwestern Historical Quarterly,* Vol. XXXVIII, No. 2 (October, 1934), 79–121; Vol. XXXVIII, No. 3 (January, 1935), 177–202.

Gautier, Peter W. "Resources and Progress of Texas," *De Bow's Review,* Vol. IV, No. 3 (November, 1847), 318–25.

Geiser, Samuel W. "A Century of Scientific Exploration in Texas, pt. 1: 1820–1880," *Field and Laboratory,* Vol. IV, No. 2 (April, 1936), 41–55.

————. "A Century of Scientific Exploration in Texas, pt. 1 b: 1820–1880," *ibid.,* Vol. VII, No. 1 (January, 1939), 29–51.

————. "Audubon in Texas," *Southwest Review,* Vol. XVI, No. 1 (October, 1930), 109–35.

————. "Ferdinand von Roemer and His Travels in Texas," *ibid.,* Vol. XVII, No. 4 (July, 1932), 421–60.

————. "Racer's Storm (1837), with Notes on Other Texas Hurricanes in the Period 1818–1886," *Field and Laboratory,* Vol. XII, No. 2 (June, 1944), 59–67.

————. "Southwestern Siftings: I. William Douglas Wallach," *Southwest Review,* Vol. XXIX, No. 2 (January, 1944), 291–97.

————. "William Douglas Wallach, Pioneer Hydrographer of Texas," *Field and Laboratory,* Vol. XII, No. 1 (January, 1944), 27–31.

Gilmer, Daffan. "Early Courts and Lawyers of Texas," *Texas Law Review,* Vol. XII, No. 4 (June, 1934), 435–52.

Graham, Philip (ed.). "Mirabeau B. Lamar's First Trip to Texas," *Southwest Review,* Vol. XXI, No. 4 (July, 1936), 369–89.

Greer, D. Edward. "A Legal Anachronism: The Married Woman's Separate Acknowledgment to Deeds," *Texas Law Review,* Vol. I, No. 4 (June, 1923), 407–22.

Greer, James K. (ed.). "Journal of Ammon Underwood, 1834–1838," *Southwestern Historical Quarterly,* Vol. XXXII, No. 2 (October, 1928), 124–51.

"Growth of Texas," *De Bow's Review,* Vol. VI, No. 2 (August, 1848), 153.

Haggard, J. Villasana. "Epidemic Cholera in Texas, 1833–1834," *Southwestern Historical Quarterly,* Vol. XL, No. 3 (January, 1937), 216–30.

Hardin, J. Fair. "An Outline of Shreveport and Caddo Parish History," *Louisiana Historical Quarterly,* Vol. XVIII, No. 4 (October, 1935), 759–871.

Harris, Helen W. "Almonte's Inspection of Texas in 1834," *Southwestern Historical Quarterly,* Vol. XLI, No. 3 (January, 1938), 196–211.

Hammeken, George L. "Recollections of Stephen F. Austin," *Southwestern Historical Quarterly,* Vol. XX, No. 4 (April, 1917), 369–80.

Hinueber, Caroline von. "Life of German Pioneers in Early Texas," *Quarterly of the Texas State Historical Association,* Vol. II, No. 3 (January, 1899), 227–332.

Hogan, William R. "Amusements in the Republic of Texas," *Journal of Southern History,* Vol. III, No. 4 (November, 1937), 397–421.

———. "Henry Austin," *Southwestern Historical Quarterly,* Vol. XXXVII, No. 3 (January, 1934), 185–214.

———. "Pamelia Mann: Texas Frontierswoman," *Southwest Review,* Vol. XX, No. 4 (July, 1935), 360–70.

———. "Rampant Individualism in the Republic of Texas," *Southwestern Historical Quarterly,* Vol. XLIV, No. 4 (April, 1941), 454–80.

———. "The Theater in the Republic of Texas," *Southwest Review,* Vol. XIX, No. 4 (July, 1934), 374–401.

Holland, J. K. "Reminiscences of Austin and Old Washington," *Quarterly of the Texas State Historical Association,* Vol. I, No. 2 (October, 1897), 92–95.

"Hooton, Charles," obituaries in *Gentleman's Magazine,* New Series, Vol. XXVII, No. [4] (April, 1847), 442–43; and *New Monthly Magazine,* Vol. LXXIX, No. 315 (March, 1847), 397–98.

Jeffries, Charles. "Early Texas Architecture," *Bunker's Monthly* (continued as *Texas Monthly* and *Texas Weekly*), Vol. I, No. 6 (June, 1928), 905–15.

Johnson, Moses. "Lavacca, Texas—Farming," *Prairie Farmer,* Vol. X, No. 9 (September, 1850), 283–84.

"Jottings from the Old Journal of Littleton Fowler," *Quarterly of the Texas State Historical Association,* Vol. II, No. 1 (July, 1898), 73–84.

Kenney, M. M. "Recollections of Early Schools," *Quarterly of the Texas State Historical Association,* Vol. I, No. 4 (April, 1898), 285–96.

Kemp, L. W. "Mrs. Angelina B. Eberly," *Southwestern Historical Quarterly,* Vol. XXXVI, No. 3 (January, 1933), 193–99.

———. "The Capitol (?) at Columbia," *ibid.,* Vol. XLVIII, No. 1 (July, 1944), 3–9.

Kleberg, Rosa. "Some of My Early Experiences in Texas," *Quarterly of the Texas State Historical Association,* Vol. I, No. 4 (April, 1898), 297–302; Vol. II, No. 2 (October, 1898), 170–73.

Kuykendall, J. H. "Reminiscences of Early Texans," *Quarterly of the*

Texas State Historical Association, Vol. VI, No. 3 (January, 1903), 236–53; Vol. VI, No. 4 (April, 1903), 311–30; Vol. VII, No. 1 (July, 1903), 29–64.

Looscan, Adele B. "Harris County, 1822–1845," *Southwestern Historical Quarterly,* Vol. XVIII, No. 2 (October, 1914), 195–207; Vol. XVIII, No. 3 (January, 1915), 261–86; Vol. XVIII, No. 4 (April, 1915), 399–409; Vol. XIX, No. 1 (July, 1915), 37–64.

McClintock, William A. "Journal of a Trip Through Texas and Northern Mexico in 1846–1847," *Southwestern Historical Quarterly,* Vol. XXXIV, No. 1 (July, 1930), 20–37; Vol. XXXIV, No. 2 (October, 1930), 141–58; Vol. XXXIV, No. 3 (January, 1931), 231–56.

McCraven, William. "On the Yellow Fever of Houston, Texas, in 1847," *New Orleans Medical and Surgical Journal,* Vol. V, No. [2] (September, 1848), 227–235.

McDonald, Abner S. To "Bro. John," March 11, 1838, in *Southwestern Historical Quarterly,* Vol. XIV, No. 4 (April, 1911), 334–35.

McKay, S. S. "Texas and the Southern Pacific Railroad, 1848–1860," *Southwestern Historical Quarterly,* Vol. XXXV, No. 1 (July, 1931), 1–27.

McMurtrie, Douglas C. "Pioneer Printing in Texas," *Southwestern Historical Quarterly,* Vol. XXXV, No. 3 (January, 1932), 173–93.

Millenial Harbinger, Vol. VI, No. 1 (January, 1835)–Third Series, Vol. VII, No. 3 (March, 1850).

[Moore, A. W.?]. "A Reconnoissance in Texas in 1846," *Southwestern Historical Quarterly,* Vol. XXX, No. 4 (April, 1927), 252–71.

Muckleroy, Anna. "The Indian Policy of the Republic of Texas," *Southwestern Historical Quarterly,* Vol. XXV, No. 4 (April, 1922), 229–60; Vol. XXVI, No. 1 (July, 1922), 1–29; Vol. XXVI, No. 2 (October, 1922), 128–48; Vol. XXVI, No. 3 (January, 1923), 184–206.

Muir, Andrew F. "The Destiny of Buffalo Bayou," *Southwestern Historical Quarterly,* Vol. XLVII, No. 2 (October, 1943), 91–106.

———. "Early Missionaries in Texas, with Documents Illustrative of Richard Salmon's Church Colony," *Historical Magazine of the Protestant Episcopal Church,* Vol. X, No. 3 (September, 1941), 219–41.

———. "The Free Negro in Harris County, Texas," *Southwestern Historical Quarterly,* Vol. XLVI, No. 3 (January, 1943), 214–38.

———. "Railroad Enterprise in Texas, 1836–1841," *ibid.,* Vol. XLVII, No. 4 (April, 1944), 339–70.

Murphy, DuBose. "Early Days of the Protestant Episcopal Church in

Texas," *Southwestern Historical Quarterly,* Vol. XXXIV, No. 4 (April, 1931), 293–316.

Nance, J. M. (ed.). "A Letter Book of Joseph Eve, United States Chargé d'Affaires to Texas," *Southwestern Historical Quarterly,* Vol. XLIII, No. 2 (October, 1939), 196–221; Vol. XLIII, No. 3 (January, 1940), 365–77; Vol. XLIII, No. 4 (April, 1940), 486–510; Vol. XLIV, No. 1 (July, 1940), 96–116.

Newsom, W. L. "The Postal System of the Republic of Texas," *Southwestern Historical Quarterly,* Vol. XX, No. 2 (October, 1916), 103–31.

Niles' Weekly Register, Vol. XXXII, No. 2 (March, 1827)–Vol. LXXV, No. 26 (June, 1849).

"Notes on Texas. By a Citizen of Ohio," *Hesperian; or, Western Monthly Magazine,* Vol. I, No 5 (September, 1838), 350–60; Vol. I, No. 6 (October, 1838), 428–40; Vol. II, No. 1 (November, 1838), 30–39; Vol. II, No. 2 (December, 1838), 109–18; Vol. II, No. 3 (January, 1839), 189–99; Vol. II, No. 4 (February, 1839), 288–93; Vol. II, No. 5 (March, 1839), 359–67; Vol. II, No. 6 (April, 1839), 417–26.

Peareson, P. E. "Reminiscences of Judge Edwin Waller," *Quarterly of the Texas State Historical Association,* Vol. IV, No. 1 (July, 1900), 33–53.

Potts, Charles S. "Early Criminal Law in Texas: From Civil Law to Common Law, to Code," *Texas Law Review,* Vol. XXI, No. 4 (April, 1943), 394–406.

Raines, C. W. "Enduring Laws of the Republic of Texas," *Quarterly of the Texas State Historical Association,* Vol. I, No. 2 (October, 1897), 96–107; Vol. II, No. 2 (October, 1898), 152–61.

Raunick, Selma M. "A Survey of German Literature in Texas," *Southwestern Historical Quarterly,* Vol. XXXIII, No. 2 (October, 1929), 134–59.

"Records of an Early Texas Baptist Church," *Quarterly of the Texas State Historical Association,* Vol. XI, No. 2 (October, 1907), 85–156; Vol. XII, No. 1 (July, 1908), 1–60.

Red, William S. (ed.). "Allen's Reminiscences of Texas, 1838–1842," *Southwestern Historical Quarterly,* Vol. XVII, No. 3 (January, 1914), 283–305; Vol. XVIII, No. 3 (January, 1915), 287–304.

———(ed.). "Extracts from the Diary of W. Y. Allen, 1838–1839," *ibid.,* Vol. XVII, No. 1 (July, 1913), 43–60.

Reid, Mary. "Fashions of the Republic," *Southwestern Historical Quarterly,* Vol. XLV, No. 3 (January, 1942), 244–54.

"Reminiscences of Captain Jesse Burnam," *Quarterly of the Texas State Historical Association*, Vol. V, No. 1 (July, 1901), 12–18.

"Reminiscences of C. C. Cox," *Quarterly of the Texas State Historical Association*, Vol. VI, No. 2 (October, 1902), 113–38; Vol. VI, No. 3 (January, 1903), 204–35.

"Reminiscences of Mrs. Annie Fagan Teal," *Southwestern Historical Quarterly*, Vol. XXXIV, No. 4 (April, 1931), 317–28.

"Reminiscences of Mrs. Dilue Harris," *Quarterly of the Texas State Historical Association*, Vol. IV, No. 2 (October, 1900), 85–127; Vol. IV, No. 3 (January, 1901), 155–89; Vol. VII, No. 3 (January, 1904), 214–22.

"Resources of Texas," *De Bow's Review*, Vol. IX, No. 2 (August, 1850), 195–97.

Rourke, Constance. "Davy Crockett," *Southwest Review*, Vol. XIX, No. 2 (January, 1934), 149–61.

Schoen, Harold. "The Free Negro in the Republic of Texas," *Southwestern Historical Quarterly*, Vol. XXXIX, No. 4 (April, 1936), 292–308; Vol. XL, No. 1 (July, 1936), 26–34; Vol. XL, No. 2 (October, 1936), 85–113; Vol. XL, No. 3 (January, 1937), 169–99; Vol. XL, No. 4 (April, 1937), 267–89; Vol. XLI, No. 1 (July, 1937), 83–108.

Shettles, E. L. "The Clark-Wells Controversy," *Texas Methodist Historical Quarterly*, Vol. I, No. 3 (January, 1910), 255–82.

Sinks, Mrs. Julia Lee. "Rutersville College," *Quarterly of the Texas State Historical Association*, Vol. II, No. 2 (October, 1898), 124–33.

Smith, Ashbel, and John S. Bowers. "Letters on Constipated Colic— Vulgarly Called 'Patent-Dry-Belly-Ache,' " *New Orleans Medical and Surgical Journal*, Vol. V, No. [5] (May, 1849), 713–19.

Smith, Henry. "Reminiscences of Henry Smith," *Quarterly of the Texas State Historical Association*, Vol. XIV, No. 1 (July, 1910), 24–73.

Smither, Harriet (ed.). "Diary of Adolphus Sterne," *Southwestern Historical Quarterly*, Vol. XXX, No. 2 (October, 1926)–Vol. XXXVIII, No. 3 (January, 1935).

———. "The Alabama Indians of Texas," *ibid.*, Vol. XXXVI, No. 2 (October, 1932), 83–108.

Smithwick, Noah. "Early Texas Nomenclature," *Quarterly of the Texas State Historical Association*, Vol. II, No. 2 (October, 1898), 174–75.

Spell, Lota M. "Anglo-American Press in Mexico, 1846–1848," *American Historical Review*, Vol. XXXVIII, No. 1 (October, 1932), 20–31.

Spirit of the Times, Vol. VIII, No. 1 (February, 1838)–Vol. XVI, No. 52 (February, 1847).

Bibliography

"Statement of the Relative Advantages and Capacities for the Culture of Sugar in Louisiana and Texas," *De Bow's Review,* Vol. V, No. 4 (April, 1848), 319–24.

Stenberg, Richard R. "Jackson's Neches Claim, 1829–1836," *Southwestern Historical Quarterly,* Vol. XXXIX, No. 4 (April, 1936), 255–74.

St. John, Percy Bolingbroke. "The Hunting Widow, or a Week in the Woods and Prairies of Texas," *Campbell's Foreign Semi-Monthly Magazine,* Vol. IV, No. 8 (December, 1843), 510–16.

Strickland, Rex W. "History of Fannin County, Texas, 1836–1843," *Southwestern Historical Quarterly,* Vol. XXXIII, No. 4 (April, 1930), 262–98; Vol. XXXIV, No. 1 (July, 1930), 38–68.

————. "Miller County, Arkansas Territory, The Frontier that Men Forgot," *The Chronicles of Oklahoma,* Vol. XVIII, No. 1 (March, 1940), 12–34; Vol. XVIII, No. 2 (June, 1940), 154–70; Vol. XIX, No. 1 (March, 1941), 37–54.

Terrell, A. W. "Recollections of General Sam Houston," *Southwestern Historical Quarterly,* Vol. XVI, No. 2 (October, 1912), 113–36.

"Texas," *Missionary Chronicle,* Vol. XI, No. 25 (July, 1843), 213–14.

"Texas," *Spirit of Missions,* Vol. VII, No. 11 (November, 1842), 341–44.

"Texas," *Spirit of Missions,* Vol. IX, No. 5 (May, 1844), 155–57.

"Texas," *Spirit of Missions,* Vol. X, No. 6 (June, 1845), 184–85.

"Texas Associations," *The Baptist,* New Series, Vol. I, No. 34 (April, 1845), 531–32.

"Texas. By an English Traveller," *The Corsair,* Vol. I, No. 27 (September, 1839), 428.

"Texas Lands," *De Bow's Review,* Vol. VIII, No. 1 (January, 1850), 63–65.

Thomas, A. O. "Money of the Republic of Texas," *The Numismatist,* Vol. LVII, No. 9 (September, 1944), 775–80.

Thomason, John W., Jr. "Huntsville," *Southwest Review,* Vol. XIX, No. 3 (April, 1934), 233–44.

Townes, John C. "Sketch of the Development of the Judicial System of Texas," *Quarterly of the Texas State Historical Association,* Vol. II, No. 1 (July, 1898), 29–53; Vol. II, No. 2 (October, 1898), 134–51.

Tryon, William M. "Texas," *The Baptist,* New Series, Vol. I, No. 16 (December, 1844), 254.

W., H. W. "Texas Sugar Lands," *De Bow's Review,* Vol. V, No. 4 (April, 1848), 316–19.

325

Walker, Olive T. "Esther Amanda Sherrill Cullins," *Southwestern Historical Quarterly,* Vol. XLVII, No. 3 (January, 1944), 234–49.

Webb, Walter P. "The American Revolver and the West," *Scribner's Magazine,* Vol. LXXXI, No. 2 (February, 1927), 171–78.

Wharton, Clarence [R.]. "Early Judicial History of Texas," *Texas Law Review,* Vol. XII, No. 3 (April, 1934), 311–25.

Wilcox, Seb. S. "Laredo During the Texas Republic," *Southwestern Historical Quarterly,* Vol. XLII, No. 2 (October, 1938), 83–107.

Wilkinson, A. E. "The Author of the Texas Homestead Exemption Law," *Southwestern Historical Quarterly,* Vol. XX, No. 1 (July, 1916), 35–40.

Williams, David R. "An Indigenous Architecture," *Southwest Review,* Vol. XIV, No. 1 (October, 1928), 60–74.

———. "Toward a Southwestern Architecture," *ibid.,* Vol. XVI, No. 3 (April, 1931), 301–13.

Williams, J. W. "The National Road of the Republic of Texas," *Southwestern Historical Quarterly,* Vol. XLVII, No. 3 (January, 1944), 207–24.

Winkler, Ernest W. "The Cherokee Indians in Texas," *Quarterly of the Texas State Historical Association,* Vol. VII, No. 2 (October, 1903), 94–165.

———. "The Seat of Government of Texas," *ibid.,* Vol. X, No. 2 (October, 1906), 140–71; Vol. X, No. 3 (January, 1907), 185–245.

Winston, R. W. "Robert Potter: Tar Heel and Texan Daredevil," *South Atlantic Quarterly,* Vol. XXIX, No. 2 (April, 1930), 140–59.

THESES

(Approximately fifty theses in the University of Texas Library were found useful. Those listed below were found indispensable.)

Crane, R. E. L., Jr. "The Administration of the Customs Service in the Republic of Texas." M.A., 1939.

Curlee, Abigail. "A Study of Texas Slave Plantations, 1822–1865." Ph.D., 1932.

Marshall, Ellen. "Some Phases of the Establishment and Development of Roads in Texas, 1716–1845." M.A., 1934.

Masters, B. E. "A History of Early Education in Northeast Texas." M.A., 1929.

May, Lucy. "The Life and Activities of Frost Thorn." M.A., 1939.

Mixon, Ruby. "William Barret Travis, His Life and Letters." M.A., 1930.

Strickland, Rex W. "Anglo-American Activities in Northeastern Texas, 1803–1845." Ph.D., 1937.

Index

Index

Horton, Alexander: 271
Hospitals: 241–42
Hotels: 48–49; food, 107, 227; listed, 106–107; see also individual entries
House-raisings: 110
Houses: log cabin, 25–26; plantation, 27–28; in towns, 28–30
Houston and Brazos Rail Road Company: 74
Houston, Sam: 53, 74, 98, 118–19, 220, 267, 276; president, 4, 5; Indian policy, 15; drinking bouts, 43–44; clothes, 51–52; represents speculators, 82–84; town promoter, 89; retrenchment policy, 95, 100; as material for folklore, 162; attacks David G. Burnet, 174; portraits painted, 179; alleged dueling challenges, 287–89
Houston (Tex.): 62, 64, 65, 94, 164, 180, 181, 231, 238, 239, 241, 250, 256, 260–61, 270, 277, 278; prepares for Mexican invasion, 13; cattle raising near, 21; early buildings, 28; fire control, 30; condition of streets, 31; saloons, 40–41; stagecoach connections with other towns, 57–60; commercial center, 67, 74; beginnings, 92; population (in 1839), 92; hotels, 106–107; professional theater, 119–25; amateur theater, 125; vaudeville and circuses, 127–28; gambling prevalent, 129; racing center, 131–32; schools, 138–40; musical activities, 185; religious activities, 193, 201, 216, 217, 218–19; yellow fever epidemics, 229–30; sanitation, 230–31; see also newspapers
Houstoun, Mrs. Matilda C. F.: writes Texas and the Gulf of Mexico, favorable to Texas, 162, 177–78; says whittling chief amusement, 133–34
Hoxey, Asa: 6
Hubert, Mrs.: 63
Huckins, Rev. James: 198, 209
Hudson, R.: 287
Hudson, Radcliffe: 277
Huff, William P., exhibits prehistoric remains: 180
Humor: 160–64, 171, 174–75
Hunt, Memucan: 285
Hunting: 111–12
Huntsville (Tex.): 117, 208
Huston, Felix: 281, 287

Ice, at Houston and Galveston: 42
Immigration to Texas: 5 ff

Independence (Tex.): 216
Indians: viii, 148; tribes in Texas, 14–15; fights with, 14, 15, 168; settlers attitudes toward, 14, 112, 169; trade with, 103
Individualism: 267 ff., 297–98
Indolence: 17, 108–109
Industries, in towns: 107–108
Industry (Tex.): 20
Ingram, Ira: 275; remarks on cotton production (in 1835), 16; describes library and plantation life, 187–88; attitude toward religion, 191–92
Ingram, Seth: 275
Ives, Rev. Caleb S.: 140, 201, 207

Jack, William H.: 253, 276
Jackson, Charles: 264
Jeffers, John E.: 251
Jefferson, Joseph, actor: 123–24
Johnston, Albert Sidney: 281, 285, 287
Jones, Dr. Anson: 89, 93, 235, 285; president, 4; opposes banks, 99; head examined by phrenologist, 182
Jones, David: 261
Jones, Levi: 91
Jones, Oliver: 283
Judiciary, Republic of Texas: 253–58

Kain, Rev. James H.: 219
Kaufman, David S.: 152, 272
Kendall, George Wilkins: 56 n., 112; writes Narrative of the Texan Santa Fé Expedition, 178; plagiarized by Frederick Marryat, 178
Kennedy, William: 217; writes Texas: the Rise, Progress, and Prospects of the Republic of Texas, authoritative book, 176–77
Kenney, Rev. J. W.: 56
Kenney, M. M., school recollections: 144
Kerr, Hugh, writes Poetical Description of Texas: 171
Ketchell, Aaron: 250
Kinney, H. L.: 35
Kneass, Charles, portrait painter: 179
Kuykendall, J. H.: 249

La Grange (Tex.): 21, 226, 282
Lamar, Mirabeau B.: 273, 285, 287, 288; president, 4; Indian policy, 15; backer of Lamar (Tex.), 89; opposes banks, 99; president during depression, 100; joke played on, 134–35; message to Congress concerning education, 137–38; as material for folk-

lore, 162; speech at La Grange, 165–66; writes poetry, 172; patron of arts, 175–76; collects historical data, 176; writes chapter of Foote's history of Texas, 176 n.
Lamar, Rebecca Ann: 146
Lamar (Tex.): 89
Land frauds: 11, 82
Land-grant policy of Republic of Texas: 10–11
Land grants to *empresarios:* 11, 12, 82
Land ownership: 10–13, 293
Land scrip, issued to soldiers and office-holders: 101
Land speculation: 82–87, 291, 293–94; public sentiment opposed to, 85–86
Land values: rise (in 1837–39), 87–88; fall (in 1840), 89
Latimer, James W.: 223
Law books: 251–52
Lawlessness: 260–66, 270–71, 297
Lawyers: 192, 246 ff.; community status, 247, 251, 260; apprenticeship, 248–50; derelections, 250–51; libraries, 251–52; leaders, 252–53; courtroom manners, 256–58; nature of practice, 258–59
Leger, Dr. Theodore: attacks prevalent methods of malaria treatment, 232–33; attacks quack doctors, 236
Leroy, Stiles: 281
Lewis, Mrs. Henry, actress: 122
Lewis, Ira R.: 276, 286; reports Mexican scare, 13
Lewis & Howell, Shreveport merchandise firm: 80
Liberty (Tex.): 77
Libraries: 149, 186–88, 189, 252
Linn, John J.: 240
Literature, Texas: 160–61, 162–63, 171–73, 175–78
Lockhart, Dr. John Washington: opinion concerning lack of opportunities of ordinary settler, 190; describes camp meeting, 212
Long, Mrs. Jane: 107
Love, James: 91
Lubbock, Francis R.: 45, 189, 271, 287
Lynching: 262–63

McCalla, Rev. W. L., educator: 149
McCoy, John C.: 56
McCullough, Rev. John: 200, 208
McFarland, John: 200
McHenry, Lydia A., school teacher: 144
McKenzie, Rev. John W. P., head of

McKenzie College: 155–57, 211–12
McKenzie College: 155–57
McKinney, Thomas F.: 275; helps develop Galveston, 91; commission merchant, 101; *see also* McKinney, Williams & Company
McKinney, Williams & Company: steamboat *Constitution,* 71; issue money, 101; mercantile-cotton business, 102; moves from Quintana to Galveston, 102; owns Tremont Hotel, 107
McLaughlin, P.: 47–48
McQueen, T.: 276
Madden, Miss A. E., school teacher: 145
Magazines, in Texas libraries: 187–88
Magnolia (Tex.): 76
Maillard, N. Doran, *History of Republic of Texas:* 266
Malaria: 224–27, 231; termed "The Shakes," 178; types, 225; theories about causes, 225–27; treatment, 232–34
Manhattan (Tex.): 89, 93; plans university, 141
Mann, Mrs. Pamelia: 107, 268
Marryat, Frederick: writes *The Travels and Adventures of Monsieur Violet,* 178; plagiarism from George Wilkins Kendall and Josiah Gregg, 178; book assailed by Texans, 179
Marshall University: 141
Martin, Wyly: 275
Mason, John T., speculator: 85; grant voided by constitution, 83; retains Sam Houston, 83
Mason, Judge, mail contractor: 63
Masonic lodges: 217
Matagorda Academy: 140
Matagorda (Tex.): 64, 189, 193, 194, 201, 258, 286; condition of streets, 31; freight line to Austin, 67; theater, 123, 125
Maverick, Mrs. Mary A.: 242–43
Maverick, Samuel A.: 54 n., 225, 226
May Day celebration: 158–59
Mayfield, James S.: 272
Medical books: 187, 188, 236
Medical practice: 232 ff.; advances in, 233–34
Medical treatments: 38, 232–35, 236–37, 242–44
Menard, Michel B.: 182; obtains grant to Galveston site, 91; organizes Galveston City Company, 91
Menifee, Judge, early sugar producer: 19

Index

Mercer, E., early sugar producer: 19
Mercer's Colony: 12
Methodist Episcopal church: supports colleges, 147–48, 152–53, 155; attitude toward instrumental music, 184–85; growth of, 194–97; supports Southern view in church split, 196–97; activities among Negro slaves, 197; attitude toward Baptists, 119, 204; circuit riders, 206–207; church services described, 212–16
Mexicans: *vii–viii*, 146, 166, 183; rumors of aggression by, 13–14; conflict with, 13–14; smoke cigarettes, 38; temperate in drinking, 41; sell land to speculators, 85; trade with, 103; amusements, 117, 127
Miasma of marshes, reputedly cause of malaria: 226
Milam Guards, Houston: 49, 74
Millard, Henry: 285
Miller, B., school teacher: 139
Mills, Andrew G., merchant: 102
Mills, David G.: 102
Mills, John T.: 251
Mills, R. and D. G., & Company: 103
Mills, Robert: commission merchant and planter, 102–103; owns extensive historical library, 186
Milroy, Colonel: 280
Mississippi Texas Land Company (Mississippi): 85
Monadelphia (Tex.): 89
Money, Republic of Texas, types of: 99–100
Montezuma (Tex.): 89
Montrose, Rev. Marcus A.: president of San Augustine University and Nacogdoches University, 149–51; controversies concerning educational methods, 151, 154–55
Moore, Edwin W.: 287
Moore, Dr. Francis, Jr.: 143, 221, 227, 243, 278, 282; *see also* Newspapers: Houston *Telegraph and Texas Register*
Moore, John W.: 275
Moorman, Watt: 265, 269
Morgan, James: 35, 288; quoted on economic prospects (in 1845), 18; early sugar producer, 19; opposes Negro slavery, 23–24; agent of New Washington Association, 90; describes medical treatment, 232
Mormons: 202

Morrell, Rev. Z. N.: 133, 197, 207, 208–209
Morrill, Amos: 251
Morris, F. A.: 44
Moscross, H.: 280
Mosquitos, regarded as nuisance: 227–28
Muldoon, Miguel: 202
Murat, Achille, land speculations: 85
Murder: 261, 263, 264, 274
Music: 45; 182–86; songs, 113, 115, 119–20, 170, 212, 222 n.; *see also* musical instruments
Musical instruments: 158, 170, 182, 183–84, 185

Nacogdoches (Tex.): 63, 64, 65, 94, 173, 217, 218, 219
Nacogdoches University: 153–54
Narbonne, Count de, swindler and subject of book by Frederick Marryat: 178–79
Nash, James P., school teacher: 140
Nashville (Tex.), reached by steamboat: 71
Natchitoches (La.), freighting to Texas: 67
Nazarenes, sect of: 202
Neches, battle of: 14
Negro slavery: opposed, 23–24; defended, 24; condemned, 109; Methodist church attitude toward, 196–97
Negro slaves: 10, 21–22; condition on plantations, 21–23; desired by farmers, 23, 24, 292; fear of insurrections by, 23; clothing, 46–47; dances, 115; religion, 197, 214
Neighborliness: 110–11
New Braunfels (Tex.): 11, 235
Newell, Rev. Chester: 192
"New School" Presbyterian church: 200 n.
Newspapers: humor, 168–71; poetry, 171–73; editorials, 171, 174–75; news columns, 173–74; *see also* Newspapers: Texas *and* Newspapers: England
Newspapers, England:
London *Atlas:* commends Maillard's history of Republic of Texas, 177
Newspapers, Texas:
Austin *City Gazette:* 175
Austin *Texas Centinel:* attacks Sam Houston, 174
Civilian and Galveston Gazette: announces arrival of organ, 185

333

Settlement, bases for choice of location: 10, 12–13
Shelby County: 240, 262, 263–65, 266
Sheridan, Francis C.: 105–106; opinion of Texans, 109
Sherman, Mrs. Sidney: 50
Shreveport (La.): 79
Sims sisters, school teachers: 145
Slaveholding, extent of: 21–22
Smith, Dr. Ashbel: 65, 94, 226, 235, 238, 239, 268, 272, 278; reports on business conditions (in 1837–40), 87–88; describes Houston horse races, 132; assails anti-Texas book in London press, 179; vice president of Texas Bible Society, 218–19; reports on yellow fever epidemic, 229–30
Smith, Henry, part owner of Aransas: 89
Smith, James N.: 8, 126, 217
Smith, Shelby: 132
Smith, Dr. William P.: 235
Smith, William R.: 95
Smithwick, Noah: 63
Smuggling of cotton into U. S.: 18
Sneed, Rev. J. P.: 206, 208
"Spanish Burying," practical joke: 134
Spanish civil law, influence of: 245–46
Splane, P. R.: 130
Springfield (Tex.): 133, 208
Stagecoach lines: 57–60
Stanley, Marcus Cicero: 279
Stanley, "Pud," barkeeper in play: 123–24
Starke, P. B., operates stagecoach line: 57–60
Starr, Dr. James H.: 237, 239, 264; describes cattle thefts from Mexicans, 21; aids in founding Nacogdoches University, 153–54; medical prescription book, 232 n.
Steamboat accommodations: 7–8, 73
Steamboats: *Columbia*, 7–8, 57, 71; *Concord*, 7, 79; *Douglas*, 7; *Elizabeth*, 7; *New Brazil*, 7; *Robert T. Lytle*, 7; *Galveston*, 8, 9; *Llama*, 7; *New York*, 8; *Alabama*, 9; *Cuba*, 9; *McKim*, 9; *Neptune*, 9; *Republic*, 9, 73; *Sarah Barnes*, 9; *Star Republic*, 9; *Ariel*, 68–69; *Cayuga*, 69–70; *Lady Byron*, 70–71; *Laura*, 70, 72; *Mustang*, 70–71; *Ocean*, 70; *Yellowstone*, 70; *Constitution*, 71, 72; *Branch T. Archer*, 72, 75; *Dayton*, 72; *Friend*, 72, 76; *Leonidas* (later *Sam Houston*), 72, 73; *Maryland*, 72; *Albert Gallatin*, 73;

Brighton, 73; *Sam M. Williams*, 73; *Spartan*, 73; *Correo*, 76; *Ellen Frankland*, 76–78; *Scioto Belle*, 76; *Trinity*, 76; *Vesta*, 76–78; *Victoria*, 76; *Wyoming*, 76; *Kate Ward*, 78; *Cotton Plant*, 79; *Frontier*, 79; *Hempstead*, 79; *Swan*, 79; *Yazoo*, 79; *Red River Planter*, 80
Steamboats built in Texas: 73, 78, 80
Steamboat transportation: on Red River, 6–7, 69, 79–80; to Jefferson, 7; New Orleans to Galveston, 7–9; New York to Texas, 9; on Rio Grande, 68; Brazos River, 68–71; Buffalo Bayou, 71–73; Trinity River, 75–78; Colorado River, 78–79; Guadalupe River, 79; Sabine River, 79
Steamboat wrecks: 73–74; the *Sarah Barnes*, 9
Steel mill: 32
Sterne, Adolphus: 36, 94, 150, 173; Nacogdoches postmaster, 63–64
Stevens, Rev. Abel: 192
Stewart, Dr. John McNeill: 263
Stiff, Edward, writes *The Texan Emigrant*: 177
Stores: 35, 41, 47, 95, 96, 103
Storms: 29, 91–92, 201
Strange, J., portrait painter: 179
Strickland, Henry: 240, 276
Stubblefield, G., Houston postmaster: 62
Stumps, in Texas towns: 31
Sublett, Phil: 150; large landholder, 87; promoter of Hamilton and Sabine City, 89
Sugar production (1830–60): 19–20
Sunday schools: 216–17
Superstitions: 244
Supreme Court, Republic of Texas: 253, 256
Surgery, amateur: 240–41
Swartwout, Samuel: land speculations, 83–84; embezzler, 84; friendship with Sam Houston, 84; obtains eleven-league grants, 85; leader in New Washington Association, 90
Swartwout (Tex.): 77; developed by New Washington Association, 90
Swearing: 269
Sweeny, John, early sugar producer: 19
Sweet, Sidney A., architect: 30
Swindlers: 279

Tall tales: 134, 162–64, 254, 268
Tanner, T. W., "strong man": 127

UNIVERSITY OF OKLAHOMA PRESS

NORMAN